Nation, Nationalism and Social Structure in Ancient India

शान्ति-पाठः

Peace Invocations

(१)

भद्रमिच्छन्त ऋषयः स्वर्विदस्तपो दीक्षामुपनिषेदुरग्रे ।
ततो राष्ट्रं बलमोजश्च जातम् तदस्मै देवा उपसन्नमन्तु ॥
अथर्व, १९/४१/१

The ṛṣis realized benedictory Heaven at the beginning of his creation. They performed penance and held devotion. From that strength of penance nation, force and vigour sprang out. Let all gods bestow their force and vigour to this (nation).

(२)

यार्णवेऽधि सलिलमग्र आसीद् यां मायाभिरन्वचरन्मनीषिणः
यस्या हृदयं परमे व्योमन्त्सत्येनावृतममृतं पृथिव्याः
सा नो भूमिस्त्विषिं बलं राष्ट्रे दधातूत्तमे ॥
अथर्व, १२/१/८

The land which was under the water of ocean in the beginning, the inner portion of which is covered with truth like that of immortal place, which earth is staying in mahat ākāśa and has been served by scholars with their aptful actions, let this our land establish vigour and strength in this eminant nation.

ॐ शान्तिः शान्तिः शान्तिः ॥

Nation, Nationalism and Social Structure in Ancient India

A Survey through Vedic Literature

by

Shiva Acharya

Decent Books
New Delhi -110059

Cataloging in Publication Data — DK

Courtesy: D.K. Agencies (P) Ltd. <docinfo@dkagencies.com>

Acharya, Shiva, 1962-

Nation, nationalism and social structure in ancient India : a survey through Vedic literature / by Shiva Acharya.

xxx, 434 p. 23 cm.

Includes bibliographical references (p.)

Includes index.

ISBN 818692129X

1. Nationalism — India — History. 2. State, The. 3. Vedic literature — History and criticism. 4. India — Social conditions — To 1200. I. Title.

DDC 954.02 21

ISBN 81-86921-29-X

First Published in India in 2005

Published and printed by:

Decent Books

D-36/A-1, Mohan Garden

Najafgarh Road

New Delhi - 110 059

Ph. (011) 2535-3435

Distributed by:

D.K. Printworld (P) Ltd.

Regd. office : *'Sri Kunj,'* F-52, Bali Nagar

New Delhi - 110 015

Phones : (011) 2545-3975; 2546-6019; *Fax* : (011) 2546-5926

E-mail: dkprintworld@vsnl.net

Web: www.dkprintworld.com

Dedicated to
The sacred memory of
The Revered offsprings of

BHĀRAT-MĀTĀ

who performed austerities
to build her
JAGADGURU

Foreword

It is indeed a pleasure to see that the Ph.D. dissertation of my pupil Dr. Shiva Acharya is under print. Dr. Acharya prepared his thesis entitled "Nation and Nationalism in the Vedic Literature: A study" under my supervision during 1993-2000. Dr. Acharya made a very extensive and intensive study of the Vedas in original and secondary sources, to bring home his point of study. His work shows that he has taken meticulous care while collecting the materials from the original source and arranged those in a very near perfect manner. He has earned praises from the external examiners for that account.

Dr. Acharya, while dealing with the subject-matter, first offers the definitions of Nation and Nationalism quoting various opinions of the reputed scholars in the fields. Then he enters into the discussion of the political aspects of the Vedic period. Then he takes care to offer his study of the assemblies called *sabhā, samiti* and *vidatha* in a critical manner. The *varṇa* and *āśrama vyavasthā,* etc., were the subject of his criticism.

Dr. Acharya has paid adequate attention to the various aspects, such as socio-political, socio-economical, civil and military, religious and philosophical, of the Vedic culture and civilization. While dealing with those aspects Dr. Acharya has cited evidences and quotations from original and secondary sources in support of discussion and opinion.

Dr. Acharya is a young scholar; but his work manifests his maturity in scholarship. And it is hoped that this young man will make profuse contribution to the Indological study. His clarity in vision is praiseworthy. I invoke blessings of god to help Dr. Acharya in doing so. I express my sincere hope that he will maintain his quest for knowledge and wisdom.

I also hope that this work of Dr. Acharya would prove a fore-runner of many of his post doctoral writings.

28-11-2003

Thaneswar Sharmah
Professor and Head
Sanskrit Deptt.
Guahati University

Preface

THE present book is an outcome of a dissertation entitled, "Nation and Nationalism in the Vedic Literature: A study," including several important additional informations and interpretations, has been compiled to present a light on the theory of Nation and Nationalism, as described in the Vedic literature. Moreover, we have attempted to present the life of the Vedic people and also a picture of the Vedic nation in all its different aspects that includes politics, economics, religion, amusement, education and thinkings as well.

The social, cultural, political and religious history of India is being interpreted on the basis of the translations and explanations made by the foreign writers who have tried their best to "uproot all that has sprung from it (the Vedas) during the last 3000 years." Such scholars interpreted the Vedic texts in such a way that the historians also started writing about the Āryan's invasion, as a result of which the present comparative philology came into being. It has divided India in south and north, plains and hills and tribes and general people. Their interpretation presented the wrong picture of cow-slaughtering, the theory of meat sacrifices and has described the *somarasa* as a type of intoxicating drink and so on. Such works increased diversities and presented a picture of a wrong and savage culture. All these were done intentionally and so we thought to compile our thesis on nation and nationalism as the Vedic literature reveals. Remarkable fact is that Maxmueller opposed to have any element of nationality in the Indian literature.

We have studied Balasastri Haradas, Satavalekar, Shri Ram Sathe, R.K. Mukherjee, Jogiraj Basu, R.S. Sharma, Dayananda Sarasvati, Vivekananda, Aurobindo, Śaṅkarācārya, Jvala Prasad Misra, M.G. Bokare, Gurudatta, P.N. Oak, Dr. Kunwarlal Vyasasisya, Khagendra Dasgupta, etc., from whom we get a new and extraordinary light and viewpoint regarding Indian literature. Thus we decided to compile a dissertation in that line.

Contents

Key to Transliteration

अ *a* (but)	आ *ā* (palm)	इ *i* (it)
ई *ī* (beet)	उ *u* (put)	ऊ *ū* (pool)
ऋ *ṛ* (rhythm)	ए *e* (play)	ऐ *ai* (high)
ओ *o* (toe)	औ *au* (loud)	ळ* ḷ
क *ka* (skate)[1]	ख* *kha* (blockhead)[1]	ग *ga* (gate)[1]
घ *gha* (loghut)[1]	ङ *ṅa* (sing)[1]	
च *ca* (chunk)[2]	छ* *cha* (catch him)[2]	ज *ja* (john)[2]
झ *jha* (hedgehog)[2]	ञ *ña* (bunch)[2]	
ट *ṭa* (start)[3]	ठ* *ṭha* (anthill)[3]	ड *ḍa* (dart)[3]
ढ* *ḍha* (godhead)[3]	ण* *ṇa* (under)[3]	
त *ta* (path)[4]	थ *tha* (thunder)[4]	द *da* (that)[4]
ध* *dha* (breathe)[4]	न *na* (numb)[4]	
प *pa* (spin)[5]	फ* *pha* (loophole)[5]	ब *ba* (bin)[5]
भ *bha* (abhor)[5]	म *ma* (much)[5]	
य *ya* (young)	र *ra* (drama)	ल *la* (luck)
व *va* (vile)	श *śa* (shove)	ष *ṣa* (bushel)
स *sa* (so)	ह *ha* (hum)	क्ष *kṣa* (*kṣatriya*)
त्र *tra* (*trishūl*)	ज्ञ *jña* (*jñāni*)	

अं (ं)*ṁ* (*saṁskṛti*) *ṁ anusvāra* (nasalisation of preceding vowel)

अः *ḥ* (*prātaḥ*) *ḥ visarga* (aspiration of preceding vowel)

* No exact English equivalents for these letters.

[1] guttural [2] palatal [3] lingual [4] dental [5] labial

Acknowledgements

SOME important personalities became the fountain of my inspiration in compiling my Ph.D. dissertation whom I must not forget to pay my gratitude after its successful completion. Moreover, the dissertation is being published. So, I cordially express my thanks to all of them who have directly or indirectly contributed in my work.

First of all I would like to express my gratitude to the Retd. Professor and the Head of the Department of Sanskrit, Guahati University, Dr. Thaneswar Sharmah who with his utmost co-operation helped me to complete the research work as my guide on the topic of "Nation and Nationalism in the Vedic Literature: A Study" during AD 1993-2000. He blessed me by giving a "foreword" for this publication.

Secondly, I express my sincere thanks to Shri Vinayak Kanetkar, the Organizing Secretary of Bharatiya Shikshan Mandal, who inspired me to enter into the research work and helped through the books he had.

I must not forget to express my sincere gratitude to Shri Tulasi Sharan Upadhyaya (Sāhityācārya and Vyākaraṇācārya), the Pradhānācārya of Rakachandra Sanskrit Vidyalaya and an authentic scholar on Sanskrit Grammar of North-East India, who encouraged me by providing his co-operation in the field of grammatical etymologies of some important terms and helped with the books of the library of his vidyalaya.

I am indebted to all those authors and writers whom I have quoted. Scholars like D.B. Tengdi, P.N. Oak, Guruji Golwalkar, Pandit Dinadayal Upadhyaya, Vivekananda, Shri Ram Sathe, Aurobindo, etc., gave a new light to my thought. I must express my cordial gratitude to all of them.

I am thankful to Late Lakshmiprapanna Bhandari, my revered uncle who looked after me when I was a child and brought me unto this state. I could have informed him about the submission of my thesis, but I could not do so because unfortunately he had left for his heavenly abode till then. Besides my uncle, I would particularly like to mention my cousin, Shri Tikaram Upadhyaya whom I respect as my guardian, for his inspirations and encouragement.

I would like to record my gratitude to Late Buddhindra Nath Sharma, the first Headmaster of Gameri High School, who allowed me to take the exams in M.A., otherwise the degree of Ph.D. would not been possible. Secondly, I express my sincere thanks to Shri Shiva Prasad Sharma, the present Headmaster of the school, along with the teaching staff including Shri Dhiren Saikia, Shri Romnath Sharma, etc., who encouraged me to work hard providing several facilities during my research period.

I am also thankful to Shri Kanak Chandra Sharma of Kawaripather and Dr. Lalu Prasad Upadhyaya of Tezpur who respectively helped me by not only providing the typewriter but also typing the dissertation with keen attention.

I express my sincere gratitude to the members of Sanskrit Prasarini Sabha, Gameri, who helped boost my otherwise sluggish work or whenever I delayed in the work. Among them Shri Vinod Dabari and Dharani Dhungel are remembered.

I will be ungrateful if I forget to express my warm gratitude to Mrs. Gita Devi, my beloved wife, who faced all the household problems without any complain and furthermore even smilingly, and thus helped me by providing enough time for my studies.

I shall remain ever grateful to the authorities of "Decent Books" who published this research within a reasonable time.

AUTHOR

Abbreviations

AA	:	*Aitareya Āraṇyaka*
AB	:	*Aitareya Brāhmaṇa*
ĀDS	:	*Āpastamba Dharmasūtra*
ĀGS	:	*Āpastamba Gṛhyasūtra*
AGVDJRUS	:	*Adhyātma Gñān se Vaiyaktik Divyajīvan Aur Rāṣṭrīya Unnati*, Sātavalekara
AHVPr	:	*The Aryans and the Holy Vedas*, Pranav Bandyopadhyaya
AIWŚ	:	*Ancient Indian Warfare*, Sarva Daman Singh
AK	:	*Amarakośa*
AMSS	:	*Atharvaveda: Mātṛbhūmi aur Svarājyaśāsana*, Satavalekara
APIIAIR	:	*Aspects of Political Ideas and Institutions in Ancient India*, R.S. Sarma
ARV	:	*Atharvaveda Rājanīti*, V.R. Ratate
Arth	:	*Arthaśāstra*, Kauṭilya
ĀpSS	:	*Āpastamba Śrautasūtra*
ĀsGS	:	*Āśvalāyana Gṛhyasūtra*
Ast	:	*Aṣṭādhyāyī* of Pāṇini
ĀŚS	:	*Āśvalāyana Śrautasūtra*
ASSK	:	*Ārjya Sabhyatār Sandhāne*, Khagendra Dasgupta

AV	:	*Atharvaveda*
AWTR	:	*Aryans: Who were They*, Sri Ram Sathe
BAIT	:	*Bhāradvājas in Ancient India*, Thanesvar Sharma
BDU	:	*Bhāratīya Darśana*, Umesh Misra
BDS	:	*Baudhāyana Dharmasūtra*
BIPK	:	*Bhāratīya Itihās ka Punarlekhan Kyon evam Purāṇon me Itihās Vivek*, Kuwarlal Vyassisya
BSS	:	*Baudhāyana Śrautasūtra*
BP	:	*Bhāgavata Purāṇa*
BU	:	*Bṛhadāraṇyakopaniṣad*
CCRVD	:	*Concept of Cow in the Ṛgveda*, Sri Nivas Doris
ChU	:	*Chāndogya Upaniṣad*
CLAIM	:	*Corporate Life in Ancient India*, R.C. Majumdar
DDO	:	*Dharma aur Darśana*, Om Shivaraj
DGCIN	:	*Development and Growth of Castes in Ancient India*, N.K. Dutta
DGKAIM	:	*Development of Geographical Knowledge in Ancient India*, M.P. Tripathi
EEAHS	:	*Ethenic Elements of Ancient Hindus*, Sukumar Chattopadhyay
GB	:	*Gopatha Brāhamaṇa*
GDS	:	*Gautama Dharmasūtra*
GGS	:	*Gobhil Gṛhyasūtra*
HDIMP	:	*Historical Development of Indian Music*, Pragyanananda
HDKR	:	*Hindu Dharmakośa*, Rajbali Pandey

HEM	:	*Hindu Economics*, M.G. Bokare
HSA	:	*Hindu Saṁskṛti Aṅka, Kalyāṇa*
HSSAJS	:	*Hindu Sāmājik Saṁsthāyen aur Ārthik Jīvan*, S.S. Sahay
HVLS	:	*A History of Vedic Literature*, S.N. Sharma
IABJr.	:	*India of the Age of the Brāhmaṇas*, Jogiraj Basu
ILSYVS	:	*Indian Life in the Śukla Yajurveda*, Sitanath Dey
INH	:	*Idea of Nationalism*, Hans Kohn
ITS	:	*The Indian Theogony*, Sukumari Bhattacharjee
ĪU	:	*Īśopaniṣada*
IVKR	:	*India of Vedik Kalpasūtras*, Ram Gopal
JGS	:	*Jaiminīya Gṛhyasūtra*
KathU	:	*Kaṭha Upaniṣad*
KB	:	*Kauśitakī Brāhmaṇa*
KenU	:	*Kenopaniṣad*
KGS	:	*Kāṭhaka Gṛhyasūtra*
KRKRN	:	*Kiṁ Rāṣṭraṁ Kaśca Rāṣṭriyaḥ*, Narahari Narayan Bhide
KS	:	*Kāṭhaka Saṁhitā*
KSS	:	*Kātyāyana Śrautasūtra*
KumS	:	*Kumārasambhavam*
MB	:	*Mahābhārata*
MRK	:	*Marxvād aur Rāmarājya*, Karapatriji Maharaj
MS	:	*Manu-Smṛti*
MU	:	*Muṇḍakopaniṣad*

Nir	:	*Niruktam*
OGCIN	:	*Origin and Growth of Castes in India*, N.K. Dutta
OHIS	:	*Oxford History of India*, Vincent A. Smith
PBRNH	:	*Prācīn Bhārat me Rājya aur Nyāyapālikā*, Hariharnath Tripathi
PGS	:	*Pāraskar Gṛhyasūtra*
PIMBN	:	*Political Ideas and Ideals in the Mahābhārata*, N.K.P. Sinha
PU	:	*Praśnopaniṣad*
PunyT	:	*Punyāhavācan*, Dattopanta Thengdi in *"Rāṣṭra"* of M.S. Golwalkar
Raghu	:	*Raghuvaṁśa* of Kālidāsa
Rām	:	*Rāmāyaṇa*
RCD	:	*Ṛgvedic Culture*, A.C. Das
RJDD	:	*Rāṣṭrajīvan Kī Diśā*, Dindayal Upadhyaya
RPVUK	:	*Religion and Philosophy in the Vedas and Upaniṣads*, A.B. Keith
ṚV	:	*Ṛgveda*
		(i) *ṚVg* : *Ṛgveda* with Griffith's commentary
		(ii) *ṚVSāt* : *Ṛgveda* with Sātavalekar's commentary
		(iii) *ṚVSāy* : Notes and commentaries of Sāyaṇa on the *Ṛgveda*
		(iv) *ṚVDay* : Notes and commentaries of Dayānanda Sarasvatī on the *Ṛgveda*
SAG	:	*Sātavalekar Abhinandan Grantha*

ŚB	:	*Śatapatha Brāhmaṇa*
ŚBG	:	*Śrīmad Bhagavadgītā*
SEDM	:	*A Sanskrit English Dictionary*, M.M. Williams
SGAIA	:	*State and Government in Ancient India*, A.S. Altekar
ŚGS	:	*Śāṅkhāyana Gṛhyasūtra*
SK	:	*Siddhānta Kaumudī*
SMHG	:	*Studies in Modern History*, G.P. Gooch
SPD	:	*Satyārtha Prakāśa*, Dayānanda Sarasvatī
SRSBN	:	*Sacrificial Rituals in the Śatapatha Brāhmaṇa*, Naama Drury
SSSIK	:	*Sanskrit Sāhitya kā Samālocanātmak Itihās*, Kapildev Dvivedi
ŚYV	:	*Śukla Yajurveda*
TA	:	*Taittirīya Āraṇyaka*
TMB	:	*Tāṇḍya Mahābrāhmaṇa*
TB	:	*Taittirīya Brāhmaṇa*
TCAIB	:	*Trade and Commence in Ancient India*, Balaram Srivastava
TS	:	*Taittirīya Saṁhitā*
TU	:	*Taittirīya Upaniṣad*
VMM	:	*Vedic Mythology*, Macdonell
VācT	:	*Vācaspatyam*, Taranath Bhattacarya
VDJRU	:	*Vaiyaktik Divya Jīvan aur Rāṣṭrīya Unnati*, Satavalekar
VDVRSS	:	*Veda me Darśāye vividh prakār ke Rājya Śāsana*, Satavalekar

VI	:	*Vedic Index*
VICK	:	*Veda and the Indian Culture*, Kireet Joshi
VIG	:	*Vedic India*, Ghurye
VJR	:	*Vedakālīna Janatantrasthānāni*, Ramanuja Tatacarya
VMB	:	*Vedic Mathematics*, Bhāratī Tīrtha Kṛṣṇa
VMSS	:	*Viśuddha Manu-Smṛti*, Surendra Kumar
VPJr	:	*Veder Paricaya*, Jogiraj Basu
VPK	:	*Vedārtha Pārijāta*, Karapatriji
VDRB	:	*Vaidik Rāṣṭradarśana*, Balasastri Haridas
VRSS	:	*Vaidik Rājnītiśāstra*, Visvanath Prasad Varma
VRVYR	:	*Viśva me Rāṣṭrīyatā kī Vikāsa yātrā*, Sri Ram Sathe
VS(L)	:	*Vivekananda Sāhitya* (Lectures)
VSNP	:	*Vaidik Sāhitya me Nārī*, Prasanta Kumar
VSR	:	*Vaidik Sāhitya*, Ram Govinda
VSSB	:	*Vaidik Sāhitya aur Saṁskṛti*, Acarya Baladev Upadhyaya
VSS	:	*Vedakālīna Samāja*, Shivadatta Gnani
VSSS	:	*Vaidik Svarājyaśāsana*, Satavalekar
VTSBA	:	*Villages Towns and Secular Buildings in Ancient India*, Amit Ray
VYBAG	:	*Vaidik Yuga ke Bhāratīya Ābhuṣaṇa*, Govinda Chandra Ray
WIB	:	*The Wonder that was India*, A.L. Basham
YV	:	*Yajurveda*

Introduction

THIS research work is aimed at the theory of Nation and Nationalism in the light of the Vedic literature, by completion of which it is expected to provoke a new line of thinking regarding Nationalism. Dr. T.P. Varma remarked,

> India is the oldest country with a continued (*sanātana*) long living tradition. It has made history since the dawn of the human civilization because it has maintained contacts with other parts of the civilized world and has recorded it.[1]

This ancient nation was able to establish the theory of Nation and Nationalism.

Selection of the Topic

Each planned action possesses its inspiration and motto. In the same way, we also have thought and planned to find out the elements of Nation and Nationalism in the Vedic literature. The facts which inspired us in the research of the above-mentioned topic are as follows:

1. Some scholars used to say that India was the nation of philosophers and the national feeling was absent in the Indian people.[2]
2. The Western political thinkers have had a firm belief that Nationalism is very modern.[3]

---

1. *Indian Conception of History Writing*, Dr. T.P. Varma Research paper presented in the seminer "Sonitpur through ages," Tezpur 1998.
2. *APIIAIR*, p. 1.
3. *Essay of Nationalism* by Heys Curlton, p. 29.

3. While the studies of such informations led us to think, the following questions jerked our mind:

   (a) We get the term *rāṣṭra* in the *Mantra saṁhitā*s frequently.[4] Was not the feeling of Nation and Nationalism at that time?

   (b) The *AB* proclaims about an undivided *rāṣṭra* surrounded by oceans.[5]

   (c) The Purāṇas also present the picture of one and undivided nation, Bhārata.[6] Can we say in such condition that the feelings of Nationalism was not in existence in India?

   (d) The poet Kālidāsa also praises the land existing between the Himālayas and the oceans.[7] Was not that the evidence of Nationalism?

These general informations which we get in everyday life led us to think as to why should we not investigate the elements of Nation and Nationalism in the Vedic literature. As a result of that, we entered into the present research.

Sources

Our sources of study may be divided into two: Primary and Secondary Sources. Primary Sources include all the Vedic *Saṁhitā*s namely *R̥V, SV, ŚYV, TS, AV*, all the

---

4. We get the term *rāṣṭra* in the Vedas as follows:
   (a) *R̥V*, 4/42/1; 7/34/11; 84/2; 10/109/3; 124/4&5; 173/1&5; 174/2&5 (11 times in 11 *r̥ks*).
   (b) *SYV*, 9/23; 10/2; 10/3; 10/4; 20/8&10; 22/22 (71 times in 7 *mantras*)
   (c) *AV*, 1/29/1; 4&6; 3/4/1&2; 3/5/2; 3/8/1; 3/19/2&5; 4/1/2; 28/4; 5/17/3, 4, 12&17; 5/19/4, 6, 7, 8 & 10; 6/39/2; 54/2; 78/2; 87/1&2; 88/2; 124/1; 134/1; 7/35/1; 8/9/13; 10/3/12&16; 10/8; 11/7/11&17; 12/1/8; 3/10; 5/8; 13/1/8&9; 13/1/34&35; 15/10/2; 19/24/1; 30/3; 41/1; 20/27/1&10 (59 times in 51 *mantras*)
5. Read, *pr̥hivyaiḥ samudraparyantāyā ekarāṭ*, *AB*, 8/4/1.
6. *VP*, 2/3/1.
7. *KumS*, 1/1.

Brāhmaṇas, with the *Āraṇyakas* and major Upaniṣads. And the classical works such as *Rām*, *MBh*, and major Purāṇas, have been presented in support of the Vedic works. Secondary Sources include the modern works of oriental and occidental scholars. Moreover, articles of some scholars in prominent magazines also have been counted and put into account accordingly.

Method Followed

In order to deal with the problem we have followed the library method in which we have studied the original texts, secondary sources and independent articles as well.

1. First of all we studied the four *mantra saṁhitās* — *R̥V*, *YV* (*ŚYV* and *TS*), *SV* and the *AV* — investigating the word *rāṣṭra* and found that it was mentioned 141 times in those texts.
2. We tried to define the term *rāṣṭra* on the basis of the above *Mantras* and the meaning hidden behind them.
3. We have chalked out the definitions of *rāṣṭra* or nation from the Eastern and Western sources which helped us to go beyond the Vedic interpretation.
4. Next, we started to collect data chapter-wise after reading the original sources. Some other informations have been collected from the secondary sources also.
5. These data have been placed orderly so that they can form chapters in several sub-points.
6. This arrangement in the end made it easy to write down the chapters orderly.

Chapter Plan

With a view to acheiving the goal of compiling the thesis we made a primary chapter plan as follows:

Introduction	:	General View — Sources — Method followed — Hypothesis
Chapter 1	:	Nation and Nationalism
Chapter 2	:	Political Aspects
Chapter 3	:	Parliament (*sabhā, samiti* and *vidatha*)
Chapter 4	:	Social Structure (*varṇa* and *āśrama vyavasthā*)
Chapter 5	:	Socio-Political Aspects
Chapter 6	:	Socio-Cultural Aspects
Chapter 7	:	Vedic Economics
Chapter 8	:	Needs
Chapter 9	:	Religion and Philosophy
Chapter 10	:	Military Aspects
Conclusion		
Appendices		

Succinct Gist of Each Chapter

***Chapter* 1**: In this chapter we have dealt with Nation and its definitions according to Western and Eastern scholars and the Vedic evidences as well. We have dealt with etymological researches also. We have discussed here the elements of Vedic *rāṣṭra* so as to have the patriotism, motherly feelings to a particular land, etc., establishment of a *rāṣṭra*, its evolution and spreading the Vedic concepts outside India.

***Chapter* 2**: Types of States such as *vairājya, rājya, sāmrājya, svārājya, bhaujya, pārameṣṭhya rājya, ādhipatyamaya rājya, samanta-paryāyī, jānarājya, sārvabhauma rājya*, etc., have been discussed elaborately. Moreover, kingship and its meaning, origin, characteristics, qualities, coronation ceremony and king's duties are discussed in this chapter.

***Chapter* 3**: *Sabhā, samiti* and *vidatha* have been discussed elaborately under the sub-points of types, qualifications of members, topics of discussions, functions, characteristics, origin and history, etc.

***Chapter* 4**: The meaning of the *varṇa* and *āśrama vyavasthā*, universality of the *varṇa vyavasthā*, *varṇa*s on the basis of function and genealogical order, the four castes, their importance, rights of a *purohita* and his functions, duties of those castes, national importance of caste system, etc., have been discussed under the *varṇa vyavasthā*. On the other hand, the *āśrama vyavasthā* comprises of its meaning, duration, characteristics, their life, duties, etc. The former conducted the society and the later led the individual life to make them run smoothly.

***Chapter* 5**: We have discussed here firstly the topics of *puruṣārtha* and *trivarga* and their national importance. Secondly, the Vedic conception of all round development of a *rāṣṭra* is presented. Motherly feelings to a particular land, importance of *kṣātra* and *brāhmateja* in nation building, are discussed in the first part of this chapter. The second part comprises of the educational system of the Vedic period where we have mentioned the explanations of the term, courses, teachers, students, uniforms, types of students, teaching methods, medium of teaching, teacher-student relationship, female education and convocations, etc.

***Chapter* 6**: We have discussed the following topics under socio-cultural aspects. In the first part of the chapter, we have discussed the Vedic view towards women. The second part includes the marriage institutions, selection of brides and bridegrooms, types of marriage festivities and the rituals, etc., where the peculiarity of the Vedic system of marriage has been presented.

***Chapter* 7**: Vedic view on the economic theories such as price, demand, supply, population, resources, production, consumption, exchange and formulation of prices, distribution, taxes, market competition, and five foot economy are in the first part of the chapter. In the second, third and the fourth part of the chapter we have discussed on agriculture, industries, and trade and commerce.

***Chapter* 8**: The first part of this chapter comprises of essential and secondary needs. Food, dresses and houses are included in primary needs where the problem of meat eating and *soma* juice have been tackled out. Several types of buildings have clearly been discussed. The second part of this chapter includes secondary needs where we have dealt with physiology. In addition to this, we have discussed on music, dance and jewellery as well.

***Chapter* 9**: This chapter deals with religion and philosophy of the Vedas. In the first part we have discussed about *upāsanā*, conception of God and Vedic prayers, etc. On the other hand, the second part comprises of *yajña*s and its types, detail about *agnyādhāna, pūrṇāhuti, cāturmāsya, agniṣṭoma*, political *yajña*s such as *rājasūya, vājhapeya* and *aśvamedha* sacrifices along with other general *yajña*s. The third part includes philosophy where we have discussed about cosmogony, creation and transmigration or rebirth.

***Chapter* 10**: The chapter deals with military aspects in which we have included army troops, types of wars, weapons, charioteering, chariots and elephants in the wars, cavalary, infantry, several types of forts and fortifications.

***Chapter* 11**: This chapter contains such topic which do not come under the purview of the above-mentioned chapters. Those have been treated in the chapter "Miscellaneous." This chapter has taken such topics as science in the Vedas, existence of *lipi*, knowledge of geography in the Vedic India and the theory of *ārya* as depicted in the Vedic literature.

We hope that it would not be an extravagant claim when we say that the thesis is an original one because of its presentation and expression.

1

Nation and Nationalism

Rāṣṭra as it is Defined

THE term *rāṣṭra* is derived from the root *rāj* "to shine" with the addition of the affix *ṣṭran* in the *uṇādi sūtra*.[1] Thus, the term *rāṣṭra* bears three meanings, (i) that which reveals all the people,[2] (ii) by which all are revealed everywhere, all with grandeur,[3] (iii) that shines over all sphere.[4] The word *rāṣṭra* is formed through a special grammatical process.[5]

Some later literatures define *rāṣṭra* as an important organ of state.[6] Organs of a state are as follows: (a) a master or a king, (b) ministers, (c) friends, (d) account of *kośa*, (e) *rāṣṭra*, (f) fort and (g) military.

Sāyaṇācārya has taken the term in the sense of

---

1. *Uṇādi Sūtra*, 4/1/151 from *Siddhānta Kaumudī*, Serial No. 598.
2. Read, *Rājayati prakāśayati sarvān lokān iti rāṣṭram* (*karmāṇi*), *rājṛ* + *ṇic* + *ṣṭran as chādi* + *ṇic* + *ṣṭran* = *chātra* in *SK Uṇādi* 598.
3. Read, *rājyate prakāśyate* (*sva mahimnā*) *sarvatra iti rāṣṭram* (*karaṇe*) as we get *pīyate anena iti pātram* in *SK* with Tatvabodhinī commentary of Gñānendra Sarasvatī, p. 281.
4. Read, *rājate sarveṣu lokeṣu iti rāṣṭram* (*kartari*) as we get *patati iti pātram* in *SK Uṇādi* 598.
5. *Rāj* + *ṣṭraṇ* = *rāj* + *ṣṭra* (*halantyam* and *tasya lopaḥ* = *rāj* + *ṭra* (*sa* is omitted according to *sa pratyayasya*. Again *j* becomes *s* according to *vrasca bhasca* . . . . Thus the term *rāṣṭra* is formed.
6. *AK*, *Kṣatriya Varga*, 36.

kingdom,[7] subjects,[8] state or *deśa*[9] and so on.

Thus, the scholars have indicated its meaning as a kingdom, realm, empire, dominion, district and country but in the Vedas it is taken in the sense of people, nation and subjects. The *BP* applies the word *rāṣṭrakarṣaṇa* to mean "distress, distressing or oppressing a kingdom."[10]

The function of *rāṣṭra* is to endow with all the wealth to the people who live in, as *rāṣṭra* was thought to be property in itself.[11]

The *aśvamedha* sacrifice has been identified with the king of all the sacrifices.[12] Therefore, the position of the *yajña* is above all in the glances of the Vedic people. On the other hand, the *AB* describes that a *rāṣṭra* is always equal to an *aśvamedha* sacrifice.[13] Such passages reveal that a *rāṣṭra* is in itself a culture, religion, inspiration, emotion and base for them. The importance of the word *rāṣṭra* appears from the fact that *rāṣṭra* is mentioned itself to be *kṣatra*,[14] subjects or *viś*,[15] deers,[16] etc. Savitā[17] and Rudra[18] were regarded as *rāṣṭrapati* and *sabhāpati*, respectively.

Pandit Narahari Narayan Bhide defines *rāṣṭra* as follows:

---

7. *ṚV*, 10/11, 3/1; 2; 5; 10/174/1-5.
8. *ṚVSāy*, 4/42/1.
9. *ŚYV*, 22/22.
10. *SEDM*, p. 879.
11. *ŚB*, 6/7/3/7.
12. Read, *rājā vai eṣa yajñānam aśvamedhaḥ*, *ŚB*, 13/2/2/1.
13. Read, *rāṣṭraṁ vai aśvamedhah*, *ŚB*, 13/1/6/3.
14. *AB*, 7/22.
15. *Ibid.*, 8/26.
16. *ŚB*, 13/2/9/8.
17. *Ibid.*, 11/3/4/4.
18. *ŚYV*, 16/24.

> The feeling of eternal goal of human life which makes the life celestial and elegant, and the race, language, literature, community of economic interest, tradition, country, administration of the state and awareness in the invasion of foreigners which are found within the psychology being expressed with those seven organs, is the Nationality or *rāṣṭrīyatā*. The people having such *rāṣṭrīyatā* is a *rāṣṭra* and the member of such *rāṣṭra* is the *rāṣṭrīya*.[19]

Nation and Nationalism: Foreign View

So far the term Nation and Nationalism in the Western world is concerned, it is still obscure. The term is not yet defined. Israel Zangwile in his *Principle of Nationalities* says, "Nationalism is one of those tropical jungles of thought in which politics and journalism flourish."[20] H.L. Featherstone goes to say in his *A Century of Nationalism* as "Nationalism is not capable of scientic definition."[21] Florian Znaniecki goes one step further and declares, "In view of the terminological confusion, the editors of several encyclopaedias have omitted the word "Nation" altogether. For example, *International Encyclopaedia, Encyclopaedia of Social Sciences, Encyclopaedia Britanica* and *Woterbuch der statt Swissensc hafte*."[22] Most of the historians today agree upon the modern origin of Nationalism. G.P. Gooch remarks, "Nationalism is a child of the French Revolution."[23] On the other hand, Carlton J.H. Hays remarks Nationalism to be a very modern theory. He writes, "Nationalism is modern, very modern."[24] John Oaksmith describes Nationalism as "What the vast majority of civilised people feels to be the most sacred and

---

19. *KRKRN*, pp. 40 & 41.
20. Quoted *PunyT*, p. 33.
21. *Ibid.*, p. 35.
22. *Ibid.*
23. *SMHG*, p. 217.
24. *Essays on Nationalism*, Curlton, J.H. Hayes, p. 29.

dominating inspiration in life." Further, he mentions it to be "The most pregnant fact of modern political evolution."[25] W.B. Pillsbury defines Nationality and says, "Nationality is an affair of the mind or spirit, not of physical relationship. The only way to decide whether an individual belongs to one nation rather than another is to ask him."[26] Robert Michels observes,

> Nationality does not consist necessarily in either language or religion or a common past, but in the will of people. The expression of this will is generally made by a synthesis of some of the constitutive elements which we have just enumerated, and sometimes all of them. However, Nationality can very well exist in the absence of several of them and can even be limited to a single element, the essential one: the will.[27]

Similarly, Arnold J. Toynbee says,

> Nationality is like all great forces in human life, it is nothing material or mechanical, but a subjective psychological feeling in living people. This feeling can be kindled by the pressure of one or several factors as a common country, language or tradition.[28]

On the other hand, Max Weber tries to define the term as follows:

> Nationalism is a common bond of sentiment whose adequate expression would be a state of his own, and which, therefore, normally tends to give birth to such a state.[29]

---

25. *Race and Nationality: An enquiry into the Origin and Growth of Patriotism*, John Oaksmith, p. 25.
26. *The Psychology of Nationality and Internationalism*, W.B. Pillsbury, p. 267.
27. Quoted from *INH*, p. 582.
28. *Nationality and the War*, Arnold J. Toynbee, p. 13.
29. Quoted from *INH*, p. 583.

Whatever the definitions of the term there may be, Hans Kohn in his *Idea of Nationalism* discuss it as the process of integration of the masses of the people into a common political form.[30] Later on, he discusses language, customs and traditions, religions, political frontiers, as some of the important elements of Nationalism. But, he confused in determining the concrete definition and wrote at last.

> Although some of these objective factors are of great importance for the formation of the nationalities, the most essential element is a living and active corporate will. Nationality is formed by the decision to form a nationality.[31]

League of Nations confessed that the word, "State" and "Nation" are synonymous. The Indian thinkers warned about the bad effects of this misinterpretation at that time. Prof. Wilson accepted the proposals of the then members and committed mistakes. As a result of this, the question of minority arouse which caused the Second World War.[32] Thengdi asks,

> Is the UNO of today untouched with such mistakes? Does it not observe a country whenever it seeks the membership of it in the basis of the definition fixed by the League of Nations?[33]

He further informs,

> The genocide of the Australian people has now been accepted as "Fait accompli." It is not known how many people were killed but it is told that there were 260 languages of those people. Their number was badly decreased after the genocide caused by the Europeans. But the question that arises here is whether they will be regarded nationless

30. Quoted from *INH*, p. 4.
31. *Ibid.*, p. 15.
32. *PunyT*, p. 19.
33. *Ibid.*

> people for their few population? Is not that an appeasement to the whites?[34]

The theory of Nationalism which the Western world had brought up, is based upon the theory of evolution. At first the people of ancient times were supposed to be roaming tribes who lived on hunting. That state of living was said Tribalism. Secondly, the system of agriculture was discovered and the settled agricultural communities started to grow. That brought the feelings of blood and soil and it was supposed to be Territorialism. The Western thinkers adopted the theory of Nationalism which came out as the synchronization of Tribalism and Territorialism.[35]

The people of Western countries soon became able to be related with the land which they lived in. For example, the administrators were said to be the "King of the English" and "King of French," etc.[36]

Exposing the fact that all the European nations are the child nations, Napoleon remarked,

> There are in Europe more than thirty million Frenchmen, fifteen million Italians, thirty million Germans . . . Out of each of these people, I wanted to make a united national whole . . . . For France unity has been wrought; in Spain, it has proved unattainable; to establish the Italian Nation I would have needed 20 years; to make the Germans a nation would have required still more patience.[37]

An Indian scholar, D.B. Thengdi remarks,

> Nationalism starts from the point where the effort of the progress from natural diversity to psychological unity comes to an end.[38]

---

34. *PunyT*, p. 21.
35. *Ibid.*, p. 22.
36. *Ibid.*, p. 23.
37. *Ibid.*
38. *Ibid.*, p. 24.

Thus, the term "Nation" itself has remained confusing. So it seems that the term *rāṣṭra* is to be explained neither through the vision of "Nation" nor of a "State." It is completely an independent term. The Sanskrit term specially used in the Vedic literature have their own meanings in themselves. They can neither be translated nor expressed in other languages properly. Vincent A. Smith confessed,

> The Vedic hymns present innumerable difficulties to the students. Even when a literal version in more or less grammatical English has been produced, the meaning behind the words eludes the translator. The idea of *ṛṣis* are so remote from those of the modern world that the most learned Sanskritist, whether Indian or Foreign, may fail to grasp them. Interpretations consequently differ to an enormous extent, and after all, possible has been and done much remains obscure.[39]

Characteristics of Rāṣṭra: A Vedic View

The term *rāṣṭra* is found frequently in the Vedic *Saṁhitās*. It was supposed to be an important factor of the social life in the Vedic era to think about *rāṣṭra*. The importance of *rāṣṭra* appears from the fact that the term *rāṣṭra* is mentioned 11, 71 and 59 times in the *ṚV*, *ŚYV* and the *AV*, respectively. As it is derived from the root *rāj*, the *rāṣṭra* becomes an enlightening and spiritual geo-cultural unit. Thus, the term *rāṣṭra* has a peculiar meaning carrying throughout the *Mantra Saṁhitās*.

It is said that the sacrificial oblations had created *rāṣṭra*. The oblations satisfied gods and they bestowed *rāṣṭra* to the people.[40] The scholars with their hard labour walked on the earth surrounded by oceans and they nomenclatured it as *rāṣṭra*. This land is prayed as a *rāṣṭra*, to bestow valour

39. *OHIS*, p. 46.
40. *ṚV*, 10/174/1.

and brightness to the people.[41] Another passage similarly declared that the learned seers did hard penance and discovered *rāṣṭra, vala* and *ojas* for which people were requested to offer their respects to the *rāṣṭra*.[42] The efforts of the Vedic sages to bring a *rāṣṭra* into its existence are scattered everywhere in the Vedic literature. Avinas Chandra Das with special references to some Ṛgvedic passages[43] remarks,

> It was the *ṛṣis* or sage-priests, the mighty, wise thinkers of old, the "brainist" among the people, who led the van of progress in the early and subsequent stages of Aryan development. It was they who domesticated the cattle, discovered the use of fire, invented the plough, learnt and taught the art of agriculture, invented and manufactured various implements, made chariots and wagons, discovered the intimate relations of the Cosmic Powers with human welfare, instituted Fire-worship and the various sacrifices calculated to promote human happiness, evolved the institution of marriages and established it on a firm and sure basis, discovered the existence of the various beneficient deities and differentiated their individual characteristics, brought them down from their distant spheres to exercise their benevolent influence on human affairs, discovered their unity in the One Supreme Deity, permeating the Universe — the premordial Source of Creation — the one and indivisible, yet manifesting itself in manifold ways, and lifted up human hopes and aspirations from the fleeting evanescent and perishable things of this world to the attainment of calm, serene and everlasting *anandam* (beatitude) that knows no flow nor ebb is centred in and co-extensive with Brahman, the Great and Undefinable. It was these great minds that in early Ṛgvedic times fused the disjointed and discordant elements into one homogeneous

41. *AV*, 12/1/8.
42. *Ibid.*, 19/41/1.
43. *ṚV*, 10/60/4; 5/86/2 and 9/101/9, etc.

> whole, and united the scattered villages into one confederacy under the supremacy of one vigorous and powerful clan whom they guided by their sage-counsels to the attainment of the blessed goal of one united people. It was through their noble and selfless exertions that there came into being in the Ṛgvedic times the Five Tribes (*pañcajanāḥ* or *pañcakṛsṭayaḥ*) who possessed a homogeneous civilisation, speaking one language, performing the same sacrifices, and believing in the same gods, and though existing as separate Tribes, were looked upon as the different limbs of the great Aryan people such that in the making the Sage-Masters, realising the ultimate destiny of the Aryans, never missed an opportunity for praying to the Great gods for the well being of the Five Tribes.[44]

Those *ṛṣi*s discussed about politics, economics, philosophy, psychology, medical science and so on. They, in the same process, discussed about Nation and Nationalism also. What they found as the characteristics of *rāṣṭra* are as follows: First of all, protection of a territory of land by the warriors (kṣatriyas) was an important element to make a *rāṣṭra*. It must be protected from all sides.[45] The territory of land must have awaken *purohita*s who could exercise control over the protectors.[46] They were responsible persons as it is seen in the *AB* when a king was coronated.[47] Another passage of the *AV* shows the importance of *purohita* when he advised the king.[48] Secondly, an important element of *rāṣṭra*, though it is confessed by some scholars as "it is little surprising to note that population as such is not mentioned as one of the constituents of the state"[49] is a well organized society.[50] The

44 *RCD*, pp. 304-05.

45. Read, *rāṣṭraṁ gupitaṁ kṣatriyasya*, *ṚV*, 10/109/3; *AV* 5/17/3.

46. Read, *vayaṁ rāṣṭre jagṛyāmaḥ purohitāḥ*, *ŚYV*, 9/23.

47. *AB*, 8/2/2.

48. *AV*, 3/23.

49. *SGAIA*, pp. 44-45.

50. Read, *rāṣṭrāṇi vai viśaḥ*, *AV*, 1/29/1; *AB*, 8/26.

society was expected to be conscious one.[51] Strong and proper administration was supposed to be another important element of a *rāṣṭra*.[52] The administrator seems to be selected or elected. He had to think of his subjects as his own limbs.[53]

People of that territory must be conscious for their culture and history that helps a territory to be recognized as *rāṣṭra*. In a passage of the *R̥V* a seer says that the knowledge of the past and present must be there.[54] This may help to establish the national feeling through which the citizen of a state become ready to omit a traitor to maintain the glory of his *rāṣṭra*.[55] The earth or *bhūmi* of the *rāṣṭra* was prayed as mother by the Vedic sages.[56] A Vedic sage never thought of his *rāṣṭra* to be a congregation of stone, land and sands only, but he saluted[57] it and invoked it as mother.[58] Thus, it proved that the motherly feelings towards a *rāṣṭra* or the conception of motherland came first in the minds of the Vedic sages.

Rāṣṭra as a living being remains under the guidance of the brāhmaṇas. Without the help of a brāhmaṇa, *rāṣṭra* was supposed to be unable to perform all the activities, because, *ṛta*, *satya*, *tapa*, *rāṣṭra*, *śrama*, *dharma*, *karma*, etc., all were supposed to be under the brāhmaṇas.[59]

A *cakravartī* was first advised by a *purohita* to be coronated and perhaps after coronation, he offered his whole *rāṣṭra* to

51. *AV*, 3/19/2-5.
52. *Ibid.*, 6/87/1 & 2: 13/1/34 & *R̥V*, 10/109/3.
53. *AV*, 12/3/10 & 13/1/1.
54. *R̥V*, 10/15/2.
55. *AV*, 10/3/16.
56. *AV*, 12/1/8.
57. *Ibid.*, 12/1/26.
58. *Ibid.*, 12/1/63.
59. *Ibid.*, 11/7/17 & 18.

God[60] and accepted again as a kind of *prasāda* of his worship. The fact clearifies that the *rāṣṭra* was thought always to be divine and cultural unit, in fact a geo-cultural territory. In *rāṣṭra*, its ruler and the subjects must have their relationships like a master and a servant, or in other words, like God and the devotee.[61] A *rāṣṭra* was supposed to continue its existence till the *samūhapati* or *vrātya* was respected.[62] In short, the above-mentioned Vedic evidences seems forming the definition of the *rāṣṭra* as follows: **A *rāṣṭra* is such a geo-cultural territory of land having warrior protectors, awaken *purohitas*, conscious and well-organized society which are conducted by a powerful administration in which the people should have their cultural heritage, national and motherly feelings for that territory of land.**

Various linguistic groups are seen even in the times of the Vedas. The duties (*dharma*) were already divided but they lived peacefully having possessed the feeling of motherland in their heart. One prays the earth, for the latter provides shelter to the groups of various languages and *dharmas*.[63]

The Vedic sages used to sing the songs in the *yajñas* which were based on national feelings.[64] Another passage of the *ṚV* tells that the intelligent people praised the land of Asamāti.[65] The political scholars were conscious to awaken the people by filling the feeling of nationalism in their heart. One of the scholars expressed his wishes that the people might respect their nation and the rulers as well.[66] The *AV*, on the

60. *ṚV*, 10/124/5.
61. *Ibid.*, 4/42/1.
62. *AV*, 15/10/2.
63. *Ibid.*, 12/1/45.
64. *ṚV*, 8/100/10.
65. *Ibid.*, 10/60/1.
66. *Ibid.*, 10/173/1.

other hand, mentions the importance of historical co-operation among the people of the state. The seer says that the land which bestowed the prosperity and shelter was made great by the forefathers . . . That shows that the actions of his forefathers or the historical consciousness was highly required.[67] The Vedic sage offers his salutations to the land purified by greats with several activities such as *yajña*, worships, eulogies, etc.[68] The following were thought to be evil things by which a *rāṣṭra* was believed to be ruined. . .

1. where the piece of *ulkā* falls[69]
2. where a brāhmaṇī is kidnapped[70]
3. where a cow is prohibited to roam freely[71]
4. where the brāhmaṇas are tortured[72] and so on.

The characteristics of a *rāṣṭra* as we find in the Brāhmaṇic literature also are vivid. In one passage of the *AB* it is said, "If a kṣatriya salutes thrice a brāhmaṇa he starts to follow him. The *rāṣṭra* will be prosperous and full of warriors if it begets strong and brave sons."[73] If we do not take the term brāhmaṇa and kṣatriya as individual, we would find that the combinations of *brāhmateja* and *kṣātrateja* make a *rāṣṭra* prosperous and the works of all round development also run swiftly.

Another passage of the *AB* indicates that the *rāṣṭra* of others should not be snatched away. If the master of a particular land or country is defeated his kingdom had to be restored to him.[74]

67. *R̥V*, 12/1/5.
68. *AV*, 12/1/38.
69. *Ibid.*, 5/17/4.
70. *Ibid.*, 5/17/6.
71. *Ibid.*, 5/17/12.
72. *Ibid.*, 5/18.
73. *AB*, 8/2/5.
74. *Ibid.*, 8/2/6.

Geographical Evidences

Some scholars of Indology have tried to prove that the Ṛgvedic Āryans settled on the banks of the river Sindhu. In *ṚV*, 10/75 the seer prays the rivers, and the Western scholars like Vincent A. Smith and others try to prove that the Āryans came into India invading upon the people of Indus Valley and settled there.[75] It seems that the Western scholars like Max-Müller and others had a conspiracy to vilify the Indian people by misleading them. According to Max-Müller "to the missionary an accurate knowledge of the sacred books was as indispensable as the knowledge of the enemy's country to a General."[76] He again wrote in 1859 that India is a nation of philosophers and Indian intellect is lacking in political or material speculation, and that the Indians never knew the feeling of nationality.[77] But, contrary to these previous researches, it is found that the sages of India could realize the theory of *rāṣṭra* and the feeling of Nationalism ran in their veins.

Not only the rivers related to the Indus are found in the hymns.[78] The next passage reveals the name of the river Gomatī also.[79] Another passage mentions the Sarayū.[80] There is an interesting passage that describes how the river Sarasvatī flowed from the Himālayas and mingled with the ocean.[81] In the same way the *AV* also speaks about the course of the river Gaṅgā.[82] The *ṚV* again informs about 21 rivers that flowed within this *rāṣṭra*.[83] Another Ṛgvedic passage

75. *OHIS*, p. 53.
76. Quoted *APIIAIR*, p. 1.
77. *Ibid.*
78. *ṚV*, 10/75/5.
79. *Ibid.*, 10/75/6.
80. *Ibid.*, 10/64/9.
81. *Ibid.*, 7/95/2.
82. *AV*, 6/24/1.
83. *ṚV*, 10/64/8.

informs "O, master of the ocean, come hither from the mountains. . ."[84] Such passages prove that the national territory of India was spread from the Himālayas to the ocean.[85] The Indian nation seems to be discovered and established after the seers of the *R̥V* did hard labour and investigation.

Macdonell in his *History of Sanskrit Literature* mentions that the Āryans had no actual knowledge of ocean, they had their beliefs upon the words only which they heard.[86] Contrary to such misinterpretation, we have ample evidences which prove that the Vedic people acquired correct and proper knowledge of ocean. Some references that prove their knowledge are as under:

1. The great seven rivers flow towards ocean.[87]
2. Wealth-wisher businessmen moved all over the ocean.[88]
3. Wealth-desirers sailed their boats (ships) on ocean.[89]
4. A ship having one hundred oars sailed on the ocean.[90]
5. The ships having sails also were used in those days.[91]
6. They had the knowledge of the pearls hidden under the water of sea.[92]
7. The sailors sometimes faced the waves in oceans.[93]

We have got a lot of such evidences which falsify the theory

84. *R̥V*, 8/34/13.
85. *AV*, 12/34/13.
86. Quoted *ASSK*, p. 124.
87. *R̥V*, 1/71/7.
88. *Ibid.*, 1/56/2.
89. *Ibid.*, 1/48/3.
90. *Ibid.*, 1/116/5.
91. *Ibid.*, 1/82/5 & 10/143/5.
92. *Ibid.*, 10/97/4 & 1/47/6.
93. *Ibid.*, 8/75/9.

that the people of Vedic age were ignorant about ocean.[94] Some important passages from the *AB* can be quoted in which it is told that the expansive land upon ocean is a *rāṭ* or *rāṣṭra*.[95] The same term is repeated in the next passage also. Such evidences give us a conception regarding the existence of a geo-cultural *rāṣṭra* that spread from the Himālayas down to the ocean upon which the emperors also tried to rule over politically. Sāyaṇācārya, while explaining this passage goes one step further and remarks, "Of the land spread upon ocean should have a single emperor."[96]

The conch which was buzzed in ancient India was found in the ocean of the south.[97] Khagendra Dasgupta after his long research has opined as follows, "The *dharma*, civilisation and culture of the Aryans got spread over the whole India including south."[98]

So far the seas and oceans are concerned, we find the four seas in all the four sides of the Indus valley,[99] the sun was described as being risen in the east sea and setting in the west sea.[100] H.D. Sankalia also supports that Rājpūtānā was a sea during the time of Indus civilization and perhaps much earlier.[101]

Evolution of Rāṣṭra

In order to go through the theory of evolution of *rāṣṭra* one must understand the term *virāṭ*. The simple meaning of this term is said to be "Ruling far and wide, sovereign, excellent and splendid." The Ṛgvedic passages mean the term as a

94. *ṚV*, 1/116/2; 1/82/5 & 7; 10/183/5; 7/88/3 and 1/55/2, etc.
95. Read, *pṛthivyaiḥ samudraparyantāyāḥ ekarāṭ*, *AB*, 8/4/1.
96. Sāyaṇa on *AB*, 8/4/1.
97. *ṚV*, 1/180/8.
98. *ASSK*, p. 131.
99. *ṚV*, 9/33/6; 10/47/2.
100. *Ibid.*, 3/55/1; 4/43/5; 5/80/4 & 5; 10/136/5.
101. *ASSK*, p. 131.

ruler, chief, king and queen. On the other hand, the *AV* means the term as excellence, pre-eminence, high rank, dignity and majesty. Other Vedic literature indicate that *virāṭ* is the first progeny of Brahmā. *Virāṭ* as a sort of secondary creator is sometimes identified with Prajāpati, Brahmā, Agni and Puruṣa.[102] We get an equation among the words *bhuvana, virāṭ* and *yajña* because *yajña* described itself as *bhuvana* and *virāṭ* as *yajña*.[103]

In a passage of the *AV* it is found that *virāṭ* was begotten from *brahmacārins*[104] and another passage declares that it was born from *puruṣa*.[105] Some other passages reveal *virāṭ* as a female phenomenon which is regarded as a cow.[106] *Virāṭ* has been explained as *yajña* and *prāṇa* which bestows life in creatures.[107] It is a deity and in the *Saṁhitās*[108] it has been explained with several meanings.[109] After all, *virāṭ* is regarded to be space, sound, creator, death and matter of actions, both the past and future act under him accordingly.[110] Finally saying, it is something abstract without which neither anything becomes visible nor it can be felt. Sukumari Bhattacharya admits,

> *Virāṭ* dies mythologically after the *saṁhitā* period but is revived in the *Vedānta* philosophy as an imaginary aggregate of gross bodies, as a base for the production of Puruṣa. *Virāṭ* perhaps symbolises the cosmic water. Like Brahman, *Virāṭ* connotes vastness or all-pervasiveness.[111]

102. *ESD*, p. 982.
103. *TS*, 3/3/7/5; Read, *virāṭ vai yajñaḥ*, *SB*, 1/1/1/22; Read, *vairājaḥ yajñoḥ*, *GB*, 1/5/24.
104. *AV*, 11/5/7.
105. *R̥V*, 10/90/5; *ŚYV*, 31/5; *SV*, 6/3/4/7; *AV*, 19/6/9.
106. *AV*, 8/10/24 & 11/8/30.
107. *R̥V*, 1/88/5 (as *yajña*); *AV*, 11/4/12 (as *prāṇa*).
108. *AV*, 33/26/3.
109. *ŚYV*, 10/13 & 13/57.
110. *AV*, 9/10/24.
111. *ITSB*, p. 329.

The theory of creation as it is found in the *MS* tells about the birth story of *virāṭ* as follows: *Brahman* split himself into male and female. As a result of combination of these two distinct powers *virāṭ* was produced, from which the first Manu sprang out.[112] *Virāṭ* was first born as Uṣā who destroyed the darkness. Sūrya and Agni depended upon *virāṭ*, in the form of Uṣā. Uṣā was known as the wife of Sūrya.[113] That *virāṭ* ascended into several power which created metres seasons and so on.[114]

Virāṭ then expressed its form as water and ascended into *gārhapatyas*[115] which indicates that the scattered people were organized and family system was developed. Secondly, it stepped into the *āhavanīya* institutions[116] which indicates that the people of the particular area started to perform *yajñas* which brought the social feelings in their mind. Its next step was to *dakṣiṇāgni*.[117] It then passed through the *sabhās*. The stepping of *virāṭ* into *sabhā* brought up the small councils[118] in the villages. Conscious people started to send their youths and ladies in the *sabhās*. Thus, the *virāṭ* rose into the *samitis*. The expert member of the *samiti* was called *sāmitya*.[119] That *samiti* or the national assembly went up to the *āmantraṇa pariṣad*[120] and the ministers were selected from that.[121] The last point was the *rāṣṭra* which came into existence in the course of such evolution. Many a critics have explained *samiti* as a national council in which

112. *MS*, 1/32 & 33.
113. *AV*, 8/9/11.
114. *Ibid.*, 8/9/12-18.
115. *Ibid.*, 8/10/2.
116. *Ibid.*, 8/10/4.
117. *Ibid.*, 8/10/6.
118. *Ibid.*, 8/10/8 & 9.
119. *Ibid.*, 8/10/11.
120. *Ibid.*, 8/10/12 & 13.
121. *VRVYRS*, p. 32.

the supreme authorities of administrations had to be presented. Such *samiti*s were the origin of national feelings.

Patriotism or Rāṣṭrabhakti

The people of the Vedic ages are found always willing to maintain the independence of their *rāṣṭra*. Once a king who had lost his *rāṣṭra* regained it after people had rooted out the foreigners and he was recoronated with grandeur. The people of the Vedas are found to be conscious in this respect.[122]

The people were conscious of the internal and external enemies. They prayed God to destroy such enemies and also the would-be enemies. The Almighty was again prayed to help the people so that they could be well organized as a *rāṣṭra*. The people wanted to live in a well-developed and prosperous *rāṣṭra*.[123] The citizens of the Vedic *rāṣṭra* protected their frontiers with their keen alertness. They were found ready with sharpened arms and ammunitions. They wished that the valour of their *rāṣṭra* should remain for good.[124] A Ṛgvedic passage informs that whenever the internal or external disturbances caused chaos in *rāṣṭra*, the citizens of the *rāṣṭra* tried to scatter the conspiracies either by spiritual sacrificial ceremonies[125] or by strong organizations.[126]

The people of the Vedic *rāṣṭra* performed their religious activities to make prosperous the individual, social and national life. There are a lot of passages in which they expressed their extreme love for motherland. They offered oblations for the enhancement of the strength of their

---

122. *AV*, 3/4/1.
123. *Ibid.*, 7/35/1.
124. *Ibid.*, 3/19/5.
125. *Ibid.*, 3/19/2/7, 10/3/16.
126. *ṚV*, 10/191/2.

rāṣṭra[127] and prayed to God to help them to continue their national life.[128]

The conception of *rāṣṭra* of the Vedic people seems to be so deep that they wished to live in a prosperous *rāṣṭra* for the whole life. They prayed to Varuṇa, Bṛhaspati, Indra and Agni to bestow stability to the *rāṣṭra* they lived in.[129] A passage of the *ŚYV*, which some scholars have identified to be national enthem, runs as follows:

> Brahma, may the brāhmaṇa in our nation overflow with brahmanical lusture and shine. May the kṣatriyas be brave, skilled in archery, efficient in shooting and warriors of highest degree. May the cow yield (abundant) milk, the bullocks (strong enough) to carry (the burden of the yoke) and the horse speedy. May the young women be a respectable matron. May the youthful son of this host be a hero, ever victorious, moving in a magnificent chariot and worthy of an assembly. May the rains shower regularly for us in seasons. May the trees bear fruits for us. May we be contented by acquisition of our needs and by preservation of the acquired wealth.[130]

Such innumerable examples indicating that the people had vast love and esteem for their motherland, can be collected.

The *bhūmi* of the Vedic *rāṣṭra* was supposed to be based upon Brahmā, *tapasyā*, *dīkṣā*, *yajña* and *bṛhat*. So the people thought that the land where they lived was a living being.[131]. They, therefore, used to say, "Let the god *rāṣṭra* (*rāṣṭradeva*) be saluted."[132] The feelings of patriotism of the Vedic people can be seen from the fact that they offered their homages to the different objects of their nations also. What a deep

127. *ṚV*, 10/174/1.
128. *Ibid.*, 7/84/2 & 10/173/5.
129. *AV*, 6/88/2.
130. *ŚYV*, 22/22.
131. *AV*, 12/1/1.
132. *Ibid.*, 19/41/1.

love for their motherland they had, is revealed from the prayer offered to the Sindhu and the Vipāśā.[133] The next passage also was used to praise those rivers but the devotee goes one step further and mentions, "They irrigated the God-created land with the water of those rivers."[134] The land in which they lived was not a land of enjoyment but it was supposed to be the gift of the Creator.

Importance of Organization and Unity

It has been described that a *rāṣṭra* was thought to be geo-cultural entity and so it was related to the hearts of the people. *Rāṣṭra* had its correlation with *samiti* also[135] which inspired people to live in a corporate organization. The people of *samiti* must have equal visions and thoughts.[136] The Vedic people sought the unity in the grassroot level. A seer through a passage advises the people to give up jealousy and unite.[137] Youngsters should respect and behave properly with the elders.[138] Jealousy causes the ruin of everything and if such thing continues to happen in a *rāṣṭra* then none can protect its grandeur. So the Vedic seers tried to remove the contradictions and bring the people in a unified form.[139] The knowledge of history and tradition also is an important factor for a strong organization. Without such knowledge, the feelings of nationalism cannot grow.[140] Perhaps that view inspired the sages of the Vedas in the

133. *R̥V*, 3/33/3.
134. *Ibid.*, 3/33/4.
135. Read, "*Samiti* denotes the central assembly of the tribe attended by the kings." Zimmer quoted from *CLAIM*, p. 109.
136. *R̥V*, 10/191/3.
137. *AV*, 3/30/2 & 3.
138. *Ibid.*, 3/30/5.
139. *Ibid.*, 6/94/1.
140. Read, "Nationalism is an actual historical process," J.H. Hays quoted from *PunyT*, p. 47.

past and also in the middle ages.[141] Unity was supposed to be established through three ways, i.e., (1) equal behave, (2) equal speeches, and (3) equal thoughts.[142] Another seer goes one step further and declares through the *AV* that the people among whom unity was required must be given equal education, because they had to achieve a common destination.[143] Another passage reveals that the unity wishers must possess same heart, same will and same mind.[144] A passage from the *AV* says that the Prajāpati Brahmā created subjects. The sage further wished that they might be organized having same mind and intellect.[145] Another passage advises that the will of others should be made well disposed with one will and all should do their works unitedly.[146] A conscious citizen who required unity wanted that all should possess same opinion. Even the enemies should not split away. All the people whether they are relatives or not, should possess same thoughts and mind.[147] All the *brahma, kṣatra* and *viś* should proceed together to achieve the goal of peace.[148]

The Vedic sages gave some formulae to the people in order to bring the society in the unified form, these were found in the Vedic texts as follows:

1. One should treat his family members with loving heart so that the father, mother, sons and daughters live without quarrel.[149] The quarrel must not take

---

141. *R̥V*, 10/15/2.
142. *Ibid.*, 10/91/2.
143. *AV*, 6/64/1.
144. *Ibid.*, 6/64/3.
145. *Ibid.*, 7/19/1.
146. *Ibid.*, 7/52/2.
147. *Ibid.*, 7/52/1.
148. *ŚYV*, 20/25.
149. *AV*, 3/30/2.

place among brothers and sisters also.[150]

2. The intellectuals were expected to be conscious to make the quarelling people calf and its mother cow.[151]
3. Sweet and attractive speeches and the consumption of enjoyable things together[152] were thought to be the key notes of organization.[153]
4. Another passage of the *AV* reveals that body and mind of the persons should be full of love and sympathy[154] and the people should give up their anger.[155]
5. A strong organization in a society brings prosperity and checks dacoities and thefts.[156] It was believed that the people of such society enjoyed victory everywhere and enemies were defeated.[157]

Thus, the Vedic sages have given a vivid description of the importance of organizations which may help the people of India to cogitate a bit. The whole Vedic *Saṁhitās* and literature have revealed the importance of organization and unity. But the *MS* also gives the same idea regarding the matter.Manu says that one should not quarrel with his *ṛtvik, purohita, ācārya,* maternal uncle, guests, sheltered people, boys of teen ages, olds, sicks, doctors, relatives, friends, parents, sisters, brothers, sons, daughters, wives and servants.[158] The *BP* goes one step further and says that a proper organization

150. *AV*, 3/30/3.
151. *Ibid.*, 3/30/1.
152. *Ibid.*, 3/30/5.
153. *Ibid.*, 3/30/6.
154. *Ibid.*, 6/74/1.
155. *Ibid.*, 6/74/3.
156. *ṚV*, 5/3/11.
157. *AV*, 8/8/24.
158. *MS*, 4/179 & 80.

is not only essential for a society and a nation but also for individuals. For example, though a tongue falls between the teeth and gets severe pain, yet it does not become angry.[159]

How this Rāṣṭra came into Existence

It seems from the *Ṛgveda* that during the most ancient times the people were scattered and used to live an isolated life. Some intelligent people planned to organize them so that a *rāṣṭra* may come into existence. It has been mentioned in the *ṚV* that the Vaśiṣṭhas prayed Indra to bestow a beautiful place to Tṛtsus and thus they were given the land.[160] Though they acquired the land, yet they were unorganized and lived isolated life for which Vaśiṣṭha organized them and they were bestowed properties and prosperities.[161] Some critics translated the term "Bharata" as the people of Bhārata by which they meant that the people then existed as a *rāṣṭra*.[162] In support of the above, some passages of the *ṚV* regarding Bharata and Bhārata may be quoted.[163] The feeling of motherland inspired the people of Bhārata and they organized themselves as *rāṣṭra*.[164] The conception is that the *bhūmi* or earth lives with the grandeur and the noble deeds of the greats.[165] The term Vaśiṣṭha is also important. Somewhere this term is found being used for a person named Vaśiṣṭha. The plural form of Vaśiṣṭha as Vaśiṣṭhāḥ has been meant as (1) Vaśiṣṭhas[166] and (2) the sons of Vaśiṣṭha.[167] Vaśiṣṭha is introduced somewhere as the son

159. *BP*, 11/23/51.
160. *ṚV*, 7/33/7.
161. *Ibid.*, 7/33/8.
162. *PunyT*, p. 91.
163. *ṚV*, 3/53/12; 33/11 & 12; 10/143/5; 6/16/5.
164. *Ibid.*, 1/164/23; 5/43/15 & 1/22/5.
165. *Ibid.*, 1/72/9.
166. *Ibid.*, 7/33/4.
167. *Ibid.*, 7/33/1.

of Urvaśī through Mitrāvaruṇa.[168] The next passage refers that he was born from *kalaśa* of a sacrifice wherein Mitrāvaruṇa threw his sperm.[169] Thus, Urvaśī seems to be a symbolical term. Again, Tṛtsus were advised to satisfy Vaśiṣṭha, for he has been presented as a good adviser.[170] On the other hand, some passages in the *SV*[171] and the *AV*[172] can be found mentioning Vaśiṣṭha in the sense of tax determiner.[173] Prof. Surendra Kumar refers to Maharṣi Dayānanda Sarasvatī who mentions Vaśiṣṭha as a well educated scholar who used to determine taxes.[174]

Vedic Nationals: Outside India

Contrary to the theory that the Āryans invaded India, innumerable evidences of India as the homeland of the Vedic people are found scattered everywhere. Though they are sixes and sevens yet they can be orderly arranged. How the people of India went outside to spread the Vedic culture and to civilize the people of the world can be collected from the Vedas.

The name of Viśvāmitra is mentioned in the third book of the *ṚV*. He has been presented there as a researcher who tried to go out and stood on the bank of the rivers Vipāśā and Śutudrī. He declares that he was going out according to the advices and suggestions of the people of Bhārata.[175] The people of Bhārata led by Viśvāmitra crossed the river, offered their prayers and thanked them.[176] Though Acharya

168. *ṚV*, 3/33/11.
169. *Ibid.*, 7/33/13.
170. *Ibid.*, 7/33/14.
171. *SV*, 3/1/5/9; 6/3/2/5; 5/2/9/3, etc.
172. *AV*, 6/21/2; 6/119/1; 20/12/1 and 20/12/6.
173. *MS*, 8/157 and 8/398.
174. Quoted from *VMSS*, p. 402.
175. *ṚV*, 3/33/11.
176. *Ibid.*, 3/33/12.

Gopal Prasad Kausik in his translation of the Vedas which follows the commentary of Sāyaṇa mentions that the term Bharata stands for the son of Duṣyanta, yet no clear evidence of that is found in the *mantras* having such terms. Thus, the terms Bharata and Bhārata are found even in the *ṚV*.[177]

While going outside, Viśvāmitra advised the people of Bhārata to protect the Vedas and to maintain the Vedic way of life. So in order to obey the suggestions and the advices of Viśvamitra, the people of Bhārata worshipped Indra. For that, they took the help from *ākāśā* and *pṛthvī*.[178] Another evidence is expressed in a passage as follows:

> A sailor tells someone that unless he would go with the ship moved with the help of machine or engine, the ship which was left to sail across, would be sunk. The sailors of the mechanised ship went and helped the sinking people. Thus, they were able to cross the ocean and performed sacrifices.[179]

What did those people do in the foreign land is not mentioned in the Saṁhitās, yet it can be guessed that they sailed across.

It must be added that the motto of the Vedic people was to purify and enlighten the whole world.[180] So it can be assumed that they went outside to educate people for standard living.

Differences between Rājya and Rāṣṭra

Sāyaṇācārya has understood the word *rāṣṭra* in the sense of *rājya*[181] or *deśa*[182] in several passages of the Vedas. On

177. *ṚV*, 3/53/12; 6/16/5 & 3/33/11.
178. *Ibid.*, 3/53/12.
179. *Ibid.*, 10/143/5.
180. Read, *kṛṇvanto viśvamāryam*, *Ibid.*, 9/63/5.
181. *AV*, 3/4/1.
182. *ŚYV*, 22/22. Sāyaṇa explains as *ārāṣṭṛe asmaddeśe*.

the other hand, Dr. V.K. Ratate explains the passages as follows: "O king, you have got this *rāṣṭra*. So acquiring this *rāṣṭra* (*varcasa*) through power (*ekarāṭ virāja*) you enjoy as an only emperor."[183] The passage explained by Dr. Ratate thus means that the emperor had to bestow a proper *rājya* or administration after he had got this *rāṣṭra*.

The two terms *rāṣṭra* and *rājya*, as their English translations supposed to be nation and state respectively, are different in the glances of the Western scholars also. The theory of "One nation One state" was established in the Vienna Congress of 1815[184] and popularity of this theory grew on. On the other hand, some scholars have critically discussed the theory and showed its futility from time to time. Discussing the futility of the theory of "One nation One state" and the differences between nation and state, Lord Acton says,

> The theory nationality (i.e., One nation One state) is more absurd and more criminal than the theory of socialism. The multinational state is one of the chief instruments of civilisation.[185]

Zimmer wrote,

> In the long run, the theory of national state will go away of Henry VIII's and Luther's theory of National Church.[186]

Bernerd Joseph writes in his work *Nationality*,

> Nationality and the state are different conceptions, and a nationality can continue to exist even after the state has been destroyed. National and state loyalty are two different things . . . they can exist side by side with each other, for all that nationality requires is the freedom for cultural and social

183. *ARV*, p. 42.
184. *PunyT*, p. 51.
185. *Ibid.*, p. 50.
186. *Ibid.*

> life and certain measure of group autonomy, particulary on common matters . . . the only hope of order and peace in world affairs is to be sought in the ultimate recognition of co-operation within a state, each at the same time following its own national life.[187]

C.J.H. Hays observes,

> A national state is always based on nationality, but a nationality may exist without a national state. A state is essentially political, nationality is primarily cultural and only incidentially political.[188]

After having analysed the passages of *ŚB* (6/7/3/7, 13/4/3/14, 13/2/9/2-4, 13/2/9/8 and 13/1/6/3), *TB* (14/9/48/, *AB* (7/22 & 8/26) and the *TB* (3/9/7/4) V.R. Ratate comes to the following points:[189]

1. A *rājya* is known through administration and importance of culture, language, blood, *jāti* and prosperity seems to be secondary things for it, whereas the *rāṣṭra* counts them as primary things.
2. A *rāṣṭra* is greater than a *rājya*. More than one *rājya* may be included in a *rāṣṭra*.
3. A *rājya* may come and go but a *rāṣṭra* is perpetual.
4. A *rāṣṭra* is connected with the theory of land or *bhūmi* where the *bhūmi* is regarded as a mother (motherland). On the other hand, there is no essentiality of motherly feelings to a territory of land for the establishment of a state.

After all, the above passages reveal that a *rājya* is a geo-political material unit and *rāṣṭra* or nation is clearly a geo-cultural spiritual entity.

---

187. *PunyT*, pp. 50 & 51.
188. *Ibid.*, p. 52.
189. *ARV*, p. 59.

2

Political Aspects — States and Kingship

Types of States

As the *ṛṣis* of the Vedic ages were the founders of *rāṣṭra* through the austerities they faced,[1] so also they were the founders of civilization, culture, agriculture and what not.[2] A.C. Das writes, "They made a persistent attempt to eliminate all discordant elements from the land and create a peaceful atmosphere, quite conducive to the growth and development of their noble ideas."[3] Such people of high intellect and education thought different types of matters. To say that the political theories and the different types of states sprung first in the Western world and the Āryans were ignorant of political theories[4] is nothing but to ignore the truth. The research of the Western scholars was mainly aimed at finding the loop-holes of the Vedic literature and not the truth at all.[5] Whatever the fact there may be, our endeavour to sketch a picture of the nature of different types of states is assisted by a passage of the *AB*. These different types of states are: *sāmrājya, bhaujya, svarājya, vairājya, pārameṣṭhya rājya, mahārājya, ādhipatyamaya, samantaparyāyī*

1. *AV*, 19/41/1.
2. *RCD*, p. 304.
3. *Ibid.*, p. 306.
4. Quoted from *APIIAIR*, pp. 1-2.
5. *SSSIK*, p. 33.

and *sārvabhauma*[6] which have been translated by scholars as kingship, overlordship, paramount rule, self rule sovereignty, supreme authority, kingship, great kingship, suzereignty, and so on.[7] Dr. Shivadatta Gyani classifies the above-mentioned systems into two parts.[8] These are kingship and democracy respectively. Kingship includes *rājya, pārameṣṭhya rājya, mahārājya, ādhipatya* and *sāmrājya*. On the other hand, the governments like *bhaujya, svarājya* and *vairājya* are of democratic pattern. Pandit Acharya Baladev Upadhyaya concludes, "The Vedic Aryans had well-established *rāṣṭra* in all types of administrative aspects."[9] Though all types of administrations were not brought into practices yet the importance of those ideas remains unchanged in the modern politics also. It has already been discussed that the creation started after *ṛta* came into existance. That *ṛta* or *satya* controlled the whole cosmos where day and nights, rivers and seas, *saṁvatsara*s and years, the sun, the moon, the space and skies all sprang from one after another.[10] After the creation of the creatures, specially of the human beings, they all were controlled by that *ṛta*. That stage of the created persons is the starting point of the human politics. We are going to discuss each term independently.

VAIRĀJYA

So far the term *vairājya* is concerned, it can be derived in three ways:

1. The state where there is no king (*vigata rājakaṁ vairājyam*).[11]

---

6. *AB*, 8/39/1.
7. Quoted from *IABJr.*, p. 87.
8. *VSS*, p. 197.
9. *VSSB*, p. 469.
10. *ṚV*, 10/190/1, 2 & 3.
11. *Vaidik Rājyaśāsan* by Sātavalekar in *HSA*, Kalyāṇ 1950, p. 348.

2. The state where special type of administration is introduced (*viśeṣeṇa rājate iti virāj, tasya idam vairājyam*).[12]
3. The state where *rāṭ* or *rāṣṭra* becomes absent (*vigata rāṭ yasmāt iti virāṭ, tasya idam iti vairājyam*).[13]

The term *vairājya* originates from *virāṭ* which has been described as the first created element.[14] Though *ṛta* is found to be the first discovery in the universe,[15] yet *virāṭ* seems to be used in the political sense wherefrom the states came out. So, the first step in evolution of state was that of the *virāṭ*.[16] The *ŚYV* on the other hand, describes *virāj* to be enriched with several meanings[17] and as the one which had been used as an adjective of *sāma*. Another passage of the same mentions *virāja* as the ascertained element of *virāṭ*.[18] After all, the *MB* gives a clear picture of *vairājya* which we find as, "Neither there was king nor state nor punishment, neither there was the punisher but they all were controlled and protected by *dharma*."[19] Such types of states were described as the states of anarchy by some scholars. A.L. Basham mentions, "Anarchy prevailed at the dawn of aeon . . . etc."[20] Dr. Hariharnath Tripathi describes it to be *vigata rāja* or the condition where the administration remains absent. But he explains that three terms *ṛta, virāṭ* and *arājaka* or anarchism were three different ideas.[21] R.C. Mazumdar informs K.P. Jayasawal stating *vairājya* as

12. *VDVPRSS*, p. 3.
13. *ARV*, p. 52.
14. *AV*, 8/10/1.
15. *ṚV*, 1/190/1.
16. Read, *vairājyam itarebhyo bhūpati śāsanam*, Sāyaṇa on *AB*, 8/2/2.
17. *ŚYV*, 10/13.
18. *Ibid.*, 15/14.
19. *MB*-Śānti, 58/14.
20. *WIB*, p. 64.
21. *PBRNH*, p. 78.

"kingless state."[22] Though the above-mentioned scholars have mentioned *vairājya* as kingless state but they have not attached importance to *ṛta* through which the people lived in discipline. On the other hand, anarchism is explained in the *AV*[23] and the words such as *aparuddha, arājata,* etc., are found in other Vedic literature also.[24]

STATE OR A RĀJYA

Origin of a State

According to the Vedic literature *ṛta* and *satya* came together before the creation took place. These were brought through the penance constituted by the Almighty.[25] Both of them started to move everywhere and created nights, seas, oceans, rivers, *saṁvatsaras* (the years), the sun and the moon.[26] *Ṛta* is an important element in the origination of a state. Thus, *ṛta* was regarded to be an unavoidable phenomenon. The importance of *ṛta* appears from the fact that Mitrāvaruṇa combined were represented as the kings in some passages and they have been mentioned as obtaining their strength from *ṛta*.[27] Thus, it can be assumed that then the administration ran according to this *ṛta*. After all, *ṛta* was thought to be at the peak.[28] In that way, it meant excellent motion and perpetual laws.[29] The studies on *ṛta* bring to the conclusion that it controlled not only the affairs of the world but also conducted the whole Universe. The social status under *ṛta* was explained by Bhīṣma in the *MB*.[30]

22. *CLAIM*, p. 212.
23. *AV*, 3/3/4.
24. Quoted from *PBRNH*, p. 7.
25. *ṚV*, 10/190/1/
26. *Ibid.*, 10/190/3 & 4.
27. *Ibid.*, 1/2/8 & 1/65/3 and 4.
28. *Ibid.*, 4/23/8 & 9.
29. *PBRNH*, p. 6.
30. Read, *na rājyam na ca rājāsīt* . . . — *MB*-Śānti, 58/14.

God created kingship when the insanity crept into society and the people started to live in chaos.[31]

Dharma and *ṛta* are mentioned as similar words in the *Brāhmaṇas*.[32] On the other hand, the word *dharma* is found in the *Saṁhitās* also[33] but here it was used in the meanings of etiquettes,[34] morality,[35] duty[36] and rights.[37] That *dharma* was the conducting element of such a state.

Theories of State

So far the theories of origin of state is concerned we find some theories as follows:

Divine Theory: The king was thought to be the God-created person who was entitled to administer the state.[38] A Ṛgvedic passage also denotes same meaning[39] when a king declares, "I am the royal ruler, mine is empire. . . ."[40] The next passage also reveals as, "I am king Varuṇa. . . ."[41] In other place of the same the seer Gautama says that the power or the strength of a king (Indra) is originated from God.[42] In the same way the *ŚB* gives a clearer evidence of it.[43]

Theory of Social Contact: The *MB* regarding the origin of the state says that people started to become traitors and as such

31. *MS*, 7/3.
32. *ŚB*, 5/3/3/9 & 5/4/4/5.
33. *ṚV*, 1/22/18; 164/43, *ŚYV*, 10/29; *AV*, 14/1/58.
34. *ṚV*, 3/17/1.
35. *Ibid.*, 7/89/5.
36. *Ibid.*, 10/58/3.
37. *Ibid.*, 8/98/1.
38. *MS*, 7/2.
39. *ṚV*, 4/42/1.
40. *ṚVg*, p. 228.
41. *ṚV*, 4/42/2.
42. *Ibid.*, 1/80/15.
43. *ŚB*, 5/1/5/3.

the weaks began to suffer because of the strongs and the condition of "no rule" prevailed. In such a condition, the people prayed to God and He, in order to protect them, created king and thus the states came into existance.[44] Swamy Karapatriji Maharaj observes the state of "no-rule" in the glances of the Western and Indian scholars as follows: The difference found in the glances of the Western and the Eastern scholars on "no-rule" or *mātsyanyāya* is as follows:

> The Indian thinkers thought that honesty was in people before the state of chaos had come into existance, whereas western scholars thought that the state was controlled through force only.[45]

The traitors caused by the *mātsyanyāya*[46] or state of "no-rule" were to be subdued so that people could live peacefully.[47] In that way a king or the protector of a *rājya* was thought to have possessed divine strength.[48] On the other hand, a passage of the *ŚB* mentions that the king acquires the strength from the people he ruled over.[49] In that way, in order to protect the *ṛta* and *satya*[50] in the daily life of the people, the social need brought *rājya* into its existence.

One of the prominent scholars of ancient Indian polity, R.S. Sharma opines,

> The social contact theory of the origin of the state should be regarded as an original contribution of ancient Indian

---

44. *MB*-Śānti, 58/13 to 22 & 88.
45. *MRK*, p. 49.
46. Read, *arājakāḥ prajāḥ pūrvam vinesuriti naḥ śrutam*
    parasparam bhāvayanto matsyā iva jale kṛṣṇan — *MB*-Śānti, 67/17.
47. *ṚV*, 10/174/5.
48. *Ibid.*, 4/12/3.
49. *ŚB*, 5/4/4/11.
50. *PBRNH*, p. 12.

> thinkers to political thought, for even the Greek thinkers, Plato and Aristotle, who had established political science practically as an independent discipline, did not think in the terms of contact between the king and the people.[51]

Though we find these two theories regarding the origin of a state, yet we find experts, such as Bhīṣma and Kauṭilya, who combined these two theories and established a new theory. Therefore, A.L. Basham remarks,

> The purpose of government is to establish order, and that the king, as Head of the government is the first social servant, and ultimately dependent on the suffrage of his subjects. Thus in ancient Indian thought, on the question of the origin of monarchy, two strands are evident, the mystical and the contractual, often rather incongruously combined.[52]

Duties of a State

As the state has been mentioned to be the protector of the people from the *mātsyanyāya*[53] or "no-rule" and it was formed with this view only, it was necessary for the state to perform some duties. The Vedic literature and other traditional documents present a picture of those duties as follows:

1. The main duty of a state was to protect the Vedic tradition and *varṇāśrama dharma*. Those were to be protected in order to protect the state. A state as the Vedic sages realized would ruin unless the state protected *dharma*.[54]
2. K.B. Ayenger mentions that it was the duty of the state to protect the people from the internal and external foes. This indicates that the state had to

---

51. *APIIAI*, p. 75.
52. *WIB*, p. 83 & 84.
53. *MRK*, p. 49.
54. *MB*-Śānti, 57/43-44.

protect the laws, justice, political behaves and etiquettes.[55]

3. Emphasis was given upon the proper conduct of the judicial courts, so that it should not break the Vedic norms.[56]
4. The state is found adopting the laws for the *viśa*s but it seems to be ignorant of adopting the laws for the *svapaca*s and the *cāṇḍāla*s.[57] On the other hand, the people of the lower classes or the *antyaja*s were freed either to change the ways of living or to live the same position as they were in.[58]
5. Society came into existance prior than the state.[59] Therefore, the state could not interfere upon the laws of tribes and societies.[60]
6. A state was responsible to protect the people by providing irrigation, medicine, safety and so on.[61] The *rājya* or a state had a vast range of duties to perform. A king, as he used to be enthroned to perform the duties on behalf of the state, was called *dhṛtavrata*.[62]
7. The state had no right to rule over the brāhmaṇas who were the scholars of the laws.[63] It had its rights to adopt the rules suggested by them only.[64]

SĀMRĀJYA

There are a lot of passages in the *ṚV* and the *AV* in which

55. *PBRNH*, p. 45.
56. *Ibid.*, p. 46.
57. *Ibid.*, p. 46.
58. *ApSS*, 1/21/6; 2/7/20.
59. *PBRNH*, p. 44.
60. *Ibid.*, pp. 89-90.
61. *MB*-Śānti, 63/25 & 91/6.
62. *ŚB*, 4/4/5/2.
63. *GDS*, 11/25.
64. *MS*, 4/41.

the terms *samrāṭ*[65] and *sāmrājya*[66] are found. Many wars for *sāmrājya* can be found in the Vedic literature. The wars of many kings against Sudās is stated in the *ṚV*[67] in which we find the king Sudās getting victory over those strong kings and establishing his empire. Taranath Bhattacharya mentions the word to be derived as *samrāṭ* + *ṣyañ* and quoted Raghu in this respect.[68] On the other hand, Sāyaṇa, giving the meaning of the word *sāmrājya*, quoted, "*Sāmrājya* is the system of the administration in which the subjects are administered according to *dharma*."[69] From the textural evidence of the *mantra Saṁhitās* also we get the meaning of the term as great fame, prosperity and glory.[70] Another passage of the *ṚV* mentions it to be a territory of land.[71] An Atharvanic passage also expresses the same.[72] Damodar Sātavalekar says, "that a king after he defeats the others by performing the *aśvamedha* sacrifice was known to be a *samrāṭ*."[73] On the other hand, the *ŚB* says that the man was entitled as a king after he performed *rājasūya* and so also to attain an emperorship *vājapeya* was to be performed.[74]

SVĀRĀJYA

As far as the different types of states are concerned the Vedic sages found that the state of *sāmrājya* system was the best of all. Though we find a lot of passages in the Vedic

65. *ṚV*, 1/25/10.
66. *Ibid.*, 8/25/8.
67. *ṚV*, 7/18; 33.
68. *VācT*, vol. VI, p. 5284.
69. *AB*, 8/2/2, See Sāyaṇa's note.
70. *ṚV*, 1/141/43.
71. *Ibid.*, 8/25/8 & 8/28/17.
72. *AV*, 14/1/43.
73. *VDVRS*, p. 3.
74. *ŚB*, 5/1/1/3.

Saṁhitās regarding *sāmrājya*[75] yet we find in the *AB* the mention of *svārājya*[76] which has been explained by Sātavalekar as, "Stress upon the purification of *sva* was given in *svarājya* whereas the endeavour to keep the rights of administering a state was mainly counted for *sāmrājya*."[77] The importance of *svarājya* has been mentioned in a passage of the *AV* itself.[78] Sātavalekar meant and explained the passage as, "There is nothing above it."[79]

Whatever the explanations of the scholars there may be, *svarājya* has been mentioned to be *bahupāyya*.[80] The term *bahupāyya* indicates the meaning of the opinion of the greater number of people.[81]

In many passages of the *mantra Saṁhitā*s the term *svarājya* itself meant to enlighten.[82] On the other hand, some other passages reveal it as to control[83] of an empire,[84] shelter,[85] prosperity,[86] and religion as well.[87]

Characteristics of an Ideal Svarājya

The *R̥V* passages reveal some characteristics of the state of a *svarājya* pattern. Our analysis, in this regard goes as follows:

---

75. *R̥V*, 1/80; 1/84/10-11 & 2/8/5; *SV*, 5/1/3/1.
76. *AB*, 8/39/2.
77. *Vaidik Rājyaśāsan* by Sātavalekar in *HSA*, p. 383.
78. *AV*, 10/7/31.
79. *Vaidik Svarājyaśāsan* by Sātavalekar, p. 6.
80. *R̥V*, 5/66/6.
81. *VSSS*, p. 6.
82. *R̥V*, 1/80 & *ŚYV*, 19/60.
83. *R̥V*, 1/84/10.
84. *Ibid.*, 1/84/11.
85. *Ibid.*, 1/84/12 & 5/66/6.
86. *Ibid.*, 5/82/24.
87. *SV*, 5/1/3/1, 2, 3, 4 & 5.

1. The system of administration must be followed and conducted on the basis of the opinion of the greater number of people which has been named as *bahupāyya svarājya*.[88]
2. A *svarājya* was thought to be free from all kinds of enemies. A passage of the *R̥V* tells that the enemies should be sent away from the *svarājya*.[89] In the same way, other passages also inform us that the enemies[90] and the conspirators[91] must be killed driving away from water. Those passages show that the stress was given to make the state free from the foes in order to strengthen the *svarājya*.
3. The administrator of the state had to concentrate his attention on the system of irrigation too. We get such an idea through a passage of the *R̥V*.[92]
4. Another passage informs that there would be a system for entertainment. This is revealed through the passage in which it has been told that there should be discussions on music also.[93]
5. The state stressed upon the strong unity of the society. Perhaps the people could realize that the *svarājya* will not be strong unless and until the people are organized. So a passage advised people to sing about the deities in the congregation of thousands of people.[94]
6. People of the Vedic India wished to have

88. *R̥V*, 5/66/6.
89. *Ibid.*, 1/80/1.
90. *Ibid.*, 1/80/2.
91. *Ibid.*, 1/80/7.
92. *Ibid.*, 1/80/5.
93. *Ibid.*, 1/80/6.
94. *Ibid.*, 1/80/7.

innumerable number of cows with them.[95] The *ŚYV* also presents the same notion.[96]

In order to attain the goal, the administrator must be an *iyācakṣa* (the person having equal glances), Mitra (a man of friendly attitude), Sūrya or wise.[97]

BHAUJYA

Another important type of state is *bhaujya*. The term *bhaujya* is derived from the root *bhuj* which meant to protect and govern.[98] The derivation indicates that the state should manage to provide boarding and lodging to the general people. Sātavalekar understands the word *bhuj* in the sense of "the state being surrounded by the natural entity."[99] For example, India and England are such lands and the sages thought the theory of *bhuj* as to rule such lands, *bhaujya* was the administrative system of the Brāhmaṇic age.[100] The *AB* informs us that such type of state was for the Yādavas and the sages provided that method of administration for the kings of southern region.[101] The administrator was supposed to be made by the Rudras who used to make the rulers concentrate on three *mantra*s for 31 days.[102] The king who was coronated for *bhaujya* was supposed to be enthroned with the Ādityas, 17 Stomas and Vairūpa Sāma.[103] Sātavalekar mentions the characteristics of such a state as to provide the facilities of *yoga* and *kṣema* and to look after his subjects. In short, the state should provide a

95. *ṚV*, 1/80/10 & *AV*, 20/109/10.
96. *ŚYV*, 22/22.
97. *ṚV*, 5/66/6.
98. *Vāc.T.* vol. VI, p. 4707.
99. *ṚV*, 5/66/6.
100. VSSB, p. 458.
101. *AB*, 8/4/5.
102. *Ibid*.
103. *Ibid*., 8/4/3.

house for shelter, clothes to wear, crops to eat and cater, water to drink, open air, proper medicines at the time of illness, internal and external protection and the management of the old people after they become unable to earn.[104]

PĀRAMEṢṬHYA RĀJYA

The word *parameṣṭhi* gives rise to the term *pārameṣṭhya*. The meaning of the word *parameṣṭhi* is the existence or a person who stays in the most esteemed place. So he is such an administrator who always appoints himself in the esteemed work of the administration of the people. He is appointed by the people and is boycotted by them whenever he becomes unable to rule over the state.[105] On the other hand, *parameṣṭhi* is a term to denote God also.[106] In such a state the king or the administrator had to think that the state over which he ruled was the *prasāda* of God. Again, Prajāpati could be depicted as the master of the subjects as it indicates. In such case a passage of the *AV* gives a conception of the king of a *pārameṣṭhya rājya* where the sage praises the residence of a person and says that *Parameṣṭhi* Prajāpati brings woods and builds it.[107] Thus, the king or the administrator was liable to the managements of the people in such a state. Remarkable matter is that time first created the subjects and then the Prajāpati.[108] So the subjects of that condition followed the *vairājya* type of living and then *rājya* came into existence. In the course of time, that type of state existed in this land. The administrator of this type of state was advised and suggested to provide the subjects with several types of wealth.[109]

104. *VDVRSS*, p. 3.
105. *Ibid.*, p. 4.
106. *AV*, 4/11/7 & 8/5/10.
107. *Ibid.*, 9/3/11.
108. *Ibid.*, 19/53/8 to 10.
109. *ṚV*, 10/121/10.

ĀDHIPATYAMAYA RĀJYA

This type of state was rarely described in the Sanskrit literature because it has been determined to be the worst type of state or administration. Sātavalekar has translated it as to be bureaucracy.[110] The meaning of the word *adhipati* is officer or a master. Hence the administration which is conducted through the officers is called *ādhipatyamaya rājya*. In such a state the suggestions and orders of the officers were strictly followed whereas the advices and the suggestions of the subjects could be ignored.[111] Dethroning or expelling a despotic or autocratic king and to replace an ideal person on throne did not come in the jurisdiction of the right of general people. Only the decisions taken by the administrative authorities came to be executed as laws.[112] A passage of the *AV* discusses *ādhipatya* to be mastery.[113] Another passage of the *R̥V* clearly mentions about *ādhipatya* of the *rāṣṭra* and Varuṇa is prayed to become the master of it.[114] Varuṇa was prayed to be the *adhipati* of the *rāṣṭra* because he was able to differentiate *asatya* or untruth from *satya* or truth.[115] A general king was not allowed to be the chief of the state. T.N. Bhattacharya gives the two meanings of it, these are master and administrator.[116] Such theory of administration thus came and was practised by several kings such as Bena and Nahuṣa in the Indian literature for which the people were compelled to revolt against them and dethroned. Thus, this type of state was thought to be a worst type of state.

110. *Vaidik Rājyaśāsan* by Sātavalekar in *HSA*, p. 348.
111. *VDVRSS*, p. 4.
112. *VRSS*, p. 6.
113. *AV*, 18/3/54.
114. *R̥V*, 10/12/5.
115. *Ibid*.
116. *VācT*, vol. I, p. 714.

SAMANTAPARYĀYĪ

Samantaparyāyī or quasi-feudalism also was a theory perceived by the ancient Indian thinkers. A.L. Basham remarks,

> Authorities differ on the definition of a feudal system. Some would confine the term to be a complex structure of contractual relations covering the whole of society from king to villain, such as that which prevailed in Medieval Europe.[117]

Further he added,

> Ancient India had however a system of overlordship which was quasi-feudal, though it was never fully developed as in Europe and it is rested on a different basis.[118]

So far the *sāmanta* system is concerned the king of the small units were called *sāmanta* and the emperor was the head of those kings. The people of the state had to follow the orders of their *sāmanta*s or small kings. If there arose any contradiction between the order given by those *sāmanta*s and the emperors, the general people had to follow the order of the latter. Therefore, such type of state also was thought to be unable to fulfil the desires of the people.[119] On the other hand, Sātavalekar gives an example of *sāmanta rājya* in which he says that Rāmacandra ruled over his state under the system of *samantaparyāyī* and could give an ideal administration to the people for which *rāmarājya* is highly respected by the politicians of the present age also.[120] Sir Monier-Williams understands the term *sāmantacakra* to be neighbouring princes.[121] He again gives the meaning of

---

117. *WIB*, p. 95.
118. *Ibid*.
119. *Vaidik Rājyaśāsan* by Sātavalekar, p. 385.
120. *Vaidik Rājyaśāsan* by Sātavalekar in *HSA* p. 385.
121. *SEDM*, p. 1025.

samantaparyāyī as "all embracing."[122] After the analysis of the above matters, we may come to conclusion that the king or the administrator used to embrace or occupy all the departments of administration in his hands. He tried to conquer over the neighbouring states also.

JĀNARĀJYA

Jānarājya is such a system of administration which has been mentioned not only in the *AB* but also occupies an important place in the other Vedic literature also. We find *janarāj* in the *R̥V* in which it has been used in the sense of a general king.[123] On the other hand, the same word in the same passage has been used to denote a pious king by Dayānanda Sarasvatī.[124] Describing the duty of an administrator of a *janarājya* or of a *janarāṭ*, a passage in the *ŚYV* mentions that his duty was to kill the demons or the conspirators and the traitors.[125] In the same way, another passage of the *ŚYV* indicates the word as referring to the state of a pious king.[126] Pāṇini in his work used *janapadin* in the meaning of a country ruler.[127] Sir M.M. Williams wrote this to be sovereignty.[128] Describing the term *janarājya* and *jānarājya*, Sātavalekar writes that the system in which the stress is given upon the reformation of *jana* or the general people is *jānarājya*, on the other hand, the system where the stress is given upon the administration is called *janarājya*.[129] In another place he writes that the administration which is conducted according to the suggestion of the general people for their

122. *Ibid.*, p. 1155.
123. *R̥VSāy*, 1/53/9.
124. *R̥VDay*, 1/53/9.
125. *ŚYV*, 5/24.
126. *Ibid.*, 9/40 & 10/18.
127. *Aṣṭ*, 5/3/100.
128. *SEDM*, p. 481.
129. *Vaidik Rājyaśāsan* by Sātavaleakr in *HSA*, pp. 348-49.

welfare through the elected members is *jānarājya*. All the rights of administration is preserved under the subjects.[130] In conclusion, it may be said that as the administrators were elected or selected by the general people and the rulers should concentrate their mind for the welfare of the people, it was the democratic system of administration, as it is known in the modern times.

SĀRVABHAUMA RĀJYA

The intellectual mind of the sages of India could be able to think about a World Government. They used the word *sārvabhauma* to denote the same. But unfortunately, India could not bring it into practice due to the downfall which was to be faced by the history of itself.[131] But yet, we have some evidences through which it can be shown that some of the ambitious and vigorous administrators or the rulers forwarded such esteemed steps.

There are many passages in the *AV* where the king is advised to overthrow his enemies and to destroy his rivals.[132] The *AB*, on the other hand, is found describing the ideals of the paramount rulership. After being experienced through experiments of ruling several types of states, the intellectuals thought of a World Government at last.[133] In one passage of the *AB* we find a king being blessed by the *purohita* as to be the head of the other kings.[134] The *AB* in some passages remarks that the ancient sages could realize the theory of the world dominion.[135]

The *ŚB* also suggests that the rulers are to observe the *rājasūya*, *vājapeya* and *aśvamedha* sacrifices in order to

130. *VDVRSS*, p. 4.
131. *VRSS*, p. 8.
132. *AV*, 19/13/28.
133. *AB*, 8/6.
134. *AV*, 4/22/2.
135. *AB*, 8/6; 8/7; 8/13; & 8/15.

acquire the status of a king, an emperor and so on.[136] Giving the meaning of the term, Monier-Williams remarks, "*Sārvabhauma* is relating to or consisting of or ruling over the whole world."[137]

Kingship

MEANING AND DEFINITION OF "KING"

The term *rājan* or *rājā* is originated from the root *rāj* which means to enlighten. Thus, the meaning of the word becomes to be a brightened and powerful existence. In a question of Yudhiṣṭhira regarding the meaning of the word *rājan*, Bhīṣma gives a very satisfactory reply. He says that a person who pleases his subjects through his good administration can only be regarded as an ideal king.[138] Secondly, the *MB* says that a person who pleases his subjects through his utmost endeavour is a king actually.[139] Thirdly, Manu says that a king yields punishments after deep consideration through which the subjects please on his rule.[140] Kālidāsa in his well-known work, *Raghuvaṁśa*, describes Raghu to have ruled according to the meaning of the word *rājā*, and so it was very fruitful by rendering his pleasing administration to the subjects as the moon and the sun had done by their deeds.[141] The picture of an ideal king is given in the *MB* as follows, "The person whose praises are sung by the people even after his death is an ideal king."[142] The same book again defines the term as, "He is a king in which the

136. *ŚB*, 5/1/1/12; 9/3/4/8; 5/1/1/14.
137. *SEDM*, p. 1210.
138. Read, *rañjitāśca prajāḥ sarvāstena rājeti śabdyate* — *MB*-Śānti, 59/125.
139. Read, *rañjayiṣyati yallokamayamātmā viceṣṭitaiḥ*
athāmumāhu rājānam manorañjanakaiḥ prajāḥ — *BP*, 4/16/15.
140. *MS*, 7/19.
141. *Raghu*, 4/12.
142. Read, *yasya vr̥ttaṁ namasyanti svargasyāpi mānavā*
paurajānapadamātyāḥ sa rāja rājasattamaḥ — *MB*-Śānti 25/36.

dharma takes an important role."[143] Sir Monier-William says, "A *rājan* is a king, sovereign, prince or chief."[144] The word is applied to gods such as Varuṇa, Ādityas, Indra, Yama, Soma, and the moon.[145] A passage of the *R̥V* applies the term in locative case and meant it "guidance."[146]

The studies of the above passages lead us to the conception that the head of the administration who rules over his subjects with great love for them, keeps his equal glances upon his subjects, tries to please his people all the times, visits *sabhā* and *samiti*, acquires strength and power by all means, subdues the traitors always and protects the educational institutions was called a king.

ORIGIN OF KINGSHIP

The Vedic literature shows that in the very beginning *sabhā* and *samiti* were the supreme authorities of administration. The importance of the king started to grow along with the importance of the *sabhā* and *samiti*.[147] The *R̥V* mentions a king named Citra who resided near the river Sarasvatī.[148]

Dharma organized and conducted the Vedic society properly.[149] In short, *sattva guṇa* played an important role among the people, but in the course of time that morality decreased and two other *guṇa*s (*tamas* and *rajas*) increased. Thus, the *mātsyanyāya* or chaos occured. Such condition was faced by the people and they felt the necessity of a king and selected accordingly.[150] The person whom the

143. Read, *yasmin dharmo virājeta taṁ rājānaṁ pracakṣate* — *MB*-Śānti, 90/318
144. *SEDM*, p. 874.
145. *Ibid.*
146. *R̥V* 10/49/4.
147. *R̥V*, 3/4/8; 5/54/7; *AV*, 4/22/3 & 5; 8/7/16.
148. *R̥V*, 8/21/18.
149. Read, *na rājyam na ca rājasīt* . . . — *MB*-Śānti, 59/5.
150. *MRK*, p. 49.

people selected for kingship must had to possess the qualities of Agni, Candra, Varuṇa, Bṛhaspati, Lakṣmī, Indra, Vāyu and Yama.[151] Whatever the fact there may be, Zimmer mentions that there are definite evidences that the kings were selected by the people in some states.[152] In the long journey from the *mantra Saṁhitā*s to the *Brāhmaṇa*s and the *Dharmasūtra*s, we find that the system of selection is absent from the later literatures, i.e., the *Dharmasūtra*s.

U.N. Ghosal remarks,

> We have concrete evidence of the general prevalence of hereditary monarchy as well as of the survival of dynastic governments during the present (i.e., later Vedic) period, but of elective monarchy there is hardly any trace. In the latest Vedic period the hereditary principle is sufficiently established to make succession, by primogeniture of the normal rule.[153]

The Vedic *Dharmasūtra*s do not give any evidence regarding the election or selection of a king. Ram Gopal writes,

> The king who was usually called *rājan* succeeded to the throne by virtue of his hereditary right, and the system of electing a king was in all probability unknown to the *sūtra* writers.[154]

The King

There were several types of admnistrations in ancient India that we have discussed above, but yet we get maximum evidences regarding kingship. Other systems are secondarily presented. The most important evidence is found in the *AB*. It says that a war between gods and demons took place in which the gods were defeated. They could realize that this

151. Quoted from *VMSS*, p. 296 & *Ṛ̥V*, 10/166/7.
152. Quoted from *CLAIM*, p. 92.
153. Quoted from *IABJr*, p. 85.
154. *IVKP*, p. 176.

happened only for the absence of a king.[155] As a result of that, the gods selected Indra as their king. It makes clear that a king was selected in ancient times. In a passage of the *R̥V* the seer Dhruva informs that a king was selected by the people. He further wishes that he should be the master of the land.[156] There is another clear evidence in the *ŚYV* in which the seer had said to the king that he had bestowed the empire upon him.[157] The *AV* on the other land, presents an evidence regarding the selection of a king in which the seer says to the king that he brought him to bestow the administration of the land. The passage follows, "O king, I have brought you."[158] The king was again advised by him to bring up his subjects.[159]

Whenever disaster followed and the king lost his kingdom, the subjects tried their best to return him again, and thus he was recoronated.[160] The brāhmaṇas used to advise and bless the recoronated king.[161] Again, a passage of the *R̥V* says that if a strong person destroyed the enemies of the country he would get the kingship.[162] Another passage warns the *rājakr̥ts* or the king-makers not to select a self-centred and a wicked person as a king.[163] In short, it is clear that the king was selected in those days. After the king had taken his seat, the *purohita* chanted *śāntipāṭha* of the God Varuṇa in which he was prayed to attribute his brightness, energy and enthusiasm to the king.[164] It was

155. *AB*, 1/14.
156. *R̥V*, 10/173/1.
157. *ŚYV*, 18/37.
158. *AV*, 6/87/1.
159. *Ibid.*, 6/87/2.
160. *Ibid.*, 3/3.
161. *Ibid.*, 3/4/1.
162. *R̥V*, 10/174/5.
163. *Ibid.*, 6/72/3.
164. *AB*, 8/2/5.

supposed that a king who was not coronated accordingly, would have to face disasters.[165]

The holy water was sprinkled upon the king from the *kalaśa*s placed in rituals. That was done by *purohita* and the king was also advised to give a proper administration to the subjects.[166]

There is another passage in the *ŚB* in which the king was told that this nation was given to him for the development of agriculture, welfare, prosperity and healthiness.[167] The subjects also sprinkled medicated and well-smelt things on the king at that time.[168]

After the coronation, the *purohita* also used to pray to gods for the long life of the king.[169] It was supposed that the king after being coronated becomes the master of the subjects[170] and he should have performed a *rājasūya* sacrifice.[171]

A king had been the Chief of the army staff at the time of war and he was respected as the protector of the subjects in such conditions.[172] He got respect from people in peace times.[173] On the other hand, a king was selected with a view to protect *dharma*, as Varuṇa used to do so among the gods.[174] For this a king was told to be a *dharmapati*[175] and *rāṣṭravrata*[176] in those days.

165. *Ibid.*, 8/2/5.
166. *ŚYV*, 9/40 & 10/18.
167. *ŚB*, 5/2/1/25.
168. *ŚYV*, 6/2.
169. *AV*, 4/23/1; 5/87 & 88; 13/1/1; 4/8/6; 13/1/20; & 3/20/1, etc.
170. *Ibid.*, 4/8/1.
171. *Ibid.*
172. *ṚV*, 3/43/5.
173. *Ibid.*, 1/67/1.
174. *Ibid.*, 7/89/5 & 10/56/3.
175. *ŚB*, 5/3/3/9.
176. *ŚB*, 9/4/1/1.

The later Vedic period shows and presents another picture. The *AB* says that if a king wants to rule over the country in his own generation only, he should spell *bhuḥ*. In the same way *bhuvaḥ* and *svaḥ* were to be spelt if he wanted the kingdom for two and three generations respectively.[177] Another passage mentions of *rājānaṁ rājapitaram*.[178] The above evidences indicate that the king of the Brāhmaṇic period was coronated on the hereditary system. R.S. Sharma mentions that the kingship was bestowed upon such a man whom it was expected that his 10 generations would continue the administration of the state.[179]

As we have got two sets of evidences regarding kingship we may mention R.S. Sharma in the conclusion as follows,

> The two sets of evidences can be reconciled only by presuming that in the beginning the tenure lasted only for a limited period, and then in course of time it became hereditary.[180]

QUALITIES OF THE PERSON TO BECOME A KING

While making a person a king, the following qualifications were sought:

1. The person should be conscious for learning and Bṛhaspati or *guru* must have a close contact with him.[181]
2. A passage of the *ṚV*, giving an example of the king Asamāti, mentions that he must be a lustrous and powerful, having the capacity of killing the enemies.[182]

---

177. *AB*, 8/2/7.
178. *Ibid.*, 8/12.
179. Quoted from *APIIAIR*, p. 201.
180. *Ibid.*, p. 168.
181. *ṚV*, 4/50/8.
182. *ṚV*, 10/60/2 & 3, *AV*, 4/12/7 & 5/2/7.

3. The person who does not escape from the battlefield and always wishes to strengthen his country is eligible for a kingship.[183] Moreover, he should be constant as the earth, space and mountains.[184]
4. A passage of the *ŚYV* remarks that he should have possessed the knowledge of sciences. He must be aware of killing wicked people. He was again expected to be a pious one.[185]
5. Another long passage of the *ŚYV* counts the nine qualities required in a man who becomes a king. These are (1) unprejudiceness, (2) making happy to others (3) dedicated towards animals, providing grazing fields to them, (4) ambitious, (5) desirous, (6) strong, (7) brave, (8) able, (9) helper of the scholars and the greats. Above all, there must be the pervasion of wisdom and *dharma* in him.[186]
6. The person must be bright as Agni and his life should be a pious one.[187]
7. He should be a scholar of perpetual and perishable things as well.[188]
8. The person should have the Brāhmanical *saṁskāra*s to be a king.[189]

CORONATION CEREMONY

The Vedas inform that the Central Assembly named *samiti* used to select a king. Acharya Baladev Upadhyaya remarks that *rājakṛt*s used to select a person for kingship and offered

183. *ṚV*, 10/173/2.
184. *Ibid.*, 10/173/3.
185. *ŚYV*, 9/2 & 12/33.
186. *Ibid.*, 10/4; 12/34 & *AV*, 4/8/2.
187. *Ibid.*, 11/27.
188. *AV*, 4/16/1 & 2.
189. *MS*, 7/2.

him the state.[190] The *rājakṛts* who took part in the selection of a king were as follows: (1) the co-ordinator or the people of royal families, (2) charioteers, (3) *grāmaṇis* or the village chiefs, (4) chariotmakers, and (5) *karmāras* or blacksmiths.[191] On the basis of such passages, we may form a concept that perhaps *samiti* had to form a committee of the above persons and then the latter selected a person for kingship. Dr. Rajabali Pandey remarks that the *rājakṛts* were able to select the king but they did not desire to become a king themselves.[192]

The selected person had to first perform some religious rituals such as *avabhṛta, anubandha yāga* and *udavasānīyeṣṭi.* Thenafter the coronation ceromony followed.[193] The *AB* gives us ample information regarding the coronational ceremony in large extent. After the completion of the above-mentioned rituals, the chosen king had to collect the following materials for his coronation.[194]

1. A chair made of *gūlar* wood.
2. Curd, honey, *ghī,* rain water fallen on a clear day, sprouts of barley, wine and *dūrvā* grass.
3. Skins of three tigers.

He had to touch the chair and say,[195]

> O chair ! let Agni climb you up with *gāyatrī* metre, Savitā with *uṣṇik,* Soma with *anuṣṭubh* and so on. I want to sit on you for kingdom, empire, prosperity, independence, sovereignty, etc. . .[196]

The people, at the time of coronation of a king, used to beat

190. *VSSB,* p. 467.
191. *AV,* 3/5/6 & 7.
192. *HDKR,* p. 547.
193. *AV,* 8/2/3.
194. *AB,* 8/2/2.
195. *Ibid.,* 8/2/1.
196. *AB,* 8/8/2.

the trumpets and drums. The seers have described the *abhiṣeka* of a prince where trumpets or *dundubhi*s were beaten.[197] Secondly, the people who gathered in the coronation ceremony threw medicated scents on the king.[198] Thus, it can be assumed that the people were very conscious and took part in the selection of their administrators. Pranav Bandhyopadhyaya remarks,

> There are Veda *mantra*s relating to the coronation of kings which clearly show that the king was crowned only after having been accepted by the every segment of the society.[199]

The *ŚB*, on the other hand, gives us some descriptions of the coronation ritual. At the time of coronation the priest gave a bow and three arrows in the hands of the king.[200] That was done because the anointed king was to be made powerful before the ceremony was performed.[201] The priest again introduced the king mentioning his race and parents.[202]

Another passage of the *ŚB* informs that the king was not entitled to be king of the land but of the people.[203]

At the time of the performance of the *rājasūya* sacrifice the priest used to beat the king with a stick,[204] perhaps to examine the strength and the power of endurance of the king. R.S. Sharma remarks,

> The ritual was probably meant to judge the physical competence of the candidate. It can be better understood if we

---

197. *AV*, 6/38/4.
198. *ŚYV*, 6/2.
199. *AHVPr*, pp. 117 & 118.
200. *ŚB*, 5/3/5/30.
201. *TS*, 1/8/12; *TB*, 1/7/7.
202. *KSS*, 15/96-97.
203. *ŚB*, 5/3/3/12.
204. *Ibid.*, 5/4/4/7.

> take into account the practices prevalent among the tribal people. The savage times of Sierraleone who elect their king reserve to themselves the right of beating him on the eve of his coronation, and they avail themselves of this constitutional privilege with such hearty goodwill that sometimes the unhappy monarch does not survive his elevation to the throne.[205]

The king, when he was to be coronated, was directed by the *purohita* to perform some royal duties. The brāhmaṇa used to say, "You are for agriculture, for providing peaceful existence, to enrich the people and for frugality."[206]

CORONATION AND PUROHITA'S BLESSINGS

After the completion of the coronation ceremony the king was blessed by the *purohita*s as follows:

1. "May you live without enemy and all the subordinate kings and subjects obey you."[207]
2. "May all the gods of water do you good and let you enjoy this state up to your hundredth years of age."[208]
3. The king might have given such an administration that the *brāhmateja* and *kṣātrateja* flourish together.[209]
4. "May the help of Savitā and the power of Agni, Mitra, and Varuṇa make you perfect in administration."[210]
5. Exposing the same meaning a passage of the *ŚYV* reveals, "O King, may Savitā quicken thee for ruling, Agni for householders, Soma for trees, Bṛhaspati for speeches, Indra for lordship, Rudra for cattle, Mitra for truth and Varuṇa for the lord of the law."[211]

205. *APIIAIR*, p. 163.
206. *ŚB*, 5/2/1/25.
207. *AV*, 3/4/1.
208. *Ibid.*, 3/4/7.
209. *Ibid.*, 3/20/1.
210. *Ibid.*, 13/1/20.
211. *ŚYV*, 19/39.

6. They purified the king with divine water for his as well as his friend's prosperity[212] and prayed gods for the permanence of the king's kingdom.[213] Moreover, the priest prayed Indra at the time of the coronation to bestow offspring, animals, chariots and wealths.[214] After the completion of such duties of the *purohita*, the king assured his subjects to protect them all, following the path of *dharma*.[215]

DUTIES OF A KING

The Vedic literature give a clear idea of an ideal king. It is found throughout the *mantra Saṁhitā*s. As the king was supposed to protect the people from the chaos or *mātsyanyāya* and keep them in peace,[216] the *Saṁhitā*s have prepared a long list of his duties. Some of them are as follows:

1. The primary duty of a king was to give a popular administration to the people.[217]
2. A passage of the *ŚYV* gives a long list and tells that a king must always be conscious to get knowledge on different matters.[218] His scholarship was expected on several wings of knowledge.[219] Manu says that he should have mastery of *trayī* (*R̥V*, *YV* and *SV*) and *daṇḍanīti*.[220] Moreover, he should manage to keep the balance among *dharma*, *artha*, *kāma* and *mokṣa*.[221]

---

212. *AV*, 4/8/6.
213. *Ibid.*, 6/87 & 88.
214. *Ibid.*, 4/23/1.
215. *ŚYV*, 9/24.
216. *MRK*, p. 94.
217. *R̥V*, 10/174/3 & *AV*, 3/4/2.
218. *ŚYV*, 7/21.
219. *Ibid.*, 27/7; *AV*, 4/8/3.
220. *MS*, 7/43.
221. *Ibid.*, 7/151 & 152.

3. Such a scholar king should treat the subjects sympathetically and bring them up accordingly.[222] The subjects must be well protected[223] and they should get shelter from the king.[224]
4. A king should not try to live a lonely life rather he should always mingle with his subjects.[225]
5. A passage of the *AV* indicates that a king should behave with *sabhā* and *samiti* like a father. They should think and realize that they were the daughters of the king.[226]
6. A king should organize the *yajña*s after becoming the king. He himself should take part in it and get it performed by the *purohita*s.[227] Manu also says that a king should organize the *yajña*s after his coronation.[228]
7. The duties of the king were to remove poverty and bring prosperity in the state. He should always take care that there should not remain a single poor scholar in his kingdom. So he was expected to give wealth frequently to such poors.[229]
8. Moreover, some passages of the *ŚYV* draw the attention of the king so that he could concentrate his mind in order to increase the prosperity of the state.[230]
9. A king should be a good judge.[231] Another passage

222. *ṚV*, 1/43/9; *ŚYV*, 26/11; *ṚV*, 9/108/10; *ŚYV*, 6/7 & *AV*, 4/8/3.
223. *ŚYV*, 27/7 & 38/19.
224. *AV*, 13/1/34.
225. *Ibid.*, 3/4/6.
226. *Ibid.*, 7/12/1.
227. *ṚV*, 1/27/1; 1/126/1 & 4/21/2.
228. *MS*, 7/79.
229. *ṚV*, 2/50/9 & *AV*, 3/4/4.
230. *ŚYV*, 26/11; 13/13 & 23/26.
231. *Ibid.*, 8/23.

of the *AV* mentions that a king should be a proper Justice in cases relating to punishment, war and studies.[232] He should always be impartial in his administration.[233] Manu also admits this.[234]

10. The king should always be aware of the educational system. He must take efforts for the spread of education so that none could disturb the teacher in his duty of teaching.[235] On the other hand, he should never forget that the educational institutions should be free from the royal control.[236]
11. The king had pervasion over *kṣetra, rāṣṭra, aśva, gau,* organs of a *rāṣṭra*, self, *prāṇa, puṣṭa, dyāvā, pṛthvī* and *yajña* which prove that a king must be aware of all those things always.[237]
12. The state of the enemies might invade one's state for which the administrator should always be alert and well-equipped. He should keep his arms and ammunitions with full consciousness.[238]
13. The public enemies were to be defeated by the king.[239] They must be frightened[240] and punished.[241] He should always subdue his foes.[242] Manu also tells that such enemies were to be subdued through *sāma, dāma, daṇḍa* and *bheda*.[243]

232. *AV*, 8/4/3.
233. *Ibid.*, 19/62/1.
234. *MS*, 7/16.
235. *ŚYV*, 15/60 & 61.
236. *VRDB*, vol. II, p. 112.
237. *ŚYV*, 20/10.
238. *ṚV*, 5/33.
239. *Ibid.*, 10/174/2.
240. *AV*, 4/8/3.
241. *ŚYV*, 26/10.
242. *ŚYV*, 11/17.
243. *MS*, 7/155.

14. He should always be ready in punishing the thieves and the enemies.[244]
15. False-speakers sometimes create national chaos. The king must be aware of such persons and he should punish them with strong action.[245]
16. If the incendiary persons create fear among people, the progress of the state stops. So in order to maintain law and order, a king should take appropriate steps so that the people might live without fear.[246]
17. He also should pay his attention in the disturbances created by thieves and dacoits. Execution of such laws were highly appreciated which subdued them. The king should give them severe punishment.[247]
18. There are innumerable passages throughout the *Saṁhitās* from which it is known that the state was well administered through the *brāhmateja* and *kṣātrateja* and the king's important duty was to protect these two *tejas*.[248]
19. The king should always be careful to protect the independence of the state from all sides. A passage of *ŚYV* reveals that a king should make the entire state free from dangers and invasions.[249]
20. In a passage of the *AV*, the seer Atharvā advises the king to pay salary to the government servants according to one's ability and merit. The passage proves that the king should have to manage for such distribution of salary.[250]

---

244. *ṚV*, 5/79/9.
245. *ŚYV*, 8/23.
246. *Ibid.*, 27/7.
247. *Ibid.*, 11/77.
248. *Ibid.*, 18/38.
249. *ŚYV*, 27/7.
250. *AV*, 3/4/2.

21. A king must have apt messengers who could move everywhere. The king should manage to have such arrangements.[251]
22. A king should conduct a welfare state with full grandeur. The politics which he conducts should also be same.[252]
23. A king should appoint some officers to administer the country. Pranav Bandopadhyaya in that context remarks, "In order to run the country, to provide protection to the people, to legislate for them, to make people follow the laws laid down, for all these what are needed are high education, sound common sense, a remarkable capacity to get things done, and most of all, an outstanding world knowledge. Hence, it is not possible to directly involve all the people in the ruling of the country but only a few who have the required qualities can be entrusted with the responsibility."[253] As the selection and the appointments were to be made by the king he had to keep his keen glances on the managements.

---

251. *AV*, 3/4/3.
252. *ŚYV*, 12/17.
253. *AHVPr*, p. 118.

3

Political Aspects — Parliament

Sabhā, Samiti and Vidatha

Sabhā

MEANING AND DEFINITION OF THE TERM

Sabhā occupied an important place in ancient politics. Specially this term is found in the *mantra Saṁhitā*s. Stating the meaning of the term *sabhā*, Monier-Williams expresses that the derivation of the term is unknown, yet he meant it to be an assembly, congregation, meeting, council, public audience, social party, society, particularly a place for public meetings, large assembly room or hall, court of king or justice, council chamber, gambling house, etc.[1] R.C. Majumdar remarks, "Without attempting to be too precise about terms, we may in general, take *sabhā* to mean the local assembly."[2] A.S. Altekar tries to define it as follows,

> The state of the Ṛgvedic period consisted of only a few square miles like the city or state of ancient Greece. It had a capital, not much larger than the few dozen villages comprised in it. Villages had their own popular assemblies known as *sabhā*s and the capital had the central assembly for the whole state which was called a *samiti*.[3]

According to Dr. R.K. Mukherjee, "The *sabhā* functioned

---

1. *SEDM*, p. 1151.
2. *CLAIM*, p. 110.
3. *SGAIA*, pp. 130-40.

as a parliament for the disposal of public business by debates and by discussions."[4] Ludwig says that the term *sabhā* was "something like the upper house where the priest and rich men were represented."[5] Zimmer explains the term in the meaning of "village assembly."[6] Hillebrandt thought that "*sabhā* and *samiti* were the same and *sabhā* is the meeting place of *samiti*."[7] Pranab Bandyopadhyay remarks,

> Vedas tell us about several methods of administration such as *sabhā* and *samiti*. It was a group of intellectuals among the people who got together, deliberated on all matters of the state and laid down the norms, only according to which the king ruled the country.[8]

Moreover, Dr. Rajbali Pandey, with the reference to Kātyāyana, mentions that the people of respected races, well behaved, aged and the riches were the *sabhya*s or the members. The places where they used to discuss several problems were called *sabhā*s.[9]

The term *sabhā* is "indebted" to the word "Sippe" of the German language according to R.S. Sharma. He further analysed the term as follows:

> It has been now established that the word *sabhā* (cf. Indo-Europeon s(u)ebho) is derived from a root closely associated with Old Europeon sub(b), Old High German Sipp(e)a, Gothic Sibja and Mid-German Sippe — all meaning an association of the kin, tribe, a family or the clan.[10]

---

4. *ILSYVS*, p. 83.
5. Quoted from *SGAIA*, p. 140.
6. *Ibid*.
7. *Ibid*.
8. *AHVPr*, p. 116.
9. Quoted from *HDKR*, p. 660.
10. *APIIAIR*, p. 105.

TYPES OF SABHĀ

There are several kinds of *sabhā*s as depicted in the Vedic literature. The first type of *sabhā* is a congregation of people.[11] Secondly, the word *sabhā* was denoted for the place where people came to meet and discuss on some administrative, agricultural and social problems.[12] Thirdly, a gambling place aslo was called *sabhā*, where the gamblers lost their wealths.[13] *Sabhā* was again compared with Rudra.[14] As *sabhā* was said to be *nariṣṭhā*, it indicates that the place of joking and chattering were also named as *sabhā*.[15] Dayānanda Sarasvatī while explaining a passage of the *ŚYV* indicates that there were another three types of *sabhā*s. These were (1) *rājasābha*, or the king's court, (2) *vidyāsabhā* or the gathering to discuss on the matters of knowledge, and (3) *dharmasabhā* or the judicial court.[16] Another Yajurvedic passage presents the respectful addressing to the president, other members of the *sabhā*s[17] and all other senior and junior members or attendants.[18]

QUALIFICATIONS OF THE MEMBERS

The Vedic passages point towards the qualifications of the members. The analysis of the *mantra Saṁhitā*s lead us to as follows:

1. The members of *sabhā* should be well educated scholars so that they could participate in scholarly discussions.[19] Sometimes he had to advise the people

11. *ṚV*, 7/4/1.
12. *Ibid.*, 8/4/9.
13. *Ibid.*, 16/34/6.
14. *ŚYV*, 16/24.
15. *AV*, 7/12/2.
16. *ŚYV*, 7/45.
17. *Ibid.*, 16/24.
18. *Ibid.*, 16/32 & 33.
19. *ṚV*, 2/24/13.

and the kings also.[20]

2. A member of a *sabhā* should be rich and prosperous. A Ṛgvedic passage mentions a member going to *sabhā* being provided with praiseworthy wealth.[21]
3. Famous and well-known prosperity also was a required qualification for the membership of a *sabhā*. Fame has been described as the prominent factor of the organization of a *sabhā*.[22]
4. A *sabhā* or an assembly, as it is seen nowadays, loses its grandeur for the back-benchers. The important qualification that the Vedic sages sought for a *sabhya* or a member of assembly was that he must have to acquire the art of elocution.[23]
5. Rising chairs and quarrelings were strictly prohibited in the Vedic assemblies. So, the members were selected according to their politeness and personality.[24]
6. The *ŚYV* informs two terms such as *sabhācara*[25] and *sabheya*[26] which indicate that the qualifications of a member were determined through the representations and behaviours in the *sabhā*s respectively. He was advised to give proper judgement to the people.[27]
7. Though only polite and noble persons were expected to be the members of a *sabhā*, yet some wicked persons also used to enter there. They were supposed to be harmful for the members with their medical chantings. The verse, "What (witchcraft) they have

20. *ṚV*, 6/2/8.
21. *Ibid.*, 8/4/9.
22. *Ibid.*, 10/71/10.
23. Read, *vṛhatvo vayaṁ ucyate sabhāsu*, *AV*, 4/21/5.
24. *Ibid.*, 7/12/1.
25. *ŚYV*, 30/6.
26. *Ibid.*, 22/22.
27. *Ibid.*, 3/45.

made for thee in the assembly (*sabhā*) I take that back again."[28]

TOPICS OF DISCUSSIONS

Sabhās were held to solve the local problems so as to find out the process of progression, to give stability to their society and so on. Therefore, the topics which were discussed there, cannot be certainly discussed and identified. Yet some passages that we find in the Vedas reveal something as:

1. Cows were thought to be the backbone of ancient Indian economy. Bullocks were used in ploughing.[29] So the protection of the cows had been the main aim of the Vedic sages and perhaps the laws and regulations regarding that, were finalized.[30]
2. Members of the assemblies were conscious about the protection of the land or *bhūmi* for which too they discussed.[31]
3. The members used to discuss about agriculture also.[32]
4. A passage of the *AV* informs that the members of Yama's assembly or *sabhā* had to divide the pious deeds of the people among themselves in the ratio of 1 : 16.[33] This indicates that the higher authorities of *sabhā* used to judge the quarrels of the people.

FUNCTIONS

The functions that a *sabhā* conducted, have been revealed in the passages of the Vedas. These are only a few yet some of them are as follows:

---

28. *AV*, 5/31/6.
29. *R̥V*, 10/27/20.
30. *Ibid.*, 6/28/6.
31. *AV*, 12/1/56.
32. *R̥V*, 6/28/6.
33. *AV*, 3/29/1.

1. A *sabhā* had to judge the quarrels of the common people. In one passage of the *ŚYV* we find that a *sabhya* should be indifferent to both the petitioner and the accused.[34]
2. The *sabhā* could collect the fines and taxes. The quantity of the collection used to be one-sixteenth of the total income of the people.[35]
3. The members of the *sabhā* had to find out the solutions for the strong protection of their king and the state for which they had to maintain the skilful military system.[36]
4. The members of the *sabhā* were responsible for the development of agriculture. So they discussed about it also. It can be guessed that they had to follow some rules for the development and welfare of the general cultivators.[37]

CHARACTERISTICS OF A SABHĀ

1. Though we have analysed the several aspects of a *sabhā* yet its characteristics also are to be discussed herein. A passage of the *ŚYV* indicates that Rudra himself is identified with *sabhā*.[38] Dr. Sitanath Dey mentions that perhaps he is identified thus because then he might cast his vigilant eyes at the performances of the members of a *sabhā* so that the decisions might be impartial and fruitful.[39]
2. A.S. Altekar admits that in some localities or states, the *sabhā* was associated with the king and it was

34. *ŚYV*, 3/45.
35. *AV*, 3/29/1.
36. *Ibid.*, 12/1/56 & 7/12/1.
37. *ṚV*, 6/28/6.
38. *ŚYV*, 26/34.
39. *ILSYVS*, p. 84.

more political than a social gathering.[40] He mentions the passage of the *AV* in support of the above-mentioned statement.[41]

3. In one of the passages of the *Ṛ̥V*, it is found that not only men but women also were the members of the *sabhā*. The educated women were the members of the *sabhā*. They were expected to become the members of the assemblies also.[42]
4. Dr. R.C. Mazumdar with special reference to the *AV* (5/19) admits, "That the assembly was no mere effete body but possessed real control over the king."[43]
5. Pranab Bandyopadhyay remarks, "Whatever we mean by legislative assembly today was the sort of set-up called *sabhā* in existence in ancient times. To such an assembly designed to do good to the common people, obeisance is paid to Rudra. The will of the people is the will of God — is a motto that was there in Vedic times."[44]
6. The Vedic literature of the later *Saṁhitā* period indicates that the *sabhā* possessed ten organs. These were : (1) A king (*dāṇḍika*), (2) *prāḍvivāk* (chief justice), (3) *sabhya* or members, (4) *smṛ̥ti* or constitution, (5) gold, (6) water, (7) *gaṇaka*, (8) writer, (9) *sādhyapāla* and (10) fire.[45]
7. *Sabhā* was supposed to be protected by Indra and Agni because they controlled the wicked people of the country.[46]

---

40. *SGAIA*, p. 142.
41. *Ṛ̥V*, 1/163/3.
42. *AHVPr*, p. 116.
43. *CLAIM*, p. 106.
44. *ĀpDS*, 2/10/25.
45. *AV*, 5/19.
46. *Ṛ̥V*, 1/21/5.

ORIGIN AND HISTORY

A passage of the *ŚYV* informs that *virāṭ*, the creator of *puruṣa*, also created *adhipuruṣa* which torn into pieces.[47] After that, the creation started. In the course of time God, as he created before, desired to bring the creation into existence.[48] Thus, dawn, season, etc., came into being. That was the process through which God created the creatures.[49] *Virāṭ* changed itself into dawn, season and so on. In the course of its progress it stepped into *āhavanīya* and then to *sabhā* as it is found in the *AV*.[50] *Sabhā* then started to follow the *samūhapati*.[51]

Thus, *sabhā* has been identified as the daughter of the Creator or Prajāpati. The passage mentions *samiti* to be the twin sister of *sabhā*. The duty of those two has been mentioned "to protect the king from all sides."[52] On the other hand, it has been named as *nariṣṭhā*[53] which according to Sāyaṇa is "the resolution of many that cannot be broken."[54]

So far the origin, evolution and history of the term is concerned we have only the literary documents starting from the Vedas. There were numbers of institutions and organizations related with politics and cultures in the Vedic time besides *sabhā*. These were *vidatha, saṅgati, pariṣada* and *samiti*. The term *saṅgati* has been explained as *samiti* by Hillebrandt, with special reference to a Ṛgvedic passage.[55]

47. *ŚYV*, 31/5.
48. Read, *dhātā yathāpūrvamakalpayan*, *ṚV*, 1/90/2.
49. *ŚYV*, 31/6.
50. *AV*, 7/10/8.
51. *Ibid.*, 15/9/2.
52. *Ibid.*, 7/12/1.
53. *Ibid.*, 7/12/2.
54. *APIIAIR*, p. 110.
55. *ṚV*, 10/141/4.

Jayaswal, on the one hand mentions that both the *sabhā* and *samiti* were originated from *vidatha*, and *sabhā* was used as the Central Judicial Body.[56] A.S. Altekar mentions that the villages constituted *sabhā*s where they assembled and discussed on several problems that needed to be tackled. He says, "Villages and their own popular assemblies were known as *sabhā*s."[57] B.M. Apte says that the *sabhā* was such an assembly where the selected persons of high personality were its members. He further mentions that the *sabhā*s were known for executive and judicial purposes.[58] Ludwig, on the other hand, compares *sabhā* with *samiti* on the basis of the membership bestowed by those institutions. For example, in order to be a member of *sabhā* one must be a *maghavān* or a brāhmaṇa whereas the *samiti* had *viśa*s as its members, yet brāhmaṇas and *maghavān*s also were allowed to be the members of *samiti* if they wanted.[59] The *R̥V* in a passage mentions that the people of the higher class only were given the membership of the *sabhā*s. The people belonging to the *dāsa* or the *kirāta* classes had no right of it.[60]

The terms such as *sabheya, rayi, sabhāvāna*[61] indicate that the members of the *sabhā* were not at all the general people. But Max Müller meant the terms to be the "customs of *sabhā*s."[62] Another peculiarity of the *sabhā* was that the people kept the fire in the assembly hall and it was treated as one of the members of the *sabhā*.[63] The term *sabhācara*

56. Quoted from *PBRNH*, p. 164.
57. *SGAIA*, p. 139 & 140.
58. *PBRNH*, p. 165.
59. *Ibid.*, p. 165.
60. *R̥V*, 7/1/4.
61. *R̥V*, 2/24/13; 1/19/20; *ŚYV*, 22/22.
62. *PBRNH*, p. 167.
63. *R̥V*, 3/23/4; 5/3/11; 7/7/5 & *AV*, 8/10/5 & 19/55/6.

and *sabhāṣada*[64] indicate *sabhā* to be a judicial court, as analysed by H.N. Tripathi.[65]

On the other hand, N.C. Bandyopadhyaya remarks that the primary form of *sabhā* was of the tribals' institution, later on it associated with the *gotra* and blood in which the king also used to participate. In course of time, it became the advisory board of the king and a judicial court as well.[66]

Later on, the arising of administrative problems led *sabhā* to take judicial actions on the quarrels regarding lands, conspiracies, killings, debts, quarrels on hereditarical rights, wars, peace and chaos originated through wealths.[67]

The term *sabhā* is obscure in the Brāhmaṇic literature. A passage of the *ŚB* tells that the friends and the subordinate kings used to go to the *sabhā* called by the monarch.[68] The *TB* on the other hand, reveals that if a young boy comes to *sabhā* and shows his expertise, then he could win the favour of others.[69]

Sketching the differences between *sabhā* and *samiti* Jogiraj Basu remarks,

> Of the two organizations *sabhā* was definitely a smaller body of representatives which functioned not only as a popular body but also as a court of justice whereas the *samiti* was the larger body — the general assembly of the people more representative in character and wide in its scope.[70]

---

64. *ŚYV*, 3/45 & 20/17.
65. *PBRNH*, p. 167.
66. *Ibid.*, p. 165.
67. *ŚYV*, 30/5.
68. *ŚB*, 3/3/4/14.
69. *TB*, 3/8/13/3.
70. *IABJr*, p. 114.

He further writes,

> It was the main organ of Voxpopuli. In that age of the *Brāhmaṇas*, *samiti* became almost obsolescent. Casual reference to the *sabhā* alone are met with in the *Brāhmaṇas*.[71]

So far the *Dharmasūtras* are concerned with those which have little references on the topic of *sabhā* and *samiti*, there are some passages describing *sabhā*[72] which mean (1) assembly of the people and (2) an assembly hall. On the other hand, *samiti* is seldom mentioned[73] in the *sūtra* literature. The *ĀpDS* gives an important and interesting information in which a student is forbidden to go to *sabhā* and so was to a graduate also.[74] Actually those passages meant it to be a gambling hall. Whatever the fact there may be, the word *sabhā* was used in several meanings but the aim of an ideal *sabhā* was to inspire the people to follow the path of virtue.[75] After all the *sabhā* seems to have performed no political functions in the *Sūtra* period, and put little check on the actions of monarch.[76]

Samiti

MEANING AND DEFINITION

Though the general meaning of the word *samiti* is to come together, meeting, assembling, etc., yet in the Vedic literature and epics, it meant to be a flock, herd, association, society, hostile, meeting, war and battle. Two different words like *samitiṅgama* and *samitiñjaya* meant "assisting a council" and "victorious in battle" or "eminent in an assembly"

---

71. *IABJr*, p. 114.
72. *ĀpDS*, 2/10/25/5 & *PGS*, 3/13/2 & 3.
73. *IVKR*, p. 178.
74. *ĀpDS*, 1/1/3/12.
75. Quoted from *IVKR*, p. 178.
76. *Ibid.*, p. 178.

respectively.[77] The derivation of the word *samiti* is as follows: *sam + in + ktin*.[78]

After the *sabhā* came into existence *virāṭ* ascended into *samiti* and it started to follow its duties such as to select the kings and control people, etc.[79]

Defining the term *samiti* in a single sentence is not an easy task. Some scattered passages from *mantra Saṁhitā*s and the endeavours of some critics are the sources through which we try to find out the definition of the term. We find two passages using the words in the context of battle.[80] Some other passages identify it as a meeting place and the meeting itself.[81] *Samiti*, on the other hand, has been introduced as the daughter of Prajāpati, the Creator. *Sabhā* and *samiti* are His twin daughters.[82] R.S. Sharma tries to define it as, "It is generally recognised that the *samiti* was a folk assembly in which the people of the tribes transacted tribal business."[83] Both the *AK*[84] and *Nir*[85] mean it to be battle. Sāyaṇa,[86] on the other hand, translated this word as battle and war. Altekar remarks, "*Samiti* sometimes denoted a social gathering, usually it rejected a political assembly at the Central Government."[87] Zimmer holds that *samiti* denotes the central assembly of the tribe attended by the

---

77. *SEDM*, p. 1164.
78. *VācT*, vol. VI, p. 5235.
79. *AV*, 8/11/10.
80. *R̥V*, 9/92/6 & *AV*, 6/88/3.
81. *AV*, 5/19/15.
82. *Ibid.*, 7/12/1.
83. *APIIAIR*, p. 111.
84. *AK*, 2/8/107.
85. *Nir*, 2/107.
86. *R̥VSāy*, 10/97/6.
87. *SGAIA*, p. 143.

king.[88] Jayaswal pointed, "The *samiti* was a sovereign body from the constitutional point of view."[89] On the other hand, Ram Gopal observes, "*Samiti* which was according to some scholars an assembly of the whole nation in the early Vedic Age is seldom mentioned in the *sūtras*."[90]

CHARACTERISTICS OF SAMITI

Samiti is found nine times in the *R̥V* and 13 times in the *AV*. So its importance cannot be neglected. The character-istics of *samiti* can be found as follows:

1. The king's representation in the *samiti* was strictly required. So it seems that the administrative business were elaborately discussed therein.[91]
2. The discussions and the deliberations were conducted and controlled by the king. The *ChU* presents a story in which Śvetaketu has been described visiting the *samiti* of Pāñcāla where he finds the king presiding it over.[92]
3. People inspired the members to debate in the *samiti* as it was known that the members of the Vedic assembly also took part in the discourses with full enthusiasm.[93]
4. Debates were constituted in the *samiti* and sometimes it grew to quarrel also.[94] Yet the emphasis was on deriving a common opinion.[95]

---

88. *CLAIM*, p. 109.
89. Quoted from *APIIAI*, p. 115.
90. *IVKR*, pp. 177-78.
91. *R̥V*, 10/97/6.
92. *ChU*, 5/3.
93. Read, *vr̥hadvadema vidatheṣu vīrāḥ*, *R̥V*, 2/24/16; 2/22/15; 8/48/14, etc.
94. *SGAIA*, p. 144.
95. *R̥V*, 10/191/3.

5. R.S. Sharma with Jayaswal's reference from the *Hindu Polity* mentions that the towns and villages were probably represented by its *grāmaṇīs* in the *samiti*.[96]
6. *Samitis* were not the places for the discussions of the political affairs only but religious and sacrificial prayers also were offered to gods.[97] R.S. Sharma in its support observed, "The *samiti* was concerned with religious ceremonies and prayers. Prayers were made reaching common agreements in the *samitis*. It has also something to do with the offerings made to the gods."[98]
7. On the other hand, as *samiti* got the right of the selection of a king,[99] so also it perhaps possessed the right of dethroning a king. Therefore, *samiti* was considered to be a great asset to the king.
8. Brāhmaṇas were highly respected in the *samitis*. A passage of the *AV* says that the scathing state of brāhmaṇas brings the destruction of the state.[100] As the main duty of a *samiti* was to protect the state and the king,[101] it becomes important for it to protect the brāhmaṇas also.

IMPORTANCE OF SAMITI

Samiti played an important role in the Vedic politics and general way of life. Some of the prominent importances are as follows:

1. The importance of the *samitis* appears from the fact

---

96. *APIIAIR*, p. 112.
97. *AV*, 18/1/26.
98. *APIIAIR*, p. 112.
99. *AV*, 6/87/1 & 2; *ṚV*, 10/173/1 & 2.
100. *AV*, 5/19; 5/19/15.
101. *Ibid.*, 6/88/3.

that it had got its right to select or elect a king.[102] *Samiti* affirmed a king for the protection of his kingdom.[103]

2. Some passages from the *ṚV* and the *AV*[104] give an essence that the members as well as the king gave importance to finding out common resolutions at all times. One of the passages tells that *samiti* should have a common opinion always.[105]
3. A king could not conduct the administration if *samiti* did not help him. Therefore a successful candidate for the royal throne wished to usher it by extreme force. He utters, "Superior am I and have come here with a force capable of doing everything. I shall make myself master of your aims, your resolutions and your *samiti*."[106]
4. *Samiti* seems to be more important for a king than those of members who assembled there. Explaining a passage of the *ṚV*, R.C. Mazumdar remarks, "What forest was to a buffalo, what a pitcher was to the *soma* juice, what a sacrifice was to a priest, so was the *samiti* to a king."[107]

POWERS AND FUNCTIONS

Powers

1. Some passages of the *ṚV* indicate that the king in the Vedic Ages was elected[108] and re-elected as

---

102. *APIIAIR*, p. 113.
103. *AV*, 7/12/1.
104. *ṚV*, 10/191; *AV*, 6/64; 6/94 & 3/30.
105. *ṚV*, 10/191/3.
106. *Ibid.*, 10/166/4.
107. *CLAIM*, p. 115.
108. *AV*, 3/4/1.

well.[109] Perhaps it was done by the *samiti*.[110] So, R.S. Sharma mentions that *samiti* enjoyed immense powers.[111]

2. "Members of the *samiti* were men of substance and exercised considerable influence over the administration."[112] This shows that they had the power of legislation and executions.
3. Though sufficient data regarding *samiti* are not much found in the Vedic literature except the *mantra Saṁhitā*s, yet one of the prominent scholars, Ram Gopal remarks, "*Samiti* which was, according to some scholars, an assembly of the whole nation in the early Vedic Age is seldom mentioned in the *sūtras*."[113]
4. One passage of the *ŚB* shows that the *samiti* has possessed the power of distributing land. It says, "To whom so ever the kṣatriya with the approval of the *viś* grants a settlement that is properly given."[114]
5. *Samiti* got the power of discussion on military affairs.[115] The passage which reveals the fact, runs as follows: "We want thee, O ! Pṛthvī, because the villages, forests, *sabhā*s, *samiti*s and wars are constituted upon you. We discuss on the skills of wars also."

Functions

1. The Vedic *samiti* conducted military functions,

---

109. *AV*, 3/4/2.
110. *APIIAIR*, p. 113.
111. *Ibid.*, p. 115.
112. *SGAIA*, p. 144.
113. *IVKR*, pp. 177-78.
114. *ŚB*, 7/1/1/4.
115. *AV*, 12/1/56.

because many passages have the word *samiti* in the meaning of war or battle.[116] The passage indicates that the members of the *samiti* were aware of the skills of wars and battles.

2. *Samiti* is found always to be loyal to the kings.[117] A remarkable fact is that the king also was the member of the *samiti*.[118] So it can be told that *samiti* had to observe its functions in such a way that a king could conquer over his enemies. He should acquire a stable state and he might have to find his friends everywhere.
3. *Samiti* is also found as the conference of scholars which used to judge the knowledge of the graduates. One passage in the *ChU* tells a story of Śvetaketu in which he has been presented going to the *samiti* of Pāñcāla after the completion of his education.[119]
4. Another important function of the *samiti* was to advise and inspire the king. Unless and until the helps and assurances from the *samiti* is got the king could do nothing. So an intelligent and respected member of the *samiti* is found advising the king to give stability to the state.[120]
5. Regarding the power and functions of the *samiti*, A.S. Altekar observes, "*Samiti* was a powerful body yielding what may be conveniently described as sovereign powers, for very often the fate of a king depended upon his ability to carry his *samiti* along with him. If the *samiti* assured an obstructive attitude, the life of the king becomes measerable,

116. *AV*, 6/88/3; *ṚV*, 9/92/6.
117. *AV*, 6/88/3.
118. *ṚV*, 10/97/7.
119. *ChU*, 5/3.
120. *AV*, 6/88/3.

the partisans of a restored king felt that their work was likely to be enduring only if his *samiti* was prepared to co-operate with him. It is quite clear that *samiti* exercised considerable control over the military and executive affairs of the central government, but how exactly it was exercised and how the *samiti*'s powers were co-ordinated with that of the king we do not know."[121]

MEMBERS AND THEIR QUALIFICATIONS

1. *Viśa*s were found to be the members of *samiti*. It is known from the fact that a kṣatriya can give or allot a piece of land only with the proper recommendation of a *viś*.[122]
2. A passage of the *AV*,[123] "After him (*vrātya*) moved out both the assembly and gathering and the army and strong drink,"[124] indicates that the army also were the members of *samiti*.
3. Another passage of the *ṚV* reveals that the kings were the members of *samiti*. The importance of *samiti* for the king is compared with the medicines scattered on earth. The purpose of the passage seems to show where there is earth there is medicine and so for the *samiti*s and the kings.[125]
4. Mazumdar, through the lines, "The persuasion of its members by supremacy in debate . . ."[126] wants to tell that the scholars also were the members of the *samiti*.

---

121. *SGAIA*, p. 143.
122. *ŚB*, 7/1/1/4.
123. *AV*, 15/9/2.
124. Quoted from *CLAIM*, p. 114.
125. *ṚV*, 10/97/6.
126. *CLAIM*, p. 117.

5. A.S. Altekar, through the lines, "The *samiti* must have, like the members of the *sabhā*, gone to the meetings in their full grandeur riding their horses or carriages"[127] indicates that the rich people also were the members of the *samiti*.
6. N.K. Dutta writes, "The *purohita* was a very important member of the state because he had to accompany the king to battles to secure his victory by means of his prayers,[128] to perform sacrifices to remove such evils as epidemic and drought."[129] So *purohita*, as a helper of the king, also must have the membership of the *samiti*.
7. So far the qualifications required to become the members of the *samiti* are concerned, we find some evidences in the Vedas as follows: (a) The members must have strong voice in the *samiti*. A strong and enthusiastic youth declares in the *samiti* as, "O enemies, of opposite opinions, I am strong enough to destroy your intellect and unity."[130] (b) Three passages of hymns in the *R̥V* reveal that the members should be well educated and qualified.[131] (c) Politeness and modesty also were required in the members of the *samiti*. A learned member prays his forefathers to bestow high intellects so that he could deliver moderate speeches in the *samiti*.[132]

Vidatha: A very important unit of administration

There was an important unit of administration or institution

---

127. *SGAIA*, p. 144.
128. *OGCIN*, p. 29.
129. *R̥V*, 10/98/12.
130. *Ibid.*, 10/166/4.
131. *Ibid.*, 10/191.
132. *AV*, 7/12/1.

named *vidatha* among the people of the Vedic society. It was, unlike *sabhā* and *samiti*, an independent institution for local administration. The importance of *vidatha* appears from the fact that the word *vidatha* is mentioned 122 and 22 times in the *R̥V* and the *AV*, respectively. Though it is difficult to give concrete definition of it yet the scholars and some Vedic passages try to define it as follows:

DEFINITIONS

1. Some passages of the Vedic *Saṁhitās* reveal *vidatha* as war. A R̥gvedic passage goes as, "When the war constituted . . ."[133] May you kill your enemies in the war . . ."[134] The same thing is expressed in the passage as, "O ! Viṣṇu please receive your prayers in the wars. . . ."[135] The term *vidatha* has been used in the meaning of war in these three passages.
2. *Vidatha* is known as *loka* in a passage of the *R̥V*[136] and the word *loka*[137] implies a tract, region, district, province, open space and the 14 worlds.[138]
3. Some passage of the *R̥V* says that the *vidatha* is a kind of sacrifice performed by the greats.[139] Sāyaṇa everywhere in his commentaries meant the word as *yajña* or sacrifice. An Atharvanic passage, "O ! Vidatha you are yourself a *yajña*."[140] gives the same meaning.

---

133. *R̥V*, 1/31/6.
134. *Ibid.*, 7/93/5.
135. *Ibid.*, 7/99/6.
136. *Ibid.*, 6/51/2.
137. *SEDM*, p. 906.
138. *Ibid.*, p. 906.
139. *R̥V*, 2/4/8 & 7/34/3.
140. *AV*, 17/1/15.

4. As the word *vidatha* has been supposed to have derived from the root *vid*,[141] it means to know, to consider, to possess and to exist. A passage of the *AV* "You should know it that . . ." explains it clearly that the term *vidatha* means "to know."[142] Rāmānuja Tatacarya refers a passage of the *ṚV*[143] and supports it to be so.
5. There is a passage in the *ṚV* in which *vidatha* has been meant to be a place of offering prayers to God.[144]
6. Another passage reveals the term as proper noun in which *vidatha* has been introduced as the sons of Marutas.[145]
7. Dr. V.R. Ratate says that *vidatha* was, "an independent committee which was formed with a view to organising military activities."[146] Thus, some scholars come to such conclusion that *vidatha* was an institution of controlling military activities in the country.
8. Bloomfield derives it from *vi-dhā* and meant to be related with "distribution, disposition and ordinance."[147]
9. Monier-Williams also writes it as the "Knowledge given to others, instruction, direction, order, arrangement, disposition, rules, etc. Secondly, he expressed it as a meeting, assembly, council, community,

---

141. *APIIAIR*, p. 87.
142. *AV*, 17/1/15.
143. *VKJSR*, p. 56.
144. *ṚV*, 2/12/15.
145. *Ibid.*, 5/33/9.
146. *ARV*, p. 98.
147. *APIIAIR*, pp. 87 & 88.

association and congregation. Thirdly, it meant a host, army, body of warriors, war and fight, etc."[148]

10. Both Bloomfield and Monier-Williams understand the term *vidatha* as to be constituted for secular, military and religious purposes.[149] On the other hand, Jayasawal thinks that the *vidatha* was probably the parent folk of assembly from which the *sabhā, samiti* and *senā* differentiated.[150]

IMPORTANCE OF VIDATHA

Vidatha was an important organization and institution of the Vedic people. The importance of the word appears from the fact that a man wants to live in order to attend the *vidatha*.[151] As Agni was an important part of a *yajña* so was the importance of *vidatha*. Agni of a sacrifice is compared with the *vidathya* of a *vidatha*.[152] A passage of the *R̥V* describes that Marutas were anxious to come in the *vidathas*.[153] When a girl was sent to the house of her husband, she was blessed to acquire the quality of the membership of *vidatha*. Blessing a newly married girl in such a way shows the importance of *vidatha*.[154] Another meaningful passage of the *R̥V* concludes that the subject-matters were discussed deeply and the final decision which was accepted unanimously was said to be the decision of the *vidatha*.[155]

The speeches of the members of the *vidatha* were held so important that he had to take oath before he delivered

148. *SEDM*, p. 963.
149. *APIIAIR*, p. 88.
150. Quoted *ibid.*, p. 88.
151. *AV*, 12/2/30.
152. *R̥V*, 1/130/1.
153. *Ibid.*, 3/59/2.
154. *AV*, 14/1/20.
155. *R̥V*, 3/54/1.

his speech, same as the oaths which we hear today. The oath is, "I am in clear sense and I am going to tell something in *vidatha* in healthy and sound condition of my mind."[156]

Yajña occupied an important role in the lives of the people in ancient times. Such *yajña* has been compared with *vidatha* which shows its importance clearly.[157]

MEMBERS OF VIDATHA

There were various types of members in the *vidatha*s. A study of the *mantra Saṁhitā*s suggests the types of members attending and discussing upon various topics.

1. A passage of the *R̥V* presents Agni as a selecting authority who selected the members of the *vidatha*. He gave the membership to the people who bestowed animals and wealths to the poors.[158]
2. Some scholars also were selected as the members of the *vidatha*. A passage of the *R̥V* reveals the fact[159] which proves that some scholarly discussions also went on.
3. Some intellectuals were allowed to be the members of *vidatha* for his whole life. His membership was thus continued.[160]
4. The expert members of the *vidatha*s used to take their sons in the *vidatha*s perhaps to make them experts in participating in the debates continued therein.[161] There are a lot of passages in the Vedas regarding that.[162]

---

156. *AV*, 8/1/6.
157. *Ibid.*, 17/1/15.
158. *R̥V*, 2/1/6.
159. *Ibid.*, 4/16/3.
160. *AV*, 14/1/21.
161. *Ibid.*, 14/1/20.
162. Read, *vr̥hadvadema vidatheṣu vīrāḥ*, *R̥V*, 2/1/16; 2/13; 11/21; 13/13;

→

5. Another important fact, which is revealed in sufficient passages, is that the ladies also were the members of the *vidatha*s.[163] An Atharvanic passage informs that when a newly married girl was sent to her husband's house, she was blessed to be a member of the *vidatha*.[164]
6. The youths also were called to participate in the *vidatha*s. So it can be guessed that the youths also were provided the membership.[165]

OFFICERS IN THE VIDATHAS

Due to the importance of the *vidatha*s the official members also were selected accordingly. The fact has been revealed through a passage of the *R̥V* which states that Maruts also were eager to come in the *vidatha*s.[166] Agni is the main diety of the Vedic people, but Agni was supposed to be the superintendent to elect the members of the *vidatha*s.[167] Perhaps the membership was bestowed in the witness of fire. Marutas are found attending *vidatha*s.[168] They used to come to the *vidatha*s on the chariots and horses which were decorated with various types of pictures.[169] They were offered milk and *ghī* there.[170] Perhaps Savitā was the supervisor of the *vidatha*s. A passage of the *R̥V* presents Savitā attending all the *vidatha*s coming through the sky.[171]

→ 14/12; 15/10; 16/9; 17/9; 19/9; 20/9; 23/19; 24/16; 27/17; 28/11; 29/7; 33/15; 35/15; 39/8; 40/6; 42/11; 43/3; *AV*, 18/3/24; 12/2/22; 2/30 and 20/34/18.

163. *R̥V*, 1/167/3; 10/85/26 & 27.
164. *AV*, 14/1/20.
165. *R̥V*, 1/186/1.
166. *Ibid.*, 5/59/2.
167. *Ibid.*, 2/1/16.
168. *Ibid.*, 5/59/2.
169. *Ibid.*, 3/26/4.
170. *Ibid.*, 1/64/6.
171. *Ibid.*, 3/54/11.

Sometimes Brahmaṇaspati, who used to formulate the universal laws of the world, also attended it. They were invited there.[172] Again the emperors also are found sometimes attending it.[173] Though Rudra has been mentioned to be the *sabhāpati* in the *ŚYV*[174] yet he has been prayed in the *vidatha*s also.[175] Perhaps he also came sometimes there. Mitrāvaruṇas are found as the executing officers who controlled the world through the *vidatha*.[176] On the other hand, Aśvins, the twin gods are said to be the performers of the *vidatha*.[177] So there were seven top officials in the *vidatha* according to the *R̥V*.[178] Thus, it can be supposed that Agni, Marutas, etc., were the seven top officials of the *vidatha*.

THE HEAD

The people were always in search of the lustrous person to conduct the work of the *vidatha*. They prayed for it and was sought to be intelligent and lustrous one.[179] He must be an energetic, expert in household works and such an ideal person who brings the fame to ancestors.[180] His main duty was to provide wealth to the people.[181]

QUALIFICATIONS OF THE MEMBERS

The qualifications which were sought for the membership of the *vidatha* can be analysed through the Vedic passages

---

172. *R̥V*, 2/23/19.
173. Read, *yasya kraturvidathyo samrāṭ, ibid.*, 4/21/2.
174. *ŚYV*, 16/24.
175. *R̥V*, 2/33/15.
176. *Ibid.*, 5/63/2.
177. *AV*, 7/73/4.
178. Read, *sapta hotrāṇi manasā vr̥ṇāna*, *R̥V*, 3/4/5.
179. *Ibid.*, 4/42/3 & 4.
180. *ŚB*, 5/1/5/3.
181. *R̥V*, 1/80/15.

as follows: A wealth bestower, active and expert in domestic activities were required to be a member of the *vidatha*.[182] As they were found discussing some scholarly discussions, the members were to be well-educated people.[183] In order to acquire the membership of the *vidatha* one must have the art of elocution and the members must have eloquency.[184]

R.S. Sharma, on the other hand, mentions,

> One or two stray references are not adequate to establish the general nature of the *vidatha* as the council of the wise. It is far more probable that it was a popular assembly in the beginning, but in course of time it came to be confined to a few people, and its membership, like that of the Anglo-Saxon National Council, Witenagemot, came to be regarded as a mark of distinction.[185]

TOPICS OF DISCUSSION

As the *vidatha* had occupied an important place in the institutional life of the Vedic people, hence the topics of discussions also were particular. The studies of the Vedic *Saṁhitā*s give the following informations:

The members of the *vidatha* used to discuss about the vigorous works of the heroes who were employed in the wars and other works.[186] Regarding this, R.S. Sharma mentions, "It was an assembly in which the clansmen discussed the virtues of horse, similarly as they dilated upon the virtues of cow in the *sabhā*."[187] The members of the *vidatha* discussed the ways through which they could drive

182. *Ṛ̥V*, 1/91/20.
183. *Ibid.*, 4/16/3.
184. *Ibid.*, 1/64/11; 159/2; & 4/6/2.
185. *APIIAIR*, p. 101.
186. *Ṛ̥V*, 1/162/1.
187. *APIIAIR*, p. 97.

away the noughts and deprivers.[188] They praised the warriors in that assembly.[189] A passage of the *Ṛ̥V* the people assembled there and praised the triumphant glories of *Agni.*[190] Thus, the people discussed on military systems also. Dr. V.R. Ratate also admits the same.[191] In the same way, a passage of the *AV* gives an information in which a strong arrow has been prayed. Such things were performed in the *vidatha*s.[192] The chariots of Ṛ̥bhus also were the topics of discussions in the *vidatha.*[193] R.S. Sharma says that the topics of discussions were not clear. He mentions,

> What was the subject of delibration can be known only vaguely. According to Oldenberg one of the meanings of the terms *vidatha* is the act of disposing of any business or the like. This meaning appears in well-known passages.[194]

He refers to the *Sacred Books of the East* in its support.

FUNCTIONS

There were many functions of the *vidatha*. It was the place where wealth was distributed among the people. It is known from the passage in which Indra has been prayed as the wealth bestower.[195] Secondly, some sacrifices were performed in the *vidatha.*[196] Oblations were offered in the *vidatha* in the second sitting.[197] On the other hand, as per a passage of the *Ṛ̥V*, *vidhata* stands for *yajña*[198] where

188. *Ṛ̥V*, 2/42/11.
189. *Ibid.*, 5/29/13.
190. *Ibid.*, 6/8/1.
191. *ARV*, p. 98.
192. *AV*, 1/13/4.
193. *Ṛ̥V*, 4/56/5.
194. *APIIAIR*, p. 91.
195. *Ṛ̥V*, 2/12/15.
196. *Ibid.*, 3/28/4.
197. *Ibid.*, 3/1/18.
198. *Ibid.*, 10/122/8.

Vaśiṣṭhas were found performing the worship of Agni. Another passage of the *ṚV* reveals *vidatha* as *yajña* in which sacrifices were also performed.[199]

Some other passages of the *mantra Saṁhitās* say that the gods such as Agni[200] and Indra[201] were also worshipped in the *vidatha*. A passage of the *ṚV* informs that the people were inspired to be busy in their works.[202] The people used to blow the trumpets and drums in the *vidatha*. Perhaps people were taught to blow those things there.[203] *Vidatha* was used as a health centre in those days, where medicines also were distributed to the people.[204] The people in those days used to enjoy the songs and dances in the *vidatha*. A passage of the *AV* also confirms this fact.[205] The members, in one passage, are found remembering their forefathers when they met in *vidatha*.[206] Moreover, that also was a place of games where Marutas are described as playing therein.[207]

MANAGEMENTS

Management of the place at that time was done according to the importance and grandeur of the *vidatha*. The people of high intellects and personalities used to come to the *vidatha* for whom the organizers also had to make arrangements accordingly.

First of all, the people brought the seats for VIPs. The seats were made of *kuśa* grass.[208] Marutas are requested to

199. *ṚV*, 7/184/3.
200. *Ibid.*, 3/3/6.
201. *Ibid.*, 7/40/1.
202. *Ibid.*, 10/110/7.
203. *AV*, 5/20/12.
204. *Ibid.*, 8/1/6.
205. *Ibid.*, 12/2/22.
206. Read, *kṛdanti kṛdaḥ vidatheṣu dhṛṣvayaḥ*, *ṚV*, 1/166/2.
207. *Ibid.*, 1/166/2.
208. *ṚV*, 6/52/7 & 7/43/3 (*devāsaḥ varhiso sadantu*).

take the seat.[209] A *yajamāna* or a general member also received the seat of *kuśa*.[210]

A *yajña-kuṇḍa* or a fireplace was made in the middle of the members.[211] Perhaps it was done for sacrifice, heat and light. There was the special system of hoisting the flags in the *vidatha*.[212]

The people in the ancient times used to drink *somarasa* or the juice of *soma* creeper. So they prepared the juice when they met each other.[213] The members of the surrounding area used to bring required articles from their houses to prepare it.[214] After its preparation the people kept a little aside for Aśvinikumāras.[215] Only thereafter people used to drink it.

The work of *vidatha* perhaps, used to begin from the morning, because Uṣā is described affecting *vidatha*.[216] Moreover, the work of *vidatha* was conducted in three sittings.[217] The organizers also provided the facilities of drinking water when the *vidatha* was conducted.[218]

---

209. *R̥V*, 7/57/2.
210. *Ibid.*, 7/12/2.
211. *Ibid.*, 4/6/2.
212. *Ibid.*, 10/122/8 & 3/3/2.
213. *Ibid.*, 3/1/1.
214. *Ibid.*, 7/12/2.
215. *Ibid.*, 7/73/2.
216. *Ibid.*, 1/92/5.
217. *Ibid.*, 2/4/8; 2/27/8; 3/38/6 & 3/56/5.
218. Read, *vidathe apsu jījanan*, *ibid.*, 1/151/1.

4

Social Aspects

(Varṇa and Āśrama Vyavasthā)

Varṇa Vyavasthā

So far the social structure of India is concerned, we find many critics engaging themselves to explain in the ugly form of it on the basis of castes. One of the prominent scholars Maxmüller wrote, "India is a nation of philosophers and Indian intellect is lacking in political and material speculation, and that the Indian never knew the feeling of nationality."[1] On the other hand, there are some critics who believe that the Indian society, though it had to face a lot of invasions of the foreign invaders from Alexender to Mountbatten, has not lost its grandeur in the pages of history.[2] Moreover, Dr. Bhagavan Das goes one step further and says,

> All this world of objects, which is named by the word "this" is made of and by ideation and hence none who knows not the science of self can carry action to fruitful issues. He also knows the inner purpose of the laws of process and its orders ideated by the self-existent, he alone can rightly ascertain and enjoin the rights and duties of the different classes of human beings, of their social occupations (*varṇa*s) and vocations and of their *āśrama*s, "stages of" life.[3]

---

1. *APIIAIR*, p. 1.
2. Hindu Saṁskr̥ti: Uskī Ajeyatā aur Ādhārśilā by Murlidhar Sharma in *HSA*, p. 195.
3. Quoted from Hindu Saṁskr̥ti aur Pāścātyavād by Acarya Naradev Sastri in *HSA*, p. 175.

An unnamed article of the *HSA* gives four kinds of objectives for which the Indian society is still held in esteem by the entire world. These are, (1) purity of women, (2) *varṇa vyavasthā*, (3) *āśrama vyavasthā*, (4) etiquettes and ideologies of Aryan culture.[4]

DIFFERENT TYPES OF CLASSES

While we go to discuss the numbers of castes in the Vedas we have to go through a passage of the *R̥V* in which brāhmaṇa, kṣatriya, vaiśya and śūdras have been told springing from the mouth, arms, thighs and feet of God respectively.[5] The same verse is repeated in the *ŚYV*[6] and the *AV*[7] as well. On the other hand, there are some other passages which mention the numbers of castes. In a passage of the *R̥V* a sage counts five *varṇa*s as brāhmaṇa, kṣatriya, vaiśya, śūdra and niṣāda.[8] Another passage of the *R̥V* mentions five *varṇas*[9] in which the sage prays Indra by saying that all the five *varṇa*s might get lusture from him.[10] Dayānanda Sarasvatī believed that the caste system came into vogue on the basis of the functions of the people.[11] That is why, he finds the thieves and *narakāka*s or the men having abominable life along with the other four *varṇa*s.[12] The *ŚYV* in its 30th chapter mentions many groups of people which was explained to have different types of trades and businesses. Two types of *varṇa*s are mentioned in another

4. Ārya Saṁskr̥ti kī Tulanātmak Gaveṣaṇā in *HSA*, p. 210.
5. *R̥V*, 10/90/12.
6. *ŚYV*, 31/11.
7. *AV*, 19/6/6.
8. *R̥V*, 3/59/8.
9. *Ibid.*, 7/72/5.
10. *Ibid.*, 10/55/2.
11. *SPD*, p. 58.
12. *ŚYV*, 30/5.

passage of the *ṚV*[13] explaining which Jogiraj Basu says that there were two types of *varṇa*s in the Vedic societies.[14] On the other hand, four livelihoods or professions have vividly been described in the *ŚYV* as (1) *rājya*, (2) *yaśa*, and (3) *yajña* and some other serving things.[15] In the same way a passage counts four *varṇa*s such as brāhmaṇa, rājā, vaiśya and śūdra[16] while some other showed brāhmaṇa, kṣatra, śūdra and ārya.[17]

Sitanath Dey writes, "The *ŚB* excludes the śūdra from the list of the original castes and mentions only three upper castes such as brāhmaṇa, kṣatriya and vaiśya."[18] Though he mentiones the passage of the *ŚB* in its support to be 2/1/4/12, but yet it mentions in other place that there were four *varṇa*s in the Vedic society, and these were brāhmaṇa, kṣatriya, vaiśya and śūdra.[19] The *Nirukta* mentions the *varṇa*s to be four in numbers.[20] A.L. Basham writes, "All Aryans belonged to one of the four classes, with the exception of children and widows who were outside the system."[21]

We come to know after this that the Vedic society was divided mainly into four parts and those parts were known to be *varṇa*s. These were brāhmaṇa, kṣatriya, vaiśya and śūdra.

---

13. *ṚV*, 4/50/8.
14. *IABJr*, p. 9.
15. Read, *kṣatrāya tvaṁ śravase tvaṁ mahīyā iṣṭaye tvam arthamiva tvamityai visadṛśa jīvitābhiḥ pracakṣa uṣā ajīgarbhuvanāni viśvā.*
    — *ṚV*, 1/113/6.
16. *ŚYV*, 18/39.
17. *ŚYV*, 14/28; 29, 7/30.
18. *ILSYVS*, p. 9.
19. Read, *catvāro vai varṇāḥ brāhmaṇo, rājanyo vaiśyāḥ śūdraśca*, *ŚB*, 5/5/4/9.
20. *Nir*, 3/8.
21. *WIB*, p. 139.

THE WORD VARṆA

Though the word *varṇa* meant to be colour but yet, it does not mean that the *varṇa*s were classified according to the colour of the skin. The *Nir* says that the meaning of *varṇa* is "to select."[22] Swami Karapatriji writes regarding it, "According to Durgācārya, someone like Agni of the golden colour is described in this definition of the *Nirukta*."[23] There are some Ṛgvedic passages in which the word *varṇa* has been mentioned clearly. One of the passages mentions about the *dāsa varṇa* and those have been described to have settled in the caves through Indra's help.[24] Another passage says that Indra might lead human beings to the path of progression.[25] In that passage we also find the term *varṇa* to denote caste. On the other hand, the term *varṇa* has been used to denote the selectable thing as it denotes through its meaning. A passage of the *ṚV* mentions Agastya wishing success and strength. Thus the both *varṇa*s were achieved.[26] A *ṚV* passage mentions about the *ārya varṇa* which was protected by Indra after the annihilation of the Dasyus.[27] Though the term meant to be the colour yet it was implied everywere in the meaning of the caste or the human group.

Sir Monier-Williams writes,

> *Varṇa* is the class of men, tribe, order, caste, in *ṚV*, especially applied to the *Ārya*s and *Dāsa*s, but more properly applicable to the four principal classes described in Manu's code, *viz.*, Brāhmaṇas, Kṣatriyas, Vaiśyas and Śūdras, the more modern word for 'caste' being *jāti*.[28]

---

22. Read, *varṇo vṛṇute*, *Nir*, 2/1/4.
23. Quoted from *VPK* II, p. 1478.
24. Read, *yo dāsaṁ varṇamadharaṁ guhākaḥ*, *ṚV*, 2/12/4.
25. *ṚV*, 1/104/2.
26. *Ibid.*, 179/6.
27. Read, *hatvī dasyūnprāryaṁ varṇamāvat*, *Ibid.*, 3/34/9.
28. *SEDM*, p. 924.

UNIVERSALITY OF THE VARṆA VYAVASTHĀ

The *varṇa vyavasthā* was employed not among the human beings only but also it was supposed to be got spread over all the animals and plants. In brief we may say that, it was made a universal system. Caste system was thus a philosophy of the Indian society. It was a way of living through which the people could conduct the social life smoothly. Vedic gods and goddesses also were divided in the *varṇa*s. Some passages of the *ŚB* and some other sources reveal that Agni and Bṛhaspati were brāhmaṇas; Indra, Varuṇa, Soma, Rudra, Parjanya and Yama were kṣatriyas; Basu, Āditya, Viśvadevāḥ and Marutas were vaiśyas and Pūṣā was śūdra.[29] On the other hand, Sātavalekar divides them as follows.[30] (1) Agni — brāhmaṇa, (2) Jātavedāḥ — *vāka*, (3) Indra — kṣatriya, (4) Antarikṣa — vaiśya and (5) Pṛthvī — śūdra.

So far other creatures are concerned, animals also are classified into groups. For example, goat has been supposed to be in the brāhmaṇa *varṇa*,[31] horse is kṣatriya,[32] ass is vaiśya and śūdra as well.[33] The *AB* mentions tiger to be of the kṣatriya group.[34] In vegetable *palāśa* is brāhmaṇa and *dūrvā* is kṣatriya.[35] The *TB* speaks about Rohiṇī star that it is brāhmaṇa by *varṇa*.[36]

VARṆA VYAVASTHĀ AND THE ṚGVEDA

Whether the *varṇa vyavasthā* was in practice in the Ṛgvedic period or not is a matter of discussion, because some deny

29. *ŚB*, 14/4/2/23-25; *AV*, 15/10/7.
30. *VDVS*, p. 4.
31. *ŚB*, 6/4/4/22.
32. *Ibid.*
33. *Ibid.*
34. Read, *kṣatraṁ vā etadarnaṇyānām paśūnaṁ yad vyāghraḥ*, *AB*, 8/6.
35. *Ibid.*, 8/37/4.
36. *TB*, 2/7/9/4.

and some confess. The *R̥V* is said to be the first Veda of the Āryans and the scholars try to sketch the social status of the then society. Thus going, R.C. Majumdar writes,

> There is only one passage in the *R̥V* about the celebrated *puruṣasūkta* which refers to the division of society into four classes. The *sūkta* is however, admittedly of late origin and cannot therefore be accepted as an evidence of the earlier period.[37]

N.K. Dutta informs that the earlier European scholars of the subject belittled the significance of the *puruṣasūkta* representation, some even suggested that the hymn was a later interpolation and tried to show that the R̥gvedic society was practically free from caste institution which according to them were later development.[38]

On the other hand, there are some scholars who oppose the above theory. As A.L. Basham says, "The four classes, priest (Brāhmaṇa), warrior (Kṣatriya), peasant (Vaiśya) and serf (Śūdra), were crystallizing throughout the period of the *R̥gveda*."[39] N.K. Dutta also writes that "class in the sense of caste distinction was unknown in the early part of the R̥gvedic period, we bound to presume that the Aryans had at one time possessed such idea, then lost them, and subsequently got them again in an inexplicable way."[40]

A prominent Indologist, Keith, opposes the Western authorities of Vedic literature and comments,

> The existence of the caste system in any form in the age of the *R̥V* has been denied by high authority (Muir, Zimmer, Weber), though it has been asserted later with increasing insistence (Gelmer, Niubarg). In one sense, indeed, presence

---

37. *CLAIM*, p. 311.
38. *OGCIN*, p. 26.
39. *WIB*, p. 36.
40. *OGCIN*, p. 26.

in the *ṚV* cannot be disputed.[41]

Some Western authorities denied the existence of caste system, yet we find the castes in the pages of the *ṚV* also. They want to explain the matter as that the 10th *maṇḍala* of the *ṚV* was added later on. There is no strength in the above-mentioned comment. Because if we suppose that the 10th *maṇḍala* was interpolated later yet we find the terms brāhmaṇa[42] in the earlier *maṇḍalas* also. The term kṣatriya or *rājanya*,[43] vaiśya or *viś*[44] also are frequently found in the earlier *maṇḍalas*. On the other hand, the seers of the 10th *maṇḍala* are found earlier also. For example, Tṛta,[45] Budha,[46] Jamadagni,[47] Vena,[48] Prajāpati,[49] Viśvāmitra,[50] Madhucchandā[51] are the seers found in the several books of the *ṚV*. Again the sons and the grandsons of the seers of the 10th *maṇḍala* are found in the previous *maṇḍalas*. For example, there is a seer Kṛṣṇa in the 10th *maṇḍala*[52] and the seer Kārṣṇi is in the eighth *maṇḍala*.[53] In the same way, Bṛhaspati is in the 10th book[54] whereas Bārhaspatya is in the sixth.[55] Viśvāmitra and Vaśiṣṭhas are the contemporary sages and

41. Quoted from "Varṇāśram kī Aitihāsiktā" by Nirajakanta Devachaudhari in *HSA*, p. 224.
42. *ṚV*, 4/50/8; 2/43/2; 9/112/1; 6/75/10.
43. *Ibid.*, 4/42/1; 8/104/13.
44. *Ibid.*, 1/69/3; 1/126/5; 4/24/4; 6/26/1 & 7/79/2.
45. *Ibid.*, 10/1; 2; 3; 4; 5; 6; 7, 8/47, 9/34 & 9/102.
46. *Ibid.*, 10/101; & 5/1.
47. *Ibid.*, 10/110, 8/101, 9/62 & 9/67.
48. *Ibid.*, 10/123 & 9/85.
49. *Ibid.*, 10/129 & 3/38.
50. *Ibid.*, 10/167 & 3/1; 2; 3; 4; 5; 6; 7; 8; 9; 10; 11 & 12.
51. *Ibid.*, 10/190 & 1/11.
52. *Ibid.*, 10/42; 43 & 44.
53. *Ibid.*, 8/86.
54. *Ibid.*, 10/71.
55. *Ibid.*, 6/2 to 42.

Viśvāmitra is found in the 10th *maṇḍala*[56] whereas Vaśiṣṭha is in the seventh.[57] The above-mentioned evidences prove that neither there was the absence of the caste system in the *ṚV* nor the 10th book was added later on. The caste system mentioned in the *ṚV* and the 10th book was rather as old as the other *maṇḍalas*.

DIVISIONS OF THE PEOPLE IN VARṆAS

The point whether the *varṇas* were determined according to their performances or the functions or they were genealogical is a contradictory matter. A lot of debates among intellectuals regarding it, have gone through but no concrete result has yet come out. But yet, an endeavour to come to a conclusion is being propelled here.

Between the two schools of thoughts, the organization Ārya Samāj mainly advocates the first theory while on the other hand, the traditional scholars support the second one.

THE FIRST THEORY: FUNCTION BASED VARṆA VYAVASTHĀ

1. First of all the name Dayānanda Sarasvatī is to be taken as an important advocate of this theory. According to him, "*Varṇavyavasthā* should be determined according to one's qualification, function and nature."[58]
2. To bestow the rights according to the qualification and functions is *varṇa*.[59] Surendra Kumar describes the term brāhmaṇa as the combination of *brahma* and suffix *aṇ*.[60] Thus, he explains it as, "The man who immerse himself in the studies of the Vedas

56. *ṚV*, 10/167.
57. *Ibid.*, 7/1 to 110.
58. *SPD*, p. 58.
59. *VMSS*, p. 54.
60. *Ibid.*, p. 55 with special reference to *Ast.* 4/2/59.

and in the worship of God along with acquiring knowledge and qualities is a brāhmaṇa."[61] Dayānanda Sarasvatī mentions Manu and says that[62] a man could become a brāhmaṇa if he engages himself in *svādhyāya, japa, homa* in acquiring *trayī vidyā*s, performing *iṣṭi,* begetting sons through *dharma,* and performing *mahāyajñas*, etc."

3. Sivadatta Gnāni says that the division of the society was according to the theory of "Division of Labour" of Economics.[63] N.K. Dutta also writes, "Ṛgvedic society had far advanced from the primitive state when one man could till his land, weave his cloth, make his own earthen pots and crude weapons, and keeps his flock. Division of labour had become a necessity and various professional classes had arisen in the society."[64]

VARṆAS IN GENEALOGICAL ORDER

On the contrary to that school, the genealogical theory also came into existence. Actually the scholars of this school advocate the genealogical caste system to be natural and eternal. Svami Karapatriji Maharaj mentions the word brāhmaṇa to be used as *jāti.*[65] The suffix *ṇis* also denotes *jāti* which is used in Brāhmaṇi.[66] He further gives the example that Paraśurāma, Droṇācārya, Kṛpācārya and Aśvatthāmā had not been made kṣatriyas and the persons like Yudhiṣṭhira and Vidura also had not been Brāhmaṇized[67]

61 *VMSS*, p. 55.

62. *SPD*, p. 59.

63. *VSS*, p. 114.

64. *OGCIN*, p. 39.

65. *MRK*, p. 284 with special reference of Pāṇini 6/4/173. He again writes, *janmanā prāpyate sā jāti.*

66. *Ibid.*, p. 284.

67 *Ibid.*, p. 283.

even by Kṛṣṇa who declared himself to be the Creator of *varṇas*.[68]

There is another passage in the *ChU* which states that the creatures get certain birth according to their deeds of the previous birth.[69] Acarya Baladev Upadhyaya says that the *varṇas*, i.e., brāhmaṇa, kṣatriya, vaiśya and śūdras were ditermined according to birth and they were genealogical. The sons of *ṛṣis* performed the activities of a *purohita*; kṣatriya and their sons administered the states; and the vaiśyas cultivated land accordingly. As a matter of fact, the *varṇa vyavasthā* was fortified with those characteristics which we find in the later ages.[70]

The *ŚB* says that Brāhmaṇism never adjusts in a kṣatriya and so the *kṣatriyatva* happens.[71] Regarding the transformation of *varṇas* with the example of Viśvāmitra has thus been clarified by Basant Kumar Chattopadhyaya. He has stated that it was due to the supernatural austerity and penance which was practised by him. Moreover, the determiner also was the *ṛṣi* like Vaśiṣṭha and not a general person. He further writes that penance can change atom also.[72]

The Western scholars like Keith admit that the caste system was in genealogical order. He writes,

> There is no actual proof in the *RV* that the priesthood was nothing than a closed hereditary class. The term Brāhmaṇa (son of Brahmā) seems, on the contrary, to show that the priesthood was normally hereditary, and there is no instance

---

68. *ŚBG*, 4/13.
69. *ChU*, 5/10/7.
70. *VSSB*, p. 421.
71. Read, *na vai kṣatram brahmavarcasaṁ ramate*, *ŚB*, 13/1/3/5. *na vai brahmaṇi kṣatraṁ ramate*, *ŚB*, 13/1/5/2.
72. *Janmanā Jāti* by Basanta Kumar in *HSA* , pp. 229 & 230.

> which can be quoted of any person who is said to be the other than a priest appearing to exercise priestly practices.[73]

He further writes,

> The *RV* certainly knows of a ruling class, the Kṣatriya, and the Vedic kingship was normally hereditary.[74]

Moreover he writes,

> There is good reason to believe that in the period of the *RV* the priesthood and the nobility were hereditary.[75]

As a matter of fact, the caste system either introduced according to the functions and qualifications or supposed to be a genealogical order, has now lost its importance, but yet, we should remember that this system was introduced to conduct the society and nation as well. Actually, the system was based on a scientific thinking.

DETAILS ABOUT FOUR CASTES

Brāhmaṇa

Brāhmaṇa has been described to be the mouth of the *puruṣa*.[76] The term mouth denotes the knowledge of the mind also. Regarding the formation of the brāhmaṇa caste A.C. Das remarks,

> These experts (scholars) formed a class by themselves who spent their time in learning and properly reciting the *mantra*s and mastering the intricate process of performing various *yajña*s strictly in accordance with long standing practices.[77]

Whatever the theory of the introduction of the brāhmaṇa caste there may be, we find two types of brāhmaṇas in the

73. Quoted from *HSA*, p. 224.
74. *Ibid.*, p. 224.
75. *Ibid.*, p. 225.
76. R̥V, 10/90/12.
77. *RCD*, p. 129.

ṚV. A group of brāhmaṇas used to study[78] while the others went to enlighten others by the knowledge of the *ṛṣis*.[79] On the other hand, we find the following duties of a brāhmaṇa after the studies of the Vedic literature.

1. A brāhmaṇa was expected to have capacity of discriminating all the worldly things.[80]
2. One of the passages of the *ṚV* mentions a brāhmaṇa to be a *soma* squeezer.[81] The passage indicates that the *soma* juice which was offered to gods in the sacrifices was to be prepared by the brāhmaṇas only.
3. He must be a scholar of the Vedas, i.e., *vāṇī*[82] to conduct the brāhmaṇical duties, because the earlier scholars stressed upon the correct pronunciation of the *mantras*.
4. The duty of a brāhmaṇa was to teach the students also.[83] As teacher, a brāhmaṇa was greater than those of the brāhmaṇas who were not a teacher.
5. As Agni has been said to be of the brāhmaṇa group[84] and it has allegorically been described as brāhmaṇa in a passage of the *ṚV* which reveals brāhmaṇa to be *hotā, potā, ṛtvik,* etc.[85] The passage indicates that the brāhmaṇas had to perform the sacrificial duties. Other evidences of the *TS* and the *TMB* are remarkable. They also relate the Brāhmaṇa with the

---

78. *ṚV*, 10/71/8.
79. *Ibid.*, 1/164/45.
80. *Ibid.*, 10/71/8 & *ŚYV*, 31/20; 21.
81. *ṚV*, 8/32/16.
82. Read, *brāhmaṇāḥ ye manīṣiṇaḥ*, *ibid.*, 1/164/45.
83. Read, *vadan brahmāvadato vanīyān*, *ibid.*, 10/117/7.
84. *ŚB*, 14/4/2/23.
85. *ṚV*, 2/1/2.

fire of *yajña*[86] and say that a brāhmaṇa is such a personality which is connected with *vrata*.[87]

6. A passage of the *ŚYV* informs that a brāhmaṇa obtained pre-eminence through power and knowledge.[88]

In the same way, Manu mentions the following duties of a brāhmaṇa: (a) Reading, (b) Teaching, (c) To get the sacrifices performed, (d) To perform sacrifices, (e) Giving or Donating, and (f) To take or receive gifts.[89] On the other hand, the *ŚBG* also mentions some qualities of a brāhmaṇa which are to be achieved by him through austerities and labours. These are as follows:

(a) Tranquillity
(b) Self-restraint
(c) Austerity
(d) Purity
(e) Patience
(f) Honesty
(g) *Jñāna*
(h) *Vijñāna* or supreme knowledge
(i) *Āstikya* or piousness.[90]

The *MB* also says that forgiveness is the prominent qualification of a brāhmaṇa.[91]

Importance of Brāhmaṇa: The importance of brāhmaṇa appears in a passage of the *AV* where it has been told that

86. *TMB*, 15/4/8.
87. *TS*, 1/6/7/2.
88. *ŚYV*, 22/22 & 27/22.
89. *MS*, 1/88.
90. *ŚBG*, 18/42.
91. Read, *brāhmaṇānāṁ kṣamā balam*, *MB*, Ādiparva, 175/28.

the states become less of intelligents and the kings lose their kingdoms, where a brāhmaṇa's wife is made faint.[92] Another passage mentions that a kṣatriya who consumes the materials of a brāhmaṇa drinks poison and as a result of that he loses his *kṣātrateja*.[93] Another passage presents an example where the descendants of *vītahavya* were destroyed for they kidnapped the cow of a brāhmaṇa.[94] Śṛñjayas were prosperous persons but they were deprived of the heavenly obtainence for they killed Bhṛgus.[95] A king who desired taxes from a brāhmaṇa and throws spittle upon him will always be sinking in the river of blood.[96] Thus there are three *sūkta*s (5/17; 18 & 19) in the *AV* which describe the importance of brāhmaṇa.

Rights of the Brāhmaṇas: The duty of a brāhmaṇa is to civilize the whole world and thus he must go everywhere to enlighten the people. So the right to move to several places was bestowed upon the brāhmaṇas. On the other hand, he could travel everywhere if he knew the meaning of the Vedas.[97] *Soma* was offered first to gods in the sacrifices and a brāhmaṇa had the right to drink it thereafter in the sacrificial ceremonies.[98] Thirdly, a brāhmaṇa got the right of being a *vaidya* or a physician. A passage of the *ṚV* mentions a brāhmaṇa doing so.[99] A brāhmaṇa specially a *purohita* had the right of dethroning a king because he had been given the right to make a king ascend the throne. An

92. *AV*, 5/17/12; 13; 14; 15; 16 & 17.
93. *Ibid.*, 5/18/4.
94. *Ibid.*, 5/18/10.
95. *Ibid.*, 5/19/1.
96. *Ibid.*, 5/19/3.
97. *ṚV*, 10/71/8.
98. *Ibid.*, 8/32/16.
99. *Ibid.*, 10/97/2.

Atharvanic brāhmaṇa brings a person into the state and makes him ascend.[100] R.C. Majumdar with special reference to the *Indische Studien* writes,

> Brāhmaṇas are called gods and gods of gods. They are even held to be identical with Brahmā. They alone can take things offered in a sacrifice. They have right to claim for four privileges, *viz.*, (1) veneration, (2) presents or gifts, (3) freedom from oppression, and (4) immunity from capital punishment.[101]

Further he says, "These privileges belong to no other class of people."[102]

So a brāhmaṇa is a man who follows the *vratas*,[103] a spiritual guide, household *purohita* and the Prime Minister of the king.[104]

Office of the Purohita: An Important Factor of Administration

A *purohita* was always a brāhmaṇa. He used to play an important role in the administrative activities. The importance of the word appears from the fact that the first human literature of the world declares Agni as a *purohita* in its first verse. On the other hand, the word *purohita* is found in the *ṚV*,[105] *ŚYV*[106] and *AV*[107] as well. Paṇḍit Dāmodar Sātavalekar gives the meaning of the word *purohita* as,

> There are five classes in a nation. These are Brāhmaṇa, Kṣatriya, Vaiśya, Śūdra and Niṣāda. Among them Brāhmaṇa

---

100. *AV*, 6/87/1 & 2.
101. *CLAIM*, p. 315.
102. *Ibid.*, 315.
103. *TS*, 1/6/7/2.
104. *ŚYV*, 11/81.
105. *ṚV*, 1/1/1; 1/2/1; 1/94/6; 3/11/1; 5/11/2; 7/18/83 & 10/97/7.
106. *ŚYV*, 11/81 & 26/9, etc.
107. *AV*, 3/19/1 & 4; 7/62/1; 18/5/5 & 6; 10/1/6.

> had to perform the activities of *purohita*. A *purohita* is a person who assists the people of the nation fully. The whole nation becomes *yajamāna* when it is thought in national level, and thus the whole Brāhmaṇa *jāti* becomes *purohita* of the nation.[108]

The root *pṛ* with which the word *purohita* has been formed means to nourish and to make full.[109] There were two kinds of *purohitas*: personal and national. We find a lot of evidences regarding the national *purohita*.

Qualifications: We get very important passage in the *Arth* by Kauṭilya in which he gives the characteristics of *purohita*. He gives the following qualifications for the selection of a *purohita*. These are: (1) He must bear the best moral character and must belong to the best race, (2) He must be expert in the *SV*, in daily activities and in economics, (3) He should be able to remove all the natural and humane calamities through the ways shown by the *AV*.[110]

A King should follow his Purohita: The Vedic king is advised to follow the path shown by the *purohita* in all problems of the state. A passage of the *ṚV* says that the king who follows the advices of a brāhmaṇa becomes happy.[111] The *AB* advises a priest or a *purohita* to advise a king in social, political, religious and economic problems.[112] Kauṭilya also suggests the king not to ignore the advice of the *purohita* but he should always be ready to follow what the *purohita* says.[113] In one place of the *AV* it has been said that a king is

108. *AMSS*, p. 257.
109. Read, *patyanta purohitādibhyo yak, Aṣṭ*, 5/1/128 and *Pāṇinikālin Bhāratvarṣa* by Basudev Saran Agrawal, p. 391.
110. *Arth*, 1/9/9.
111. *ṚV*, 3/50/8.
112. *AB*, 8/40/3.
113. *Arth*, 1/9/10.

made with the lustures got from lion, tiger, snake, Agni, brāhmaṇa and the sun.[114] So the spiritual importance of a brāhmaṇa or a *purohita* was properly felt by the ancient *ṛṣis* of India. There are some examples in the various passages of the Vedas.

The *ṚV* mentions Vaśiṣṭha and Viśvāmitra as the priests of king Sudās.[115] Another passage of the same mentions Devāpi as the *purohita* of the king Śāntanu.[116] On the other hand, Bṛhaspati has been presented as the *purohita* of Indra[117] who through the graces and boons could get victory over the *asura*s or the demons. Vaśiṣṭha was the *purohita* of Bharata also. The Bharatas were not organized well and they were not so strong to stand as a strong state. But Vaśiṣṭha became their *purohita* or a leader who made them organized, strengthened and established.[118] The *purohita*s were highly esteemed after Vaśiṣṭha's welcome by the Bharatas.[119] As a mater of fact, they played the part of the Prime Minister as they used to advise the king.

Function of the Purohita: As an important factor of the administration, the *purohita* of the Vedic Age used to bear such important role which are reflected in the passages of the Vedas. The evidences are as follows:

1. He had to be ready to advise the kings in the national problems. The *purohita* was expected to advise the king in political, social and religious problems.[120]
2. A *purohita* was to be present and take important

114. *Ibid.*, 6/38/1.
115. *ṚV*, 2/33/53 & 7/18/83.
116. *Ibid.*, 5/10/98.
117. *Ibid.*, 4/50/7 & 8.
118. *Ibid.*, 7/33/6.
119. *Ibid.*, 7/33/14.
120. *AB*, 8/40/3.

part in the coronation ceremony of the king. We find such *purohita* advising the king to strengthen the kingdom, and is also seen the king requesting the *purohita* to fasten the *abhivarta maṇi* in his right hand so that he might be able to get victory over his enemies.[121]

3. If a king or a *yajamāna* of a *purohita* loses his kingdom, then the latter used to try his best to restore it and to submit it to the *yajamāna*.[122]
4. The *purohita*s used to teach the importance of laws to the general people. So in a passage of the *R̥V* we find Dīrghatamā telling about the greatness of the royal laws. He says, "Law is greater than divine power."[123]
5. A *purohita* had to perform the activities of a Commander or *senāpati*. A passage of the *AV* reveals the fact and the *purohita* said that Agni should defeat his enemies.[124]
6. The *purohita* even used to return the weapons or the witched chanting thrown by the enemies of his *yajamāna*.[125] Another passage of the *AV* advises and suggests the *purohita* to do the same.[126]
7. The *purohita*s used to conduct the domestic rituals of the king.[127]

Oath of Purohita: The *purohita*, must take an oath after his appointment. The *AV* explains the fact as follows:

121. *AV*, 1/29/4.
122. *Ibid.*, 6/87/1 & 2.
123. *R̥V*, 1/164/1; 30 & 31, 1/141/9.
124. *AV*, 7/62/1.
125. *Ibid.*, 8/5/5 & 6.
126. *Ibid.*, 10/1/6.
127. *MS*, 7/78.

1. I shall try my best not to misuse the wisdom, zeal, strength, power, courage, etc., in the state where I have been appointed as a *purohita*.[128]
2. I shall increase the vigour, zeal, strength and power in the state in which I have got the priesthood.[129]
3. I shall destroy the enemies of the state who invade upon the Maghavāns or the riches and the *sūrīs* (the scholars) through the knowledge I obtained.[130]
4. I make the weapons sharpened in the state where I am appointed as a *purohita*.[131]
5. I shall increase the power of fighting (*kṣātrateja*) in the people of our state. That will help the *rāṣṭra* to be developed.[132]

The *purohita* mentions some conditions to the king before his coronation ceremony is constituted. For example, he says that the king must not envy others after he gets kingship.[133] The *purohita* says, "I enthrone you for the welfare of the people."[134] Manu also admits as such: "A well-learnt Vedic scholar only has got the right of being a commander of army, administration, judge and the leader of general people, etc."[135]

Kṣatriya or Fighting Class

The Word Kṣatriya: The second class of people was of the kṣatriyas. The word kṣatriya is originated from the root

---

128. *AV*, 3/19/1.
129. *Ibid.*, 3/19/2.
130. *Ibid.*, 3/19/3.
131. *Ibid.*, 3/19/4.
132. *Ibid.*, 3/19/5.
133. *ŚYV*, 20/1.
134. *Ibid.*, 20/3.
135. *MS*, 12/100.

kṣaṇu which means to commit violence. The suffix *kta* makes it *kṣataḥ* and *train* is added there. The meaning of *train* is "to bring up." Again a *sūtra* adds a suffix *aṇ*[136] and it becomes *kṣatraḥ*. Further, *kṣatrād ghaḥ*[137] makes it kṣatriya. Therefore, we find the following meaning of the term kṣatriya according to the grammatical interpretation.

1. He who protects people.[138]
2. He who destroys and violates the things of others is *kṣatṛ* and the person who protects people from such problems is a kṣatriya.[139]

Monier-Williams, on the other hand, gives the meaning of the term as, "The rank of member of the releasing or military order, authority of the second class."[140] In that way, the meaning of the word indicates the duties of the kṣatriya which are to be performed by him. Again, the Vedic literature admit that the word *kṣatra* is synonym of *rājanya* itself. The *ŚB*[141] and the *AB*[142] declare the fact vividly. Thus we find *kṣatṛ*,[143] *kṣatra*,[144] kṣatriya[145] and *rājanya*[146] to denote the military class.

Characteristics of a Kṣatriya: As Indra has been described as

---

136. *Aṣṭ*, 3/2/101.
137. *Ibid.*, 4/1/138.
138. Read, *kṣadati rakṣati janān iti kṣatraḥ kṣatriyo vā*, *VMSS*, p. 56.
139. Read, *kṣamyate hiṁsyate naśyate padārtho yena saḥ kṣataḥ ghaṭādiḥ tatastrāyate rakṣatīti kṣatraḥ*, *ibid.*, p. 56.
140. *SEDM*, p. 325.
141. Read, *kṣatraṁ rājanyaḥ*, *AB*, 8/2.
142. Read, *kṣatraṁ rājanyaḥ*, 5/3/1/1 and *kṣatrasya vā etad rūpam rājanyaḥ*, *ŚB*, 13/1/5/3.
143. *ṚV*, 6/13/2, *AV*, 3/24/7, etc.
144. *ṚV*, 1/157/2; 8/35/17.
145. *ṚV*, 4/42/1; 5/69/1 and others.
146. *Ibid.*, 10/90/12 & *ŚYV*, 26/2.

a kṣatriya,[147] so the Vedic seers are found describing about a kṣatriya in the form of Indra.[148] Sātavalekar also admits the fact.[149] Whatever the fact there may be, the following are some of the characteristics that a kṣatriya had to possess in the Vedic Age. The evidences have been taken from various sources.

1. A kṣatriya should be unified with his kingdom, because the word kṣatriya itself denotes motherland.[150]
2. Another passage of the *R̥V* mentions kṣatriya to be strength itself, which indicates that a kṣatriya should have strong personality.[151]
3. Again, a R̥gvedic passage mentions kṣatriyas to be *dhr̥tavratas*. The passage says that the *dhr̥tavrata* kṣatriyas should acquire strength.[152]
4. The *AV*, in one passage, informs that a kṣatriya should be expert in charioting, because the passage mentions *kṣatr̥* as charioteer.[153]
5. A kṣatriya should never take the shelter of untruth, because if done so, Soma would kill such a kṣatriya.[154]
6. On the other hand, an *AV* passage informs that a kṣatriya is the master of others. He has been said to be *viśāṁ pati*.[155]

---

147. *ŚB*, 14/4/2/23.
148. *R̥V*, 4/21, 4/30, etc.
149. *AMSS*, p. 89.
150. *R̥V*, 1/57/2.
151. *Ibid.*, 8/35/17.
152. *Ibid.*, 8/25/8.
153. *AV*, 3/24/7.
154. Read, *mithuyā ghārayantaṁ kṣatriyaṁ somo hinoti*, *R̥V*, 7/104/13.
155. *AV*, 1/21/1.

Describing the characteristics of kṣatriya, Kireet Joshi remarks,

> The Kṣatriyas represented the qualities not only of courage, heroism, but also of power and strength, the ambition and desire for rule. The kṣatriyas represented, predominantly, the principle of vital force, if left unbridled or untransformed could easily become a source of misadventure and even of destruction.[156]

Functions of a Kṣatriya: The kṣatriya class is an important class and it plays an important role in the nation-building. As a class of administrators it ought to be conscious from the foreigners' aggression, internal disturbances and so on. Therefore, the duties and the functions of a kṣatriya bear some importances. These are as follows:

1. The main function of a kṣatriya is to defend his nation.[157] The class, as it has been described to be the arms of *puruṣa* or society[158] allegorically, has occupied the place of *viśāṁ pati.*[159]
2. A kṣatriya should manage the sacrifices. An *AV* passage says that the person who knows the *sandīpani āhuti*s to perform in the fire established by the kṣatriyas need not fear from lions and tigers.[160] The passage thus informs that the kṣatriyas should participate in the sacrifices also.
3. Thirdly, a kṣatriya is advised to do the works in such a manner so that the national glory would grow.[161] The passage shows that the works whatsoever a

156. *VICK*, p. 42.
157. Read, *rāṣṭraṁ gupitaṁ kṣatriyasya*, *R̥V*, 10/109/3; *AV*, 5/17/3.
158. *R̥V*, 10/90/2.
159. *AV*, 1/21/1.
160. *Ibid.*, 6/76/3.
161. *R̥V*, 6/13/2.

kṣatriya does, should be analysed from the national point of view.

4. As *vīra* is the synonym of the word kṣatriya[162] so the duty of a kṣatriya becomes to acquire valour[163] by which he could be able to do the works of the nation properly. For that noble purpose he should perform the never-ending accomplishments to acquire strength.[164]
5. The word *kṣatra* itself means to be prosperous in a passage of the *R̥V*[165] and it has been used in plural form so that the term indicates that a kṣatriya should try to be prosperous always.
6. An ideal person follows the path of virtue to acquire strength but never adheres to fowl means.[166] Doing so, he beautifies the earth where he resides. On the other hand, a king prays to his god to bestow the *kṣātrateja* so that he might be able to maintain the freedom of his motherland or nation through it.[167]
7. A kṣatriya, after getting the rights of administration and the duties of defence, must not be mad with power. He should always respect his father[168] instead of rebelling against him. On the other hand, he should be aware of the fact that he should not consume the wealth of a brāhmaṇa. If he does so, he would loses his *kṣātrateja*.[169]

---

162. *R̥V*, 3/35/17.
163. *Ibid.*, 7/64/2.
164. *Ibid.*, 4/12/3.
165. *Ibid.*, 4/4/8.
166. *Ibid.*, 3/38/3.
167. *AV*, 3/5/2.
168. *Ibid.*, 5/1/8.
169. *Ibid.*, 5/18/4.

Describing the duties of a kṣatriya, the *ŚBG* says that a kṣatriya must possess bravery, lustre, patience, cleverness, not to escape from battle, giving and expressing the feelings of mastery.[170] On the other hand, the *MS* also has indicated some duties of the kṣatriyas. These are (1) protection of people, (2) giving or donating, (3) performing *yajña*, (4) studies, (5) not adhering to worldly pleasures.[171]

Kauṭilya also mentions some duties of a kṣatriya specially of a *rājarṣi* and says that he, after getting victory over worldly pleasures should avoid the envy of the others' property and women. In the same way, he should avoid slumbering, unstability, untruth, obstentation in dresses, relation with the unnecessary people and unauspicious activities.[172]

Dr. Rajabali Pandey remarks that the kṣatriyas of the Vedic states had to consider the fight as their main duty. He further classifies the kṣatriyas into three groups. These were, (a) the race of the kings, (b) administrators, and (c) soldiers.[173]

Qualities of a Kṣatriya: Sātavalekar writes that wherever the characteristics and the qualities of Indra are found, one should know that there lies the qualities of a kṣatriya.[174] Accordingly, he refers to some passages and mentions the following qualities:

1. He should be *In + dra* or the destroyer of the enemies.[175]

---

170. *ŚBG*, 18/43.
171. *MS*, 1/89.
172. *Arth*, 1/7/2.
173. *HDKR*, p. 215.
174. *AMSS*, p. 87.
175. *AV*, 2/5/1.

2. *Śūra* or a brave one.[176]
3. *Cakānaḥ* or a satisfied one, lustrous and enlightening.[177]
4. He should be the friend of the people and should always be helpful.[178]
5. He must be an enthusiastic in his duties.[179]
6. *Bhr̥gu* or the man who parches his enemies.[180]
7. *Turāṣāṭ* or a man who might be able to attack upon enemies quickly.[181]
8. *Śakraḥ* or able, powerful and strong.[182]
9. *Vajrī* or he who takes sharpened weapons such as *vajras*.[183]
10. *Vr̥ṣāyamāṇa* or the man who always increases his strength in all sides.[184]
11. *Maghavā* or a rich person.[185]

Thus, after the analysis of these characteristics, duties and qualities of a kṣatriya, we come to know that this class of society occupied an important place in the national life of India which in times was able to maintain the independence of it.

Vaiśya

Vaiśya — The word: The word vaiśya has been originated

---

176. *AV*, 2/5/1.
177. *Ibid.*
178. *Ibid.*, 2/5/3.
179. *Ibid.*
180. *Ibid.*
181. *Ibid.*
182. *Ibid.*, 2/5/4.
183. *Ibid.*, 2/5/5.
184. *Ibid.*, 2/5/7.
185. *Ibid.*

from the word *viś*. The *Nighanṭu* gives the meaning of *viś* to be "man."[186] The word can be formed in two ways: there will be *ṣyañ* suffix[187] after the uninflected noun or *prātipadika viś* and the word is formed.[188] The meaning according to the derivation given above, is, "He who enters into the several businesses and becomes apt in those is called a vaiśya."[189]

The Vedic passages mention of some characteristics of a vaiśya through which we may come to a conclusion later on. These evidences are as follows:

(a) *Viś* has been used to denote general people in some places.[190]

(b) Another passage informs us that the *viśa*s had to perform sacrifices.[191]

(c) He had to look after the cattle also.[192]

Importance: The vaiśyas have occupied an important place in the society in ancient India and they tried to develop its prosperity. Their importances that have been drawn in the pages of the Vedic literature are found as follows:

1. Other *varṇa*s were created from the *viśa*s. The *viśa*s were told to be the source of all classes.[193] On the other hand, the *ŚB* says that the *kṣatra* and *brahma* were originated from the *viśa*s.[194]

---

186. *Nighanṭu*, 2/3.
187. Read, *guṇavacana brāhmaṇādibhyaḥ karmaṇi ca, Pān*, 5/1/124.
188. Read, *tasyāpatyam, Pān*, 6/1/92.
189. Read, *yo yatratatra vyavahāravidyāsu praviśati saḥ vaiśyaḥ vyavahāravidyākuśalo jano vā*, quoted from *VMSS*, p. 58.
190. *ṚV*, 1/69/3.
191. *Ibid.*, 4/24/4.
192. Read, *etadvai vaiśyasya samṛddhaṁ yad paśavaḥ, TMB*, 18/4/6.
193. *TS*, 5/3/3/4.
194. *ŚB*, 11/2/7/16.

2. *Kṣatra* may continue its grandeur only on the basis of *viś*. *Viś* is the base and that base supports the administration and others.[195]
3. A king or the kingship remains safe when *viśa*s are alert. A passage of the *TB* reveals the fact[196] and shows the importance of the vaiśyas in the Indian society.
4. Again another passage of the *TB* goes one step further and says that not only king but also the *rāṣṭra* cannot exist without *viś*.[197] There must be the *viśa*s to continue the national life properly.

Functions and Duties of the Vaiśyas: Duties of the vaiśyas are described below:

1. The duties of the vaiśyas have been divided according to the characteristics they possessed. Their main duty was to follow the path of virtue.[198] A Ṛgvedic passage mentions this and indicates the word to be a "good man."
2. Their second duty was to look after the cattle[199] so that these may contribute in the noble purpose of nation building proving wealths and consuming commodities.
3. Their another duty was to conduct the agricultural activities.[200] The Vedic people cultivated several crops and adopted several methods.[201]

---

195. Read, *bhūma vai viṭ viśi tad bhīmānam dadhāti, ibid.*, 6/6/1/8.
196. *TB*, 2/6/5/4.
197. *Ibid.*, 3/9.
198. *ṚV*, 7/79/2.
199. *TMB*, 18/4/6.
200. *MS*, 1/90.
201. *ṚV*, 8/22/6, 4/57/4 & 6.

4. The *viśa*s have been advised to go to the battlefields to fight wherever and whenever needed. A passage from the *ṚV* is used to pray Indra to protect a *viś* in the battlefield.[202]
5. The *MS* mentions some duties of the vaiśyas as follows:
   (a) Protection of the cattle,
   (b) Giving,
   (c) Performing sacrifices,
   (d) Studies,
   (e) Trade and commerce,
   (f) Taking interest, and
   (g) Cultivation are the duties of the vaiśyas.[203]
6. The *ŚBG* mentions the following duties of the vaiśyas:
   (a) Cultivation,
   (b) Protection of cows, and
   (c) Trade and commerce.[204]

While going to explain the verse of the *ŚBG*[205] Jayadayal Goyandaka mentions the following duties of a vaiśya,[206]

> The base of trade and commerce, wealth, cattle and grains all are in the hands of the vaiśyas. He earns wealth and gets it increased but never for his own sake. He, being protected with the strength obtained from the wisdom of the Brāhmaṇas and the power of the Kṣatriyas, applies the wealth for the welfare of the *varṇa*s accordingly. He has neither any right

---

202. *ṚV*, 6/26/1.
203. *MS*, 1/90.
204. *ŚBG*, 18/44.
205. *Ibid.*, 8/44.
206. *Ibid.*, 18/42 to 44, *ŚBGI*, p. 906.

upon administrative businesses nor there is any necessity of that. The fact is that neither the Brāhmaṇas nor the Kṣatriyas interfere in his duties. They never take their wealth but protect their rights through the wisdom and strength in such a way that he might continue his trades without difficulties. So he has no dissatisfaction in this and confesses the superiority of the Brāhmaṇas and the Kṣatriyas. He pays the taxes to the king, serves the Brāhmaṇas and helps the Śūdras by giving them their ample financial helps.

Viśpati

There is another term *viśpati* found in the Vedas. The word has several meanings.

1. A passage of the R̥V mentions the word *viśpati* and means it to be the guardian or the protector of the subjects.[207]
2. Another passage indicates it to be a king.[208]

The Śūdras

Term and definition: Śūdra is one of the four *varṇa*s occupying the fourth place in the Indian society. It is found in the R̥V in one place only.[209] The word is derived from the root *śuc* that means "to grief." This root of the *bhvādi* group takes *rak* suffix[210] and the word śūdra is formed. Thus, the term śūdra means "He who has not obtained the esteemed status is a śūdra."[211] On the other hand, he who has come out or sprung from *asat* or unexistence is a śūdra.[212] Again, with the reference of the *Vāyu Purāṇa* (VIII. 165) N.K. Dutta

207. R̥V, 1/12/2.
208. *Ibid.*, 1/31/11 & 7/55/5.
209. R̥V, 10/90/12.
210. Read, *sucerdaśca uṇādi*, 2/19.
211. Read, *śocanīyaḥ śocyam sthitimāpanne manuṣya śūdraḥ*, quoted from *VMSS*, p. 58.
212. Read, *asato vā eṣaḥ saṁbhūto yat śūdraḥ*, *TB*, 3/2/3/9.

remarks, *śuc* and *dru* to be the root of the word. The meaning of the word *dru* is "to run."[213]

Again the word śūdra is formed from the root *sucya* which has threefold meanings, (1) Weakening the body, (2) Preparing drinking things, and (3) Bathing. Briefly, the root means to press out (*soma* juice).[214] Thus, the term śūdra means as follows:

1. He who weakens body through his works is the śūdra.[215]
2. He who makes or prepares drinking things like *soma* is the śūdra.[216]
3. The man who feels like bathed through his services is the śūdra.[217]

Importance of Śūdras: Even śūdras were given importance in the Vedic society:

1. The importance of the śūdras in the Indian society appears from the fact that it has been described to be sprung out from the feet of the *puruṣa* wherefrom the brāhmaṇas, kṣatriyas and the vaiśyas also are said to have sprung from its mouth, arms and thighs, respectively.[218] This passage says that the śūdras were so important as the feet of a man.
2. A passage of the *ŚYV*[219] mentions the importance of the śūdras in which a sage says that the śudras also

213. *OGCIN*, p. 41.
214. Read, *śūcyabhiṣave, SK Dhātupāṭha* 513.
215. Read, *śūcayati pariśrameṇa avayavān śithilīkaroti iti śūdraḥ, avayavānāṁ sithilīkaraṇam abhiṣabaḥ, ibid.*, 513.
216. Read, *śūcayati surā sandadhāti iti śūdraḥ surāyāḥ sandhānam abhiṣavaḥ, ibid.*, 513.
217. Read, *śūcayati sevāratena sarvadā snātaiva pratīyate iti śūdraḥ, ibid.*, 513.
218. *R̥V*, 10/19/12.
219. *ŚYV*, 14/30.

were the Āryans who were the creation of the same creator. They have the same right to perform the duties as the others do.

3. The *ŚB* says that the śūdras have been originated from *svaḥ* whereas the brāhmaṇa, kṣatriya and vaiśyas sprang from *aum̐*, *bhuḥ* and *bhuvaḥ* respectively.[220] That also indicates that the śūdras also were counted to be the part and parcel of the Indian society.
4. The *TS* says that the śūdra is one of the important members of the nine *ratni*s who select the kings.[221]
5. Considering the importance of the śūdras, the *rathakāra*s were kept in the esteemed position and they had been mentioned to be the persons of good standing.[222]

Duties and functions of the Śūdras: It was the common duty of every citizen to develop their morality in all respects. Besides those duties, the śūdras were indicated to perform some other duties and activities for the sake of the society.

1. A passage of the *ŚYV* says that the śūdras should purify themselves through austerities. Thus, the first and foremost duty of a śūdra is to purify himself through noble deeds.[223]
2. N.K. Dutta describes the duty of the śūdra as, "Aryan community was complete with Brāhmaṇas, Kṣatriyas and Vaiśyas and no particular work was assigned to the Śūdras except to serve their masters as slaves."[224]

220. *ŚB*, 5/4/6/9.
221. *TS*, 1/8/9/1.
222. *ŚYV*, 30/6; *AV*, 3/5/6; *ŚB*, 13/4/2/17.
223. *ŚYV*, 30/5.
224. *OGCIN*, p. 41.

3. The Śūdras have not to serve the other people only but they were given sufficient opportunities for their spiritual development also.[225] The aim of doing so was perhaps to give them the better way of life.
4. The king makers or *rājakr̥ts* were included of chariot makers, carpenters, blacksmiths, wise persons, ministers, charioteers, leaders of the villages, chiefs, etc.,[226] among which chariot makers, carpenters, blacksmiths and charioteers belonged to the śūdras. In such conditions the duties of the śūdras became more important.
5. The *MS* says that the main duty of the śūdras is to serve others without any grief. He should be satisfied in the duties indicated by God.[227]
6. A śūdra has been indicated by the *ŚBG* to serve the people. It says that the serving activities are the natural duties of a śūdra.[228] Explaining the verse Jayadayal Goyandaka writes about the duties of the śūdra as follows:[229]
   (a) A śūdra should serve other three castes, brāhmaṇa, kṣatriya and the vaiśyas.
   (b) To follow the orders and become loyal to them.
   (c) To supply the needs such as food and water to the other classes.
   (d) His another duty was to make other three classes bathed.
   (e) The śūdras had to make convenience in the activities of others.

225. *VSS*, p. 123.
226. *AV*, 3/5/6 & 7.
227. *MS*, 1/91.
228. *ŚBG*, 18/44.
229. *ŚBGJ*, p. 903.

(f) Their another duty was to help the people of other castes in their daily works.

(g) The śūdras had to look after the cattles of other three classes.

(h) The śūdras should serve the other classes so that their things might be kept orderly.

(i) The śūdras had to wash the clothes of the three upper classes.

(j) Their important duty was to serve the people by sharing them in all their activities.

Rights of the Śūdras: The duties of a śūdra have been mentioned in several branches of the Vedic literature but these have given some rights to them on the other hand.

The śūdras have got the rights of studying the Vedas according to Dayānanda Sarasvatī's interpretation of a passage of the *ŚYV*.[230]

There is a passage in the *ChU* in which a brāhmaṇa is found advising śūdra for religious activities.[231] The fact proves that the śūdras also got the rights of performing religious activities. On the other hand, a brāhmaṇa received the daughter of a śūdra also.

Another passage of the *TB* informs that the fire for sacrifices were not only for the *dvija*s (brāhmaṇa, kṣatriya and vaiśyas are called *dvija*s) but also for the śūdra. The passage mentions the rights to have for *rathakāra, takṣaṇa, karmāra*, etc.[232]

Some of the śūdras had got the rights of selecting a king, for there were some śūdras in *rājakṛt*s and *ratnins*.[233]

230. *ŚYVD*, 26/2.
231. *ChU*, 4/2.
232. *TB*, 1/1/4/8.
233. *TS*, 1/8/9/1.

Place of the Śūdras in the Society: So far the relationship of the śūdra with the other *varṇa*s are concerned, we find scholars of the śūdra groups whom all other sages of the so-called higher classes respected. Some of the examples are as follows: Kavaṣ Ailuṣa was the son of a maid servant.[234] But he, for his noble character, was highly respected by the sages like Gṛtsamada, Viśvāmitra, Vāmadeva, Atri, Bharadvāja and Vaśiṣṭhas. They greeted him by saying *namaste astu* and *tvam vai naḥ śreṣṭho hsi.*[235] A.C. Das remarks,

> We, thus, find that in the early Vedic times, recruitments to the rank of the brāhmaṇas and *ṛṣi*s were made from all classes on the basis of superior spiritual culture and acquirements and there were no hard and fast rules about classes.[236]

On the other hand, we find Kakṣivān as śūdra's son.[237] But in course of time, we find him as a king[238] and a *ṛṣi* as well.[239] He performed the sacrifices also.[240] He is the son of Uśija[241] and was made intelligent by Indra.[242] He is the seer of many passages of the *ṚV*.[243] Kakṣīvatī Ghoṣā, the daughter of Kakṣivān, also was a female seer of some *sūkta*s.[244] Suhastya Ghauṣeya, as he is known to be the son of Ghoṣā by name, was a seer of a Ṛgvedic *sūkta*.[245] Thus, it is clear that the

234. *AB*, 2/8/1 & *KB*, 12/3.
235. Quoted from *RCD*, p. 132.
236. *Ibid.*, p. 132.
237. VSS, p. 122.
238. Kākṣivatī tells her to be the daughter of a king, *ṚV*, 10/40/5.
239. *ṚV*, 4/26/1 & 9/74/8.
240. *Ibid.*, 8/9/10.
241. *Ibid.*, 1/18/1.
242. *Ibid.*, 10/2/10.
243. *Ibid.*, 1/116; 117; 118; 119; 120; 121; 122; 123; 124; 125 & 126.
244. *Ibid.*, 1/39 & 40.
245. *Ibid.*, 10/41.

śūdras, as they are thought today, were not in such condition in the Vedic Age as it is found in the *Ṛgveda*.

NATIONAL IMPORTANCE OF CASTE SYSTEM

Though the Vedic way of life was divided people into four groups, yet the Vedic sages did not want to isolate them from the mainstream of the Indian society. They were aware of the social evils that could arise in the course of time. So they advised the people to outrage the vaiśyas and the śūdras.[246] The sages used to pray God to keep equal glances at the brāhmaṇa, kṣatriya, vaiśyas and the śūdras.[247] The ideal king also wished to be loved by both the śūdras and Āryas.[248] The *KSS* admits that *rājanya*, vaiśyas and brāhmaṇas are of equal status.[249] Perhaps considering the problem of clash, the seer in a passage of the *ŚYV* says that the auspicious speeches should be told to the brāhmaṇas, kṣatriyas, vaiśyas and the śūdras.[250]

So far untouchability is concerned, N.K. Dutta remarks, "There was no Not-me-touchism" in the relation between the Āryans and the *dāsa* or the śūdra slaves.[251] Rāmānuja Tatacārya classified[252] (a) brāhmaṇa, (b) kṣatriya, (c) vaiśya, and (d) śūdras to be the benefectors of the other castes. They were the protectors and protected respectively, which later on came to be existed as castes.

As a matter of fact, the *varṇa vyavasthā* was made to lead the society towards perfection. It was not introduced here for hatred and abhorrence. Jayadayal Goyandaka writes,

246. *ŚYV*, 20/17.
247. *Ibid.*, 18/18.
248. *AV*, 18/62/1; 4/20/4.
249. *KSS*, 6/4/12.
250. *ŚYV*, 26/2.
251. *OGCIN*, p. 14.
252. *VKJSR*, p. 16.

> The four castes always do their works as the four sons of a family do, for the development of their family. A Brāhmaṇa does it through the establishment of the *dharma*, Kṣatriya through his strength, Vaiśya through his wealth and Śūdra through his service. They help each other and grow the strength of society. They neither want to do the same work nor feel any superior or inferior complex in doing so. This balances the strength of society and the *dharma* also becomes stronger and stronger. These were the characteristics of *varṇavyavasthā*.[253]

The Western scholars have seen the word with the Western glances and translated this as fiendish, demonical, barbarous, impious, slave and servant.[254] But the slavery, which was introduced in the Western world through which the above-mentioned meanings are found to be correct, did not exist in India at any cost. Deen Dayal Upadhyaya writes, "*Varṇavyavasthā* cannot be explained and understood through the western glances. The western world had introduced the classes in their societies on the foundation of rivalry, competition and hatred."[255] As the society is the main element of a *rāṣṭra* to be formed, it has been explained as a *virāṭ puruṣa*[256] having thousands of heads, eyes and bellies from which the four *varṇa*s sprung[257] and came to exist in India.

On the other hand, the feeling of nationalism was in the *varṇa*s mentioned in the Vedas. As a kṣatriya's duty was to protect the *rāṣṭra,* he also is found saying, "We are the kṣatriyas and this *rāṣṭra* is ours."[258] Again a brāhmaṇa is

---

253. *SBGJ*, p. 909.
254. *SEDM*, p. 477.
255. *RJDD*, p. 132.
256. *Ṛ̥V*, 10/90/12.
257. *Ibid.*, 10/90/12.
258. *Ibid.*, 4/42/1.

found to concentrate his mind in the welfare of the nation where he resides. He selects the king and gives him the kingship.[259] Moreover, he performs sacrifices to stabilise the nation and and to destroy the enemies.[260] Such sacrifices were not only for the destruction of the enemies but also for the welfare of the *yajamāna*.[261] He had to go everywhere to educate the people for the protection of the nation.[262]

Thus, from the above-mentioned passage, it is clear that the division of the society in the form of *varṇa vyavasthā* was for the protection of the nation and society as well. That was the fact for which our nation could face the invasion of the foreign invaders for a long period of time but did not lose the national identity of India.

Swami Vivekananda in the letter to Mary writes,

> If there will be possibility to establish such a state where there is knowledge of the Brāhmaṇas, civilization of the Kṣatriyas, publicity of the Vaiśyas and equality of the Śūdras, avoiding their faults, then that would be an ideal state.[263]

He further writes that, "the *purohita*s (in the meaning of opportunist and greedy priests) had composed the books where the *varṇa*s have been described as *jāti* but the books composed by God is lacking. I shall follow the path shown by God."[264]

Āśrama Vyavasthā

A man can improve in his life if he improves his four objects,

---

259. *ṚV*, 10/173/1.
260. *AV*, 3/19/2.
261. *Ibid.*, 6/54/2.
262. *Ibid.*, 19/24/1.
263. *VS*(*L*), vol. V, p. 387.
264. *Ibid.*, vol. VI, p. 327.

i.e., *ātman, mana, śarīra* and *buddhi*. It has been described in the Upaniṣads in a very attractive manner.[265] The first two are related with *jñāna* or wisdom and the last two are related with *karma*.

Again the Vedic concept of human life is of hundred years.[266] So, Vātsyāyana divides *āśrama*s in four equal durations.[267] On the other hand, the word *āśrama* is lacking from the *Brāhmaṇa*s and the *mantra Saṁhitā*s.[268] But we find it in the Upaniṣads,[269] Smṛtis,[270] and epics.[271] So far the names and chronology of the *āśrama*s are concerned, we find it at first in *Jābāla Upaniṣad*.[272] Later on the chronology is found in the *sūtra* literatures.[273] The *GDS*[274] also mentions the four *āśrama*s where we find the word *vaikhānasa* in the place of *vānaprastha*. The same declares that a *brahmacārī* spends remaining part of his life in any of the *āśrama*s for which he got absolute liberty.[275] The *MB* explains them to be four stages of life.[276] To say that the system of the *āśrama*s was not known to the sages of the *mantra Saṁhitā*s is not the fact. Though we do not find the terms as we find today, in most of the *mantra Saṁhitā*s yet the words like

---

265. *KaṭhU*, 1/3/3.
266. *IU* 2nd verse, *ŚYV*, 40/2, 36/24.
267. *HSSAJS*, p. 101.
268. *Ibid.*, p. 99.
269. *ChU*, 2/23/1.
270. *MS*, 2/230 & 6/1.
271. *Rām*, 2/196/22 and *MB* Śānti parva, 242/15.
272. Quoted from *HSSAJS*, p. 99.
273. *ĀsGs*, 1/20/11, *ĀpGs*, 4/10/1.
274. *GDS*, 3/2.
275. *Ibid.*, 3/1.
276. *MB* Śānti, 242/15.

brahmacarya,[277] *gṛhapati*,[278] *yati*,[279] and *muni*[280] are found frequently.

IMPORTANCE OF THE ĀŚRAMAS

Shiv Swarup Sahay mentions the three bases of the *āśramas*[281] as follows: (1) The *āśrama* system was based on supernaturalism or spiritualism as Sahay quoted thus from Prabhu, "Here, therefore practically start with supernatural basis, upon this, we erect the supernatural structure of man's early career." (2) He mentions three types of debts which, as Manu describes (6/35) are the debts related with sages, forefathers and gods. All these debts were supposed to disburse in the *āśramas*. Mentioning Prabhu from the *Hindu Social Organisation* (page 97), he concludes that the third base was *yajña*. Both *varṇa* and *āśrama* differ in meanings. Rajabali Pandey informs, "The *varṇa* system was related with the human nature whereas the *āśrama-vyavasthā* was related with culture which was used to purify the human life."[282] Thus, the word *āśrama* bears three meaning (1) The position or place where labour is done, (2) Labour or penance itself, and (3) A place for rest.[283]

At last, we can quote from the *Encyclopaedia of Religion and Ethics* which proclaims the grandeur of the *āśrama vyavasthā* as follows,

> We cannot tell it that how far this *āśrama* system described in the *MS* and the other *Smṛtis* came into practice, but we are free to confess that there is no any conception in the entire

277. *ṚV*, 10/109/5, *AV*, 11/5/18.
278. *Ibid.*, 2/1/2.
279. *Ibid.*, 8/3/9, 8/6/18 & 10/72/7.
280. *Ibid.*, 10/166/2.
281. *HSSAJS*, p. 93.
282. *HDKR*, p. 93.
283. *Ibid.*, p. 94.

human literature which can compete it.[284]

BRAHMACARYĀŚRAMA

First of all, the *brahmacaryāśrama* was followed. But a child could not be sent to the forest for studies for which he had to stay with his parents for some years. But we do not get such clear description regarding that in the most of the Vedic literature. On the other hand, a boy was admitted in the *āśrama* of his *guru* for his studies after his *upanayana* and hence one had to search the time of *upanayana* to determine the age of the boys to enter into *brahmacarya āśrama*. The *AGS* mentions that a boy should be given *yajñopavīta* in the age of eight in case of a brāhmaṇa, while the 11th year is fixed for a kṣatriya and the 12th year for a vaiśya.[285] The last limitation for it has been mentioned in the same as follows: 16th year for a brāhmaṇa boy, 22nd years for a kṣatriya boy and 24th years for a vaiśya boy.[286] Again Manu in one place mentions that brāhmaṇa should be of five years, kṣatriya of six years and a vaiśya boy should be of eight years when he would be given *yajñopavīta*.[287] Dayānanda Sarasvatī also admits the second one.[288] Thus, we may come to the conclusion that a Brāhmaṇa boy could enter into the *brahmacarya āśrama* between the age of 5th to 16th, a kṣatriya in the 6th to 22nd of age and a vaiśya could enter into it after the age of eight years.

Duration of Brahmacaryāśrama

So far the duration of the *brahmacaryāśrama* is concerned,

284. *HDKR*, p. 94.
285. *ĀsGS*, 1/19/6, *MS*, 2/36.
286. *ĀsGS*, 1/19/6, *MS*, 2/38.
287. *MS*, 2/37.
288. *SPD*, p. 31.

the *ChU* mentions that they should be of 24,[289] 44,[290] and of 48,[291] years of age. Secondly, Dayānanda Sarasvatī says that a young boy should get married in the age of 25 with a girl of 16[292] which indicates that the *brahmacaryāśrama* continued up to the 25th year of age of a *brahmacārī*. Of course, that may be varied according to the suggestions of the *ChU*[293] Thus, the duration of *brahmacaryāśrama* is uncertain.

Characteristics of a brahmacārin

The main purpose of *brahmacarya* life was to acquire education from his *guru* or the teacher.[294] In order to get success in it, he must be an obedient student for which he has been advised to bow down in the teacher's front and offer his prostration to him by saying, "I . . . (mentioning his father's name to introduce himself) the son of . . . do hereby offer my prostration to you."[295] He always had to be ready to go in search of *bhikṣā*.[296] The remarkable characteristics of an ideal student was thought to be loyalty to his *guru* in such deep manner that he should even go away from the place where his *guru* would be criticized.[297] Such kind of student was regarded as the foundation for the existence of the whole universe.[298]

289. *ChU*, 3/16/1.
290. *Ibid.*, 3/16/3.
291. *Ibid.*, 3/16/5.
292. *SPD*, p. 32.
293. *ChU*, 3/16/1, 3/16/3, 3/16/5.
294. *Arth.* by Kauṭilya 1/3/12/1.
295. *ĀpDS*. 1/5/2/20.
296. *ŚB*, 11/3/3/5 & 7.
297. *MS*, 2/200.
298. *AV*, 11/5/2.

Daily Life of a Brahmacārin

A *brahmacārī* had to touch the feet of his *guru* after he had left his bed.[299] The *TS* and the *TB* mention that a *brahmacārī* had to leave his bed early in the morning.[300] Perhaps he then had to clean his rooms and the entire *āśrama* along with his friends.[301] After his studies he had to go the village to collect foods and fuels for *yajña*.[302] His another duty was to perform some religious functions through which he could protect the Vedic and divine wealths.[303] He had to bath and perform *tarpaṇa* thrice a day.[304] The students were not ignorant in the social matters. Though they had to spend their busy life in the *āśrama*s yet they were conscious in the day-to-day happenings of the state.[305] Thus, it is clear that the routine of the daily life of a *brahmacārī* was very rigid and hard to follow. In fact, it was a kind of penance through which a *brahmacārī* got the proper training to conduct the next *āśrama*s smoothly.

GṚHASTHĀŚRAMA

Gṛhasthāśrama was the second stage of life of the Indian people as it has been reflected in several Vedic literature.[306] After the *brahmacarya āśrama* was over, some wanted to stay in the same *āśrama* and these were called *naiṣṭhika*s while the others who wanted to enter into *gṛhasthāśrama* were called *upakurvāṇa*s.[307] He was said to be the

299. *GDS*, 1/52-4.
300. *TS*, 6/4/3 & *TB*, 2/15.
301. *HSSADS*, p. 111.
302. *AV*, 11/5/9.
303. *Ibid.*, 11/5/10.
304. *Rām*, 1/23/2, 1/35/9 & 1/23/18.
305. *Ibid.*, 6/124/16.
306. *ĀsGS*, 1/20/11 & *ĀpGS*, 4/10/1.
307. *HDKR*, p. 239.

jyeṣṭhāśramī, gṛhamedhī, gṛhī, gṛhapati and *gṛhādhipati*, etc.[308]

Why Gṛhasthāśrama

The *gṛhasthāśrama* was thought to be a very important *āśrama* among others because it was thought that only *gṛhasthāśrama* can beget the people for other *āśramas*.[309] Secondly, the *gṛhasthāśrama* was maintained to perform *karma*. On the other hand, the *karma* should be good.[310] Thirdly, the ideal *karma* has been told to be the *yajña*.[311] On the other hand, a man becomes indebted with some worldly and divine existence for which he got the chance to repay the debts at the time when he stays in the *gṛhasthāśrama*. So, he was advised to perform five types of *yajña*s in the life of a *gṛhastha*.[312] Again, the *gṛhasthāśrama* is the place for the penance to get success on the three *vargas*.[313]

How to enter into Gṛhasthāśrama

So far the system of the entrance in the *gṛhasthāśrama* is concerned, a man should get married with a girl in order to unfold a new chapter in the book of holy life.[314] The second important work was to make a house and a man is suggested to build his house just after marriage.[315] As the important religious and cultural activities were to be performed in this *āśrama*, he had to build the house specially.[316] In this respect, our Vedic literature gives sufficient descriptions. The *ŚYV* says that a house must have

308. *HDKR*, p. 238.
309. *GDS*, 3/2.
310. *ŚYV*, 1/6.
311. Read, *yajña vai śreṣṭhatamaṁ karma*, *KaṭhU*, 3/10.
312. *MS*, 4/21.
313. *HSSAJS*, p. 105.
314. *ṚV*, 10/85/24.
315. *ĀsGS* 2/7 & *GGS* 4/7.
316. *ŚYV(D)* 29/5 & 6.

some comfortable doors wherefrom air may come and go. On the other hand, the *AV* speaks about the house fixed with strong pillars,[317] where a place for gods also was to be made.[318] Moreover, a Vedic *gṛhastha* was expected to have cows in his life for which they felt the necessity of separate place for those cows.[319] The houses were to be smeared frequently.[320] After the management of those things he had to place two-three types of Agni or fires namely *āhavanīya, gārhapatya* and *dakṣiṇāgni*.[321] After that he had to follow his household activities.

Duties of a Gṛhastha

Gṛhasthāśrama is the important *āśrama* among the four *āśrama*s. It has some hard and fast rules to observe. First of all, a *gṛhastha* had to get up early in the morning,[322] i.e., an hour before the sun rises.[323] Then his duty is to perform the *yajña*s early in the morning.[324] Such functions helped a *gṛhastha* to keep the air[325] in his surroundings pure and auspicious. His another duty was to perform the five kinds of *yajña*s in his daily life.[326] On the other hand, a *gṛhastha* had to follow the path of truth and he was inspired for that.[327] Mutual co-operation and co-progress[328] was the motto of the Vedic society for which the system of gifts or *dāna* was

317. *AV*, 3/12/1.
318. *Ibid.*, 3/12/3.
319. *Ibid.*, 3/12/2.
320. *Ibid.*, 3/12/8.
321. *ŚB*, 1/1/1/1.
322. *MB* Anuśāsan 17/14, Jagadisvarananda's commentary.
323. *Ibid.*, 17/14.
324. *Ṛ̥V*, 7/65/1.
325. *Ibid.*, 1/140/7.
326. *MS*, 4/21 & *MB* Anuśāsan, 17/22.
327. *AV*, 7/60/6.
328. *Ṛ̥V*, 10/191.

introduced and mainly the men of *gṛhasthāśrama* were inspired for that. An *ṚV* passage says that a charitable person is equal to a king and he is invited in all auspicious activities.[329] Another passage mentions that the charitable person is compared with God.[330] The *MS* also praises a charitable man.[331] Another important duty of a *gṛhastha* is to cater others before he takes meal.[332] His responsibility to perform the *saṁskāras* is the remarkable factor. All other people of the *āśramas* are ignorant of it. All the *saṁskāras* from *jātakarma* to *vivāha* of a boy was to be performed by the father.[333] The sufficiency of milk was thought to be the characteristics of the well-to-do family.[334] So, the management of the cattle-shed was primarily thought.[335] Another passage of the *AV* mentions clearly about the shed for cows.[336] Secondly, an *ārya* must have a comfortable residence[337] as well as sufficient milk and food to eat.[338] Describing the importance of *gṛhasthāśrama*, P.N. Prabhu writes, " . . . Where by he is to fulfil his obligations to his wife, to his children, to his family, to his departed ancestors and his community."[339]

VĀNAPRASTHĀŚRAMA

Vānaprasthāśrama follows after *gṛhasthāśrama*.[340] A

---

329. *ṚV*, 10/107/5.
330. *Ibid.*, 10/107/8.
331. *MS*, 2/229 to 233.
332. *GDS*, 5/25.
333. *HSSAJS*, p. 106.
334. *AV*, 3/14/2.
335. *Ibid.*, 3/14/1.
336. *Ibid.*, 3/12/2.
337. *Ibid.*, 7/60/1.
338. *Ibid.*, 7/60/2.
339. Quoted from *HSSAJS*, p. 108.
340. *ChU*, 2/23/1.

vānaprasthī is somewhere found as *vaikhānasa*[341] and somewhere as *yati*.[342] Vedic Index mentions that *vaikhānasas* were a group of sages.[343] On the other hand, the *GDS*[344] mentions some duties of a *vaikhānasa* where we have been informed that a *vaikhānasa* should perform penances by eating only the fruits of the forests. The *TS* also says that a *vaikhānasa* should eat only the fruits of forests.[345]

Entering into the Vānaprasthāśrama

So far as entering into the *vānaprastha āśrama* is concerned, we find a distinct instruction of the *ŚB* where it has been said that a man should enter into the *vānaprasthāśrama* only after his *gṛhasthāśrama* is over.[346] On the other hand, the *ṚV* also mentions that when a person have his grandson and his hair become grey then he should go to forest with the things of *agnihotras*.[347] The same thing is discussed in the *MS* also.[348] His life of the *vānaprasthāśrama* starts after he leaves his wife to his sons or takes her with him to forest and avoids the village diet and clothes.[349]

Importance and Functions of a Vānaprasthī

As the word *vānaprastha* denotes, he should stay in the forest,[350] taking fruits[351] as his meal. He cannot use aristo-

341. *GDS*, 3/2.
342. *ṚV*, 8/3/9, 8/6/18 & 10/72/7.
343. VI, 1/368.
344. *GDS*, 3/26.
345. *TS*, 5/2/5/5.
346. Read, *brahmacaryāśramaṁ samāpya gṛhī bhavet, gṛhī bhutvā vanī bhavet, banī bhūtva pravrajet*, *ŚB* 14, quoted from *SPD*, p. 85.
347. *ṚV*, 10/4/5, Explained in *VMSS*, p. 259.
348. *MS*, 6/2.
349. *Ibid.*, 6/3.
350. Read, "He goes for ascetic life in wood." *SEDM*, p. 940.
351. *TS*, 5/2/5/5.

cratic clothes or other worldly things.[352] He has been advised to wear the barks of tree and the skins of the animals.[353] He should have long beards[354] and stay always in austerity.[355] His another duty was to study the Vedas and the Upaniṣads[356] and perform five types of sacrifices or *pañcamahāyajñas*.[357] He has been forbidden to go to the villages.[358] His another duty was to serve the guests[359] though he had to collect food by begging.[360] On the other hand, he should be free from fear and woes.[361] A *gṛhastha* may go alone or with his wife to the forest for *vānaprasthāśrama*.[362] Comments of some scholars on *vānaprasthāśrama* is also an important matter to mention here. S.N. Sharma mentions,

> The third stage (*vānaprastha*) indicates that the man leaves homes and retires to the solitude of the forest, and devotes to meditation on the problems connected to the soul, the life beyond; but he does discord the affairs of life.[363]

Kireet Joshi says,

> The preparation to leave ordinary life by enlargement, by travel, and by detachment, symbolised by dwelling in the forest.[364]

---

352. *MS*, 6/3.
353. *GDS*, 3/34.
354. *AB*, 7/13/5.
355. *ChU*, 2/23/1.
356. *MS*, 6/29.
357. *Ibid.*, 6/9.
358. *VSR*, p. 213.
359. *Ibid.*, p. 213.
360. *MS*, 6/5-7.
361. *Ibid.*, 6/32.
362. *Nir*, 3/14.
363. *HVLS*, p. 104.
364. *VICK*, p. 52.

Pranab Bandyopadhyay writes,

> *Vānaprastha* literally means going to forest to live a detached life there. But the real spirit of the stage involves the cultivation of a broader vision even while living in the society. The detachment one has to cultivate, does not mean shunning all activity. It should rather be a period of self refining acitivity with a service oriented vision that transcends the limited family boundaries. It is a period of training for expansion of consciousness. The spirit of a *vānaprastha* broadens the vision to experience the riped sweetness of (as age advances) life, and leads onto *sanyāsa*, the last phase of life. The inner expulsion achieved through *vānaprastha*, enables one to transcend the cravings for worldly positions and to physical limitations of the body and mind to enter into a blissful communion with the all-pervading and internal supreme consciousness within.[365]

SAṀNYĀSA ĀŚRAMA

A man entered into the *saṁnyāsa āśrama* after he had completed the *vānaprastha āśrama*.[366] But the word *saṁnyāsa* is not found in the *Saṁhitā*s. The word *brahmasaṁsthā* of the *ChU*[367] has been guessed by the scholars to be used in the sense of *saṁnyāsa*.[368]

Definition of the Words Saṁnyāsa and Saṁnyāsin

Before defining the word *saṁnyāsa* we may refer to *ŚBG* which says, "Scholars say that he, who leaves the resulting works or the *kāmya karma* is a *sanyāsin*."[369] On the other hand, it has also been told that a *saṁnyāsin* is he who, leaves all the worldly attractions and partialities and wanders in

365. *AHVPr*, p. 89.
366. *ĀsGS*, 1/20/11; *ĀpDS*, 4/10/1; *MS*, 6/33.
367. *ChU*, 2/23/1.
368. *VSS*, p. 131.
369. *ŚBG*, 18/2.

the world for the welfare of the people.[370] Again, Jaydayal Goyandaka explains the term as follows:

> The word *saṁnyāsa* has been formed with the combination of the prefix *sam* and *nyāsa* which mean "properly" and "abandonment," respectively. So, the abandonment of the arrogance created from the feelings of all the mental, vocal and physical activities and secondly, the complete abandonment of self conceit and affection to the whole world are the meanings of the word *saṁnyāsa*.[371]

The *ŚBG* in another place says that, he who performs proper works without the expectation of the results of those works is a *saṁnyāsī*.[372] Swami Vivekananda meant the word *saṁnyāsa* as the man who abandons all the laws and searches the *brahma* theory.[373] In another place, he says that the abandonment of dignity, fame and wealth, and attaching himself in the continuous search of the spiritual knowledge[374] are the characteristics of a *saṁnyāsī*. Kireet Joshi defines the terms as the "Final renunciation of ordinary life for the exclusive pursuit of spiritual life."[375]

How to enter into Saṁnyāsāśrama

After completing the 3/4 part of the life one often entered into *saṁnyāsāśrama* for the remaining part of his life.[376] The *BU* in one place mentions,

> On knowing Him, in truth, one becomes an ascetic. Desiring Him only, their world monks wander forth. Verily because they know this, the ancient sages did not wish for offspring.

---

370. *VMSS*, p. 266 Commentary on *MS*, 6/33.
371. *ŚBG*, 5/2 (See Jaydayal's note).
372. Read, *anāsṛtaḥ karmaphalaṁ kāryam karma karoti yaḥ*, *SBG*, 6/1.
373. *VS*(L), IV, vol. p. 234.
374. *Ibid.*, pp. 236 & 231.
375. *VICK*, p. 52.
376. *MS*, 6/33.

> What shall we do with offspring (they said), we who have attained this self, this world. They leave the desire of sons, the desire for wealth, and the desire for worlds and lead the life of a medicant.[377]

A.L. Basham informs that a *vānaprasthī* left his hermitage and became a homeless wanderer with all the earthly things broken.[378] He had to ensure to keep his *śikhā*[379] and he had to take an oath as follows,[380] "I have left the wish of offsprings, wealths and worlds. Let all the creatures of this world be free from fear." Thus, a man became a *saṁnyāsin*.

Characteristics of Saṁnyāsāśrama

As the men of the *āśrama* were regarded as the most respected persons,[381] so they had some peculiarities. They had such boundary of abandonment that they could not keep anything for them.[382] A *saṁnyāsin* never wished to enjoy the worldly happiness though he got them easily.[383] He neither looked into the faults of people nor discussed about them.[384] But instead, he kept the feelings of friendship with all and stays far from envies.[385] He had neither any acceptibles nor to be abandoned.[386] He should not accumulate anything with him.[387] His another characteristic was to control over speeches, glances and actions.[388] An ideal

377. *BU*, 4/4/22.
378. *WIB*, p. 160.
379. *GDS*, 3/22.
380. *ŚB*, 16/6/4/1.
381. *VSS*, p. 128.
382. *GDS*, 3/11.
383. *MB* Śānti, 56/3 commentary of Jagadisvarananda Sarasvati.
384. *Ibid.*, 56/4.
385. *Ibid.*, 56/5.
386. *ĀpDS*, 2/9/21/12.
387. Read, *anicayoḥ bhikṣuḥ*, *GDS*, 3/11.
388. *Ibid.*, 3/17.

saṁnyāsin puts on the clothes thrown by others.[389] He had to stay in a lonely place[390] and should not stay more than one night in a place.[391] So, the question of building a hermit did not arise.[392]

Duties of Saṁnyāsin

So far the main duty of a *saṁnyāsin* is concerned, he had to engage himself in the austerities[393] and should leave all the worldly activities (*karma-kāṇḍas*).[394] His another duty was to contemplate upon God through *yoga*.[395] Lastly, we may quote, S.N. Sharma:

> *Sanyāsa* is the last stage, where all actions are cast aside and the man becomes a *sanyāsī* who thinks only of *Brahman*; and the ultimate merging of the soul with the Universal One was his subject.[396]

A man had to throw all the worldly ties and thus being enlightened became a *saṁnyāsin*. So they wandered from one place to another and spread the theory of perpetual way of life. Moreover, they advised the people how to remove their faults. Service to the society was everything for them.[397]

After a study of the Vedic and other related literatures we may come to the conclusion that the people of ancient times had owned the system of *āśrama* and the people had both worldly and spiritual knowledge. This *āśrama* system

389. *ĀpDS*, 2/9/21/11.
390. *MB* Śānti, 56/8 Commentary of Jagadisvarananda Sarasvati.
391. *GDS*, 3/21.
392. *ĀpDS*, 2/9/21/10.
393. *AB*, 7/13/5.
394. *VS*(L), vol. IV, p. 298.
395. *MS*, 6/65.
396. *HVLS*, p. 104.
397. *VSS*, p. 83.

is seemed to have been introduced in order to balance the both ways of life. That was the only cause for which India could stand even against the continuous attacks of the foreign invaders. A nation is made with individuals. The purity of a nation depends upon the purity of the people for which the system of *āśrama* played an important role to maintain it.

5

Socio-Political Aspects

All Round Development and Education

All Round Development

So far the development of a *rāṣṭra* is concerned, the ancient sages of India have cogitated vast. They actually advanced the theory of *rāṣṭra* in order to bring prosperity and welfare among the people of this land.[1] Therefore, they got the conception of *trivarga* in the course of time. "The theory of *trivarga* may not be traced in the Vedic *Saṁhitas*,"[2] says N.K.P. Sinha. Yet the elements of *trivarga* include *dharma*, *artha* and *kāma* which are frequently found in the entire Vedic literature. Though these were not discussed as *trivarga* but yet, we find them in individual or other forms. As a matter of fact, *artha* and *kāma* were controlled by *dharma* in the politics.

"*Dharma* in its original form is found 56 times in the *ṚV* either in noun or in adjective forms in neuter gender in general" says P.V. Kane.[3] On the other hand, Rajabali Pandey mentions Vaiśeṣika definition of *dharma* and writes that the thing through which a person can obtain worldly and divine success in life is called *dharma*.[4] As the word *dharma* is derived from the root *dhṛ* and the suffix *man* is added to that, the

1. *AV*, 19/41/1.
2. *Political Ideas and Ideals in the Mahabharata*, N.K.P. Sinha, p. 73.
3. Quoted from *DDO*, p. 4.
4. *HDKR*, p. 338.

word means "to maintain." So far the Vedic meaning of the word is concerned, M.M. Williams writes, "it is to be that which is established or firm, steadfast decree, statute, ordinance, law, usage, practice, customary, observation or prescribed conduct, duty, right, justice virtue, morality, religion, religious merit, good works, etc."[5] On the other hand, N.K.P. Sinha finds *dharma* in *ṛta* and writes, "The earlier Vedic concept of *ṛta* contains in embryonic form some of the connotations which were later on attached with *dharma*."[6]

Describing the first *dharma* introduced in the world, a Ṛgvedic passage says that the gods originated *yajña* through another *yajña* and the rules through which they did so were the first *dharmas*,[7] *virāj* ascended into *āhavanīya* institution[8] and thus *ṛta, satya*, etc., came into existence as a result of that. Thus, in order to originate or establish a *dharma*, a new *yajña* was performed. The word *dharma* means duty also. According to it, the *yajña* was to create a new *yajña* and these were the first human *dharmas*. Such human *dharmas* were originated just after the human civilization had come into being. So *dharma* played an important role in the Indian life.

Artha, as it is known through the general meaning of it, is economy but in Sanskrit the term *artha* has frequently been used in the meaning of politics where entire administrative conduct is described.[9] So far economy is concerned, we find the people wishing crops from his

5. *SEDM*, p. 510.
6. *Political Ideas and Ideals in the Mahabharata*, N.K.P. Sinha, p. 73.
7. Read, *yajñena yajñamayajanta devāḥ tāni dharmāṇi prathamānyāsan*, *ŚYV*, 31/16.
8. *AV*, 8/10/4.
9. The term *arthaśāstra* denotes a vast range of politics and administrations but not mere economy. Kauṭilya's *Arthaśāstra* is the example of it.

motherland[10] and the king or Prajāpati being expected to build houses for his subjects.[11] The people expected lot of facilities from their kings or gods.[12] Moreover, it was thought that prosperity should be provided to all the people.[13] The people thought of seeds, water, progeny, and the sunlight as the key of progress.[14] The economy, as depicted in the Vedic literature, will be discussed separately later.

Kāma was first created when the supreme authority or God wished to create this cosmos.[15] On the other hand, a R̥gvedic passage tells that desire or *kāma* arose in the beginning.[16] An Atharvanic passage describes Br̥haspati as having the fulfilling capacity or *kāma*.[17]

The above-mentioned passage shows that the ancient Indian intellectuals realized the importance of *artha* and *kāma* though they wished those elements to be controlled by the *dharma*. *Yajña*s were conducted for the same.[18]

CONCEPTION OF ALL ROUND DEVELOPMENT

So far all round development of a *rāṣṭra* is concerned, the ancient sages of India went through the idea of it. We can find the conception that has been found by the ancient sages in a passage of the *SV*.[19] The passage reveals the element through which a nation can undergo all round development. It gives a long list of those things which may bring all round prosperity in the nation. These are:

10. *AV*, 10/5/45.
11. *Ibid.*, 9/3/11.
12. *R̥V*, 1/159/5.
13. *Ibid.*, 1/160/1.
14. *Ibid.*, 6/31/1.
15. *R̥V*, 10/129/3.
16. *Ibid.*, 10/129/4.
17. *AV*, 11/3/3.
18. *Ibid.*, 19/4/4.
19. *ŚYV*, 22/22.

1. A brāhmaṇa, though it is used to address the Almighty God, yet, it denotes that there should be the existence of a spiritual knowledge and belief.
2. Brāhmaṇas that overflow Brāhmaṇical lustre.
3. Kṣatriyas or the soldiers of the country should be brave, skilled in archery, efficient in shooting and are warrior of highest degree.
4. Abundant milk and sufficient cows for that.
5. Carrying things such as bullocks in the passage.
6. Speedy carrier for communication which has been expressed in the passage to have the speedy horses.
7. The young women should be responsible matrons.
8. The young should be hero, ever victorious, moving in magnificent chariot and they were expected to be worthy of assemblies.
9. Irrigation facilities.
10. Plantation.
11. Satisfaction.

Another passage of the *MB*[20] mentions the following attributes for a well-organized and an ideal state. The list is as follows:

1. Desire to acquire the knowledge of *brahmatattva.*
2. Sufficient supply of water perhaps through irrigation, etc.
3. The subjects should be of good character and they should have speedy process in the state.
4. Try to maintain the self right and etiquettes.

On the other hand, the Vedas used to advise the people to acquire the qualification of getting prosperity. The man is advised to have so, through the help of lustre.[21] The duties

---

20. *ŚYV*, 1/1.
21. *AV*, 17/1/7.

of citizens to achieve that goal of all round development of the state are very important yet, the Vedas suggest the king or an administrator to protect the people through the non-subdued lusture from all sides. He has been told to be the protector of all kinds of happiness.[22] Another Atharvanic passage shows the importance of organization for the prosperity of a nation.[23] Again the same mentions the following qualifications for a *rāṣṭra* to become a well prosperous one. These are: (1) Truth, (2) Generosity, (3) *Ṛta*, (4) Valour, (5) Dexterity, (6) Austerities, (7) Absolute knowledge, and (8) *yajña*.[24]

A long chapter of the *ŚYV*[25] gives a list of several types of officials of the state. We may mention some departments as follows:

1. Education Department: *śruta, sabhya, suta, rudra,* etc.
2. Military Department: The master of the world, the master of all directions, Minister for Animals, Minister for Forest Reservation, etc.
3. Medical Department: A doctor or *bhiṣak,* Master of trees, Divine doctors, etc.
4. Ministry for Trade: A Trademan, A Collector, Master or Manager of the collected Food and Crops, Master of the Animals, etc.

CONCEPTION OF MOTHERLAND

So far the duties of citizens to bring the state and nation to the highest peak of progression is concerned, they should always be aware of the historical importance and grandeur

22. *AV*, 17/1/9.
23. *ŚYV*, 40/11.
24. Read, *satyaṁ bṛhaṭ ṛtaṁ ugraṁ dīkṣā tapo yajñaḥ pṛthivīṁ dhārayanti*, *AV*, 12/1/1.
25. *ŚYV*, 16th chapter.

of the nation.[26] In addition to it, they should have the revered heart for their motherland.[27] The intellectual and learned persons composed the poems of patriotism for the *yajñas* which advised that the poets of all the ages also should compose the poems, songs, essays and other wings of literatures to inspire the people in their duties.[28] Griffith has translated the Ṛgvedic passage as follows:

> An erst Kakṣivān and the Rai Vyāśva, as erst Dīrghatamas invoked your presence, or in the sacrificial chambers Vainya Pṛthu, so be yet mindful of us here, O ! Aśvins.[29]

Intellectuals, along with other general people used to sing the patriotic songs.[30] Such feeling of motherland was the keynote of "progress of the people of Japan even then when they were destoryed badly in the Second World War."

The USSR came to be known as a communist union of states after AD 1917 and it propelled atheism. Yet, its Constitution proclaims its land to be the "mother". It says,

> Defence of the socialist motherland is the sacred duty of every citizen of U.S.S.R. Betrayal of motherland is the parent crimes against the people.[31]

On the other hand, China also is a communist country but it also could not think of progression without establishing the theory of motherland and added such clause in its constitution as,

---

26. *ṚV*, 10/90/2; *ŚYV*, 30/2 & *AV*, 12/1/5.
27. *ṚV*, 10/173/1.
28. *Ibid.*, 8/9/10.
29. *ṚVg*, p. 400.
30. Read, (a) *yasyāṁ samudra uta sindhurāpo, AV*, 12/1/2.
    (b) *viśvambharā vaśudhāni pratiṣṭhā, AV*, 12/1/6.
    (c) *sa no bhūmistvisiṁ valaṁ rāṣṭre dadhātūttame, AV*, 12/1/8.
    (d) *sā no bhūmirvisṛjātam mātā putrāya me payaḥ, AV*, 12/1/10.
    (e) *mātā bhūmiḥ putro ahaṁ pṛthivyāḥ, AV*, 12/1/12.
31. *Constitution of USSR*, Article 62, Moscow 1977.

> It is the sacred duty of every citizen to defend the motherland and resist aggression.[32]

So we the people of India are proud of finding the theory of mother-land in the very dawn of human civilization. On the other hand, it is our ill-luck that we have given the conception of motherland nowhere in our Constitution of free India.

THE COMBINATION OF *KṢĀTRA* AND *BRĀHMATEJA*: A KEYNOTE FOR SUCCESS

There are so many instances in the history of India which reveals that the combination of *kṣātrateja* and *brāhmateja* had played important roles in defeating the enemies and protecting the identity of the nation.

A sage in a Ṛgvedic passage declares that Indra become strong through the help of the lustres got from the sages.[33] A sage is met in a passage of the *ŚYV* who prays that Mitrāvaruṇa might bestow the lustre of *brahma* and *kṣatra*.[34] Three passages of the *ŚYV* pray at a time for the protection of *brāhmateja* and *kṣātrateja*.[35] Another passage of the same says that if the both, *brahma* and *kṣātrateja*, can progress then the prosperity and success may also run in the same way.[36] Another important passage says that where both the *brāhma* and *kṣātrateja* run simultaneously, such state is known as a pious state.[37] In the same way, an Atharvanic passage wishes the *brahma* and *kṣatra* to be the state of fearless and immortality.[38] Another passage goes to say that

32. *Constitution of Chinese Republic*, Article 55, Hongkong 1982.

33. *ṚV*, 8/3/4.

34. *ŚYV*, 5/27 & 6/3.

35. Read, *sa na idam brahma kṣatram pātu tasmai svāhā*, *ŚYV*, 18/40, 41 & 42.

36. *Ibid.*, 18/44.

37. Read, *yatra brahma ca kṣatrañca samyañcau carataḥ saha*
taṁ lokaṁ pūṇyaṁ prajñeṣaṁ devā yatra sahāgninā, *ŚYV*, 20/25.

38. *AV*, 2/15/4.

a man becomes lustrous through the *brāhmateja*.[39]

There are a lot of instances regarding the improvement of both the *teja*s through which an administrator could administer the state properly.

OTHER ATTRIBUTES

An *ŚYV* passage presents[40] the following attributes to make the nation well-developed and an ideal one. These are: (1) The king should be a scholar of the worldly things, (2) The women of the concerning state should be lustrous, (3) The women may choose her husband properly and accordingly, (4) There must be the ponds and wells for water. Another passage of the same[41] mentions that if the subjects follow the path according to the king's advice, become desirous to learn various *śāstra*s, and follow the path shown by the scholars, then the state may develop rapidly. Dayānanda explains a verse of the *ŚYV*[42] and mentions that the people should always be aware of freedom but they should not be beyond control. An Atharvanic passage stresses upon expert messengers for the rapid progress of the nation.[43] The decentralization of power was also a factor of a nation's progress. A passage of the *BU* informs us that the emperor used to appoint several officers in the several places.[44] Its view was to administer the kingdom in a proper way. Such was done and the administrative system was brought into practice by Prajāpati, who created several departments of administration and appointed the officers therein.[45]

At the very end of this discussion, it is clear that the

39. *AV*, 10/5/31.
40. *ŚYV*, 10/3.
41. *Ibid.*, 17/86.
42. *ŚYVD*, 15/5.
43. *AV*, 3/4/3.
44. *PU*, 3/4.
45. *BU*, 1/5/21.

Vedic sages sought two types of progress: (1) *yoga* or worldly progress, and (2) *kṣema* or spiritual progress.[46] The spiritual progress seemed to reach the peak when we hear a sage singing, "I am Indra, nobody can defeat me, I am immortal and never die."[47] Such spiritualism led the people to the national awakening and the Vedic people became well organized is order to defend their motherland. They thought that the human body is the hermitage of seven *ṛṣis* which has been described as the temple of God.[48] On the other hand, the Post-Buddhist era is the declining history of India where the people started to pray God supposing themselves as sinful persons.[49]

A chapter of the *AV*, identified as the national anthem of the Vedic people, by Satavalekar, gives a clear conception of the all-round development of a *rāṣṭra*. The elements which a *rāṣṭra* should possess[50] are: (a) suggestion for organization, (b) feeling of respect for our towns[51] and forefathers,[52] (c) devotion towards the motherland,[53] and (d) the feelings to make the country most powerful,[54] etc., are found in this *sūkta*.[55] A sage in an Atharvanic passage, expresses his view while describing the duties of bridegroom and bride, that they should develop their own glories along with the glories of the *rāṣṭra*.[56] It seems that whenever and wherever the

46. Read, *yogakṣemo na kalpatām*, *ŚYV*, 22/22.
47. *ṚV*, 10/48/5.
48. *ŚYV*, 34/55.
49. With special reference to *pāpo ahaṁ pāpakarmā aham*, etc., from *AGVDJRUS*, pp. 2 & 3.
50. *ṚV*, 12/1/1.
51. *Ibid.*, 12/1/44.
52. *Ibid.*, 12/1/29.
53. *Ibid.*, 12/1/56.
54. *Ibid.*, 12/1/62.
55. *AVMSS*, p. 11. There he says that the *AV*, 12/1 *sūkta* is the national anthem of the Vedic India.
56. *AV*, 6/78/2.

Indian sages performed any religious ritual they had the feeling of nationality behind such rituals. In such condition, the history of India tells us that the kings of several ages ruled over it accordingly and the subjects also treated in the same way. For example, we may mention a verse of *ChU* where a king proclaims, "Neither thief, drunkard, foolish, nor curses of society like prostitutes are in my state."[57]

Education

This topic includes a very vast range of discussion. In the discussion of the branches of education and its institutions, we get some sub-topics that need to be discussed but we have to go through the terms *śikṣā, vidyā, guru, śiṣya* and *chātra,* etc., first.

DEFINITION AND MEANING OF ŚIKṢA

1. The term *śikṣā* was mainly used in the Vedic literature as the first organ of the six *vedāṅga*s which is meant to be related with the science of "pronunciation." It is, in the other words, a *dhvaniśāstra*.[58]
2. What we are going to discuss here, does not mean that. A broad range of knowledge and education, its evolution, and the systems are the topics of the present discussion. So *śikṣa* in such broad sense can be analysed as follows: The term mainly originated from the root *śikṣa* which means to receive *vidyā*.[59] Such *śikṣā* helps people to achieve success by making them worthy.[60]

---

57. *ChU*, 5/11/5.
58. *MunU*, 1/1/5.
59. Read *śikṣā śikṣyate anayeti varṇādyuccārana lakṣaṇam śikṣyanta iti vā śikṣā varṇādayaḥ śikṣaiva śikṣā dairghyaṁ chāndasam*, Commentary of Śaṅkarācārya on *Śikṣā of TU*, 1/2/1. Quoted from *Śikṣāṅka*, *Kalyāṇa* Gorakhpur, p. 86.
60. *Sikṣā evaṁ guru śabdon kī nirukti* by Jagannath Vedalankar in *Sikśāṅka*, *Kalyāṇa*, p. 263.

3. Another word *vidyā* was used in the meaning of *śikṣā*. This has some other meanings. The meanings differ according to the various branches of philosophy, *dharma* or eternal rules, and *kalā* or art.[61] The meanings as they reveal are as follows:
   (a) According to *darśana* — *adhyātma śāstra* or Spiritual knowledge
   (b) According to *dharma* — *vedatrayī* and *dharma-śāstras*.
   (c) According to *kalā* — Art, Architecture and Industries, etc.
4. *Vidyā* has been identified as spiritual education in some passages.[62] Nagesh Bhatta also is found admitting the fact.[63]
5. Monier-Williams means the term *śikṣā* as "Desire of being able to effect anything and wish to accomplish."[64]
6. Same author in the other place defined *vidyā* as knowledge, science, learning, scholarship and philosophy.[65]

TYPES OF VIDYĀ OR ŚIKṢA

1. Types of education were different according to the different thinkers, *Muṇḍaka* refers two types of *vidyās*.[66] These are (i) *parā* and (ii) *aparā*.
2. *Arthaśāstra*, on the other hand, mentions four types of education.[67] These are: (i) *anvikṣikī* (logic or

61. *HDKR*, p. 589.
62. Read, *vidyāñca avidyāñca yastadveda ubhayaṁ saha avidyayā mṛtyuṁ tīrtvā vidyayāmṛtamaśnute, IU*, 1/11
63. Read, *paramottama puruṣārtha sādhanībhūta vidyā brahmagñāna-svarūpā*, Nagesh Bhatta.
64. *SEDM*, p. 1070.
65. *Ibid.*, p. 963.
66. *MU*, 1/1/4.
67. Quoted from *HDKR*, p. 589.

philosophy), (ii) *vedatrayī* (three Vedas), (iii) *vārtā* (economics), (iv) *daṇḍanīti* (political science).

3. Manu has added another type of *vidyā*, that is *ātmavidyā*.[68]

The *vidyā* or *aparā vidyā*s are, in fact synonymous to the term education.[69]

COURSES OF STUDIES

The following subjects were taught to a student. The evidences of which are scattered everywhere in the Vedic literature and other works also.

1. The Vedas were most important subjects in those days.[70] Pranab Bandyopadhyaya remarks, "The four Vedas, *R̥V*, *SV*, *YV* and the *AV*, were considered the materials of knowledge and education."[71]
2. The *MU* refers that the four *Saṁhitās*, *śikṣā*, *kalpa*, *nirukta*, *chanda* and *jyotiṣa* are the *aparā vidyā*. These can be learnt but the *parā vidyā* can be achieved by realizations and penance only.[72] The passage indicates that those subjects were taught as a part of the course to the Vedic students.
3. We get a long list of the courses of studies in the *ChU* in which Nārada reveals what he had studied.[73] The list informs us that the four *Saṁhitās*, *itihāsa*, Purāṇa, *deva-vidyā*, *brahma-vidyā*, *bhūta-vidyā*, *kṣatra-vidyā*, *nakṣatra-vidyā*, *devayajana-vidyā*, etc., also came into being in the Vedic education.

---

68. *MS*, 7/43.
69. *MU*, 1/1/5.
70. *AV*, 11/5/17.
71. *AHVP*, p. 85.
72. *MU*, 1/1/5.
73. *ChU*, 7/1/2.

4. The knowledge of industry[74] and literature[75] also are found in the Vedas which prove that these subjects also were taught in those days.
5. Science subjects such as mathematics,[76] medical science,[77] military education,[78] and other technical education[79] also were found as courses of studies.
6. In a long chapter of the *Vedic Society*: *Socio-Cultural Aspect*, Ghurye admits that the Vedic people enjoyed songs and dances.[80] This gives a conception that perhaps some were taught dancing and singing also.
7. Balasastri Haradas counts 20 subjects as the courses for the Vedic students. These were : 1. *veda-vidyā*, 2. *itihāsa Purāṇa*, 3. *nārāśaṁśis*, 4. *chanda*, 5. sacrificial rituals, 6. *bhūmiti*, 7. *jyotiṣa*, 8. military education, 9. singing, 10. art of secrecy, 11. carpentry, 12. *citikarma*, 13. archery, 14. charioteering, 15. charioting, 16. medical science, 17. education for goldsmiths, 18. mining, 19. snake-charming or *sarpa-vidyā*, and 20. *guru-vidyā*.[81]
8. Dr. Sitanath Dey remarks, "Besides the knowledge of the four Vedas, the knowledge of *yajña-śāstra*, astronomy, geography, geology, hydrostatics,

---

74. *ṚV*, 10/130/1; 2 & 3.
75. *Ibid.*, 10/130/4 & 5.
76. *Ibid.*, *ŚYV*, 17/2 and *VM* by Bhāratī Tīrtha Kṛṣṇa Śaṅkarācārya of Gobardhan Maṭh, Purī is a surprising discovery. He gives 16 Vedic formulae to solve the hard mathematical problems in easy manner. Published by Motilal Banarsidass, Delhi, 1989, 11th edition.
77. *AV*, 1/3, 1/24 and 1/23, etc.
78. *ṚV*, 6/35 & 10/103, etc.
79. *Ibid.*, 1/116/6; 10/143/5, etc.
80. *VIG*, p. 254.
81. *VRDB*, vol. II, p. 109.

medicines and navigation were also included in the syllabus.[82]

A TEACHER, GURU, OR ĀCĀRYA

Definition

The root '*gṝ*' (to spray, to destroy, to give proper knowledge) and '*gṝ*' (to sound) form the word *guru*. These give four meanings:

1. He, who imparts knowledge to the disciple.[83]
2. He, who destroys the darkness of innocence of a pupil.[84]
3. He, who advises about the *dharma* to the students.[85]
4. He, who teaches the meaning of the Vedas to his *śiṣyas*.[86]
5. He, who inspires a student to follow the path of truth.[87]

On the other hand, the word *ācārya* has been analysed as he, who defines the meaning of *śāstras*, executes them as *ācāras* and follow them.[88] The root *car* with the prefix *ā* also means the same.

---

82. *ILSYVS*, p. 24.
83. Read, *girati siñcati karṇayorjñānāmṛtam iti guruḥ* (*gṝ, secane*) *bhuvādi*, quoted from *Śikṣāṅka*, p. 263.
84. Read, *girati ajñānāndhakāram iti guruḥ* (*gṛ, nigaraṇe*) *tudādi*, quoted *Śikṣāṅka*, p. 263.
85. Read, *gṛṇāti dharmādi rahasyam iti guruḥ* (*gṝ, śabde*) *kriyādi*, quoted *ibid.*, p. 263.
86. Read, *garayate vijñapayate sastrarahasyam iti guruh* (*gṝ, śabde*) *kriyādi*, quoted *ibid.*, p. 83.
87. Read, *gurate śatpathe pravartayati śiṣyam iti guruḥ* (*guri udyamane*), quoted *ibid.*, p. 83.
88. *HDKR*, p. 75.

Several terms were used in the later period to denote a teacher. These are *kulapati, ācārya, upādhyāya* and *guru*.[89]

Characteristics of a guru

1. A teacher's duty is to educate the ignorant people. He is aware of his duties always.[90]
2. A teacher is like a mother who gives birth to a child since he takes him to his hermitage to educate him. The *guru* keeps the student in his womb for three nights and begets him.[91] Of course, it is symbolic in meaning. He was respected as a God.
3. *Ācārya* has been identified as Yama, Varuṇa and Soma for its grandeur.[92]
4. Describing Varuṇa as a teacher, a passage of the *R̥V* reveals that the intellectual Varuṇa teaches hundred names of Pr̥thvī to his students.[93] The passage thus implies that a teacher must be an intellectual and expert in teaching.
5. Varuṇa has been mentioned as a *guru*[94] and he was prayed by the students to bestow the knowledge.[95] The meaning of the word Varuṇa becomes important. Dayānanda Sarasvatī says that the root *vr̥ṇa* adding the suffix *uṇan* becomes the word Varuṇa. He, who owns the *ātmayogin*s, and is pious and wishing salvation or he who is received by salvation wishers and pious persons is called Varuṇa.[96] Thus, it is clear

89. *Bhāratīya Prācīn Śikṣāvyvasthā* by Acarya Ramnath Suman in *Sikṣāṅka, Kalyāṇ*, Gita Press, p. 114.
90. *R̥V*, 7/4/4.
91. *AV*, 11/5/3.
92. *Ibid.*, 11/5/14 & 15.
93. *R̥V*, 7/87/4.
94. *Ibid.*
95. *Ibid.*, 1/86/6.
96. *SPD*, p. 10.

that a teacher should always be ready to receive the persons, who are anxious to acquire knowledge. Perhaps the students who approached to the teacher were to be taught first.

6. Though the *guru*s were married persons[97] yet they were expected to stay in *brahmacarya* when they used to teach.[98]
7. An *ācārya* have to compulsarily follow, the *ṛta, satya, tapa, dama, śama* and *mānuṣya*.[99]
8. Deriving the word *ācārya, Nir* says that an *ācārya* teaches *dharma* and *artha*. He tries to mould the character of his students in a good form. He has to teach the mysteries of *śāstra*s and develop the intelligence of students.[100]
9. A *śloka* of the *MB* mentions that none can acquire knowledge without a *guru*. He is a boatman of the worldly ocean who helps his students to cross it.[101]
10. A teacher should wear the saffron coloured clothes when he performs his duties.[102]
11. Though they were visible to the common eyes but their soul was so great that they appeared to be distinct from the worldly beings.[103]

A STUDENT OR ŚIṢYA

To denote a student, we have four special words: *chātra, vidyārthin, brahmacārin* and *śiṣya* in the Sanskrit world whereas two words *śiṣya* and *brahmacārin* were used in the Vedic works specially.

97. *ILSYVS*, p. 30.
98. *AV*, 11/5/17.
99. *TU*, 1/9.
100. Read, *ācinoti hi śāstrārthānācārya sthāpayatyapi*, quoted *HDKR*, p. 75.
101. *MB* Śānti, 326/22-23.
102. *ṚV*, 10/136/2.
103. *Ibid.*, 10/136/3.

The term *śiṣya* is derived as *śās* + *kyap*[104] and it means he who is efficient to be administered or ruled.[105] Another word *chātra* means the student who covers the faults of his *guru* and spreads his fame.[106] The student who went to his *guru* to be prosperous with *vidyā* and begged this from him, was known as *vidyārthin*.[107] On the other hand, the pupil who followed his life being connected with Brahmā was called a *brahmacārin*. Another typical word *antevāsin* was implied to denote a student. It indicated those students who lived with *guru* and acquired knowledge by rendering their services in the *guru*'s hermitage.[108]

Duties of a Student

A Vedic student had to follow some duties. His main duties were to be a worthy *śiṣya* which are found scattered in the Vedic literature.

1. A student should live and conduct his student life in austerity. He, if lives and stays in that way, gets the blessings from the gods.[109]
2. (a) From the *Saṁhitopaniṣada*, Yāska has quoted a passage in the *Nir* in which it is said that the teachers of the Vedic Age wanted such students.

   (b) A student must not be fault-finder in the qualities of others specially of his colleagues.

   (c) A student must be able to control his general and sensitive desires.[110]

---

104. *Ash*, 3/1/109.
105. Read, *śāsituṁ yogyaḥ śiṣyaḥ*.
106. Read, *gurordoṣānām āvaraṇaṁ chatram. tacchīlamasya chātraḥ (chatrādibhyo ṇaḥ)*, *Aṣṭ*, 4/4/62.
107. Read, *vidyām arthayate tacchīlaḥ vidyārthin, vidya + ṇini, Aṣṭ*, 3/2/78.
108. *ante gurusamīpe vasati tacchīlaḥ, Aṣṭ*, 4/3/18 for *ṇini*.
109. *AV*, 11/5/1.
110. *Nir*, 2/1-4.

3. The life of a *brahmacārī* or a student should be kept auspicious by baths and austerities.[111]
4. His duty was to collect food for his teacher also. The teacher seems to have lived on the materials begged by his disciples.[112]
5. A student had to follow honesty, truth, austerity, kindness, daily sacrificial rituals and humanity, etc.[113]
6. A student had not to remain limited in his studies of courses only. He had to be able to achieve the *ātma-jñāna*.[114] Nārada, in this context, tells Sanatkumāras that he had studied the worldly education but not achieved the knowledge of *ātman* (*ātma-jñāna*).
7. A student had to go for begging and secondly he had to look after the fire meant for sacrificial rituals.[115]
8. Another main duty of a student was to protect the hermitages of his *ācārya*.[116]

Thus, the student who studied under a *guru* performing all such duties was able to achieve the ultimate goal of perfection.

Uniform

1. The students of the Vedic Age used to wear the girdle or *mekhalā* that was specially made of *muñja* grass. Wearing such clothes he maintained his austerities and accomplished his studies.[117]
2. Another verse of the *AV* tells that a student must

111. *AV*, 11/5/26.
112. *Ibid.*, 11/5/1.
113. *TU*, 1/9.
114. Read, *so ahaṁ bhagavo mantravidevāsmi nātmaviśrutaṁ hyeva*, *ChU*, 7/1/3.
115. *Ibid.*, 4/10/2.
116. *ŚB*, 3/6/2/15.
117. *AV*, 11/5/4.

have the skin of an antelope when he goes on with his religious functions and studies.[118]

3. Ram Gopal with special reference to *SGS, ĀpGS, PGS, BGS, GGS* and *GB* writes that a student uniformed himself with an animal skin (*ajina*), a piece of cloth (*vāsas*), a gridle (*mekhalā*) and a stuff (*daṇḍa*).[119]
4. The *JGS* in one place refers that a brāhmaṇa should wear the girdle of *muñja* grass, a kṣatriya of *murvā* grass and a vaiśya a mixture of *tamāla* and *muñja* grass.[120]

Types of Brahmacārin

There were three types of *brahmacārins* mentioned in the Vedic literature. Specially the *ChU* indicates that (1) The lower type of *brahmacārī* should study under a *guru* for 24 years. (2) Those, who stay for 44 years in *brahmacarya* studies along with other physical trainings are the students of medium class. (3) The third or the best type of student studies from the early age and lives for 48 years in *brahmacarya*.[121] Sitanath Dey in the light of Devichand mentions that these three types of *brahmacārins* were known as Basu, Rudra and Ādityas.[122]

Daily Life

The daily routine of the student is found as follows:

1. They got up in the *brāhma-muhūrtta* (the period that included between the 4th *ghaṭikā* and the second before sunrise).[123]

---

118. *AV*, 11/5/6.
119. *IVKR*, p. 293.
120. *JGS*, 1/12.
121. Quoted from the *SPD*, p. 31.
122. *ILSYVS*, p. 29.
123. *VRDB*, vol. II, p. 93.

2. They had to take bath and thereafter perform their daily sacrificial rituals.[124]
3. After the completion of the sacrificial rituals they had to study upto noon, after which they took their meal and had little rest.[125]
4. In the evening, they were sent to collect fuels in the forests. Without fuels in the hand, one was thought to be unfit to take lessons.[126]
5. The students used to gather and offer their oblations to gods in the evening also.[127] The students who did not perform the daily rituals was considered a sinner and was called a fool.[128]
6. Sometimes they had to go to collect their materials from the villages. The students were highly respected in the villages and the villagers offered the materials humbly. If a women abused and dispelled the *brahmacārī* from her home, then, it was supposed that the *brahmacārī* had taken all the human qualities from her home.[129] A most important point is that the students were kept bound with a strong ring of sanctified daily routine and they were inspired for that. As a result of that, the brightness of his lusture dazzled in his face.[130]

Qualities of a Student

1. The qualities of an ideal student can be found in the story of Naciketā mentioned in the *KaṭhU*. There are

124. *AV*, 11/5/6.
125. *VRDB*, vol. II, p. 93.
126. Read, *saḥ gurumevābhigacchet samitpāṇi śrotriyam brahmaniṣṭham*, *MU*, 1/2/12.
127. *AV*, 11/5/6.
128. *ṚV*, 10/71/9.
129. *ADS*, 1/1/3/24.
130. *AV*, 11/5/26.

two kinds of things, *śreyas* and *preyas*. The meaning of the two words can be expressed as the satisfaction originated from the distinguished knowledge or *ātma-jñāna* and worldly enjoyment, respectively. A real student wishes *śreyas* and kicks the mortal and worldly wealths.[131]

2. The path of knowledge is as sharp as a razor yet a thirsty of real knowledge does not hesitate to follow such path.[132]
3. A real student was respected like a God. He was supposed to be those rays of the sun of nights under the earth which shines after rising and mingle in the space. The lustre created by those two is acquired by a student.[133]
4. A perfect student is protected by his forefathers and gods such as Indra and Viśvāvasu, etc. So a *brahmacārī* or a student worships him through his austerities.[134]
5. In a passage of the *R̥V* it is said that a *brahmacārī* is the member of the god's own body.[135]

SYSTEM OF TEACHING

The term "teaching" or *sikṣaṇa* has been defined by Śaṅkarācārya as the knowledge, endeavour and austerity for an acquirable knowledge or education.[136] The Vedic sages adopted some methods to bestow knowledge to the students in their *āśramas*.

1. The course was divided and taught accordingly. The brāhmaṇa students were taught religion, philosophy,

131. *KaṭhU*, 1/2/2.
132. *Ibid.*, 1/3/14.
133. *AV*, 11/5/11.
134. *Ibid.*, 11/5/2.
135. *R̥V*, 10/109/5.
136. Quoted from *Śikṣāṅka Kalyāṇa*, p. 86.

astronomy, astrology and rituals. A kṣatriya got the education of archery, fighting, religions and laws. The vaiśyas were mainly educated on trade, commerce and artisan, etc.[137]

2. While going to teach a student, a teacher should behave with him like his parents. Teaching is like making a hole in the ear. When a student is taught he may feel pain but after the action is over, he is thought to become as good as one wears the beautiful *kuṇḍala*s in his ears.[138]
3. Students were not allowed to take scents, necklaces, shoes, umbrellas and had to avoid dances, gambling, sleeping in daytimes and going to crowd, etc. They were kept in the *āśrama*s under hard rules.[139]
4. Periods of teaching were conducted after the rituals of the *āśrama*s. Both the teachers and the taughts performed those religious function together.[140]
5. The teacher taught the students by pronouncing what they wanted to teach. The students also followed him. Those teacher and students have been compared with frogs in which others make sound after one.[141]
6. The art of writing also seems to be developed in those days. Pranab Bandyopadhyay remarks, "In Vedic Age it is known that *ṛṣi*s in their hermitages taught not in oral but reading, writing were also the part of their curriculum."[142]

---

137. *AHVP*, p. 86.
138. Read, *yatṛṇatya vitathena karṇāvaduḥkhaṁ kurvannamṛtaṁ saṁprayacchan taṁ manyeta pitaraṁ mātarañca tasmai na druhyet katamacchanāha*, *Nir*, 2/4.
139. *ĀpDS*, 1/2/5; 9 & 10.
140. *ṚV*, 7/3/5.
141. *Ibid.*, 7/103/5.
142. *AHVP*, p. 83.

Khagendra Dasgupta also admits and firmly urges that the Vedic *ṛṣi*s taught their students with the help of scripts.[143]

7. A student had to touch the feet of his teacher at the beginning and the end of his lesson.[144]
8. Discipline was the most important matter for the students of the Vedic era. Kireet Joshi remarks, "The life of pupil began with a resolve to impose upon himself the ideal and practice of *brahmacarya* which meant not only physical continence, but also a constant burning aspiration for the knowledge of *Brahma*. This one ideal uplifted the physical, vital and mental energies, unified concentration to achieve self- knowledge and self-mastery. For this reason, the pupil came to be called *brahmacārin*, one who has resolved to follow the discipline of *brahmacarya*. *Vratam cariṣyāmi* — I shall resolutely follow my vow, is what the pupil resolves when he embarks upon his journey of disciplineship."[145]
9. The teachers emphasized upon correct pronunciation. It was supposed that Indra, Varuṇa, Mitra and Aryamā stay in such *mantras*.[146]
10. The students were advised to sing the *mantras* loudly. One *ṚV* passage says that the sound of *soma* preparation is heard from distance same as the sound of the Vedic *mantras*.[147]

MEDIUM OF TEACHING (LANGUAGES)

Many languages are found to have existed in the Vedic period. A passage of the *AV* reveals that the earth gives the

143. *ASSK*, pp. 75, 77.
145. *VICK*, p. 33.
146. *ṚV*, 1/40/5.
147. *Ibid.*, 9/111/2.

shelter to the people of various languages.[148] On the other hand, there was another language existing among people, to whom they used to think that the language was bestowed by gods and sages through their austerities and penances, and thus that was brought in use.[149]

The *ŚB* in one place mentions that there were four types of languages in the world spoken by men, animals, birds and creeping creatures.[150] It is also found that there were *daivī vāk* and *mānuṣī vāk* as two main divisions of languages.[151]

Thus, it is found that the people of the Vedic ages used to speak many languages, yet a prominent language, which was known to be divine one, existed. That particular language came into existence as a result of the hard labour of intellectuals.[152]

Ram Gopal writes, "There is no doubt that Sanskrit was the medium of instruction in the Vedic Universities." He again adds, "Sanskrit was understood and spoken by all so much so that even the Śūdras conversed in Sanskrit."[153]

TEACHER-STUDENT RELATIONSHIP

Relations between teachers and taughts are found very cordial in the Vedic ages. The Vedic passages and the other sources reveal the fact as follows:

1. A student was supposed to be regenerated,[154] and the *upanayana saṁskāra* gave him second birth. So, he was called a *dvija* or twice-born. Therefore, the

148. *AV*, 12/1/45.
149. *TB*, 11/88.
150. *ŚB*, 4/1/3/16.
151. *HDKR*, p. 581.
152. *ṚV*, 10/71/2.
153. *IVKR*, p. 342.
154. *AV*, 11/5/3 & *ŚB*, 11/5/4/12.

view of an *ācārya* or teacher became like the view of a father. The student also behaved well with his teacher like an obedient son.

2. The teacher always expected that his and disciple's fame should spread together. He further prays God to bestow the Brāhma lusture in both of them. Thus, the teacher and the taughts were not thought to be different but one soul.[155]
3. Both the teacher and the taughts were directed to follow eternal laws, truth, austerities, kindness, humanity, etc., whenever they taught and learnt.[156] So, it is clear that from such strong disciplines and rules a sweet relation was built up.
4. The people in those days thought that the *vedātmaka* Brāhma comes out from teacher and it is established in the disciple. A passage of the *AV* indicates that a student cannot be a perfect one without the advices and teaching of a teacher. As a thirsty person wants water so was the teacher for a student.[157]
5. The *śāntipāṭha* of the *KaṭhU* focuses a very important light upon the teacher-student-relationship in which it is expected that God should protect and nourish them together. They wanted to get strength, bright knowledge, sweet co-relation and non-zealous life together.[158]
6. A teacher was expected to have possessed the fine qualities such as utmost devotion, piousness and scholarship.[159] The student considered him as

155. *TU*, 1/3/3.
156. *Ibid.*, 1/9.
157. *AV*, 11/5/22.
158. Read, *sahnāvavatu, sahanau bhunaktu, saha vīryaṁ karavāvahai . . .*, etc., *Śānti pāṭha* in *KaṭhU*.
159. *ŚYV*, 11/37.

guardian. He prayed him to lead him towards an austere life.[160]

7. The teacher used to visit the residence of the students sometimes. The people highly respected him. In a passage of the *ŚYV* a host welcomes the teacher when he visits to his home.[161] Such passage proves that they kept all round relations with the students.
8. The teacher was always aware of the health of his student. In a passage of the *ŚYV* he declares that he is ready to protect all the organs of the student and develop good character and behaviour.[162]
9. Dayānanda Sarasvatī while explaining a passage of the *ŚYV* means a teacher for *auṣadhī* and says that a teacher should not punish a student improperly.[163]
10. As *saha nāvavatu*[164] reveals in the Upaniṣads, so also the *AV* tells that a student must be a protector of his teacher at all times.[165] The passage tells us that the teacher is the creator of sky and earth implying that the teacher should be an expert in the theories of creation.
11. After research on the Vedic *Kalpasūtra*s, Ram Gopal concludes, "The student lived with the teacher as a member of his family. Loving the student like his own son the teacher taught him attentively without concealing anything from him, and the teacher did not use the student for his own purpose to the detriment of latter's education."[166]

---

160. *ŚYV*, 5/40.
161. *Ibid.*, 6/14.
162. *Ibid.*, 6/15.
163. *Śānti pāṭha* in *KaṭhU.*
164. *AV*, 11/5/8.
165. *IVKR*, p. 325.
166. *ṚV*, 8/6/31.

12. Pranab Bandopadhyaya gives a distinct picture of the teacher-student relationship in the Vedic Age. He writes, "There was, however, no intervening medium between the *guru* and the disciples. The *guru* fully influenced the life of his pupils, although not intentionally but naturally. He was the only source of knowledge available in the country. Hence, the relationship between the *guru* and his disciple was very pure and warm and essentially very cordial which was based on love, affection and unpretentious sympathy. The main function of the teacher was to ensure the all-round and complete development of the personality of his pupils. There was always personal touch, a human element, a living inspiration in the matters of instructions, creating a communion of soul."[167]

CONVOCATION

After the completion of the studies or the *brahmacarya āśrama*, a student used to go to the *ācārya* where he was advised by his *ācārya*.[168] thus,

> Speak the truth. Follow the path of *dharma*. Never leave the studies or *svādhyāya*. Do not avoid the *gṛhasthāśrma* after *brahmacarya āśrama* is over. Do not avoid the truth. Never turn away from *dharma*. Do not avoid the auspicious duties. Be not proud of worldly wealths. Never neglect in offering oblations to gods and forefathers. Respect mother as Goddess. Respect father as God. Respect the guests as gods. Perform the unblamed duties. Follow our good and ideal deeds only. Not others. . . . [169]

---

167. *AHVP*, p. 87.
168. *TU*, 1/11/1.
169. *TU*, 1/11.

FEMALE EDUCATION

Education was not only for male students in the Vedic India, but emphasis was given on female's education too. We get such examples everywhere in the entire Vedic literature.

1. In one passage of the *ṚV* we find the wife of Mudgala roaring in the battlefields.[170] That was possible for the military education which she got in her student life. Later on, she got victory over their enemies also.[171] Likewise the above passage, Viśpalā in the other one, is found in the war where her thigh is cut.[172] Thus, the military education is found among the female students also.
2. In a passage of the *ŚYV*, the female students are advised to go to *sabhā*s and were expected by the teachers that they could enlighten everywhere.[173]
3. Several *sūkta*s themselves reveal that some scholarly women are the seers of the *mantra*s. Some of them are Apālā, Lopāmudrā, Aditi, Ghoṣā, Gaurī, Rātri, Saramā and Urvaśī, etc. Such evidences say that the women also were educated as the boys in those days.
4. Learned women were found everywhere, because the female students were advised to mingle with the educated ladies whenever they had to go.[174]
5. The women of the Vedic India got such education through which they could control the household problems in their life. We get a lady warning her husband for his evil deeds.[175]

---

170. *ṚV*, 10/102/6.
171. *Ibid.*, 10/102/11.
172. *Ibid.*, 10/39/8.
173. *ŚYV*, 6/24.
174. *Ibid.*, 11/64.
175. *Ibid.*, 8/48.

6. Dayānanda Sarasvatī explaining a passage of the *ŚYV* remarks that the female education also ran along with the male education.[176]
7. Appointment of female teachers[177] is mentioned in the *R̥V*. Iḍā, Piṅgalā and Sarasvatī or Bhāratī are the goddesses of learning.[178] The evidences denote that the female education was not only introduced but continued in full vigour in the Vedic India.
8. In a passage of the *R̥V* it is mentioned that the educated women were expected to attend the *sabhā*s.[179] Thus, to make eligible for the membership of the *sabhā* a women or a girl was to be educated.
9. Dayānanda Sarasvatī remarks that the education of the Vedas was given to women without disturbances.[180]
10. Acarya Baladev Upadhyaya mentions that there were two kinds of female *brahmacārin*s. These were *sadyodvāhā* and *brahmavādinī*s.[181]
11. With the references of the *AB* and the *ŚB*, Jogiraj Basu informs that the women not only participated in sacrifices but they even watched and warned when the mistakes were commited by the priests at the time of the singing the *sāma*s.[182]

---

176. *ŚYV*, 10/6.
177. *Ibid.*, 11/59.
178. *Ibid.*, 21/19.
179. *R̥V*, 1/167/3.
180. *SPD*, p. 52.
181. *VSSB*, p. 424.
182. *IABJr*, p. 50.

6

Socio-Cultural Aspects

Women and Marriage Institution

Women in Vedic India

WE find only a few instances regarding women in the *ŚYV*, whereas the *SV* has not any at all. On the other hand, though we find a lot of passages in the *AV* yet it is not greater than that of the number of the *ṚV*. Women have not been ignored in the Indian heritage. The *ŚBG* may be mentioned in this respect.[1] There is a story found in the *BU* regarding the origin of women. The story is as follows:

Though the Supreme Power or the *virāṭ vigraha* possessed all the powers and energies within Him yet he was not satisfied and was afraid as because the loneliness created fear in Him.[2] That fear caused the fall of *virāṭ*. It splitted into two parts, named as husband and wife.[3] Those two parts of Bŗahmā, *sukha* or happiness and *ākāśa* or sky[4] also were divided into man and woman respectively.[5] The *ka* or *sukha* divided into two groups and formed the bodies

---

1. Read, *striyo vaiṣyāstathā śūdrāste api yānti parām gatim*, *ŚBG*, 9/3.
2. Read, so *abibhet tasmād ekākī bibheti sahāyamīkṣamcakre yanmadanyannāsti kasmānnu bibhemi iti tata evāsya bhayam vīyāya BU*, 1/4/1.
3. Read, *strī pumāṁsau samparṣvaktau sa imām eva ātmānaṁ dvedha pātayat*, *BU*, 1/4/3.
4. Read, *kaṁ brahma khaṁ bradma*, *ChU*, 4/10/5.
5. *BU*, 4/10/5.

of man and woman.[6] The man was Manu and the woman was Śatarūpā. Later on Manu got married with her.[7]

THE WORDS USED FOR WOMEN

We get a word *menā* to express women in the Vedic texts which has been derived by Yāska as, "She, who is respected by others."[8] The *gnā* also denotes women in the *R̥V*. That has been explained in the *Nir* as, "She, to whom people approach."[9] The word *gane* of Germany and *gomus* of Greek seems to be its cognate. The word *strī* is the most prevalent word to denote women in the Sanskrit language. She is known for her shyness.[10] On the other hand, the root, *stai*, from which the word *strī* is derived does not mean to be so rather it denotes "talk loudly."[11] Mahīdhara writes, "She is *strī* who has breasts and hair."[12] Patañjali gives two important meanings of woman which are:

(1) She is *strī* because she holds embryo in her.[13]

(2) She is known as *strī* because she is the aggregate of the five *guṇas*.[14]

Explaining 1/16/16 of the *R̥V* Yāska remarks, "They who carry and remove the *guṇas* are the women."[15] Another word

6. Read, *kasya rūpamabhud dvedhā yatkāyam adhigacchate tābhyaṁ rūpavibhāgābhyāṁ mithunam samapadyata, BP,* 13/12/52.

7. Read, *śatarūpā ca tam nārī taponirdhūtakalmaṣām svayambhuvo manurdevaḥ patnītve jagr̥he prabhuḥ, VP,* 1/7/17.

8. *Nir,* 3/21/1.

9. *Ibid.*

10. *Ibid.*

11. Read, *styai śabdasaṅghatayoḥ,* Pān. *Dhātupāṭha,* 1/935.

12. Read, *stankeśavatī strī syāt,* Mahīdhara's commentary on *Aṣṭ,* 4/1/3.

13. *Ast,* 4/1/3 Patañjali's commentary as *styāyati asyāṁ garbha iti.*

14. Read, *śabdasparśarūparasagandhānaṁ guṇānāṁ styānaṁ strī, Ibid.,* 4/1/3.

15. Read, *striyaḥ eva etāḥ śabda-rūpa-rasa-sparśa gandha-hāirṇyaḥ, Nir,* 14/20.

is *yoṣā*. It is used to denote beloved[16] and women in general.[17] She is *yoṣā* because she mingles herself with a man.[18] The word *nārī* is absent in the *R̥V* but *nāryaḥ* is found in the meaning of sacrifice. The word *nr̥* means to perform the activities of bravery, to give and to lead.[19] The word indicates that the woman of the Vedic Age used to help their husbands in the battlefields like Viśpalā[20] and Mudgalānī[21] for which perhaps they had been named as *nārī* later on. We find *nārī* first in the *AV*.[22] We get the term in the *PGS* after that.[23] The word *sundarī* for a woman is not found in the *sūkta*s of the *R̥V* yet it mentions Uṣā to be *sundarī*[24] in the meaning of a beautiful woman. *Nir* explains the word to be pleasure.[25] So it is clear that the word *sundarī* is the other term that comes into existence later on. The word *jāyā* is to be the ideal wife.[26] It is said that the house becomes meaningless without a *jāyā*.[27] The *AB* also mentions *jāyā* and says that she is the real friend of a man.[28] It again clears the meaning of the term *jāyā* by referring to that she begets others.[29] An important and mostly used word to denote the wife in the Vedic literature is *patnī*. A *nārī* tries to become a *patnī* through some activities for which

16. *R̥V*, 1/18/91.
17. *ŚB*, 3/6/1/4.
18. *Nir*, 3/15/1.
19. *TB*, 4/2/1.
20. *R̥V*, 1/116/15.
21. *Ibid.*, 10/102.
22. *AV*, 14/2/64.
23. *PGS*, 1/6/2.
24. *R̥V*, 1/48/5.
25. Read, *suṣṭhu nandayati iti*, *AK*, 3/1/52.
26. *R̥V*, 3/53/6.
27. *Ibid.*, 3/53/4.
28. *AB*, 8/3/13.
29. Read, *tajjāyā jāyā bhavati yadasyāṁ jāyate punaḥ*, *ibid.*, 7/13.

she would be able to get the consequences of the deeds of her husband. Discussing the word terminologically, Pāṇini also wants to mean the same.[30] She has been described to be the better-half of the man.[31] The man is incomplete without *patnī*[32] and the sacrifices without her, goes in vain.[33] Another passage of the *ŚB* mentions her to be *Lakṣmīsvarupā*.[34] The word *duhitā* was used to denote a daughter. It is so because the daughter stays away from her father and assists her parents if needed.[35] The *AV* mentions *sabhā* and *samiti* to be the daughter of the king.[36] Some other words to denote "woman" are *vāmā, abalā, pramadā, lalanā, māninī, mahilā* and *mātā*. The first six are though rare in the Vedic literature but are found frequently in the Classical literature. Again the word *mātā* is found everywhere in the Vedas to address space, river, water and earth. Each of the above terms carries the sense and the feelings of people towards women in the Vedic India.

TREATMENT OF SON AND DAUGHTERS

Referring to a passage of the *KS* some scholars want to say that the Vedic people threw their daughters just after she had taken birth.[37] Westermark mentions a passage of the *ṚV*[38] and steps forward by saying that the people assasinated the newly born girls. But there is no such instances found to have referred.

A father in the Vedic time did not want to distinguish

30. *Aṣṭ*, 4/1/33.
31. *TB*, 3/3/5.
32. *ŚB*, 5/2/1/10.
33. *TS*, 2/2/2/6.
34. *ŚB*, 13/2/6/1.
35. Sātavalekar on *Nir*, 3/1/4 in *Mātṛ bhūmi : aur Svarājyaśāsah*, p. 61.
36. *AV*, 7/21/1.
37. *KS*, 27/9.
38. *ṚV*, 2/29/1.

between his son and daughter. He treated them equally.[39] A person who did not have any daughter wished to get it through sacrifices.[40] A verse of the *BU* mentions that there should be a daughter having wisdom, knowledge and long age.[41] If a father would not have any son he had been advised to admit the daughter as son.[42] The girls who had no brothers stayed to serve her parents without marriage.[43] The *ṚV* says that the daughter is an esteemed member of the family.[44]

WOMEN EDUCATION

The girls were given perfect education so that they could be able to conduct her social and personal life with full grandeur. A.C. Das mentions,

> Her education, such as it was in those days, was not neglected, and the cultured classes went so far as to give her a very liberal education equally with the son, which made her rightful place in society.[45]

As the first step to their education, they were given the holy thread. It was thought that only such girls were able to perform the hard works who are *upanītās*.[46] The *PGS* mentions about *upanītā* and *anūpanītā* girls,[47] to whom perhaps *HārDS* has classified to be *brahmavādinī* and

---

39. *ṚV*, 3/31/1.
40. Read, *tatraśraddhā manoḥ patnī hotāraṁ samayācata duhitārthamupāgamya praṇipatya payovratāḥ*, *ŚBG*, 9/1/14.
41. *BU*, 6/4/17.
42. *TB*, 1/5/5/6.
43. *AV*, 1/17/1.
44. *ṚV*, 3/31/2.
45. *RCD*, p. 248.
46. Read, *bhīmā jāyā brahmaṇasyopanītā*, *ṚV*, 10/109/4.
47. *HSSAJ*, p. 264.
48. Read, *dvibidhāḥ striyo bramhavādinyaḥ sadyobandhūśca*, *HārDS*, 21/20.

*sadyobadhū*s[48] respectively. Such *anūpanītā*s or *sadyobadhū*s did not get their education as the *upanītā*s got, for which it has been told that such girls should be given the *upanayana* at the time of their marriage.[49]

We have already discussed the women education in the Vedic times in the chapter of education. Yet the instances of the educated girls appeared from the fact that the ladies such as Ghoṣā,[50] Sūryā,[51] Mamatā,[52] Lopāmudrā,[53] Śārparājñī,[54] Viśvavārā,[55] Indrāṇī,[56] Apālā,[57] and Sacī[58] became *ṛṣikā*s by seeing the Vedic hymns. Viśvavārā was a *ṛtvik* in a sacrifice also.[59]

AN IDEAL WIFE

A girl was got married after she took her education. *Sadyobadhū*s were given the *yajñopavīta* at the time of their marriage and the *brahmavādinī*s were given at the time of their *vidyārambha* or at the beginning of their education.[60] After a girl of the Vedic Age got married, she was expected to be an ideal wife so that their family life might run smoothly.

CHARACTERISTICS OF AN IDEAL WOMAN

The Women of the Vedic society were given high respect.

49. *Ibid.*, 21/21; 22; 23 & 24.
50. *ṚV*, 10/39/40.
51. *Ibid.*, 10/85.
52. *Ibid.*, 6/10/2.
53. *Ibid.*, 1/179.
54. *Ibid.*, 10/189.
55. *Ibid.*, 5/28.
56. *Ibid.*, 10/145.
57. *Ibid.*, 8/91.
58. *Ibid.*, 10/159.
59. *Ibid.*, 5/28/1.
60. *HārDS*, 21/20-24.

They were the members of the family, a conscious part of society who used to go to *sabhās* and participate there skillfully. Their characteristics as found in the Vedic literature are as follows :

1. She was supposed to be the half of the man.[61] A man was not supposed to have incomplete personality unless and until he would have his wife.[62]
2. She was supposed to be the mistress of the family.[63] Perhaps she could or would help the man by her valuable suggestions. That is found to be true from the fact that a passage of the *AB* mentions a woman to be the friend of man.[64]
3. The women were responsible for the financial conduct of the family in the Vedic ages. She is said to be *lakṣmīsvarūpā* according to the *ŚB*.[65]
4. The wife herself has been supposed to be the house. The term *jāyedastam* mentions the truth.[66] It was said so because she is told to be the co-operator of her husband in all matters.[67]
5. She is the prominent element of the society as it is reflected in the *AV*.[68]
6. Another Atharvanic passage mentions a women to be the snare of affection.[69] The passage indicates that

61. *BU*, 1/4/3.
62. *ŚB*, 5/2/1/10 & *TS*, 2/2/2/6.
63. *ṚV*, 10/85/30.
64. *AB*, 1/4/3.
65. *ŚB*, 13/2/6/7.
66. *ṚV*, 5/53/4.
67. *Ibid.*, 8/31.
68. *AV*, 14/2/27.
69. *Ibid.*, 6/77/1.

the women in those days were kept in an esteemed place.

DUTIES AND RIGHTS OF WOMEN

Duties

As the woman was regarded to be the head of the family,[70] she had some important duties to perform by which the family might run swiftly. The duties of a woman as it is reflected from the various sources of the Vedic literature are found as follows :

1. Her duty was supposed to have ideal behaviours towards others. She should have sweet voice[71] while speaking to others.
2. Her another duty was to look after the animals and the members of the family. One *R̥V* passage mentions the four-footed and two-footed creatures to be looked after by a Vedic woman.[72]
3. She had to weave and make clothes[73] for her sons[74] and husband.[75]
4. Nursing and taming children was one of the important duties to be followed by a woman.[76]
5. A passage of the *R̥V*[77] mentions some other important duties of a woman. It informs that she should perform the sacrifices, weave clothes, water in the plants and to fulfil the desires of the members of her family.

---

70. *AV*, 14/1/43.
71. *Ibid.*, 3/30/2.
72. *Ibid.*, 10/85/44.
73. *Ibid.*, 14/1/45 & *R̥V*, 2/38/4.
74. *R̥V*, 5/40/6.
75. *AV*, 14/2/51.
76. *R̥V*, 5/2/1.
77. *Ibid.*, 2/3/6.

6. Her another duty was to awake her husband in the morning always.[78] Moreover, she should respect[79] and serve her husband.[80]
7. An Atharvanic passage instructs a woman to stay at home and not to wander in vain.[81]

At last, a passage declares that a woman who follows her duty would become famous, and as a result of that the people would praise her.[82] All these passages show that the Vedic sages clearly described the duties of the woman.

Rights

Since the woman were advised to perform some duties, so were the rights bestowed upon her which she could enjoy according to her ability and qualifications. The rights of women, that have been found through the Vedic literature, are as follows:

1. She could give whatever she wanted to someone. A passage of the *R̥V* mentions that she could give anything to a brāhmaṇa without asking others.[83] Nobody opposed it because all confessed that she was the mistress of the family.[84]
2. She is found having the liberty of visiting and enjoying the festivals if she wanted.[85] On the other hand, she had rights to participate in the *vidatha*s and the *sabhā*s.[86]

---

78. *R̥V*, 3/51/3.
79. *Ibid.*, 10/32/2.
80. *AV*, 5/12/5.
81. *Ibid.*, 7/77/3.
82. *R̥V*, 1/79/1.
83. *Ibid.*, 10/85/30.
84. *AV*, 14/1/43.
85. *R̥V*, 1/124/8.
86. *Ibid.*, 1/124/8 & 1/167/3.

3. She had some religious rights under which she could perform the sacrifices.[87] She was given important place in the sacrifices.[88] We find Viśvavārā taking place of a *ṛtvik* in a sacrifice.[89]
4. The Vedic ladies had the military rights also. We find Viśpalā[90] and Mudgalānī going to the battle-fields.[91] Viśpalā lost her one leg in the war which was cured by the Aśvins by adding an iron leg.[92]
5. Women were appointed as messengers also. We have one such evidence in which Saramā had been appointed to carry the messages to the Paṇis. She was successful in the responsibility bestowed upon her.[93]
6. The Vedic women used to sing the songs in the tasks.[94] On the other hand, there were some girls in the society who used to dance,[95] perhaps in the festivals.[96]

QUALITIES OF AN IDEAL WOMAN

The Vedic sages imagined the life of an ideal woman. They had advised the woman to be so. We find many passages in the Vedic literature regarding it.

1. An ideal Vedic woman never wept. She used to put ornaments and remained clean always.[97] Her smiling

---

87. *AV*, 11/1/17 & 19/58/6.
88. *ŚB*, 3/8/2/2.
89. *ṚV*, 5/28/1.
90. *Ibid.*, 1/112/10.
91. *Ibid.*, 10/102.
92. *Ibid.*, 1/116/15.
93. *Ibid.*, 10/108.
94. *Ibid.*, 1/92/3.
95. *Ibid.*, 10/29/2.
96. *Ibid.*, 10/86/10.
97. *ṚV*, 10/18/7.

face enlightened the house[98] and she wore ideal dresses.[99]

2. She had to be a wise woman[100] for which she had to be educated. Without proper education, she could not be a wise lady as expected.
3. She was supposed to be a devotee of her husband.[101] The *PGS* also supports the fact.[102]
4. She was like a queen for her brother-in-law(s), daughter-in-law(s), father-in-law and the mother-in-law.[103] An Atharvanic passage says that the women of that age were really conscious in performing their duties.
5. Another Atharvanic passage mentions some qualities of an ideal lady in which it has been told that she must be soft, angerless, woman of sweet speeches, and follower of the *vratas*.[104]
6. She offered her prayers through the Vedic passages. An evidence of Sitā can be mentioned in the case. Sitā used to offer the Vedic hymns in her prayers.[105]
7. An ideal lady was alert in the social activities[106] and used to go to the *sabhās* and the *vīdathas*.[107]

Thus, an ideal Vedic woman was supposed to be an important factor of the nation. They could do everything for the sake of society and the nation.

---

98. *ṚV*, 3/58/8.
99. *Ibid.*, 10/71/4.
100. *Ibid.*, 1/28/3.
101. *Ibid.*,10/85/47 & *AV*, 14/1/42.
102. *PGS*, 1/8/8.
103. *AV*, 14/1/42.
104. *Ibid.*, 3/25/4.
105. *Ram* 5/15/48.
106. *AV*, 14/2/27.
107. *ṚV*, 1/124/8 & 1/167/5.

GREATNESS OF WOMEN DESCRIBED IN THE VEDAS

As said earlier, woman in the Vedic Age was thought to be the mistress[108] of the house. She was thus treated by the other members of the family. Another passage of the *AV* mentions a woman to be queen of the house.[109] The passage says that a woman is like an ocean in which many rivers mingle and the ocean gets the mastery by being mingled. So it was thought about a woman. The same passage on the other hand, informs that a woman is the mistress of a person in both the earth and heaven. The smiling faced woman[110] should always be a thoughtful one.[111] She used to respect her husband highly[112] and kept herself with softness in behaviour, angerlessness in the heart and sweet speaking. She was the follower of the *vrata*s.[113]

PHYSICAL STRUCTURE OF A WOMAN

There were some ideal descriptions regarding the physique of a woman in the Vedas. A passage of the *R̥V* describes darkness which represents a beautiful girl allegorically.[114] Her fingers are slender but long and the arms are attractive. Another passage of the *R̥V* says about the thickness and length of the hairs of a woman and also the thickness of her thighs[115] while describing the beauty of Indrāṇī. Her middle portion along with her waist[116] is emaciated.[117]

---

108. *R̥V*, 10/85/30.
109. *AV*, 14/1/43.
110. *R̥V*, 3/58/8.
111. *Ibid.*, 1/28/3.
112. *Ibid.*, 10/85/47.
113. *AV*, 3/25/4.
114. *R̥V*, 2/32/7.
115. *Ibid.*, 10/86/8.
116. *ŚB*, 3/5/1/11.
117. *Ibid.*, 1/2/5/16.

A.C. Das describing the Vedic views towards woman writes,

> The status of women in Ṛgvedic society was ordinarily high and honourable. Though, she was obedient to her husband, and subservient to his will, she was treated by him with proper respect.[118]

Marriage Institution

Indian national life is keeping its grandeur from the time immemorial due to some characteristics. One of them is marriage system which has been performed with full purity and faith. The Indian marriage is not only a social contract rather it is believed that a wife is found as a result of several good deeds of several births. It appears from the importances that have been traced in the Vedic passages.

IMPORTANCE OF MARRIAGE

A passage of the *ṚV* mentions that a house without a wife cannot be regarded as house. On the other hand, a wife is the house.[119] Again an Atharvanic passage declares that the conjugal life is the base of the peace and happiness of a woman.[120] Another passage of the *ṚV* says that the married people only can unfold a new chapter in the book of holy life.[121] The *TB*[122] and the *ŚB*[123] declare that an unmarried person is not worthy to participate in the sacrifices. Describing the discovery of the marriage tradition the *TMB* says, "Heaven and earth were once together, when they were separated"; they said, "Let us bring about a marriage, let

---

118. *RCD*, p. 250.
119. *ṚV*, 3/53/4.
120. *AV*, 1/14/1.
121 *ṚV*, 10/85/24.
122. *TU*, 2/2/2/6.
123. *ŚB*, 5/1/6/10.

there be co-operation between us".[124] After all, marriage was regarded as an indissoluble bond between them.[125] So far the conjugal life is concerned a wife was supposed to be wedded to Soma, Gandharva, Agni and the man.[126] A passage of the *R̥V* mentions that a person should not get married with two girls.[127] A.L. Basham mentions three purposes of marriage, these were (1) The promotion of religion by the performance of household sacrifices, (2) Progeny by which the father and his ancestors were assured of a happy life after and the line was continued, and (3) *Rati* or sexual pleasure.[128]

SELECTION OF A BRIDEGROOM OR A BRIDE

There are many systems of the selection of a bride or a bridegroom as reflected in the Vedic literature. Some scholars say that the system of *svayaṁvara* was in existence. They forward their argument after a passage of the *AV* where the word *pratikrāmya* is found mentioning *svayaṁvara*.[129] The next passage also has the same word.[130] Another passage says that a girl should stay in *brahmacarya*[131] which is supported by a passage of the *ŚYV*[132] mentioning that a girl after being educated in the *brahmacarya āśrama* should select a worthy lifemate. On the other hand, an Atharvanic passage declares that the bride and the bridegroom select each other according to their wishes.[133] The same thing is reflected in the *R̥V* also.[134]

---

124. Quoted from *IVKR*, p. 204.
125. *R̥V*, 10/85/57.
126. *AV*, 14/2/4.
127. *R̥V*, 1/105/8.
128. Quoted from *WIB*, p. 167.
129. *AV*, 2/36/5.
130. *Ibid.*, 2/36/6.
131. *Ibid.*, 11/5/18.
132. *ŚYN*, 34/10.
133. *AV*, 2/30/2.

We find another story in the *AB* where Prajāpati is mentioned declaring the *svayaṁvara* of his daughter Sūryā-Sāvitrī.[135]

We find a festival *samana* in the *R̥V*.[136] The meaning of the term is meeting, assembly, concourse and festival.[137] Some scholars say that the young girls used to go and participate in the festivals.[138] So far the festival *samana* is concerned, Prasanta Kumar Vedalankara mentions that the imagination of the festival *samana* is of the Western scholars and no Indian scholar has supported the theory of festival.[139] On the other hand, we get such a passage in the *R̥V* that badly criticises the woman who let herself subdued by a man for wealths. It further advises a gentle lady to select her husband once in the life for which finding should not be money centred at all.[140]

Another passage informs that the brother, in the absence of father guided his sister in finding a partner for her.[141] On the other hand, Acarya Baladev Upadhyaya says that the system of *svayaṁvara* was only for the daughter of the kṣatriyas.[142] He mentions such a passage in which the father of a girl is found in happiness after he managed a bride-groom for his daughter.[143]

Sukanyā in the *ŚB* also declares that she would not leave

134. *R̥V*, 10/27/12.

135. Read, *prajāpatirvai somāya rājñe duhitāraṁ prāyacchat, Sūryāṁ sāvitrīṁ tasmai sarve devāḥ varā agacchan*, *AB*, 4/7.

136. *R̥V*, 1/48/6, 1/124/3, 4/58/8, 7/2/5, 10/168/2, etc.

137. *SEDM*, p. 1154.

138. *R̥V*, 7/2/5.

139. *VSNP*, p. 151.

140. *R̥V*, 10/27/12.

141. *Ibid.*, 10/126.

142. *VSSB*, p. 421.

143. *R̥V*, 3/31/1.

her husband until her death to whom her father had bestowed her.[144] Thus, it is clear that the Vedic sages had given two types of systems of the selection of the partners of girls. On the other hand, some Atharvanic passages reveal that the father used to give his daughter to marriage.[145] In a passage of the *AV*, a bridegroom is found saying, "O the father of the girl, please isolate the feelings of the enmity and hatred from the heart of your daughter and give her to me".[146] The contract ritual would take place after the father of the girl confessed the proposal.[147] The *AB* mentions that the father has full right in the selection of the bridegroom.[148]

FORMS OF MARRIAGES

So far the forms of marriages are concerned, we find many types of marriages in the Vedic literature. The word *vivāha* itself occurs in the *AV*.[149] Moreover we find it in the *TS*,[150] *KS*,[151] *TMB*,[152] *AV*[153] and others. The Vedic evidences tell that there were (1) *brāhma*, (2) *daiva*, (3) *prājāpatya*, (4) *ārṣa*, (5) *gāndharva*, (6) *āsura*, (7) *rākṣasa* and (8) *paiśāca*,[154] systems of marriage.

We must refer to the *MS* for its better clarification. It says that the first four types are better than those of the last four ones.[155] Though we did not find the term in the *mantra*

144. *ŚB*, 4/1/5/9.
145. *AV*, 14/1/9.
146. *Ibid.*, 3/25/6.
147. *Ibid.*, 14/1/13.
148. *AB*, 8/6.
149. *AV*, 12/1/24, 14/1/65.
150 *TS*, 7/2/8/7.
151. *KS*, 25/3.
152. *TMB*, 7/10/4.
153. *AV*, 4/27/5.
154. *BDS*, 1/11/20; *GDS*, 4/6, 7, 8, 9, 10, 11, 12 & 13; *ĀsGS*, 1/6; *R̥V*, 1/112/19, 1/116/1, etc.
155. *MS*, 3/27.

Saṁhitās and *Brāhmaṇas*, yet the terms are explained in the *Kalpasūtras* and Smṛtis. The *MS* is the authentic Smṛti where all these have been elaborately discussed.[156]

On the other hand, we find three more forms of wedding in the *ṚV* which are as follows :

(1) An intermediatory takes active part in arranging the marriage.[157]

(2) Stealing and capturing a bride also is described in the *ṚV*.[158]

(3) A.C. Das mentions that the *ārṣa* system of marriage also was in vogue at that time.[159]

After the analysis of the Vedic literature, as the forms of marriages are found, we may come to the conclusion that the latter four systems were hated and the former four systems were respected. Thus, the marriage system was neither a mere social contract nor a means of satisfaction of sexual passions, rather it was the sacred duty of the people to continue the system of divine creation.

MONOGAMY AND POLYGAMY

Although, the Vedic system of life depicts monogamy yet we find some instances of polygamy also. Therefore, it is a controversial matter. For example, monogamy is evidently found in the passages of the *ṚV*[160] in which it has clearly been mentioned that the marriage with two ladies is unlawful and so it advises to abandon such things.[161] Prof. Macdonell and Keith admit that the highest thought of morality on the

156. *MS*, 3rd Chapter.
157. *ṚV*, 10/85/18.
158. *ṚV*, 1/112/19; 116/1; 117/20; 10/39/7; 65/12.
159. *RCD*, p. 252.
160. *ṚV*, 1/124/7, 4/3/2, 10/71/4, 10/104/3, 10/105/8, 10/186/7, 4/3/2 & 10/71/4, etc.
161. *Ibid*., 1/105/8.

marriage institution came into being in the Ṛgvedic period.[162]

On the other hand, we find the mentioning of polygamy also in the passage of the Vedic literature.[163] A passage of the *ṚV* mentions[164] that Śacī, the wife of Indra, is found defeating her co-wives so that she might be able to get the mastery over Indra. We find another passage where Tṛta is found shouting in grief caused by his co-wives.[165] The *TS* also mentions about polygamy.[166] It says that one may have two wives sometimes but a lady could not marry with two persons. The same thing is found in the *AB* also.[167] It gives an example of Hariścandra in which he has been mentioned having hundreds of wives.[168] The *ŚB* mentions of four wives who used to sit by their husband while performing the *aśvamedha* sacrifice.[169]

Though, we find both monogamy and polygamy in the Vedic literature yet it advises human society to follow monogamy. The *ṚV* mentions about *dampati* for referring husband and wife together and they are described to go forward unitedly.[170] Through another passage, the *AV* also mentions that Indra must bless the husbands and wives to be unseparated like an ostrich bird.[171] The *ĀpDS* abhores polygamy and says it to be punishable.[172] The Vedic sages

162. *VI*, 1/536.
163. *ṚV*, 1/62/11, 71/1, 104/4, 105/8, 122/19, 186/7, 6/53/4, 7/18/2, 7/26/3, 10/43.
164. *Ibid.*, 10/159/5 & 6.
165. *Ibid.*, 10/105/8.
166. *TS*, 6/6/5/4.
167. *AB*, 12/11.
168. *Ibid.*, 33/1.
169. *ŚB*, 13/4/1/9.
170. *ṚV*, 5/3/2.
171.. *AV*, 14/2/6.
172. *ĀpDS*, 2/5/11/12.

realized that the plurality of wives never leads to a smooth society system and rather makes life miserable and unhappy.[173] Thus, it seems that the Indian nation could realize the theories of monogamy and brought it into practice through experiments.

MARRIAGE FESTIVITIES

So far the pre-wedding rites are concerned, these are not found in the four Vedas clearly. These are vividly found in the *Kalpasūtra*s where the bride has been mentioned to have ceremonial bath in the night preceding the wedding day.[174] After bath she (the bride) wears new garments and takes her seat to the west of the fire and cooks food to offer in ritual sacrifices.[175] The *KGS* gives a long list of festivities which are to be performed in the wedding ceremony.[176] On the day of the marriage, the bridegroom has to perform sacrifices with the Vedic formulae.[177] He, then should be anointed with perfumes and garlanded after bath.[178] After that, the wedding procession departs[179] towards the bride's residence.[180] The marriage is conducted in the presence of the families of the both, bridegroom and bride and the processioners[181] as well. The presence of an *udvāhaka* is indispensable.

The religious functions start after the bride offers a seat to the bridegroom and presents *pādya, arghya,* and

173. *R̥V*, 1/105/8 & 10/32/2.
174. *SGS*, 1/11/1/4; *KGS*, 21/1.
175. *Ibid.*, 1/11/3-4.
176. *KGS*, 17/18.
177. *Ibid.*, 23/1-4.
178. *BSS*, 1/1/24.
179. *R̥V*, 2/36/1.
180. *R̥V*, 10/17/1.
181. *AV*, 11/8/1.

ācamanīya, etc.[182] The bridegroom then sings the following *mantras*, "Let the airs, rivers, medicines, nights and mornings, the soil of this land, God, vegetables, the sun and cows be charming."[183]

The *pāṇigrahaṇa* ritual is started after this, for which *śilārohaṇa* and *keśamuñcana* functions are performed, then they walk around the sacrificial fire.[184] Before mounting the stone, the bridegroom says, "I am he, thou art she, I the *sāma*, thou art *r̥k*. I, the heaven, thou the earth, here will we unite ourselves and produce offspring."[185] As she will be mounting the stone, the bridegroom says to the bride, "Mount upon the stone, be stable and get victory over your enemies."[186] Next the ceremony of the opening of hair *(keśamuñcana)* follows and then the bridegroom says, "I am going to free you from the ties of your father."[187]

After that, the bridegroom catches the hand of the bride and says, "I have caught your hands for your fortune. O lady, God has combined us today and I am going to give you the mastery of my family."[188] He further says, "Let us tighten ourselves with the thread of marriage and give worthy sons to this earth."[189] Moreover, we can see other six passages in the *AV* which are chanted by the bridegroom at the time of *pāṇigrahaṇa*.[190]

Another ritual is the *lājāhoma* which was performed with

182. *PGS*, 1/3.
183. *VSNP*, p. 52.
184. *Ibid.*, p. 53.
185. *AV*, 13/2/71; *RCD*, p. 253.
186. *VSNP*, p. 53.
187. *R̥V*, 10/85/25.
188. *AV*, 14/1/50 & *R̥V*, 10/85/36.
189. *AV*, 14/1/52.
190. *Ibid.*, 14/1/53-58.

an Atharvanic passage.[191] The same thing is found in the *PGS* also.[192] After that, the bride touches the bride-groom[193] and reads the passage. Thus the Vedic marriage is completed musically, poetically and dramatically and it bears the importance of the Indian society.

The bride was blessed by both the *purohitas* and parents as follows : She must have worthy children and fortunes and live with her husband peacefully.[194] She should be like a queen to her father-in-law, mother-in-law and sister-in-laws.[195] She might get ample milk, kingdom and she should be wealthy.[196] Her glances should be charming and happy.[197] She might develop herself as the worthy member of the *vidatha.*[198] The couple was blessed to have a healthy life, to get tasty diet, to beget the worthy offsprings and live happily.[199] The bride was again blessed to be fortunate,[200] sweet sounded,[201] to remain unwidowed, to be decorated with ornaments always and to remain healthy and tear-less.[202]

The ritual of *saptapadī* plays an important role in the ceremony. The bride is suggested to take seven steps for food, strength, prosperity, happiness, cattle keeping, becoming suitable for all seasons and love respectively.[203]

191. *AV*, 14/2/63.
192. *PGS*, 1/6/2.
193. *AV*, 14/1/21.
194. *Ibid.*, 14/1/42.
195. *Ibid.*
196. *Ibid.*, 6/78/2.
197. *Ibid.*, 14/2/17 & 14/2/27.
198. *Ibid.*, 14/1/21.
199. *Ibid.*
200. *Ibid.*, 14/1/18.
201. *Ibid.*, 14/1/19.
202. *AV*, 18/3/57.
203. *ĀsGS*, 1/8/9.

At the time of taking the steps, a passage of the *GGS* is pronounced.[204]

POST-MARRIAGE RITUALS

After those rituals and festivities were over, the bridegroom was permitted to be ready for departure with bride to his home on a well-adorned chariot alongwith the procession.[205] Then the father of the bride sends her to the bridegroom's house[206] decorating her with ornaments and dresses.[207]

The wedding procession reaches the home of bridegroom and some rituals follow in which the bride says to the bridegroom, "You should prosper here along with your children and have your loving things. Let the household duties be followed properly and keep your attention in those."[208]

Moreover, the last ritual seems to be the *caturthīkarma.*[209]

Macdonell and Keith write, "The ceremony started from the house of the bride where their friends used to be introduced with the bridegroom's party and cows were slaughtered to feed them." Moreover, they write that the bride mounted stone and her hands are grasped by the bridegroom. Thus, he leads the bride to his residence in a car with a marriage procession.[210]

GIFTS TO THE BRIDEGROOM

Some scholars like U.M. Apte,[211] Prasanta Kumar,[212] etc.,

---

204. *GGS*, 1/2/1.
205. *R̥V*, 10/85/7, 8, 10, 24, 25, 26, 27 & 42.
206. *R̥V*, 9/46/2.
207. *AV*, 14/2/12.
208. *Ibid.*, 10/85/27.
209. *IVKR*, pp. 242 to 247.
210. *VI*, 1/549.
211. *VSNP*, p 12.

mention that the dowry system was in existence in the Vedic period. A passage of the *ṚV* mentions that the bride is well decorated with ornaments and dresses at the time of grasping the hands.[213] It was done at the time of sending her with the bridegroom[214] because the people felt the importance of decorating the bride with dresses and ornaments.[215] A bridegroom is found in the *AV* telling that his bride was provided with wealth[216] and again a passage of the *ṚV*[217] says about the boy who wished to get wife, wealths and coins. An Atharvanic passage speaks about bride's father, bridegroom and the Brahmā of the sacrifice who sat together to fix the gifts.[218] The *AV* advises the bride's father to offer good dresses and attractive ornaments so that the newly married couple may be happy.[219] A list of pillow, collirium and coins are suggested in a passage.[220] The next passage mentions about clothes.[221] On the other hand, we find the mentioning of gold, sacrificial materials, cows and oxen.[222] The same says that the box of wealth[223] a bed,[224] and six types of wealths[225] were to be given to the bridegroom. Moreover, we find a king named Svanaya who gave the following things to the bride of Kakṣivān in the

212. *VSNP*, p 55.
213. *ṚV*, 10/39/14.
214. *Ibid.*, 9/46/2, 10/39, 10/14.
215. *Ibid.*, 5/30/14.
216. *AV*, 14/2/4.
217. *ṚV*, 1/126/1-3.
218. *AV*, 2/36/2.
219. *Ibid.*, 14/2/12.
220. *Ibid.*, 14/1/6.
221. *Ibid.*, 14/1/7.
222. *AV*, 2/36/7.
223. *Ibid.*, 14/2/30.
224. *Ibid.*, 14/2/31.
225. *Ibid.*, 2/36/17.

marriage:[226] (1) hundred of *niṣka*s, (2) hundred of horses, (3) hundred of oxen, (4) 10 chariots, (5) 60,000 cows.

Though the bridegroom and the party received the wealth given in the house of the bride yet it is worthnoting fact that the *ŚYV* hates the temptation clearly.[227]

To conclude this discussion, we may quote A.C. Das as follows :

> The *ṚV mantra*s clearly describe the status of the newly wedded wife, the duties that she was expected to perform in her new sphere and environment and the necessity of uniting her heart with her husband for ever. It appears that the bride came to her husband's house to live there permanently though she was permitted to visit her parents occasionally.[228]

---

226. *ṚV*, 1/126/2-4.
227. *ŚYV*, 40/1.
228. *RCD*, p 254.

7

Vedic Economics

Theories

AIM OF ECONOMICS

So far the Vedic view in Ecomomics is concerned, our attention centralises on a *ŚYV* passage[1] which gives the following ideas:[2]

1. All kinds of resources exist on earth for the living of all creatures.
2. Give your earnings to others.
3. Consume your earnings.
4. Do not tempt to other's wealth.
5. Whose wealth? What is wealth?

The above-mentioned aphorism reveal the vast range of Vedic economic thoughts which was reflected in the Vedic literature. The importance of the passage appears from the fact that Sātavalekar has written an essay titled *Vaidik Arthavyavasthā* on its basis.[3] The base of Economics and the economic activities are to acquire happiness.[4] A sage prays God for that.[5]

---

1. *ŚYV*, 40/1.
2. *HEM*, p. 12.
3. *Vaidik Arthavyavasthā* by Sātavalekar *SAG* pp. 119 to 131.
4. *ṚV*, 10/64/1.
5. *Ibid.*, 4/42/2.

WANTS

People are not satisfied with what they have and as such one approaches the rich in order to get some more wealth.[6] In this respect, we may quote R. Sharma for better illustration. He says,

> One who possesses one quantity of wealth, tries to emulate the man who has two quantity of wealth. One who has two quantities of wealth ran after the man who has three quantities and the man who has four tries to secure maximum importance in wealth so that he should also possess wealth.[7]

So, it was obvious to the sages of India that wants of people are unlimited. The fact is more clearly expressed in the *MS* which says that the desires cannot be fulfilled no matter however it is comsumed just like the fire that consumes *ghī* as much as it is thrown into it.[8]

THEORY CONCERNED WITH RECEIVING AND GIVING

First of all, the people are advised in the Vedas to earn honestly. A passage of the *R̥V* mentioned that the wealth earned with honesty is pure.[9] Moreover, another *R̥V* passage advises that a beggar also should offer something from his collected wealth.[10] Another passage of the same *sūkta* lays that the grandeur of a charitable person is greater than that of the person who is famous and learned but not charitable.[11] Again at another place it has been mentioned that the ideal God Indra always gives but never takes anyhing from others.[12]

---

6. *R̥V*, 10/117/8.
7. *HEM*, p. 94.
8. *MS*, 2/94.
9. *R̥V*, 5/70/4 & 10/117/6.
10. *Ibid.*, 10/117/2.
11. *Ibid.*, 10/117/7.
12. *Ibid.*, 6/28/2.

DEBTLESSNESS

The sages of the Vedic Age advised the people not to debunk in debts. A Ṛgvedic seer prays Varuṇa to make him free from his and his forefather's debts.[13] Again, we find another passage in the *ṚV* which mentions of a devotee praying to God to bestow him wealths so that he might be free from debts.[14] A whole *sukta* of the *AV* describes the evil results of debts.[15] We find the following three important points from the passages:

1. The people of this era confessed their faults of indebtness if they were really indebted.
2. The people took crops in debts.
3. The people had the conception of two kinds of debts (i.e., worldly and divine) so they wanted to be free from both the debts so that they might follow the pleasant path after death.

ECONOMY BASED ON MORALITY

One of the important characteristics of the Vedic economics is that it was based on morality. A Ṛgvedic passage declares[16] that an ideal Vedic person never utilises other's wealth for one's own sake or to nourish himself. Moreover, the poet seer mentions that his sons also did not take anything in debts. The sages of the Ṛgvedic India advised their people to be honest and gentle. They related the economic theories with morality and told that a licentious person remains poor always.[17] Thirdly, to say, they describe that the distribution of wealth is equivalent to performing of a *yajña*.[18] Again, the snatched wealth from the wicked

13. *ṚV*, 2/28/9.
14. *Ibid.*, 7/4/7.
15. *AV*, 6/117/1,2,3.
16. *ṚV*, 5/70/4.
17. *Ibid.*, 5/2/5.
18. *Ibid.*, 10/117/3.

persons should be distributed among the gentle beings.[19]

SUBJECT-MATTER OF ECONOMICS

M.G. Bokare mentions some subject-matters of economics as follows :

> Any textbook on modern economics is suitably divided and sub-divided into the chapters as under :1. Population, 2. Resources, 3. Production, 4. Consumption, 5. Exchange and formation of price, 6. Distribution [(a) Rent, (b) Wages, (c) Interest and (d) Profit.] 7. Taxes i.e. Public Finance.[20]

We may discuss the Vedic economics also on these points.

Population

The Vedic people were conscious in politics and economics as well. The main factor of all the sciences is man. Without man, neither economics nor any other progress may occur. So, the Vedic people stressed upon well-organised society.[21] Moreover, an Atharvanic passage mentions that there must be a conscious society for the prosperity of the people.[22] There are a lot of passages in the Vedic Saṁhitās in which the devotee begged worthy sons from them.[23] Thus, this factor of economics is found in the Vedas vividly.

Resources

Resources in the Vedic India to conduct the Aryan's economic way of life were many. They made their income through husbandry,[24] collection of gold,[25] and perhaps through

---

19. *R̥V*, 1/19/6.
20. *HEM*, p. 72.
21. *AV*, 1/29/1 and, *rāṣṭrāṇi vai viśaḥ*, *AB*, 8/26.
22. *AV*, 3/19/2.
23. *ŚYV*, 22/22 & 1/1.
24. *R̥V*, 1/29/2 to 5.
25. *Ibid.*, 1/30/17.

trades.[26] Mainly the milk of cow[27] and oxen[28] seems to be the main resources of the Vedic economy. Moreover, the Vedic people collected their earnings through agriculture.[29] Industrial activities also were the sources of income of the people of Vedic time. Chariot-makers[30] and potters[31] also are found in the Vedic literature.

Production and Labour

Mainly the land has been described as the means of production in the Vedas but yet, we get other evidences also. The *AV* gives a clear description of land and all the functions which could be performed through it.[32] Secondly, the Vedic sages have regarded the land as mother.[33] Thus, land was highly esteemed for it gave water,[34] cows and food,[35] and milk.[36] Land looks after the people[37] and gives a lot of wealth.[38] The people of Vedic Age were aware that land possessed minerals and precious metals like gold and pearls.[39] On the other hand, the factor of labour is very important in the Vedic economics. The R̥gvedic passage mentions of different types of labours which were to be

---

26. *AV*, 7/60/7.
27. *R̥V*, 1/30/13.
28. *AV*, 4/34/8.
29. *R̥V*, 1/176/2, 2/5/6; 1/117/21, etc.
30. *TB*, 7/55/8.
31. *ŚB*, 9/8/7.
32. *AV*, 12/1.
33. *Ibid.*, 12/1/40.
34 *Ibid.*, 12/1/3.
35. *Ibid.*, 12/1/4.
36. *Ibid.*, 12/1/9.
37. *Ibid.*, 12/1/13.
38. *Ibid.*, 12/1/40.
39. *Ibid.*, 12/1/44.

treated accordingly.[40] Our analysis of the passage is as follows:

1. All labourers are equal.
2. The value of their result of labour differs always.
3. The value of their labour is to be determined according to their output.

Moreover, we find some passages in the Vedic literature which reveal the strong existence and importance of capital. The grazing fields of animals,[41] the bags to keep the instruments,[42] a kind of reed and canes for cottage industry[43] are found everywhere. Again, so far the organization is concerned, the words like *vrāta* and *gaṇa*[44] themselves are the examples of the Āryan's idea of organization in production. At last we may mention that the Vedic people offered their prayers to God for their better production.[45]

Consumption

Vedic view of consumption is remarkable. A passage of the *ŚYV* suggests that a person should consume anything after he offers to others.[46] On the other hand, the poors were

---

40. Read (i) Griffith's translation : "The hands are both alike : their labour differs. The yield of sister milch-kine is unequal. Twins even differ in their strength and vigour : even two kinsmen, differ in their bounty."

    (ii) Sāyaṇa's commentary : "The strength of two hands, though possessed by a same person, differs. Two calves of a cow also do not give equal quantity of milk after they beget their calf again. The twins also differ in strength. In the same way between two persons of a race, one may become charitable and the other may be a selfish one." *R̥V*, 10/117/9.
41. *R̥V*, 10/10/3 & 4.
42. *HSSAJS*, p. 405.
43. *AV*, 6/138/5.
44. *R̥V*, 5/53/11.
45. *Ibid.*, 1/1/3; 1/29/6; 1/30/5, etc.
46. *ŚYV*, 40/1.

looked after by the riches always.[47] It was forbidden in the consumption of the wealth snatched from the wicked persons but that was to be distributed among the humble persons of the states.[48] On the theory of consumption as reflected in the Vedas, Sātavalekar mentions, "A man had to consume the things remained after *yajña.*"[49]

Exchange

From the studies of the Vedas we come to the conclusion that there were three types of systems for exchange. (1) Barter system, (2) Using cows as the medium of exchange, and (3) Purchasing with coins. We find the system of barter in a passage of the AV in which a *ṛṣi* changes rice with the skin of an antelope.[50] An example of purchasing Indra's statue with two cows[51] may also be seen. On the other hand, the existence of coins appears from the fact that Kakṣivat received hundred *niṣka*s from the king Bhāvayavya.[52] *Śatamāna* was discussed in the *ŚB*,[53] *TB*,[54] etc. Thus, the medium of exchange was found in Vedic literature. Selling and purchasing are found in the *ṚV*,[55] *ŚYV*,[56] and *AV*[57] also.

Market Competition and Price

After the analysis of a Ṛgvedic passage we come to know

47. *ṚV*, 10/117.
48. *Ibid.*, 1/19/6.
49. *Vaidik Arthavyavasthā, SAG*, p. 126.
50. *AV*, 3/24/4 17; 4/7/6.
51. *ṚV*, 4/24/10.
52. *Ibid.*, 3/47/4.
53. *ŚB*, 5/4/3/24; 26 & 5/5/5/16, etc.
54. *TB*, 1/7/6/2 & 1/2/7/3.
55. *ṚV*, 4/24/9.
56. *ŚYV*, 3/50.
57. *AV*, 3/15/2.

that the people of the Vedic era had proper knowledge on market, competition, price, demand and supply, etc. The passage[58] has been translated by several scholars[59(a)] by which Bokare came to the following points.[59(b)]

1. The goods flow in the market.
2. The bid for price may be small or high.
3. Buyers and sellers are both simple and clever.
4. Both buyers and sellers get benefit according to supply, demand and price.
5. The buyers get benefit of more total supply and small price. Buyers get benefit if the sellers are more than the number of buyers of the total supply.
6. The seller gets benefit if the price is high. It can be high, if the supply is low or purchasers are more than sellers.

Distribution

Distribution of wealth seems to be a personal matter[60] because it was known to the people that wealth is not a stable thing.[61] Yet, we have divided it into rent, wages,

---

58. *R̥V*, 4/24/9.
59. (a) Read, (i) Griffith's commentary : "He bid a small price for a thing of value: I was content, returning, still unpurchased. He hightened not his sufficient offer. Simple and clever, both milk out of the udder."

    (ii) Sāyaṇācārya's commentary : "One gets a little wealth through his virtue or begs the remaining wealths from the buyer by saying, 'I have not sold'. Then the buyer does not give him more wealth."

    (iii) Sātavalekera's commentary : "Somebody gave more price and obtained less quantity of goods. When the goods are not sold, he again demanded his money back. The seller was not willing to give more price for less goods. Weak and the clever man obtained the price which they have bargained."
59. (b) *HEM*, p. 86.
60. *R̥V*, 10/117/2, 3 & 7.
61 *Ibid.*, 10/117/5.

interest and profits. These things are the matters of administration.

Taxation

We sometimes get taxless administration[62] and sometimes people are advised to give 1/16 of the total income to the king.[63] In a place of the *ŚYV*, it has been told that tax is collected in order to protect people in the wars.[64] So far the taxation is concerned it is not the subject of economic theory. In this regard, M.G. Bokare remarks,

> The state collects taxes for its expenditures. There is no economic theory as such for taxation. It is the policy. The principles of taxation are described in the textbook in the realm of policy. To tax the citizens, is not an eternal law. It is historical movement in the economy. It has, therefore, a historic-legal status in the economy. Like the historical laws that disappear in the economy, taxes can also disappear. We have to study taxation of the state governed by the theoretical results of the Hindu economics. These illustrations in the literature should be studied to know the connotation of Eternal Law in the *Ṛgveda*.[65]

Whatever the fact there may be, M.G. Bokare mentions about the Vedic theories of economics,

> I believe, I have substantiated the thesis. Holy Vedas are the beginning of economics in the history of economics of the world. The blessings of abundance in Holy Vedas is also the end of modern economics in the Western corpus of the studies. ***Hindu Economics*** traces the theories of economics in the holy Vedas and the course of analytical exercises

---

62. *ṚV*, 6/28/2.
63. *AV*, 3/29/1.
64. *ŚYV*, 9/17.
65. *HEM*, p. 80.

transcends the western economics. It realises eternal economic order for mankind.[66]

Five Footed Economy

A single passage of the *Ṛ̥V*[67] unfolds five aspects of inter-connected theories in economics. M.G. Bokare mentions it and explains as follows:[68]

1. Economy without state is one-footed. All production that is income belongs to the man.
2 Economy with state is Biped economy. It has sources of state as independent entities in the economic life of society. It is two-footed economy.
3. Economy is found with state owners and hired labourers. This is the three-footed economy. Tax, wages and income of ownership are cognized in three parts.
4. When capital is sub-divided into owned and borrowed capital, interest and profit as separate entities emanate in economy. Rent of land, wage, interest and profit thus become four-footed economy.
5. Steadily, the state introduces taxes, rent, wages, interest and profit and thus emerges the five-footed economy.

The lesson has alternatively been stated by the same writer as follows :[69]

One foot economy : Man produces and consumes all his income. This is one-foot economy.

Two feet economy : Trades are needed to organize goods in the market for different times and places. Two-feet economy is thus engendered in living. This is trader's profit.

66. *HEM,* p. (iii) preface.
67. *Ṛ̥V,* 10/117/8.
68. *HEM,* p. 97.
69. *Ibid.*

Three feet economy : Due to various causes, people become propertyless. They depend upon others for work and income. The lease, rent and wages as income emanate in the economy. This is three-feet economy.

Four feet economy : All need money for their increasing activities. The money lenders and credit on interest, emerge in economy. This is four-feet economy.

Five feet economy : The government needs money. Tax on citizens by the state emerges in the economy. This is five-feet economy.

Agriculture

HISTORY AND IMPORTANCE

The history of agriculture of the Vedic Age is found as follows : The agriculture was first introduced in India by Aśvins.[70] They taught the method of agriculture to the Āryans. Before that, they had taught Manu as to how to sow the seeds in the land.[71] In the course of time, when people were educated in cultivation, the problem of cultivating land arose. Perhaps it was then that the king or ruler, who has been presented as Indra, provided such land for agriculture.[72] On the other hand, through an Atharvanic passage, Macdonell informs that the system of agriculture was first introduced by Pṛthu Vainya in the world.[73] Whatever the history of agriculture there may be, it had vast importance in the life of the people of India. The *ŚB* praises agriculture in the following words "Agriculture itself is ritual."[74] A passage in the *ŚYV* says that ploughing brings prosperity.[75]

70. *ṚV*, 1/117/21.
71. *Ibid.*, 1/112/6.
72. *Ibid.*, 4/26/2.
73. *VI*, 1/201.
74. Read, *annaṁ vai kṛṣiḥ*, *ŚB*, 7/2/2/6.
75. *ŚYV*, 12/71.

The *Ṛgveda* advises not to be gambler but instead, he should be a cultivator so that he might be satisfied on getting wealth that would further result in getting cows and a beloved wife.[76]

Thus, we find the mentioning of the importance and historical evidences of agriculture in the Vedic India.

Agriculture was an important factor of production in India. It appears from the fact that the word, *kṛṣi* has frequently been used in all the Vedic literature. The people of Vedic Ages knew about several seasons, system of irrigation, performing cultivation frequently in a plot of land, etc. One *ṚV* passage[77] mentions the fact. The verse shows the following points :

1. People had knowledge of six seasons, which indicates that they divided their works according to those seasons.
2. People used to cultivate a plot of land more than once in a year.
3. Such was not possible unless people were conscious in irrigation. So, we find people irrigating the land.[78]

TYPES OF CROPS

We find *dhānya*,[79] *dhāna*,[80] *yava*,[81] in the *ṚV* as main crops of agriculture. But on the other hand, a passage of the *ŚYV*[82]

---

76. *ṚV*, 10/34/13.
77. Read (i) Griffith's commentary : "And may be duly bring to me the six bound closely, through these drops. As one who ploughs with streers brings corn."

    (ii) Ṣāyaṇācarya's commentary : "May that Puṣā provided all the six seasons through Soma as a cultivator gets barely frequently."
78. *ṚV*, 10/101/5.
79. *Ibid.*, 5/53/13; 6/13/4; 10/94/3, etc.
80. *Ibid.*, 1/16/2; 3/35/3; 3/52/5 & 6/29/4.
81. *Ibid.*, 1/23/15; 1/66/3; 1/117/21, etc.
82. *ŚYV*, 18/12.

lists the crops which were sown in the fields during the Vedic period. These were (1) *vṛhī* (Paddy), (2) *yava* or barley, (3) *māṣa* or beans, (4) *tila* or sesamum, (5) *mudga* or kidney beans, (6) *khalva* or vetches, (7) *priyaṅgu* or millets, (8) *aṇu* or wild rice, (9) *śyāmaka* or *Panicum furmentaceum*, (10) *nīvāra* or wild rice, (11) *godhūma* or wheat, (12) *masūra* or lentil. Moreover, we find *sarṣapa* or mustard, *kulaṭṭha*[83] and sugar cane[84] in the Sūtra period.

IRRIGATION AND MANURES

The system of irrigation and application of manures was present. We find that the people used to irrigate their fields in three ways : (a) through the rainfall, (b) through canals, and (c) through pulling water from wells and spraying in the fields. That the sun sucks the water from earth and returns it in the form of rain,[85] was clearly known to the Vedic seers which indicates that the people were dependent on rain. Secondly, a mention in the *ṚV*, "The Sindhu river flows through the green fields of corps"[86] shows that the people were able to use the rivers for cultivation. The third system of irrigating land was by pulling water from well. We may illustrate a Ṛgvedic passage[87] for clear description.

The studies of the verse leads us to the following points:

1. After irrigation the fields were thought to be well prospered.
2. As Indra is able to give glory, strength and wealth to the people so were the fields filled with water.

---

83. *IVKR*, p. 134.
84. *BGS*, 3/10/4.
85. *ṚV*, 1/85/10.
86. *Ibid.*, 10/75/2.
87. Read, (i) Sāyaṇācarya's commentary : "We salute Indra, because he is wealth, strong and glory himself. O Indra, let ours prayers satisfy you like the water fill in the fields." *ṚV*, 8/49/6.

3. Irrigation was an important factor of the cultivation of Vedic people.
4. People of those times used the water of wells to irrigate lands.

Avata was a kind of well for which a special kind of bucket tied with a rope[88] was used to pull water.[89] Those wells were used for irrigation on the one hand and to make drunk the oxen on the other.

Again a passage[90] in the *AV* says that the people wanted natural manure for good production. On the other hand, the *ŚB*[91] mentions about cowdung which was used as manure in the cultivation.

PROCESS OF PERFORMING CULTIVATION

First of all, the people of the Vedic Age used to plough on a new plot of land.[92] An astonishing fact found in a passage of the *AV* is that a seer says that six and even eight oxen were fastened on a yoke when someone went to sow barley.[93] The process of performing cultivation has clearly been explained in a Ṛgvedic passage[94] which needs a broad illustration.

---

88. *ṚV*, 10/101/6.
89. *Ibid.*, 10/25/4.
90. *AV*, 3/14/3.
91. *ŚB*, 2/1/1/7.
92. *ṚV*, 10/101/4.
93. *AV*, 6/91/1.
94. Read, (i) Griffith's translation : "lay on the yokes, and fasten well the traces : formed is furrow, sow the seed within it. Through the song may we find hearing fraught with plenty : near to the ripened grain appraoch the sickle."

    (ii) Sāyaṇācārya's commentary : "O Ṛtvijas, Faster the plough, lift the yokes, sow the seeds, we produce crops through prayers after that, sickles approach to the ripened paddy fields."

1. Ploughs were used in the Vedic Age in which a sharp blade of iron was used.
2. People were expert in making yokes in the ploughs.
3. After ploughing the fields, the seeds were sowed.
4. Grain was produced after the prayers.
5. People then used sickles to harvest the crops.

A passage of the *R̥V* informs us that the barley was harvested in slow motion[95] and collected in small bundles.[96] The peasant separated grains by crushing and the husk thus produced was thrown away through winnowing.[97] The clean and actual grains measured in *urdara*[98] were stored in the *sthivi*.[99]

INSTRUMENTS OF CULTIVATION

The plough was made of wood in which a furrow was fixed.[100] The said furrow was made of iron.[101] We find several passages which state about the use of plough. The plough was called *lāṅgala*.[102] A hole was drilled on the plough and long shaft was fixed.[103] The shaft, on the other hand, was fixed on a yoke which has been described in the several passages of the Vedas.[104] An *AV* passage mentions *sīrā* to be yoke.[105] The rope that used to tie the shaft with

95. *R̥V*, 10/131/2.
96. *Ibid.*, 8/78/10.
97. *AV*, 12/3/19.
98. *R̥V*, 2/14/11.
99. *Ibid.*, 10/68/3.
100. *Ibid.*, 4/57/8; 10/117/7; *AV*, 3/17/5.
101. *AV*, 3/17/3.
102. *R̥V*, 4/57/4; *TS* 6/6/7/4; *Nir*, 6/26; *ŚYV*, 12/17.
103. *VI*, 2/213.
104. *R̥V*, 1/84/16, 1/100/16, 1/134/3; *AV*, 5/17/18; *AB* 6/188; *ŚB* 1/1/2/10.
105. *AV*, 3/17/1.

yoke[106] or oxen with the yoke was called *varatra*.[107] On the other hand, one kind of goad was used[108] to control the oxen at the time of ploughing.

Industry

INDUSTRIES IN THE VEDIC INDIA

So far the industries in the Vedic India are concerned, we find some industries like that of a blacksmith, laundryman, charioteer, etc.[109] On the other hand, G.S. Ghurye informs us about 20 types of economic activities in the Ṛgvedic period.[110] These were, (1) rower, (2) boatman, (3) corn grinder or grinder of a mill, (4) priest, (5) *ṛṣi*, hymner, poet, (6) smith, (7) smelter and welder (*dravitṛ dhmātṛ*), (8) ploughman, (9) herdsman, (10) village headman, (11) carpenter, (12) chariot builder, (13) charioteer, (14) barber, (15) merchant, (16) weaver, (17) vinter, (18) *bhiṣaj*; physician, (19) *kari*, singer, poet, and (20) brāhmaṇa, priest. Ghurye clearly mentions, "The principal economic activity of the Ṛgvedic people would appear to have been agriculture or plough culture."

Sivadatta Gnani, on the other hand, informs of 23 types of sources of income specially mentioned in the *ṚV*.[111] Whatever the fact there may be, we find a lot of ways of income listed in the *ŚYV*.[112] These are as follows : 1. mistrel or *magadha*, 2. actor or *śailuṣa*, 3. herald, panegyrist or *sūta*, 4. counsellor or *sabhākāra*, 5. chariot maker or *rathakāra*, 6. carpenter or *takṣa*, 7. potter or *kulāla*, 8. blacksmith or

106. *ṚV*, 4/57/4, 10/60/8.
107 *Ibid.*, 10/102/8.
108. *Ibid.*, 4/57/4, 6/53/9, 6/58/2.
109. *AV*, 3/5/6.
110. *VIG*, p. 224.
111. *VSS*, p. 251.
112. *ŚYV*, 16th and 30th chapters.

karmāra, 9. jeweller or *maṇikāra*, 10. Barber or sower or *vapa*, 11. arrowsmith or *iṣukāra*, 12. bow-maker or *dhanuṣaskāra*, 13. bow-string maker or *jyākāra*, 14. rope-maker or *rajjusarja*, 15. hunter or *mṛgayuḥ*, 16. dog-keeper or *śvanin*, 17. bird-catcher or *puñjiṣṭha*, 18. basket-maker or *vidālakarī*, 19. female workers in thorns or *kaṇṭakīkarī*, 20. female expert in embroidery or *peśākarī*, 21. physician or *bhiṣaja*, 22. astronomer or *nakṣatradarśa*, 23. elephant-keeper or *hastipa*, 24. horse-keeper or *aśvapa*, 25. cowherd or *gopāla*, 26. shepherd or *avipāla*, 27. goatherd or *ajapāla*, 28. cultivator or *kṛṣaka*, 29. distiller of liquor or *surākāra*, 30. house-keeper or *gṛhapa*, 31. charioteer or *kṣattā*, 32. assistant charioteer or *amukṣattā*, 33. fuel-fetcher or *dāvāhāra*, 34. image-maker or *paśitā*, 35. washerwoman or *vāsapalpulī*, 36. female dyer or *rajayitrī*, 37. spy or informer or *piśuna*, 38. door-keeper or *kṣatta* 39. assistant door-keeper or *anukṣattā*, 40. horse-man or *aśvasada*, 41. tax collector or *bhāgadugha*, 42. a female expert in preparing unguents and cosmetics or *añjanīkārī*, 43. female scabbard-maker or *koṣakarī*, 44. furrier or *ajinasandha*, 45. tanner or *carmakāra*, 46. fisherman or *dhīvara*, 47. dealer in dried fish or *śauṣkala*, 48. goldsmith or *hiraṇyakāra*, 49. merchant or *vaṇija*, 50. forest keeper or *vanapa*, 51. lute player or *vīnāvāda*, 52. flute player or *tūṇavāda*, 53. conch-blower or *saṅkhadhmā*, 54. acrobat, a pole dancer or *baṁśanartin*, 55. headman of a village or *grāmaṇi*, 56. astrologer or *gaṇaka*, and 57. the herald or announcer or *abhikrośaka*.

Here we are going to discuss some of the important industries of the Vedic Age.

CARPENTRY

The carpenters of the Vedic Age made very attractive things such as arrows,[113] *camasa*[114] or a vessel used at sacrifices for

113. *ṚV*, 9/112/2.

114. *Ibid.*, 1/161/9.

drinking *soma.*[115] *Ṛbhus* who have been mentioned in a passage to indicate the carpenters[116] distributed the vessels among the sacrificers. Moreover, they were certainly busy and attentive while they were appointed in the works of building the thousand doored buildings.[117] We find such chariots even in the Ṛgvedic period where the warrior's chariots were described to be well cultured and strong ones.[118] We find a word *proṣṭha* in the *TB* which means a bench.[119] Another passage of the *ṚV* mentions about such a carpenter who could bend the wood and make circle.[120] We find them using axes[121] and spades[122] to cut the woods and used them in the battles. They used the axes in making the wooden vessels,[123] repairing chariots[124] and building wooden houses.[125] On the other hand, S.S. Sahay mentions that the word *brahmā* was used to denote them.[126] A passage of the *ŚYV* offers salutations[127] to them and wishes to get more carpenters.[128]

CHARIOT BUILDERS

The importance of the chariot builders appears from the fact that they were regarded as *rājakṛt*s or king makers.[129]

115. *SEDM*, p. 388.
116. *ṚV*, 3/60/2.
117. *Ibid.*, 7/88/5.
118. *Ibid.*, 1/38/12.
119. *TB*, 7/55/8.
120. *ṚV*, 7/32/20.
121. *Ibid.*, 10/53/9.
122. *Ibid.*, 10/53/12.
123. *Ibid.*, 10/53/10.
124. *Ibid.*, 10/39/4.
125. *Ibid.*, 10/53/10.
126. *HSSAJS*, p. 405.
127. *ŚYV*, 16/27.
128. *Ibid.*, 30/6.
129. *AV*, 3/5/6.

On the other hand, they were thought to have extraordinary intellect[130] for which they were counted among the respected persons.[131] A passage of the *ṚV* mentions that the art of making or building a chariot is equivalent to the intellect of composing Vedic verses.[132] Again another *ṚV* passage describing the method of chariot-making says that a chariot-maker joins the part of the chariots after he makes them.[133] After the chariot is completed, he fastens the horses to the chariot[134] and takes it to its master.[135]

Expert chariot-makers used to build the three-storeyed chariots,[136] electric chariots or *vidyudratha*s,[137] horseless chariots[138] or *anaśva ratha*s, tri-wheeled chariots, etc.[139] Other passages mentioning of *aśvaparṇa ratha,*[140] sledges[141] which were pulled by deers,[142] also are met.

JEWELLERY

The jewellers in the Vedic Ages are found to have been occupying respectable place in the society. We generally find six names of jewellers mentioned in the Saṁhitās as follows : *hiraṇyakāra* or *svarṇakāra,*[143] *karmakāra,*[144]

---

130. *ŚYV*, 30/6.
131. Read, *rathakārebhyaścabo namo namo, ŚYV*, 16/27.
132. *ṚV*, 4/16/20.
133. *ṚV*, 1/62/13.
134. *Ibid.*, 1/130/6.
135. *Ibid.*, 1/61/4.
136. *ṚV*, 9/62/17.
137. *Ibid.*, 3/14/1.
138. *Ibid.*, 1/120/10.
139. *Ibid.*, 1/118/2.
140. *Ibid.*, 1/88/1.
141. *Ibid.*, 8/7/29.
142. *Ibid.*, 1/37/2; 39/6; 85/4; 3/26/4; 1/39/6, etc.
143. *ŚYV*, 30/17.
144. *Ibid.*, 16/27.

maṇikāra,[145] *rajjusarja,*[146] *vaṇija,*[147] *saṇaśca.*[148]

We find some names of the ornaments in the Vedic passages as follows : *hiraṇyaśiprā*[149] or ornaments for head,[150] *hiraṇyaśṛṅga,*[151] *sraja.*[152] all these are the ornamnets used by the males. On the other hand, women used the following ornaments : *opaśa*[153] to which M.M. Williams calls the top knot.[154] *Karṇaśobhana*[155] *sucakra,*[156] *hiraṇyakarṇa,*[157] etc., were the ornaments for ears. In the same way *niṣka*[158] *hiraṇya urvaśī,*[159] *rukma,*[160] etc., were used as garlands in which the pearls such as *hiraṇyamaṇi,*[161] etc., also were attached therewith. Rings like *ānūka*[162] also was found. *Hiraṇyavartanī* was used to tie the waist.[163] *Khādi*[164] and *hiraṇyapava*[165] were used as the ornaments of feet.

---

145. *ŚYV*, 30/7
146. *Ibid.*
147. *Ibid.*
148. *AV*, 2/4/5.
149. *ṚV*, 2/34/3.
150. *Ibid.*, 5/54/11.
151. *Ibid.*, 1/163/9.
152. *Ibid.*, 4/38/6.
153. *Ibid.*, 1/173/6; *AV*, 9/3/8; *ṚV*, 8/14/5; *ŚYV*, 11/56.
154. *SEDM*, p. 235.
155. *ṚV*, 8/78/3.
156. *Ibid.*, 10/85/20.
157. *Ibid.*, 1/122/14.
158. *Ibid.*, 2/33/10.
159. *Ibid.*, 7/31/3.
160. *Ibid.*, 2/34/2.
161. *Ibid.*, 1/33/8.
162. *Ibid.*, 5/33/9.
163. *Ibid.*, 5/75/3.
164. *Ibid.*, 5/54/11 and 1/64/10.
165. *Ibid.*, 9/83/43.

We have come to know about the ornaments as found in the *ṚV*. In the same way, the *Saṁhitās*, *Brāhmaṇa* literatures, and *Sūtra* literatures have a lot of passages describing about the ornaments and jewellery. To say briefly, the Vedic literature have ample informations about ornaments and jewellery.

CLOTH INDUSTRY

Sivadatta Gnani remarks, "The most important industry in the Vedic Age was to spin and warp round the thread and to weave clothes."[166] We find a weaver in the *ṚV* as being described as *vāsovāya*.[167] Some informations for proper weaving has thus been explained that there must be knowledge in (1) margin of the cloth, (2) marked margin, (3) well arrangement of thread, and (4) expertness in weaving.[168] The tools for this industry were (1) some wickets to roll the thread,[169] (2) suttle,[170] (3) loom,[171] etc. The male weaver was called *vāya*[172] whereas a female weaver was called *vayitrī*.[173] A Ṛgvedic passage says,"I know not either warp or woof, I know not the web they weave when moving to the contest."[174] This proves that a keen attention was paid while weaving a cloth. It was not easy to warp and woof for only Vaiśvānara is described to be the expert in this.[175]

166. *VSS*, p. 249.
167. *ṚV*, 10/26/6.
168. *AV*, 14/2/21.
169. *ŚYV*, 19/80.
170. *ṚV*, 10/130/2 and *ŚYV*, 19/83.
171. *Ibid.*, 10/71/9.
172. *Ibid.*, 2/3/6.
173. *PB*, 1/8/9.
174. *ṚV*, 6/9/2.
175. *Ibid.*, 6/9/3.

Method of weaving as we find in the Ṛgvedic books include warping and woofing,[176] pulling and fastening the thread[177] in the wickets.[178] A Ṛgvedic passage clearly mentions about the method of weaving in which it is said, "This do this fathers weave no hitherward are come: they sit beside the warp and cry, weave forth, weave back."[179] Perhaps in the large scale industries of clothes a group of people was appointed to weave length-wise while the another group was appointed to weave the breadth.[180] The same passage says that the weaving suttle made the *Sāma* hymns. Moreover, an Atharvanic passage informs[181] that the garments were woven with the one after another thread. The people used the wool of sheeps[182] for sweaters and *sana*s for sacks.[183]

TANNERY

The word *carman* or skin was frequently used in the Vedic literature. We meet the term in some Ṛgvedic passages in different meanings such as rays.[184] We find the word *'go'* in the meaning of *carman* in a Ṛgvedic passage where it has been described as the means of throwing the weapons. It says,

> From (the slings) leather strap you hurlet the metal bolt brought by the skillful from the sky. When assisting Kutsa, O much invoked one, you surrounded *śuṣṇa* with never ending

176. *ṚV*, 6/9/2.
177. *TS*, 6/1/1/4.
178. *ŚYV*, 19/80.
179. *ṚV* 10/130/1. (See Griffith)
180. *Ibid.*, 10/130/2.
181. *AV*, 10/7/42.
182. *ṚV*, 10/26/6.
183. *AV*, 2/4/5.
184. *ṚV*, 4/13/4.

deadly weapons.[185]

Secondly, we find a word *dhmātari*[186] where *dhmā* or tanner[187] did his work of tannery. On the other hand, we find the word *'go'* in the meaning of *carman* or leather strap in some of the passages of the *R̥V*.[188] So far the usage of leather is concerned we find the deer's leather having been used for seats in the sacrifices.[189] Thirdly, the warriors also are found wearing leather armours.[190] They generally used leathers to cover the chariots also.[191] Leather was used in making bags and the roof of the huts.[192] A R̥gvedic passage[193] which has been translated by Griffith as follows, "Her tooth a deer, dressed eagles feathers, bound with cowhide, launched forth, she flieth onward there where the horses speed hither and thither there may be arrows shelter and protect us" gives a description of the usage of the leather in the arrow. In the footnote for, "Her tooth a deer" he explains, "The point of the arrow is made of a piece of deer's horn attached to the shaft with leather strings."[194] In making strings of the bows[195] and the altars of the sacrifices, the leather is found being frequently used.[196]

185. *R̥V*, 1/121/9.
186. *Ibid.*, 5/9/5.
187. *VPJr*, p. 210.
188. *R̥V*, 6/46/14; 6/53/9; 1/121/9, etc.
189. *AV*, 11/1/8.
190. *R̥V*, 6/47/26.
191. *Ibid.*, 6/47/27.
192. *Ibid.*, 10/106/10.
193. *Ibid.*, 6/75/11.
194. *R̥Vg*, p. 331.
195. *R̥V*, 1/121/9.
196. *AV*, 10/9/2.

Leather was wet and melted[197] so that it might become smooth.[198]

IRON INDUSTRY

Studies of the Vedic literature leads one to the point that the people of Vedic ages were well acquainted with the usage of iron in their daily life. Blacksmith was respected as an intellectual.[199] A passage of the *ŚYV* informs us that blacksmith had to possess intellect for his works.[200] Their importance appears from the fact that they were counted as one of the respected class as that of the chariot builders.[201] The *ṚV* also describes the blacksmith as Brahmaṇasapati who is able to build new things.[202] Large scale usage of iron is found in the Vedas. A Vedic seer prays the Aśvins, "There are the pillars set upon it (the chariot) for its support."[203] This shows that the people of the Vedic Age used iron in large scale. Secondly the passage, "This stream of the Sarasvatī with fostering current comes forth, our sure defence, our fort of iron"[204] means that the forts and even the towns also were made with iron in those days. Later on the *TA* says that the warriors had the chariots having thousand of hubs.[205] People in their everyday life used iron in triturating *soma*,[206] abolishing diseases,[207] and also using it in a consecrated instrument.[208] On the other hand, the

197. *AV*, 8/55/3.
198. *Ibid.*, 6/48/18.
199. *AV*, 3/5/6 and *ŚYV*, 16/27.
200. *ŚYV*, 30/7.
201. *AV*, 3/5/6.
202. *ṚV*, 10/72/2.
203. *Ibid.*, 1/34/2.
204. *Ibid.*, 7/95/1.
205. *TA*, 1/31/1.
206. *ṚV*, 9/1/2.
207. *AV*, 9/5/4.
208. *Ibid.*, 5/28/1.

arrows were made of iron which were poisoned before throwing them to the enemies.[209] Another passage informs us that iron was used in making axes and it was later on sharpened.[210] The covers of the iron were pasted on the hoof of horses.[211] The passage, "Straight ye gave Viśpalā a leg of iron that she might move what time the conflict opened"[212] shows that iron was used in operation also.

WEAPON INDUSTRY

One of the important industries was the industry of weapons as because a large number of weapons were used in the Vedic Age. Many metals were used in making weapons and other arms.[213] The word *dhanuṣakāra*[214] and thus the other word *dhanuṣakṛt*[215] are found to denote bow-makers. As we find different types of weapons in the Vedic Age, it is sure that the weapon-makers did it in large scale. The list of some weapons is as follows : (1) *hastaghna* or a hand armour,[216] (2) *dhanuṣa* or a bow,[217] (3) *vakra* or a carved bow,[218] (4) *iṣu* or an arrow,[219] (5) *ṛṣṭi* or a spear,[220] (6) *rambhinī* or a spear,[221] (7) *sṛk* or a lance,[222] (8) *asi* or a sword,[223] (9) *paraśu* or an

209. *ṚV*, 6/75/15.
210. *Ibid.*, 6/3/5.
211. *Ibid.*, 1/163/9.
212. *Ibid.*, 1/116/15.
213. *Ibid.*, 1/31/15.
214. *ŚYV*, 30/7.
215. *Ibid.*, 16/46.
216. *ṚV*, 6/7/5.
217. *Ibid.*, 8/72/4; 77/5; 9/99/1; *AV* 4/4/6; 6/6; 5/18/8; *ŚB*, 1/5/4/6.
218. *AV*, 4/6/4.
219. *ṚV*, 2/24/8; 8/7/4; *AV* 1/13/4; *ŚYV* 16/3; *Nir*, 9/18.
220. *ṚV*, 1/37/1; 64/4; 64/8; 64/11; 5/52/2, etc.
221. *Ibid.*, 1/168/3.
222. *Ibid.*, 1/32/12; 180/2.
223. *Ibid.*, 1/120/20, 10/79/6; 10/86/18; *AV*, 11/9/1.

axe,[224] (10) *kuliśa* or an axe,[225] (11) *vajra* or a fetal weapon,[226] (12) *drughaṇa* or a club,[227] and (13) *pināka* or a club.[228] All these, except *vajra*, are general weapons which were used in the Vedic Age. Some other vital weapons were as follows : (1) *cakra*,[229] (2) gun powder,[230] (3) bullet of lead,[231] (4) electrical weapons,[232] (5) bullet throwing machines,[233] etc.

POTTERY

So far the pottery in the Vedic age is concerned, at first the Vedic culture should be analysed. The Vedic culture mainly depended upon *yajña* for which an *ukhā*[234] or the fire pan was strictly needed. The prepararion of the *ukhā* was as follows:

> The clay for this article was to be specially prepared. The clay was to be kneaded with boiled water by means of resin of the *palāśa* tree. Some goats' hair, sand of gravel, stone and iron-rust were to be mixed with the clay. Out of this kneaded clay the *ukhā* was made in three tiers welded together.[235]

The *ŚB* again mentions that there must be four nipples on the *ukhā*.[236] Secondly, *carman*[237] or the pot to heat milk, *kalaśa*[238] or a beaker to keep the *somarasa*, *kośa* or a type of bucket to hold *soma*, etc., also were found in the society.

---

224. *R̥V*, 1/27/3; 7/104/21; 10/28/8; 10/53/9, etc.
225. *Ibid.*, 1/32/5; 3/2/1.
226. *Ibid.*, 10/27/1; 1/32/5; 1/55/5.
227. *Ibid.*, 7/28/1.
228. *Ibid.*, 1/27/2.
229. *Ibid.*, 8/96/9.
230. *AV*, 8/8/2.
231. *Ibid.*, 1/16/2; 1/16/3; 1/16/4.
232. *Ibid.*, 9/2/14.
233. *Ibid.*, 1/26/1.
234. *R̥V*, 1/162/13 & 15.
235. *VIG*, p. 216.
236. *ŚB*, 6/5/2/16 & 19.
237. *R̥V*, 3/53/14; 5/30/15, etc. *AV*, 7/73/6; *ŚYV*, 8/61.

COINAGE

We find that the people of the Vedic Age conducted their economic exchanges through barter, using cow as the medium of exchange and also the coins. So far the coins are concerned, we find some special terms in the Vedic literature. First of all, we get evidence of buying and selling in a passage of the *R̥V* as follows :

> He bid a small price for a thing of value : I was content, returning, still unpurchased. He heightened not his insufficient offer. Simple and clever, both milk out of the udder.[239]

Another evidence of giving and taking is found in a passage of the *ŚYV*.[240] An Atharvanic passage also runs thus,

> Let the roads to the countries where our trades go on, be easy-going through which we may bring wealth to our homes as a result of selling and purchasing.[241]

We find some terms used for coins. But yet some scholars do not confess that the people of the Vedic Age had coins. Whatever the fact there may be, we find the following terms used as the means of exchange.

1. ***Niṣka :*** The term *niṣka* is confusing because at some place it denotes ornaments.[242] While at other place, it denotes coins.[243] The word *suniṣka* of a passage[244] denotes golden coin according to Khagendra Das Gupta.[245] But Griffith on the other hand, takes the

238. *R̥V*, 9/96/9.
239. *Ibid.*, 4/24/9.
240. *ŚYV*, 3/50.
241. *AV*, 3/15/2.
242. *R̥V*, 2/33/10; 8/47/15; 5/19/3, etc.
243. *Ibid.*, 1/126/2.
244. *Ibid.*, 4/37/4.
245. *ASSK*, p. 102.

term[246] in the sense of chain of gold. The *GB* in one place mentions of *niṣka* which meant as something placed for bet.[247] Likewise, we find it in the *ŚB* also.[248]

2. ***Manā*** : We find a word *manā* in the *ṚV* in a place[249] which has been translated as follows, "O Indra, you gave us cows, horses, oxen and golden *manā*s." Like the word *niṣka* its meaning also differed. For example, the word bears the meaning of desire' in some place of the *ṚV*[250] and the *ŚYV*.[251] The same word denotes "evil purpose" in a different passage.[252] Again the word *manāvasu*[253] is met in a *ṛk* which means perhaps "rich in constancy."[254] In the footnote of the same passage Griffith quotes Wilson as follows : "Rich in constancy : faithful friends of your worshippers."
3. ***Rayi :*** The term *rayi* is found frequently in the Vedic literature. Some scholars meant it to be the silver coins.[255] On the other hand, A.C. Das says, "Probably silver coins, called *rayi*s, also were in vogue in Ṛgvedic times."[256] The term to denote such "silver coin" were found in many passages.[257] Again,

---

246. *ṚVg,* p. 226.
247. Read, *tasya ha niṣka upahito babhūva, upavadāt bibhyato,ṚV,* 1/3/6.
248. *ŚB*, 11/4/1/1 & 4.
249. *ṚV*, 8/78/2.
250. *Ibid.*, 1/73/2.
251. *ŚYV*, 4/11.
252. *ṚV*, 2/33/5.
253. *Ibid.*, 5/74/1.
254. *ṚVg,* p. 276 and footnote on 5/74/1.
255. *ASSK,* p. 102 note on 5/74/1.
256. *RVCD,* p. 141.
257. *ṚV*, 5/33/6.

wealth was also expressed through the word *rayi*.[258]

4. ***Hiraṇyapiṇḍa and śatamāna :*** Some other words like *hiraṇyapiṇḍas*[259] also were used to denote the golden coins. In the same way, the word *śatamāna* is found in some places of the Vedic literature.[260]

The Vedic people not only used the above-mentioned coins rather they used even the living things such as cows and sheeps which were made the medium of exchange. For example, the passage, "Who for 10 milch kine purchaseth from me this Indra who is mine"[261] clearly says about the cows that were used as the means of transactions.

Trade and Commerce

From the study of the system of agriculture and industry, we come to know that the people of the Vedic Age made ample production for which they generally required markets and thus brought the system of selling and purchasing into practice. Generally, this condition created the atmosphere for trade and commerce.

We found the word *vaṇik*[262] in a passage of the *R̥V*. The passage shows that trade was popular in those days. The passage says,

> Whereby the clouds ye Bounteous Givers shed sweet rain for Dīrghaśravas for the merchants Auśija. Wherewith ye helped Kakṣīvān singer of your praise, Come hither into us, O Aśvins, with those aids.[263]

258. *R̥V*, 10/121/10.
259. *Ibid.*, 6/47/23.
260. Read, *hiraṇyam suvarṇaṁ śatamānam, ŚB*, 11/7/2.
261. *R̥V*, 4/24/10, see Griffth.
262. *Ibid.*, 1/112/11 & 5/45/6.
263. *Ibid.*, 1/112/11 see Griffith.

A seer prays Agni as the deity of the trades.[264] Aśvins were told to be the protectors of traders.[265] Another passage describes Bṛbhu to be the head of the trades. The passage goes thus : "Bṛbhu hath set himself above the Paṇis over their highest head, like the wide bush on the Ganges bank."[266]

The places where the selling and purchasing took place were called *prapaṇa*s.[267] The passage says, "O Agni, let the wealth which I want to take to the *prapaṇa*s get increased through your blessings." We find a mention of quarrel[268] in one such *prapaṇa*s. Griffith translated the passage as follows:

> He bid a small price of a thing of value : I was content, returning still unpurchased. He hightened not his insufficient offer. Simple and clever both milk out the udder.[269]

So far the trade and commerce of the Āryans are concerned, we may divide it into two parts : naval and regional. As we take naval trade for discussion, we find a passage in the *ṚV*[270] where Agni has been told to be the teacher for teaching the navigation art to the people. There is a *sūkta* in which a trader prays Prajāpati to bestow him wealth so that he might be able to collect several types of wealths.[271] The Western scholars denied the Āryans having the knowledge of voyage and naval trades. Basudevsaran Agrawal writes,

---

264. *ṚV*, 10/156/3.
265. *Ibid.*, 1/112/11.
266. *Ibid.*, 6/45/31.
267. *AV*, 3/15/5.
268. *ṚV*, 4/24/9.
269. *ṚVg*, p. 218.
270. *ṚV*, 2/13/5.
271. *AV*, 3/24.

> Did the naval trade take place in the Vedic Age? The Western scholars cogitated over it very deeply. They certainly came to the conclusion that the Aryans did not have any knowledge of sea and naval trades, but the studies of the *R̥V* is able to root it out.[272]

We find several evidences in the passage of the *R̥V* in which the Aśvins are described as the protectors of the Bhujyus. Some such passages are, firstly, : "Where with ye rescued Antaka when languishing deep in the pit and Bhujyus with unfailing help."[273] Secondly, "So ye with birds out of the sea and water bore Bhujyus."[274] Thirdly, "to Bhujyu and to Vasa ye come near with help. . . . "[275] Fourthly, "O, Aśvins, ye delivered Bhujyus from distresses." On the other hand, voyages for business are found frequently in the *R̥V* itself. "The pearl-desirers paid their attention to the sea."[276] The *yajamāna* seeks wealth and for that he gets into the sea."[277] "Tugra left Bhujyu in the seas."[278] A wealth-wisher merchant goes for voyage,[279] etc., are sufficient examples which we find in the R̥gvedic passages. Moreover, pearl which is named as *kr̥sana* in the *R̥V* is found in many passages.[280] The *AV* also mentions about the pearls which is found in the conches of the seas.[281] We get another term *guggulu or gulgul* in *AV*.[282] This has been described as to have been found in the seas. The western and the eastern

272. *VSSV*, p. 461.
273. *R̥V*, 1/112/6.
274. *Ibid.*, 6/62/6.
275. *Ibid.*, 10/65/12.
276. *Ibid.*, 1/48/3.
277. *Ibid.*, 1/56/2.
278. *Ibid.*, 1/116/3
279. *Ibid.*, 4/55/6.
280. *Ibid.*, 1/35/4; 10/68/1; 1/126/4 etc.
281. *AV*, 4/10/1.
282. *Ibid.*, 19/38/2, 2/36/7.

seas have been described in some places.[283] A very important evidence of the voyage of the Indians appears from the fact that they were able to use the ships having hundred oars.[284] Again, we find a person desirous for trade for earning money being made to cross the sea or river.[285] Not only these passages but several others are found everywhere in the Vedic passages.[286] That the seas also have the routes was known to the sages properly.[287] We find references to innumerable ships in the Ṛgvedic passages.[288] The regional trade was spread all over the country specially in Pāṭaliputra, Vārāṇasī, Sāket, Kauśāmbī, Mathurā and Takṣaśilā, etc.[289] As the evidence regarding production and trades are concerned we find a large number of Vedic passages relating to it. The people used some effective carriers to carry the things from one place to the another. For the purpose, they used oxen,[290] horses, camels, dogs[291] and buffaloes[292] in general. Moreover, chariots, *anas*,[293] bullocks or *anaḍvāḥ*,[294] carriages drawn by horses[295] also were in existence. On the other hand, we find *aśvaparṇa*[296] and

283. *AV*, 11/5/6 & *ŚB*, 1/6/3/1.
284. *ṚV*, 1/116/5.
285. *Ibid.*, 2/5/5.
286. *Ibid.*, 7/88/3; 7/33/8; 1/71/1; 6/20/12, etc.
287. *Ibid.*, 1/25/7.
288. *Ibid.*, 1/56/2.
289. *HSSAJS*, p. 422.
290. *ṚV*, 8/46/30.
291. *Ibid.*, 8/46/48.
292. *Ibid.*, 9/33/1.
293. *Ibid.*, 4/30/16; 8/91/7; 10/102/6; *AV*, 12/1/47; 14/1/41; *ChU*, 7/15/1; *ŚB*, 1/1/25.
294. *Ibid.*, 4/30/10; 10/86/18; *ŚYV* 22/22; *ChU*, 7/15/1.
295. *ŚB*, 3/4/35.
296. *ṚV*, 1/88/1.

anaśva[297] chariots. From the above evidences it seems clear that those things were commonly used in trade of those times.

ROUTES

"Thy seeketh in thy course Krumu and Gomatī"[298] — thus, the routes of rivers are seen mentioned here. The people expected to have unobstructed paths.[299] A Ṛgvedic passage describes the method of making the routes by Indra in which it has been told that he left the blackened path where he went.[300] The verse indicates that Indra burnt the forests into ashes and made the route. In the *ṚV*[301] and the *AV*[302] Indra, Agni and Soma are mentioned as *pathakṛt* or the road-builders. Somewhere Soma is found to be the guardian of roads[303] whereas the same respect goes to Pūṣan in many of the Ṛgvedic passages.[304]

QUALITIES OF THE ROADS

Mentions about such roads which were well-built and were without dust[305] has been found. On the other hand, a passage of *AV* describes about the straight roads.[306] Improper roads also come into description.[307] Whenever, people got rough roads and felt uneasy in gaining speed,[308] whenever the travellers felt the journey insecured, they

297. *Ibid.*, 3/66/7.
298. *ṚV*, 10/56/6, see Griffith.
299. *Ibid.*, 2/34/5.
300. *Ibid.*, 1/140/9.
301. *Ibid.*, 6/21/12.
302. *AV*, 18/2/53.
303. *Ibid.*
304. *ṚV*, 1/43/3; 6 & 8; 3/62/13; 8/28/6.
305. *Ibid.*, 1/35/11.
306. *AV*, 14/1/34.
307. *Ibid.*, 12/1/46.
308. *ṚV*, 1/106/1.

generally prayed the divine power to protect them from danger.[309] So far the types of roads are concerned, we find *patha*[310] and *prapatha*.[311] While mentioning *patha* and *prapatha*, Griffith translated the 10/17/6 of the *Ṛ̥V* as follows:

> Pūṣan was born to move on distant pathways on the road far from the earth and far from heaven. To both most wanted places of assembly he travels and returns with perfect knowledge.[312]

On the other hand, *mahāpatha* is found in the Vedic literature in many places.[313] We find the mentioning of *āvasatha* or rest houses.[314] Perhaps the bridges were built over the rivers.[315] People in some places fixed pillars[316] on the way so that the travellers might get the direction and signal.

COMMODITIES

So far the commodities mention in the Vedic literature are concerned we find a lot of evidences scattered hither and thither. But yet the commodities as listed by Balaram Srivastava from the Vedic literature[317] are as follows : (1) ass, (2) antelope, (3) bull, (4) cow, (5) lamb, (6) horse, (7) ox, (8) honey, (9) clothing, (10) *drāpi*, (11) leather bag, (12) leather bottle, (13) pearl, (14) pearl-shell, (15) shoes, (16) wooden garments, (17) barley, (18) basket, (19) beans, (20)

---

309. *Ṛ̥V*, 1/42/7 & 8; 4/32/4; 6/47/7; 8/82/10; *AV*, 12/1/47; *ŚYV* 16/10.
310. *Ṛ̥V*, 10/17/6.
311. *AV*, 7/9/1; 18/2/55; 18/2/49; *Ṛ̥V*, 10/63/16; *AB*, 8/15.
312. *Ṛ̥Vg*, p. 541.
313. *AB*, 4/17/8; *ChU*, 9/6/5; *Ṛ̥V*, 1/166/9; *ChU*, 4/1/1.
314. *AB*, 3/12; *AV*, 9/6/5; *Ṛ̥V*, 1/166/9; *ChU*, 4/1/1.
315. *Ṛ̥V*, 9/41/2; *AB*, 3/35; *ŚB*, 13/2/10/1.
316. *AV*, 14/2/6.
317. Quoted from *TCAIB*, p. 270.

coverlet, (21) cord, (22) fan, (23) fibre plants, (24) cotton, (25) hemp, (26) flax, (27) garment, (28) under-garment, (29) turban, (30) silk garment, (32) wool, (33) millet, (34) mustard, (35) *oṣadhī*, or pipper red, pipper black and pipper, (36) rope, (37) *śarkarā* or candied sugar, (38) sugar-cane, (39) *taṇḍula*, (40) *vrīhi*, (41) vessel or wood (42) wheat, (43) *masūra*, (44) *madya*, (45) arrow, (46) bow, (47) bronze, (48) bucket, (49) copper, (50) copper-razor, (51) collyrium, (52) cymbal, (53) flute, (54) gold, (55) jewel, (56) lance, (57) lead, (58) *lohita lavaṇa* or red salt, (59) lute, (60) mirror, (61) needle, (62) ornaments, (63) anklet, armlet, (64) necklace, (65) ring, (66) gold-chain, (67) diadem, (68) head ornament, (69) ear-ring, (70) plough share, (71) *paraśu*, (72) sickle, (73) silver, (74) trapu (?) (75) umbrella, (76) vessel, (77) drinking vessel, (78) cooking vessel, and (79) pots. Such things were thought to be the trading commodities in general. Moreover, the ships and the chariots also were perhaps exported to the other lands. This analysis of the trade in the Vedic period presents a landmark in the history in general. In one place, we find a seller selling an idol of Lord Indra.[318] Perhaps such idols also were sold in the markets. Another passage informs us about the *soma* plant[319] becoming a trading commodity.

PAṆIS

We find a lot of passages in the Vedas regarding Paṇis. "Who were they is difficult to determine"[320] but yet we may go through the *Nir* and grammar to determine the term. *Nirkuta* says,[321] "Paṇi is *vaṇik* or a merchant, he keeps the

318. *Ṛ̥V*, 4/24/10 & 8/1/5.

319. *Ibid.*, 4/32/20.

320. *VI*, 1/534.

321. Read, *paṇiḥ vaṇik bhavati, paṇi paṇanāl, vaṇik paṇyaṁ nenekti* — *Nir*, 2/17.

things to be sold cleanly." Again the root *paṇ* when used with suffix *ij* the word *paṇij* is got. After a *sūtra* of the *uṇādi* chapter,[322] *pa* changes into *va* and thus the word *vaṇij* is got. So, it seems that the Paṇis were the traders who went abroad for trade and commerce.

The conversation between Saramā and Paṇis gives a description of the Paṇis. The bitch Saramā is found in many books of the *ṚV*. She is a messenger,[323] hound of Indra,[324] clever[325] who dedicated herself in the service of Indra. Paṇis, on the other hand, were *mṛdhravāca*[326] and *ayajvan*[327] or those who did not make oblations to the gods. The term *mṛdhravāca* means sweet spoken people.[328] Some passages mention Paṇis to be greedy[329] and as such were not held in high esteem.[330] They were desirous in eating[331] and *arādhasa* or he who never donated.[332] Somewhere they are called usury[333] for which they were identified as *bekanat*.[334] They were "foolish, faithless, rudely speaking, niggards, without belief or sacrifice or worship."[335] All those above-mentioned adjectives for Paṇis were used because the well-cultured people hated them and prayed gods to kill them. They

---

322. Read, *paṇerijādeśca vaḥ, Uṇādi-sūtra,* 228.
323. *ṚV*, 1/72/8.
324. *Ibid.*, 10/108/2.
325. Griffith's footnote on *ṚV*, 1/62/3 & 3/31/6.
326. *Ibid.*, 7/6/3.
327. *Ibid.*, 1/182/3.
328. *Nir*, 6/13.
329. *ṚV*, 6/51/14.
330. *Ibid.*, 1/182/3 Griffith's note.
331. *Ibid.*, 6/51/10.
332. *Ibid.*, 8/64/2.
333. *Ibid.*, 8/66/10.
334. *Nir*, 6/06.
335. *ṚV*, 7/6/3.

somewhere prayed gods to seize their wealths[336] and somewhere to harm them.[337] The result of that envy and hatred, led them to defeat the Paṇis in the wars.[338] Divodāsa[339] and Indra[340] are found in two different passages fighting against the Paṇis. In the fights, Indra took away their wealth.[341]

The Paṇis did not know about Indra, because they were found saying,[342] "What is that Indra-like. What is his aspect whose envoy, Saramā, from a far thou comest?" They had stolen the cows of Indra for which Saramā was appointed to approach to the Paṇis as a messenger.[343] Another passage informs that they assimilated with the other people of society later on. Balaram Srivastava on this matter remarks,

> Gradually in the Vedic economy trade found a place and the Paṇis were assimilated in the Vedic society. The process of assimilation was almost complete by the time of completion of *R̥V*. Therefore, in the post-R̥gvedic period the expression of antagonism between the Paṇi and the *r̥ṣi* becomes very rare.[344]

The assimilation of the Paṇis appears from the fact that once aPaṇi, Br̥bhu by name, became laudable even for the *r̥ṣis*.[345] Not only so, even Indra was once prayed as Paṇi in a R̥gvedic passage.[346]

336. *R̥V*, 8/45/15.
337. *R̥V*, 3/53/1; 9/22/6; 10/48/1, etc.
338. *Ibid.*, 6/39/2.
339. *Ibid.*, 6/61/1; 6/61/2; 6/61/3.
340. *Ibid.*, 6/39/2.
341. *Ibid.*, 4/25/7.
342. *Ibid.*, 10/108/3.
343. *Ibid.*, 10/108.
344. *TCAIB*, p. 19.
345. *R̥V*, 6/46/31; 6/46/32 and 6/46/33.
346. *Ibid.*, 8/45/14.

8

Needs

Primary Needs

It is obvious to all that man cannot live by bread alone, but equally obvious is the fact that man has to first and foremost fulfil the needs of food, dress and residence. After that he goes to fulfil other needs such as medicines, music, ornaments, etc. We are going to discuss in this chapter about those needs and how the Vedic nation met up those problems.

FOOD AND DRINKS

Food

The main food, as described in the Vedas, is barley or *yava*[1] which was sowed in the fields before rain.[2] Perhaps the newly germinated bud was planted in rain.[3] In course of time, barley got ripened[4] and then it was harvested. The field after harvest was ploughed again.[5] Many a things made from barley have been found, such as *yavāgu*,[6] barley mixed *soma*,[7] *karambha*,[8] a special type of juice prepared after barley

1. *R̥V*, 1/23/15, 1/66/3, 1/14/11, 7/3/4, etc.
2. *Ibid.*, 2/5/5 & 5/35/3.
3. *Ibid.*, 1/111/21.
4. *Ibid.*, 1/135/8.
5. *Ibid.*, 1/176/2.
6. *TB*, 2/8/8.
7. *R̥V*, 1/187/9, 2/21/1, 8/94/4.
8. *Ibid.*, 1/187/6, 3/52/7, 6/56/1; *AV*, 1/4/7, 6/16/1.

was triturated.[9] Moreover, we find sweet breads oiled with *ghī*[10] in the *R̥V* named as *apūpa*. These were made of rice[11] and barley both.[12] The existence of several types of rice is found as *odana* in the Vedic literature. The word *odana* is met in the *R̥V* first.[13] Again we meet the word in the *AV*.[14] Rice was boiled in the milk[15] and curd respectively.[16] The rice was cooked mixing sesamum,[17] horse beans[18] and kidney beans.[19] The cooked rice has been named as *pakva*[20] and *pacata*.[21] The cook was said *pakṭr*.[22] The *ŚB*[23] also says about *pakṭr*. On the other hand, the people of the Vedic society used to eat bread also.[24] An Atharvanic passage informs us about curry fried in mustard oil.[25] The next one informs us about the curry prepared of leaves of the mustard plants.[26] After all, people used barley in their food frequently.[27] On the other hand, milk also played an important role in making food tasty.[28] The *AV* presents a

9. *ŚB*, 2/5/2/14, 4/2/4/18.
10. *R̥V*, 10/45/9.
11. *ŚB*, 2/2/5/12.
12. *Ibid.*, 4/2/5/19 & *ChU* 3/1/1.
13. *R̥V*, 8/69/14 & 8/77/10.
14. *AV*, 4/14/7.
15. *ŚB*, 2/5/3/4, 11/5/7/5; *BU*, 6/4/13.
16. *BU*, 6/4/14.
17. *Ibid.*, 6/4/15.
18. *Ibid.*
19. *Ibid.*, 6/4/16 & *ŚB*, 11/5/7/5.
20. *R̥V*, 6/63/9.
21. *Ibid.*, 1/61/7 & 10/16/8.
22. *AV*, 11/1/17 & 12/3/17.
23. *ŚB*, 3/3/4/17 & 10/4/2/19.
24. *R̥V*, 4/24/5; 7; 25/6, etc.
25. *AV*, 6/16/1.
26. *Ibid.*, 6/16/2.
27. *R̥V*, 7/3/4 & 1/187/9.
28. *Ibid.*, 6/45/7.

list of ideal diet such as of rice, barley, kidney bean and sesamum.[29] Again, parched barley,[30] milk, curd and *ghī*[31] powder of the parched beans having mixed with curd[32] were the items of food of the Āryan people.

Drinks

So far the drinks of the Vedic people is concerned, we find the mention of the *soma*-juice in the pages of Vedic literature. The characteristics, its preparation, and after-effects of drinking it are such aspects which has left a very eligible landmark in the history of India. So our aim is to find out some data regarding the *somarasa.* First of all, *somarasa* has been described a thick drinking material.[33] Secondly, we find six qualities of juices[34] such as, "For us the *soma* juice flow, the drops best furthers of our weal, effused as friends with a spot, benevolent, friends of light."[35] On the other hand, *soma* has said to have minerals within it. We find the word *tridhātu* for these minerals,[36] which has been translated as "triply-mingled" by Griffith.[37]

So far the preparation of juice is concerned, first of all the *soma* plant was needed. A. Chinnaswamy Sastri writes,

> This plant was available only on mountain tops. A Brāhmaṇa was sent to fetch it, and it was bought from him

---

29. *AV*, 6/140/2.
30. *ṚV*, 3/52/4.
31. *Ibid.*, 3/30/4.
32. *Ibid.*, 3/52/7.
33. *Ibid.*, 9/98/2.
34. *Ibid.*, 9/101/10.
35. *ṚVg*, p. 522.
36. *ṚV*, 9/86/46.
37. *ṚVg*, p. 510.

on the second day of the sacrifice after paying the stipulated price.[38]

Mainly, the plant was found on the top of the Muñjavān mountain.[39] Whatever the fact there may be, but it is believed that after the collection of the *soma* plant it was crushed and squeezed into water. Thirdly, it was filtered and the things like milk and honey were mixed into it and then, finally, the prepared *soma* was kept in earthen pitchers. This whole process of the preparation of the *soma* juice has been mentioned in two passages of the *R̥V*.[40] The second process of the preparation of the *soma* juice was very simple. The squeezed juice of the plant was perhaps put into a pot and covered with a piece of cloth.[41] It seems that it was churned then for which we find a passage in the *R̥V* which mentions about the sound of the *soma* plant produced during its preparation.[42] It takes green colour then.[43] After that, curd was mixed and purified.[44] On the other hand, we find mixing of *ghī*,[45] milk and barley[46] also. Juice was then filtered through "the sheep's fair bright fleece."[47] It took yellow colour and finally it was put into the vats of wood.[48]

---

38. Synopsis of the *soma* plant by A. Chinnaswamy Sastri. Our Heritage — a Bulletin of the Department of Post Graduate Training and Research, Sanskrit College, Calcutta, vol. I part I, Jan-June 1953, p. 85.
39. *TS*, 1/8/6/1; *ŚB*, 2/5/3/17.
40. *R̥V*, 8/2/2 & 3.
41. *Ibid.*, 6/69/5
42. *Ibid.*, 9/18/7.
43. *Ibid.*, 9/19/3 & 9/33/4.
44. *Ibid.*, 9/22/3 & 7/32/4
45. *Ibid.*, 5/42/3.
46. *Ibid.*, 3/42/1.
47. *Ibid.*, 9/69/4 & 9/10/1.
48. *Ibid.*, 9/28/4.

Is Soma Juice a kind of wine?: Some of the Western and Eastern scholars have expressed their views regarding *soma* juice that it was a kind of wine.[49] But as per our researches the *soma* juice was not intoxicating drinks rather an inspiring and strengthening tonic.

1. It has been told as *durmada* in a passage of the *ṚV*.[50] The word *durmada* itself reveals that it was not an intoxicating drink.
2. Another passage of the same says that[51] dice, wine, and anger pulls a man towards sin. On the other hand, we find a lot of passage in the Vedic literature praising *soma* juice.
3. Intoxicating things do not make a man strong whereas *soma* juice is found being described as a strengthening tonic.[52]
4. *Soma* has been praised as a purifying drink in the Vedas.[53] The whole ninth book of the *ṚV* has been allotted to describe the qualities of the *soma* juice.
5. Drinking wine is prohibited in the Vedas[54] whereas people were inspired to drink *soma*.
6. People were advised to drink *soma* before they sat for worship.[55] Had it been a kind of wine, the seers would not advise to drink it before the worship of God.
7. On the other hand, *soma* has been enlisted as an ideal drink in ideal meal.[56]

---

49. *Somasvarūpa Vimarśa* by A. Chinnaswamy Sastri. Our Heritage vol. I 1953, p. 94.
50. Read, *durmadā na surāyām, ṚV*, 8/2/12.
51. *Ibid.*, 7/86/6.
52. *Ibid.*, 8/48/3.
53. *Ibid.*, 9/67/25 & 26.
54. *Mai. Sam.*, 2/4/6; *TS*, 1/3/3/6; *MS*, 11/93.
55. *ṚV*, 8/46/16.
56. *Ibid.*, 3/17/3.

8. A *yājñika* was advised to use *surā* as well as *soma* in the *sautrāmaṇi* sacrifice. Had *soma* been a kind of *surā* how the existence of the both is found?[57]

Again, the word *mada* in the Vedas means "delight" but not intoxication. For example, a passage of the *ṚV*[58] has the word *mādàyasva* which has been explained by Sāyaṇācārya as *hṛsto bhava* or, "be delighted". In the same way we find *mandīnām madamānam* in another passage.[59] An Atharvaṇic passage also reveals the truth.[60] A. Chinnaswamy Sastri in the synopsis of his article, *Somasvarūpa-vimarśa* writes,

> Western scholars and some Indian scholars think that this juice produces intoxication. Nothing can be farther from truth than this. The *soma* is neither an intoxicant nor a stimulant. On the other hand, the Vedas attribute some good qualities to it. It contributes to mental peace and increases vigour, it keeps the brain cool, offers inspiration to work, helps endurance, assures longivity and prevents old age. Further, it is not correct to hold that only the taking of wine in the ordinary way had been prohibited, and there was not prohibition against taking that which remained after sacrifice.[61]

Problem of meat eating in the Vedas

Some references such as of the *ṚV*[62] mention that the ancient Āryans ate the buffalo flesh. Jogiraj Basu referring that particular passage of the *ṚV* translated it as follows, "Gods organised a feast with three hundred buffaloes."[63] He

---

57. Quoted from *VSR*, p. 107.
58. *ṚV*, 10/104/3.
59. *Ibid.*, 10/96/6.
60. *AV*, 20/36/6.
61. Synopsis of *Somasvarūpavimarśa* by Chinnaswamy Sastri in Our Heritage by Sanskrit College Calcutta, Jan-June, 1953, p. 85.
62. *ṚV*, 5/29/7.
63. *VPJr*, p. 215.

secondly refers the *ŚB*[64] in which it has been mentioned to have, "I shall eat if the beef is soft."[65] Vedic Index with the reference to a Ṛgvedic passage[66] informs, "The marriage ceremony was accompanied by the slaying of oxen, clearly for food."[67]

Griffith in the footnote of a Ṛgvedic passage remarks,[68] "The corpse is addressed. Flesh, the caul and other parts of a slaughtered animal which covered the corpse to prevent to quick and complete crimation."[69] Whitney translated a Vedic passage[70] as "the heroes cooked a spotted ox."[71] The same has been translated by Griffith as, "The mighty man have dressed the spotted bullock."[72] On the other hand, the same passage is found in the *AV* which has been translated by him in the other way as, "The heroes cooked and dressed the spotted bullocks."[73] The *BU* also has been brought into account to prove meat-eating tradition of the Aryans.[74] The *Vedic Index* in one place mentions,

> The usual food of the Vedic Indians, as far as flesh was considered can be gathered from the list of sacrificial vicitm, what man ate he presented to God — that is the sheep, the goat and the ox.[75]

Acarya Baladev Upadhyaya also admits the fact[76] and

64. *VPJr*, p. 215 with the referance to *ŚB*, 3/1/2/21.
65. Read, *aśnāmi evamahamaṁśalaṁ cet bhavati*, *ŚB*, 3/1/2/21.
66. *VI*, 10/85/13.
67. *Ibid.*, 1/549 & *CCRVD*, p. 73.
68. *ṚV*, 10/16/7.
69. *ṚVg*, p. 540.
70. *ṚV*, 1/164/43.
71. Quoted from *KPAMS*, p. 23.
72. *ṚVg*, 113.
73. Quoted from *KPAMS*, p. 24.
74. *BU*, 6/4/18.
75. Quoted from *KPAMS*, p. 36.
76. *VSSB*, p. 438.

presents some passage of the *ṚV*[77] in the support of that argument.

1. The passage through which Dr. Jogiraj Basu wants to express the meat-eating incident of the Āryan gods has been translated by Sāyaṇa in some other way. He writes, "Agni made three hundred buffaloes active." Sāyaṇa says that the word *apacat* means making active[78] but not "to cook".
2. *Aśnāmi evamahamaṁśalam cet bhavati* of the ŚB[79] has been used by Basu to show beef-eating incident.[80] But the whole passage is used to hinder beef eating. This particular sentence is only of Yājñavalkya but not of the writer of the *Brāhmaṇa* or of the Indian people in general.
3. *Hanyante gāvo*[81] has been translated by Griffith as "cows were slain"[82] but we find the root *han* in the meaning of sending also.[83] Hence the meaning of this line is "cows were sent" but not "cows were slain."
4. The line, *gobhiḥ śriṇīta matsaram*[84] has been translated by the Western and some Indian scholars as "Beef was boiled with *soma* juice." But the word *go* denotes cow, milk, curd, *ghī*, cowdung and its urine also. So here in this passage, "people were advised to cook *soma* juice in milk,"[85] is the meaning.

---

77. *ṚV*, 1/64/10, 5/54/15.
78. *Ibid.*, 5/9/7 see Sāyaṇa's note.
79. *ŚB*, 3/1/2/21.
80. *VPJr*, p. 215.
81. *ṚV*, 10/85/13.
82. *ṚVg*, p. 594.
83. *ṚVSāy*, 10/85/13.
84. *ṚV*, 9/46/4.
85. *ṚVSāy*, 9/46/4.

5. In the same way, while translating the passage[86] Griffith and other scholars have mentioned that the crops was covered with beef. But on the other hand, some scholars have meant it as to give *ghī* in the kindling fire.[87]
6. The part of the passage, *ukṣānam pr̥ṣṇim apacanta* has been translated by scholars as "spotted ox was cooked"[88] but the word *ukṣā* meant clouds according to *Nir.*[89] Hence the meaning of the lines is "the clouds were made matured." Again Sāyaṇa meant the word *ukṣā* to be *soma.*[90]
7. The direct meaning of the passage of the *BU* is[91] "He who wishes to have a scholar, eloquent and expert in the Vedas and also a long living son, should cook meat and rice mixing together and eat with *ghī* otherwise they should cook with the flesh of *ukṣā* or of an ox. Here the word *māṁsa* denotes, the flesh of fruit."[92] Satyananda Sastri reads it as *māṣaudanam.* Secondly, *ukṣā* is *soma* according to Sāyaṇa.[93] *Vr̥ṣabha* is a plant collected from the Himālayas.[94] On the other hand, our studies lead us to some other points to think.
   (i) The Āryans thought, "Think that all living beings have oneness with you.[95] Consider others with

86. *R̥V*, 10/16/7
87. *KPAMS*, p. 17.
88. See Witney on *R̥V*, 1/164/43.
89. *Nir*, 12/9/1.
90. See note of *R̥VSāy*, 1/164/43.
91. *BU*, 6/4/18.
92. Read, *mā hiṁsyāt sarvabhūtāni, Kalyāṇ : Go Seva Aṅka*, Vignanananda Sarasvati, p. 147.
93. See Sāyaṇa on *R̥V*, 1/164/43.
94. Quoted from *KPAMS*, p. 28.
95. *ŚYV*, 40/7.

friendly glances.[96] Do not kill men.[97] Do not kill other creatures,[98] etc." Now, a question arises how such people supported the killings of others for a little enjoyment?

(ii) A R̥gvedic passage says that a cow-slaughterer must be treated as a man-slaughterer.[99] The *R̥V* says, on the other hand, that a cow slaughterer should be sentenced to death.[100] He must be punished by killing with cannon.[101]

(iii) A cow is *aghnyā* or "non-worth killing" in all literatures.[102]

We feel that a large field of research in this field is lying vacant. In the conclusion we want to say that the people in the Vedic age wished to have such food which could create purity and energy in men,[103] that must bestow good health[104] and for that, people wished very sapid diet.[105]

DRESSES

The word *vastra* is found first of all in the *R̥V*.[106] The passage is used to pray Agni to keep its radiance covered like clothes. The rays of Uṣā have been described as golden pieces of clothes in another passage of the *R̥V*.[107] So, in the very beginning of the Vedic literature we find the existence of

---

96. *Ibid.*, 36/18.
97. *Ibid.*, 16/6.
98. *Ibid.*, 12/32.
99. *R̥V*, 7/56/17.
100. *Ibid.*, 10/87/16.
101. *AV*, 1/16/4 & *ŚYV*, 13/45.
102. *ŚYV*, 12/73; *R̥V*, 8/102/19; *TS*, 3/3/9/2; *Nir*, 11/43; *AV*, 5/18/1.
103. *R̥V*, 1/187/1.
104. *Ibid.*
105. *Ibid.*, 1/187/2.
106. *R̥V*, 1/26/1.
107. *R̥V*, 1/134/4.

clothes among the Vedic people. A.C. Das thinks, "Thou art *vastra* probably originally meant the skin which protects the *basā* or fat, and afterwards come to mean a covering or clothing."[108] On the other hand, why people used to put on beautiful clothes is expressed in a passage of the *ŚB*[109] as follows: "Outward appearance is the main garment of a man." A well dressed person is often asked "Who can this person be? It is so only because of his outward appearance." A Ṛgvedic passage says that cloth itself is a kind of ornament.[110] While being dressed, attention was given to the fact that the clothes must be auspicious[111] and delighting.[112] People wore new[113] and embroidered[114] clothes while going out. Such beautiful and attractive clothes were worn at the time of going out of home[115] and on festivals.[116] The wife of a sacrificer must wear the garment of *kuśa* at the time of sacrifices.[117] Women also put on beautiful clothes to attract their husbands.[118] Ladies wore turban at the time of sacrifices as Indrāṇī also is found wearing turban in a passage of the *ŚB*.[119] On the other hand, a king put on *uṣṇīśa* while sitting for *rājasūya* sacrifice.[120]

The importance of clothes appears from the fact that a

---

108. *RCD*, p. 211.
109. *ŚB*, 114/4/1/15.
110. *ṚV*, 5/30/14.
111. *AV*, 14/1/30.
112. *Ibid.*, 14/1/30.
113. *Ibid.*, 14/2/44.
114. *ṚV*, 5/55/6.
115. *AV*, 14/2/44.
116. *ṚV*, 1/124/8.
117. *ŚB*, 5/2/1/8.
118. *ṚV*, 5/3/2, 10/71/4, 10/107/9.
119. *ŚB*, 14/2/1/8.
120. *PGS*, 2/6/25 & *KSS*, 15/5/3.

father presented cloth to his son.[121] Mainly mother used to weave clothes to present him.[122] Weaving seems to take an important part in the life of the Vedic woman.[123] A woman also was advised to cover her body with clothes.[124] We have some informations about various clothes in the Vedic literature. Those are as follows :

Atkā : *Atkā* was a kind of cloth which is found mentioned twice in the *ṚV*.[125] We find this word used as armour in one place[126] while its another use is obscure.[127]

Adhivāsa : *Adhivāsa* as we find in the *ŚB*[128] seems to be a loose long shirt used by people. Griffith translated the term to be "mantle."[129] A passage of the *ṚV* says that an *adhivāsa* was used for a horse also.[130] Another important passage of the same[131] describes grass as an *adhivāsa* of the mother earth. After all, Baladev Upadhyaya seems correct when he says it to be an upper garment to cover the body.[132]

Upavasana : *Upavasana* seems to be a kind of cloth having many colour in it. Perhaps the cloth was given to the bridegroom in the marriage.[133]

Uṣṇīśa : *Uṣṇīśa* was a kind of turban which was used at the

121. *ṚV*, 1/160/2.
122. *Ibid.*, 5/47/6.
123. *Ibid.*, 10/26/6.
124. *Ibid.*, 8/33/3.
125. *VI*, 1/49.
126. *ṚV*, 10/49/3.
127. *Ibid.*, 10/99/9.
128. *ŚB*, 5/4/4/9.
129. *RVg*, 10/5/4.
130. *ṚV*, 10/5/4.
131. *Ibid.*, 1/104/9
132. *VSSB*, p. 443.
133. *AV*, 14/2/49.

time of *yajña* or sacrifice. We find Indrāṇī using *uṣṇīśa*.[134] Another passage of the *ŚB*[135] informs us that a king used to wear *uṣṇīśa* at the time of the *vājapeya* sacrifice.[136]

Drāpi : The word *drāpi* is frequently found in the Vedic literature. But so far the proper meaning of the term is concerned there is contradiction. For example, Sāyaṇa meant it to be armour[137] whereas Macdonell meant it to be a kind of upper garment.[138] A passage of the *R̥V* mentions the golden *drāpi* used by Savitā which has been later described as a yellow colour *drāpi*.[139] An Atharvanic passage also mentions of golden *drāpi* used by general women.[140]

Nīvi : *Nīvi* was a kind of petticoat which was used by both the gents and the ladies. A passage of the *ŚB* informs the matter.[141] On the other hand, two passages of the *AV* have expressed the matter that *nīvi* was "doned" on the waist.[142]

Peśas : *Peśas* seems to be an important garment in the Vedic age as we find about it in the *R̥V*. It had high price and only the aristocratic society could afford to wear it.[143] Another passage of the same mentions that it glittered like the rays of the sun.[144] We came to know that to weave a *peśas* minimum two weavers were needed and they should

---

134. *ŚB*, 14/2/1/8.
135. *Ibid.*, 5/3/5/23.
136. *PGS*, 2/6/25.
137. *R̥V*, 1/25/13, 1/116/10, 4/53/2.
138. *VI*, 1/429.
139. *R̥V*, 4/53/2.
140. *AV*, 5/7/10.
141. *ŚB*, 1/2/4/13.
142. AV, 8/2/16 & 14/2/50.
143. *R̥V*, 8/31/8.
144. *Ibid.*, 7/34/11.

centre their attention very keenly.[145] A passage of the *ŚYV* describes Sarasvatī as the weaver of the *peśas*.[146] The existence of the black *peśas* also is found in the same.[147] Two Ṛgvedic passages in a place say that *peśas* were also used by the dancers at the time of dancing.[148]

Pratidhi : *Pratidhi* seems to be a sewed cloth. This type of cloth is mentioned in the reference to the description of a bridegroom.[149] The next passage mentions about *pratidhi*.[150] Baladev Upadhyaya supposes it to be a bodice.[151]

Mala : We find a passage in the *ṚV* where *mala* has been used to denote *valkala* or the skin of a tree.[152] On the other hand, Atharvanic passages give no such clear picture on the matter.[153] A.C. Das informs us that the word *mala*, occurring in the verse X/136/2, has been interpreted in the St. Peterburg Dictionary as a leathern garment; interpretation being derived from the root *mlā* to tan. But Ludwig and Zimmer think that it means only a "soiled garment" which was probably consistent with the character of the hermits.[154]

Vāsas : The word *vāsa* denotes cloth in general. We find the word in the *ṚV* mentioning the same.[155] Another passage expresses the importance of clothes in the winter season.[156]

145. *ṚV*, 2/3/6.
146. *ŚYV*, 19/82.
147. *Ibid* , 19/89.
148. *ṚV*, 1/92/4 & 5.
149. *AV*, 14/1/6 & 7.
150. *Ibid.*, 14/1/8.
151. *VSSB*, p. 443.
152. *ṚV*, 10/136/2.
153. *AV*, 6/115/3; 7/89/3; 10/5/24.
154. *RCP*, p. 210.
155. *ṚV*, 10/102/2.
156. *Ibid.*, 1/34/1.

Perhaps the word *vāsa* denoted linen also.[157] This passage has been translated by Griffith as follows : "Night spreadth out her garments."[158] *Vāsa* was used to cover a horse also.[159] On the other hand, a R̥gvedic passage informs us that a *vāsa* was raiment of body.[160] Those *vāsas* were embroidered and presented to esteemed persons and gods.[161]

Ajina : So far the term *ajina* is concerned, Monier-Williams informs us that it is (1) the skin of goat, (2) the hairy skin of a tiger.[162] A.C. Das says, "The skin seems to be the clothing of the Aryans in the primitive times."[163] He further mentions, "The word *ajina* is derived from *aja*, a goat."[164] An Atharvanic passage mentions the *ajina* of a deer.[165] A passage of the *ŚB* has been used to denote the person who has more skin.[166]

Moreover, we find *sica*, a particular type of cloth, which was used to cover the body of a bady.[167] *Śāmūlya* was perhaps a type of *sārī*[168] used in those days.

So far the different types of clothes are concerned, A.C. Das remarks,

> During the time of composition of the R̥gvedic hymns, the Aryans had greatly advanced in civilisation, and learnt the process of manufacturing clothes from sheep's wool. Their

157. *R̥V*, 1/115/4.
158. *R̥Vg*, p. 76.
159. *R̥V*, 1/126/16.
160. *Ibid.*, 8/3/24.
161. *ŚYV*, 11/40, 2/32.
162. *SEDM*, p. 10.
163. *RCD*, p. 212.
164. *Ibid.*, p. 210.
165. *AV*,5/21/7.
166. *ŚB*, 5/2/1/21
167. *R̥V*, 10/18/11, 1/95/7.
168. *Ibid.*, 10/85/29.

garments mainly consisted of woollen clothes, showing that the climate was still very cold and necessitated the use of warm clothing.[169]

HOUSE-BUILDING

The importance of the house in the Vedic literature appears from the fact that a passage of the *ṚV* advises a man not to stay in the house of others.[170] The house should be looked like a person's own wife.[171] Mainly the purpose of the house was to protect from hot, cold and rain.[172] Another passage also from the same text informs that the main purpose to build a house was to protect man from cold.[173] A Ṛgvedic passage advises people not to build a clay-house if they were able to afford.[174]

People wanted to build the permanent houses of their own,[175] for which they tried to select a proper and suitable plot of land for construction. We get no such certain methods in the *mantra Saṁhitā*s for the selection and demarcation of certain plot of land for the construction of the house. But later on, we find formulae of the selection of the plot in the Sūtra literature.[176]

An Ideal House

An ideal house can bestow a man peace and happiness. People of the ancient time, specially of the time of the Vedas, wished that the house of a person should yield happiness

---

169. *RCD*, p. 212.
170. *ṚV*, 7/1/11.
171. *AV*, 9/3/24.
172. *ṚV*, 8/18/21.
173. *Ibid.*, 6/67/2.
174. *Ibid.*, 7/89/1.
175. Read, *dhruvaṁ chardiḥ*, *ibid.*, 7/74/5.
176. *ĀsGS*, 2/7/1 to 4, 9 & 7/17/1.

to its master.[177] It must be full of milk and crops always.[178] The next verse wishes to have a house full of attractive things.[179] In the end we find the seer wishing sweet speeches from the members of the family.[180] On the other hand, the house must be majestic, ornamented with several form, long and wide, echoing and having attractive and beautiful doors.[181] The house must have pillars.[182] There should be a cattle house,[183] a temple,[184] and that it should be easy to clean and manage for women.[185] Emphasis was given in making cattle house[186] because people of that time gave importance upon milk.[187] Moreover, a firehouse was required for the performances of religious activities.[188] The necessity of the sacrificial house also was felt by the people of the Vedic Ages.[189] Such sacrificial house was told *duroṇa* and *duryā* also.[190] With special reference to the *Vedic Index*, A.C. Das wrote;

> In connection with the house, mention is made of four terms which though primarily sacrificial in meaning seem to designate parts of building : *Havirdhāna* or oblation-holder, *agniśālā* or fireplace, *patnīnāṁ sadanam* or wives' room and *sada*s or sitting room. Each house had two wings or sides

---

177. *AV*, 7/60/1.
178. *Ibid.*, 7/60/2.
179. *AV*, 7/60/3.
180. *Ibid.*, 7/60/6.
181. *ŚYV*, 29/5.
182. *AV*, 3/12/1.
183. *Ibid.*, 3/12/2, 1/3/4, 9/3/13; *ṚV* 7/56/16.
184. *Ibid.*, 3/12/1.
185. *Ibid.*, 3/12/8.
186. *Ibid.*, 3/14/1.
187. *Ibid.*, 3/14/2.
188. *Ibid.*, 3/4/4.
189. *ŚYV*, 32/72.
190. *Ibid.*, 1/11.

> called *pakṣa* which probably resembled our veranda. The post of verandas were, of course made of wood, upon which images were curved.[191]

A house consisted of outer apartment, called the sitting room, where the male members of the family assembled, talked and rested; store room in which the articles needed in a sacrifice as well as the grains required for the daily consumption were stored; an inner apartment set apart for the exclusive use of the ladies; and a room where sacred fire was burning, called *astri* in the *ṚV*. Besides these rooms there were separated bedrooms for married couples and for grown-up children. The cattle-shed was, of course, situated within the compound of the house, but at a safe distance from the living rooms. Besides these rooms or houses, there was one called *āvasatha* or dwelling.[192] *avasatha* has been explained in the *Vedic Index* as,

> (It) appears to be a place for the reception of the guest, especially for Brāhmaṇas and other on the occasion of feasts and sacrifices.[193]

Words used for house

We find many words used for "house" in the Vedas. Some of them are as follows : *gṛha*,[194] *sadma*,[195] *prasadma*,[196] *dīrghaprasadma*,[197] *vṛhanta*,[198] *duroṇa*,[199] *duryā*,[200] *pastya*,[201]

191. *VTSBAIA*, p. 46.
192. *RCD*, p. 190.
193. *VI*, 1/75.
194. *ṚV*, 6/2/8, 8/22/3, 1/81/9.
195. *Ibid.*, 7/18/22.
196. *Ibid.*, 7/8/22.
197. *Ibid.*, 8/10/1.
198. *Ibid.*, 7/88/5.
199. *Ibid.*, 1/174/7, 5/29/10, 5/32/8; *ŚYV* 33/72.
200. *ŚYV*, 1/11.
201. *ṚV*, 1/25/10.

harmya,[202] *dama*,[203] *śālā*,[204], *bṛhacchandā*,[205] and *mahāśālā*.[206]

Types of Houses

So far the types of houses in the Vedic Age is concerned, we find a lot of description used in this matter. General houses were built on the pillars made of bamboos.[207] Only the poors made the houses of clay.[208] Translating a passage of the *ṚV*, Griffith goes as follows, "Let me not yet, King Varuṇa enter into the house of clay, have mercy, spare me mighty Lord."[209] Perhaps the same feeling has been reflected in the passage of the *AV* also.[210]

1. People seems to build the houses of stones in the ancient times because a complete *sūkta* of the *AV* not only describes the house made of stone[211] rather such houses have been prayed to protect its owner from all sides.
2. Common buildings were constructed with the forest materials. Regarding the formation of such houses, Zimmer says that four pillars (*upamita*s) were set up on a good site and against them beams were leant at an angle, as props (*pratimita*s). The upright pillars were connected by cross beams (*parimita*) resting upon them. The roof was formed of ribs of bamboo cane (*vaṁśa*). A ridge called *viṣuvanta* and a net (*akṣu*) which may mean thatched covering over

202. *ṚV*, 7/56/16 & *AV* 18/4/53.
203. *Ibid.*, 1/1/6.
204. *AV*, 9/3/1.
205. *Ibid.*, 3/12/3.
206. *ChU*, 5/11/1.
207. *AV*, 3/12/6.
208. *ṚV*, 7/89/1.
209. *ṚVg*, p. 178.
210. *AV*, 5/30/14.
211. *Ibid.*, 5/10.

the bamboo ribs. The walls were filled up with grass in bundles (*palada*) and the whole structure were held together with ties of various sorts (*nahana, prāṇāha, saṁaṁśa, parisvañjalya*).[212]

3. We get an information regarding the rooms inside a room.[213] Perhaps such houses were called *bṛhacchandā*.[214] Two such buildings *sadas* and *patnī sadan* are mentioned in the *ŚB*.[215] After all, architecture of the ancient Āryan was undoubtedly highly developed.[216]
4. A Ṛgvedic passage gives us an information regarding a house of 1000 portals.[217] Griffith also writes, "I, Varuṇa, thou glorious lord have entered thy lofty home, thine house with thousand portals."[218]
5. We find another type of building which is erected upon one thousand pillars.[219]
6. An Atharvanic passage says of a building having two, four, six, eight and 10 storeys.[220]
7. Another passage informs us about a three storeyed building also.[221]
8. The existence of the iron houses and forts are also found in the *ṚV*.[222] Of course, such houses seems to

212. *Vedc Index,* 1/256.
213. Read, *kulāye adhikulāyam, AV,* 9/3/20.
214. *AV,* 3/12/3.
215. *ŚB,* 5/1/19.
216. *VSSB,* p. 434.
217. *ṚV,* 7/88/5.
218. *ṚVg,* p. 378.
219. *ṚV,* 5/62/6 (see Griffith's translation).
220. *AV,* 9/3/11.
221. *ṚV,* 8/50/12.
222. *Ibid.,* 7/3/7.

be forts.[223]

9. The word *tridhātu* of the *R̥V* is obscure.[224] The term *trivarutha* of the same,[225] according to Griffith, is "triply guarding."[226] A.C. Das trying to give a solution to the problem, remarks,[227] "The sage Bharadvāja prayed Indra for the gift of a house which should be of *tridhātu* and *trivarutha.* Some say that it seems as if the house were constructed of more than one material, i.e., wood, bricks, and stone." Further he says, "The meaning is not very clear. Had *tri* or triple been metaphorically, or literally in the sense that three materials like bricks, stone and wood were used in the construction of the house? The latter sense seems probable. But Sāyaṇa explains *tridhātu* as *tribhūmikam,* i.e., three storeyed or possessing three courtyards or separate apartments. The first that was in the front was probably constructed of stones to make it sufficiently strong against the attacks of enemies or robbers, and second and third though constructed of different materials, were equally strong. This may be probable meaning of the words *tridhātu* and *trivarutha.*[228]

Though we find that there were the houses of stones,[229] but yet Macdonell and Keith, with the reference of Zimmer say that perhaps the people of that time did not have the houses of stones.[230] We get the R̥gvedic verse,[231] like two

223. Read, *adhā mahī nāyasyanādhr̥ṣṭo nr̥pītaye, purbhavā śatabhujih, R̥V,* 7/15/14.
224. *Ibid.,* 6/46/9.
225. *Ibid.,* 10/666/5.
226. *R̥Vg,* p. 311 & 580.
227. *RCD,* p. 190.
228. *Ibid.,* p. 191.
229. *AV,* 5/10.
230. *VI,* 1/256.
231. *R̥V,* 4/32/23.

slight images of girl's unrobbed upon a new wrought post."[232] In the footnote of the above verse Griffith writes, "Perhaps as caryatids, but the passage is obscure. Professor Wilson translates : Like two puppets of an arranged, new and slender stage."[233]

Secondary Needs

MEDICINE AND EXORCISM

Mainly the word *bhiṣaj*[234] and *bheṣaja*[235] are found in the *mantra Saṁhitās* to denote doctors. Dr. Jogiraj Basu counts two more words *bhiṣak* and *bheṣajyati* for the same.[236] The doctors were well trained and in an Atharvanic passage,[237] according to Bloomfield, a doctor advised that it was better to use the proper medicines instead of using a general and ordinary home-made medicines.[238] The people who accomplished the study of physiology, perhaps, were entitled as *bhiṣaj*. Some informations about physiology in the Vedic literature are found as follows:

PHYSIOLOGY

An Atharvanic *sūkta*[239] gives descriptions of the parts of the body. We find the following parts of body mentioned in the *sukta* : Heel, flesh, ankle, finger, holes, middle portion of the feet and the ankle joint, stitch of knees, thigh, joints of knees, *śithira* or the portion which can be twisted easily, shoulder, headless body, trunk based on thighs, heart, throat, breast, elbow, jaws, tongue, skin, brain and forehead

232. *R̥Vg*, p. 223.
233. *Ibid.*, footnote on 4/32/23.
234. *R̥V*, 2/33/4, 6/50/8, 9/112/1; *AV*, 5/29/1, 6/24/2; *ŚYV* 16/5.
235. *R̥V*, 10/16/14 & *AV*, 18/3/60.
236. *IABJr*, p. 64.
237. *AV*, 5/30/5.
238. *IABJr*, p. 64.
239. *AV*, 10/2/1 to 8.

are such words as we find in the passages. Moreover, we find the names of more organs in the *ŚYV*.[240] We get the description of the skeleton of horse in a passage of the *ŚYV*.[241] The *AB* also presents the list of the limbs of the human being in which it has been stated that the man is formed with hundred and one organs in the body.[242] *Kaṅkuṣa* or a part of ear,[243] *kakṣa* or lurking organs,[244] teeth, nails, private organs, *prapada*[245] and *halīkṣṇa*,[246] also are found in the passages of the Vedic literature. While describing the disease *yakṣmā* or pulmonar,[247] a passage of the *AV* counts some organs such as bones and *kakud* or brain.[248] There are 55 spots in the nerve of throat.[249] In the same way, we find 77 and 99 spots in the nerves of neck and shoulders respectively.[250]

We find a description of womb and the method of the body formation of a child.[251] Another passage of it gives an information that there are 100 arteries in the heart of a man.[252]

The medical service somewhere is found to be a professional and commercial matter.[253] It is believed so because one of the passages reveals the fact that a doctor

240. *ŚYV*, 19/81 to 93.
241. *Ibid.*, 25/1 to 9.
242. *AB*, 1/2/2.
243. *AV*, 9/8/2.
244. *Ibid.*, 6/127/2.
245. *Ibid.*, 2/33/5.
246. *Ibid.*, 2/33/1.
247. *SEDM*, p. 838.
248. *AV*, 7/76/3.
249. *Ibid.*, 6/25/1.
250. *Ibid.*, 6/25/2 & 3.
251. *Ibid.*, 1/11.
252. *Ibid.*, 1/17/3.
253. *Ṛ̥V*, 9/112/3.

received fees. The medicine which was prescribed to a patient by the one who was professional was considered far better than that of a village medicine.[254]

Doctors as we Find in the Mantra Saṁhitās

We find the following famous doctors in the Vedic era. They were : 1. Aśvins,[255] 2. Aṅgirā and Raghat,[256] 3. Kaṇva,[257] Atharvā,[258] 4. Somadeva,[259] 5. Rudra,[260] and some other unnamed *ṛṣis*.[261] In one place, we find Indra to have been referred as doctor.[262]

LIST OF DISEASES

The names of some diseases which were found in the Vedic literature are as follows :

No.	Name of Disease	Reference
1.	*Āśarika*	*AV*, 19/34/10
2.	*Viśarīka*	*Ibid.*
3.	*Balāja*	*Ibid.*
4.	*Pṛṣṭya*	*Ibid.*
5.	*Takmā*	*Ibid.*
6.	*Viśvaśārada*	*AV*, 19/34/10
7.	*Viskandha*	*Ibid.* 19/35/1
8.	*Pāṇḍu*	*Ibid.* 19/11/2 & 7
9.	*Kṣaya*	*Ibid.* 8/7/12,3/7/1,7/ 76/3,3/11/1,2/33

254. *AV*, 5/30/5.
255. *Ibid.*, 20/140/1; *ṚV*, 10/39/5; *ŚB*, 1/7/2; *AB*, 1/4/1.
256. *ṚV*, 8/7/24.
257. *Ibid.*, 6/52/3.
258. *Ibid.*, 2/9/5.
259. *Ibid.*, 1/6/2.
260. *Ibid.*, 2/33/4.
261. *Ibid.*, 7/70/4.
262. *Ibid.*, 8/1/12.

10.	*Yakṣmā*	*AV*, 8/7/5,6/85/1 to 3, 1/12/1,1/25/1 & 2
11.	*Āli*	*Ibid.* 8/6/1
12.	*Samvarta*	*Ibid.*
13.	*Durnāma*	*Ibid.* 8/6/3
14.	*Keśī*	*Ibid.* 8/6/5
15.	*Stambaja*	*Ibid.* 8/6/5
16.	*Tuṇḍika*	*Ibid.* 8/6/6
17.	*Pramṛśa*	*Ibid.*
18.	*Amjṛghra*	*Ibid.*
19.	*Reriha*	*Ibid.*
20.	*Kravyādi*	*Ibid.*
21.	*Atisāra*	*Ibid.* 6/55/7
22.	*Visarpaka*	*Ibid.* 6/127/1
23.	*Balakṣayī*	*Ibid.*
24.	*Kṣipta vāta*	*Ibid.* 6/109/1
25.	*Jvara* (Cold)	*Ibid.* 5/22/10
26.	*Javara* (Cough)	*Ibid.* 5/22/11 & 1
27.	*Vidradhi*	*Ibid.* 6/127/1
28.	*Kṣetriya*	*Ibid.* 3/7/1 & 2/25/1
29.	*Kuṣṭha*	*Ibid.* 3/7/1
30.	*Bahumūtra*	*Ibid.* 2/3/2
31.	*Nāḍi braṇa*	*Ibid.*
32.	*Viśalpa*	*Ibid.* 9/8/6
33.	*Visvāṅgaya*	*Ibid.*
34.	*Hariman*	*Ibid.* 9/8/9
35.	*Yakṣmodhā*	*Ibid.*
36.	*Balāsa*	*Ibid.* 9/8/10
37.	*Kāhābāha*	*Ibid.*, 9/8/11
38.	*Vātisāra*	*Ibid.* 9/8/20
39.	*Alaji*	*Ibid.*
40.	*Gaṇḍamālā*	*AB*, 1/4/8
41.	*Mahodara*	*Ibid.* 7/33/3
42.	*Viśara*	*AV*, 2/4/2

43.	*Viśūcikā*	*AV*, 7/42/2
44.	*Mandāgni*	*Ibid.* 4/17/2
45.	*Tīkṣṇāgni*	*Ibid.* 4/17/7
46.	*Rājayakṣmā*	*Ibid.* 3/11/1 & *ṚV* 10/162
47.	*Jāyānya*	*AV*, 7/76/5
48.	*Harimā*	*Ibid.* 1/22/1
49.	*Tṛṣṇā*	*Ibid.* 6/29/1-7
50.	*Jamma*	*Ibid.* 8/1/76
51.	*Apacī*	*Ibid.* 6/25/1,6/83/1,7/77/1
52.	*Aśmarī*	*Ibid.* 1/3/6-9
53.	*Agotā*	*Ibid.* 4/17/3
54.	*Pāmana*	*Ibid.* 5/22/12
55.	*Bhūda garbha*	*Ibid.* 1/11/5
56.	*Mānasa*	*Ibid.* 6/43/1-3
57.	*Akṣiroga*	*Ibid.* 4/20/1-9
58.	*Āsrāva*	*Ibid.* 1/2/4; 2/3/2
59.	*Braṇa*	*Ibid.* 6/57/1-3
60.	*Kāsa*	*Ibid.* 1/12/3

Six types of treatments

So far the treatment of the patient is concerned we find mainly six types of treatments in the Vedic literature. These are being discussed below:

1. ***Exorcism*** : Exorcism is seen in an entire *sūkta* of the *AV*.[263] Medicines were given to the patients after enchanting *mantras*.[264] People invited the experts to remove the poison from a snake-bitten-person.[265] Sometimes *mantras* were used to cure the wounded portion of the body.[266] Exorcism was used to cure a

263. *AV*, 9/8.
264. *Ibid.*, 8/7/5.
265. *Ibid.*, 6/12 & 5/13/1.
266. *Ibid.*, 4/12/7.

worm sufferers.[267] The treatment of *kṣaya* also was performed through exorcism.[268] A R̥gvedic passage informs us that there are 99 methods of exorcism for the recovery from poisons.[269]

2. ***Oblation and worships*** : An Atharvanic passage informs us that the people believed in the fact that fever got cured through oblations[270] in sacrifices. A *sūkta* itself presents the description and further says that people organised *yajña* to recover *kṣaya*.[271] A particular passage is there to mention the fact.[272] In one place we find a reference that all kinds of diseases are removed if people perform sacrifices with *ghī*.[273] Again the sick people were advised to worship sun if they felt victimised from *yakṣmā*.[274] A R̥gvedic passage,[275] on the other hand, says that the principal *yakṣmā* also would get cured through oblations in sacrifices.

3. ***Enchanted globules*** : In order to make a man free from diseases, people used to wear such globules which were enchanted and "purified." We find *tilakamaṇi*[276] which was thought to be capable of destroying the bewitching of the witches. We find another plant, named *pāṭhā*, which has been translated by Macdonell and Keith as *Clypea*

267. *AV*, 2/31/3.
268. *Ibid.*, 2/33.
269. *R̥V*, 1/191/13.
270. *AV*, 5/22/1.
271. *Ibid.*, 3/11.
272. *Ibid.*, 3/11/1.
273. *Ibid.*, 2/13/1.
274. *Ibid.*, 1/12/1.
275. *R̥V*, 10/161/1.
276. *AV*, 2/11/1 & 5.

herendifolia.[277] This was used to hang on the neck, when a man suffered from poison,[278] weakness, etc.[279] The fact that an enchanted globule was used and it was hung on the neck, appears in an Atharvanic passage.[280] In the same way a *maṇi* was used to destory the *jaṅgiḍa maṇi*.[281] *Hiraṇya* or the globule[282] of gold is found in other places. In the same passage, we find the globule of eight minerals which could remove fever and increase age. The particular word *maṇi* for an enchanted globule appeared in the *R̥V*[283] and the *AV*[284] as well. The adjective *maṇi-grīvā* denotes that this *maṇi* was hung on the neck of the patient.[285]

4. ***Natural treatment*** : The people perhaps used naturopathy in the ancient times for their treatment of some diseases. It appears from the fact that the sun has been described as the bestower power of sight.[286] Hot water was used for the treatment of *yakṣmā*.[287] A passage of the *AV* says that Somadeva was a doctor and he used water in the treatment of the patient. It has been said that all types of medicine are present in water.[288] On the other hand, people thought that the fire was able to remove the diseases

---

277. *Vedic Index*, 1/687.
278. *AV*, 2/26/2.
279. *Ibid.*, 3/19.
280. *Ibid.*, 2/27/3.
281. *Ibid.*, 2/4/1.
282. *Ibid.*, 1/35/1.
283. *R̥V*, 1/33/8.
284. *AV*, 1/29/1, 2/4/1 & 2, etc.
285. *R̥V*, 1/122/14.
286. *AV*, 2/16/4.
287. *Ibid.*, 1/25/1.
288. *Ibid.*, 1/4/4. Read, *apsu bhesajam*, *ŚB*, 5/4/1; *R̥V*, 10/9/6.

of women.[289] The sun rays were thought to be able to destory the germs of diseases from the human body.[290] "Rain water charged with the rays of the sun is a medicine or a potent drink."[291]

5. ***Surgery*** : Our attention have centred on some datas of surgery. First of all, the expert examined the poison of the patient and performed needful treatment.[292] A doctor assures a patient to make the urine out.[293] A Ṛgvedic passage gives an information as, Maghavān or Indra recovers him before the blood comes out of his (*etasa*s) neck. The same Indra adjusts and recovers the isolated or infirm organs of the body."[294] On the other hand, we find a very important description of *viśpalā* in the *ṚV*.[295] *Viśpalā* was cured by adding a duplicate foot of iron in the place of her broken foot.[296] Aśvins were the doctors appointed for the treatment.[297] So far the surgical activities in the Vedic Age is concerned, Macdonell and Keith remarked that actually surgical system was not in existence in the Vedic Age,[298] and it was not more than an impossible inference.[299]

6. ***Medicines*** : While entering into the matter of medicines, we find a lot of evidences. The medicines of *kṣaya* were introduced thus : "Sky is their father,

289. *ṚV*, 1/162.
290. *Ibid.*, 10/37/4.
291. *AB*, 8/37/4.
292. *AV*, 4/7/6.
293. *Ibid.*, 1/3.
294. *ṚVg*, p. 389, 8/1/11.
295. *ṚV*, 1/112/10, 116/15, 117/11, 118/8, 10/39/8.
296. *Ibid.*, 10/39/8.
297. *Ibid.*, 10/39.
298. *Vedic Index*, 2/116.
299. *Ibid.*, 2/346.

the earth is the mother and seas are their roots."[300] On the other hand, a Ṛgvedic passage describes that *iṣkṛti* was the mother of medicines.[301] Whatever the fact there may be, we have collected the names of some medicines from the *mantra Saṁhitā*s. These are as follows : *jaṅgiḍa,*[302] *darbha,*[303] *śākti-mantha,*[304] *kācmāci,*[305] *palāśa,*[306] *pippali,*[307] *varṇa vṛkṣa,*[308] *haridrā,*[309] *rohiṇīlatā,*[310] *kaith,*[311] *apāmārga,*[312] horns of the black deers,[313] *pāṭhā,*[314] *pṛsṇiparṇī,*[315] bile of Garuḍa,[316] *vīrut* or *vīrudh,*[317] *madhukalatā,*[318] *muñja,*[319] *śalmalī* tree,[320] *gulmalatā,*[321] mountain

300. *AV*, 7/8/2.
301. *ṚV*, 10/97/3.
302. *AV*, 19/34/3, 10; 35/1, 2/4/1.
303. *Ibid.*, 19/32/10, 8/7/20.
304. *Ibid.*, 7/45/1.
305. *Ibid.*, 6/137/1.
306. *Ibid.*, 6/127/1, 6/15/1; *ṚV*, 10/97/5.
307. *AV*, 6/109/1; *ṚV*, 10/97/5.
308. *Ibid.*, 6/85/1 to 3.
309. *Ibid.*, 6/21/3, 1/23/1.
310. *Ibid.*, 4/12/1 to 7.
311. *Ibid.*, 4/4/1.
312. *Ibid.*, 4/17/, 4/18/, 4/19 *sūkta*s.
313. *Ibid.*, 3/7/1.
314. *Ibid.*, 3/19 & 2/27/2.
315. *Ibid.*, 2/25/1 to 3.
316. *Ibid.*, 1/24/1.
317. *Ibid.*, 8/7/20/ & 1/34/1.
318. *Ibid.*, 1/34/1.
319. *Ibid.*, 2/3/2.
320. *ṚV*, 7/50/3.
321. *Ibid.*

grass,[322] *aśvavatī*,[323] *somavatī*,[324] *urjavantī*,[325] *usojaśā*,[326] *arundhatī*,[327] *madhumatī*,[328] *soma*,[329] etc.

MUSIC

Music was not alien to the Aryans in the Vedic India. We get sufficient datas regarding music in the Vedic literature scattered in its several pages. Swami Pragnanananda writes,

> The Vedic music *sāmagana* evolved through the medium of songs and singing process of the chanters and singers, and their laws, materials and processes were contained in the three main books, *grāme geya gāna*, *araṇye geya gāna*, and *uha* and *uhya gāna*s. These four Vedic song books were really composed of four kinds of *r̥ks* or collection of verses, and those *r̥ks* were : *pūrvārcika*, *āraṇyaka saṁhitā* and *uttarārcika*. These verses were the womb of song.[330]

A R̥gvedic passage informs that the songs were sung at *yajña* or sacrifice.[331] Generally people sang the songs at the time of *soma* preparation.[332] At that time, women also sang the songs.[333] They used to hum and sing even at the time of their busy tasks.[334]

---

322. *R̥V*, 5/4/11.
323. *Ibid.*, 10/97/7.
324. *Ibid.*
325. *Ibid.*
326. *Ibid.*
327. *Ibid.*, 8/7/6.
328. *Ibid.*
329. *Ibid.*, 8/7/20.
330. *HDIMP*, p. 372.
331. Read, *tasmāt yajñāt sarvahutaḥ r̥caḥsāmāni jagñire*, *R̥V*, 10/90/9.
332. *R̥V*, 7/103/7 & 8.
333. *Ibid.*, 9/66/8.
334. *Ibid.*, 1/92/3.

G.S. Ghurye comments thus :

> Probably even in the Ṛgvedic society singing was not only a desired object but was a domestic accomplishment and accompaniment of some of the daily routine.[335]

Secondly, Hillebrundt preserves his views regarding the Vedic song as :

> We are indebted for the Vedic songs and prose (chant) to the poets and *ṛṣis* of ancient India who composed their hymns for the solemn sacrifices by the kings and nobles of the time and also for the praise of gods, worshipped by patrons. The priests and kings were not stranger to the people; they stood above, but not outside their objects and we fairly assume that the hymns did reflect the opinions; not only of the higher but also of the lower classes, and the popular traditions of the different ages.[336]

The Words Used for Songs

The importance of music in the Vedic society appears from the fact that the Vedic literature has possessed some terms for songs. We find the word *sāmagāna* first of all in the *ṚV*.[337] Thereafter it has been mentioned in several places.[338] *Gāthā* is occurred in many passages in the *ṚV*. In some places *gāthā* meant for song and specially for eulogical songs.[339] In another passage the same term has been used to denote speech or *vāk* according to Sāyaṇa.[340] In yet some other places we find it.[341] Another important word *ṛju gāthā*[342] perhaps

335. *VIG*, p. 259.
336. Quoted from *HDIMP*, p. 372.
337. *ṚV*, 1/2/14.
338. *Ibid.*, 1/81/5, 6/69/2.
339. *ṚVSāy*, 1/167/6 & 9/11/8.
340. *ṚV*, 8/32/1.
341. *Ibid.*, 8/71/14, 4/98/9, 9/99/4.
342. *Ibid.*, 5/44/5.

meant singing correctly and easily. Moreover, Jogiraj Basu counts some of the words such as *gān, gīti, udgāna* and *udgāta* for songs in the Vedic literature specially in the *mantra Saṁhitā*.[343] The *AB* mentions that a *ṛk* was supposed to be connected with divine existence whereas *gāthā* was supposed to be related with human beings.[344]

Musical Instruments

We get a long list of the musical instruments in the Vedic literature. *Vīṇā* among them seems to be a familiar musical instrument.[345] The *AB* describes *vīṇā* in detail.[346] It was believed that the *daivī vīṇā* was practised by gods and the mortal man practised *mānuṣī vīṇā*.[347] The passage again informs us that both types of *vīnās* were played with fingers. A *ṛk* informs about *vāṇa*[348] about which Pragnanananda informs,

> The *vāṇa* is an instrument of wood, according to Śāṅkh. (?) consisting a kind of crate and handle (cross bar?); it is covered with the skin of red ox, hairs on solitude, it has 10 holes at its backside, over each of which 10 strings are fastened; the strings are manufactured of *muñja* and *durbā* grass.[349]

Another instrument seems to be *dundubhi* or a trumpet like instrument, which we find in the *ṚV* also.[350] Another *bhūmi-*

343. *VPJr*, p. 261.
344. *AB*, 7/18.
345. *ṚV*, 1/85/10.
346. *AV*, 3/2/5.
347. Read, *atha khalviyaṁ daivī vīṇā bhavati, tadanukṛtirasau bhavati.*
yathāsyāḥ śirāḥ eva manuṣyāḥ śiraḥ.
yathasyā udaramevamanuṣyā ambharam.
yathāsyai jihvā eva manuṣyai vādanam, yathā ..... vāco bhāṣante vidureṇa tatra iti. — *AA*, 3/2/5.
348. *ṚV*, 1/85/10.
349. *HDIMP*, p. 450.
350. *ṚV*, 1/28/5, 6/47/44 & 31.

dundubhi also is met.[351] But so far the difference between the two is concerned, we may quote Swami Pragnanananda as follows:[352]

> *Dundubhi* was afterwards made up of a hollow trunk of a tree, which was covered with rough skin of animals. The *bhūmi-dundubhi* was made out of the *bhūmi* or earthen ground, covered with skin. It can be asked as to when those rude drums evolved, or were created. Now when we study the music materials of the primitive times, we find that the uncultured savage nations of the most antique days used to sing and dance to please themselves after retiring from their works. The songs and dances of the primitive people were very simple and monotonous, and drums like *bhūmi dundubhi* and *dundubhi*, etc., were also in use to keep the rhythms and beats of songs and dances. In the pre-historic times we find also some remanents of crude drums and whistles of bone. It is most probable that the use of drums *bhūmi-dundubhi* and *dundubhi* etc., were revived. Besides the drums, many musical instruments of *vīṇā* and *veṇu* classes were devised to suit the purpose of singing and dancing in the developed Vedic times. We also find that like the primitive days *bhūmi-dundubhi* and *dundubhi* drum were struck with rough wooden club, so as to produce grave and deep sounds.

Moreover, we find *karkarī*,[353] *aghaṭi*,[354] *kṣoṇī*,[355] *nādī*,[356] *vanaspati*,[357] *ādambara*,[358] etc. On the other hand, we get some informations about the existence of the musical instruments. A Ṛgvedic passage describes three musical

351. *TS*, 1/5/9/30.
352. *HDIMP*, p. 54.
353. *ṚV*, 2/43/3 & 3/37/4.
354. *Ibid.*, 10/146/2 & *ŚYV*, 5/35.
355. *Ibid.*, 2/35/13.
356. *Ibid.*, 10/135/7.
357. Read, *vanaspatayo vimucadhvam*, *ŚYV*, 9/12.
358. *Ibid.*, 30/10 & 19.

instruments named *gargara, godhā* and *piṅga*.[359] Some other instruments *vīṇā, veṇu, vaṁśa, mṛdaṅga, paṇava, puṣkara* and *bhāṇḍa* also are found.[360] Jogiraj Basu counts two more instruments : *śatatantrī* and *vīṇāgāthī*.[361]

The Usual Singers

Several persons in different rituals and activities used to sing songs. For example, we find a *purohita*[362] and some women[363] singing the songs at the time of the preparation of *soma*. Moreover, *udgātā*,[364] *gāthāpati*,[365] *gāthāni*[366] and *gāthina*[367] also are mentioned. A *paṇighna* was the *dundubhi* blower whereas a *śaṅkhadhmā* was called *śaṅkha* blower.[368] On the other hand, we find a description about the professional musicians in the two Yajurvedic passages.[369] Uṣā has been described to be like a singer.[370] A *paṇighna* or *dundubhi* player and a *śaṅkhadhmā* or a *śaṅkha* blower are found together in a passage.[371]

Singing

The word *oṁ'* was supposed to be the origin of songs in the ancient times.[372] Another passage of the *ṚV*[373] mentions

359. *ṚV*, 8/69/9.
360. Quoted from *HDIMP*, p. 53.
361. *VPJr*, p. 216 & 217.
362. *ṚV*, 7/103/7 & 8.
363. *Ibid.*, 9/66/8.
364. *VPJr*, p. 216.
365. *ṚV*, 1/43/4.
366. *Ibid.*, 1/190/1; 8/92/2.
367. *Ibid.*, 1/7/1.
368. *ŚYV*, 31/20.
369. *Ibid.*, 30/19 & 20.
370. *ṚV*, 1/92/3.
371. *ŚYV*, 31/20.
372. Read, *oṁ, ityetad akṣaram udgūham upāsū*, *ChU*, 1/1.
373. *ṚV*, 10/32/4.

about *satadhātu* about which we may guess it to be nothing but seven sounds. People developed some rules through which a *ṛk* was transfered into a *sāman*. We find the following rules.[374] Pragnanananda remarks as follows :

1. ***Vikāra :*** Changes in the letters of the Ṛgvedic words in the Sāmavedic setting, i.e., Agni of the *ṚV* becomes *ognāi* in Sāmavedic rendering.
2. ***Viśleṣaṇa :*** A Ṛgvedic word is broken into parts in Sāmavedic setting, e.g., *vītaye* of the Ṛgvedic text becoming *voi-taya 2 yi* in Sāmavedic song.
3. ***Vikarṣaṇa :*** The vowel of the Ṛgvedic word being lengthened in Sāmavedic song, e.g., *ye* becoming *ya 2 3 yi* in Sāmavedic rendering.
4. ***Abhyāsa :*** Repetition, e.g., singing *toya 2 yi* twice as *toya 2 yi, toya 2 yi.*
5. ***Virāma :*** Meaning pause, singing part of a word after a pause, e.g., of the phrase *Gṛṇānohavyadataye,* one is to sing *graṇāno ha* and then after a short pause *vya-dātaye.*
6. ***Stobha :*** Introduction of exclamatory words in the midst of a son, for example, the introduction of exclamatory words like *auhovā, hāu hāu* etc. in the midst of a particular song.

Regarding the Vedic songs, Prof. A. Hillebrandt opined as :

> We are indebted for the Vedic songs and prose (chante) to the poets and the *ṛṣi*s of ancient India, who composed their hymns for solemn sacrifices of the kings and nobles of the time, and also for the praise of the gods worshipped by the patrons. The priests and kings were not strangers to the people, they stood above, but not outside their objects, and we may fairly assume that the hymns did reflect the

374. *HDIMP,* p. 65.

opinions, not only of the higher but also of the lower classes, and the popular traditions of the different ages.[375]

ORNAMENTS

Generally, people are fond of decorating their bodies from the very beginning of the human civilization. Thus, ornamentation came into being. We get a lot of evidences regarding several types of ornaments, and also of the astonishing aptness of the Āryan people in making ornaments. Here we are going to reveal some datas in this context. The importance of the ornaments appears from the fact that the people used several words to denote ornaments and ornamentation. The words are as follows : *araṅkṛta*[376] or *alaṅkṛta*,[377] *svaraṅkṛta*,[378] *bhūṣat*,[379] *abhivarta*,[380] *dhātā*,[381] *sambhāra*,[382] *hiraṇya*,[383] and *bandha*.[384] We have the names of several types of stones and pearls found in the Vedic society. These were *hiraṇya*,[385] *svarṇa*,[386] *rajata*,[387]

375. *HDIMP*, p. 48.
376. *ṚV*, 1/2/1.
377. *Ibid.*, 8/67/3.
378. *AV*, 10/1/25.
379. *ṚV*, 8/90/1.
380. *Ibid.*, 1/35/4.
381. *AV*, 8/5/18.
382. *ŚB*, 2/1/1/3.
383. *AV*, 4/10/6; *ŚYV*, 15/50, 20/37.
384. *ŚB*, 6/1/7/17.
385. *ṚV*, 1/35/4; 43/5; 122/14; etc. *ŚYV*, 30/50 & 52; *AV*, 5/4/5; *AB*, 2/15; *ŚB* 2/1/1/5; 3/1/5/20, 3/3/2/2, etc.
386. *ṚV*, 4/23/6.
387. *ṚV*, 8/25/22; *ŚYV*, 23/37; *AV*, 5/28/1, 13/4/51, etc.

ratna,[388] *kṛśana*,[389] *hasti*,[390] *laṅkā*,[391] *śaṅkha*,[392] *jātarūpa*,[393] *muktā*,[394] *vajra*,[395] etc., from which different kinds of ornaments were made by the people.

The goldsmith or the person who made the several types of ornaments was named as *dhamātṛ*,[396] *karmāra*,[397] *sukarmāṇa*,[398] *hiraṇya peśas*,[399] *hiraṇyakāra*,[400] *maṇikāra*[401] and *rajjusarja*.[402]

Ornaments for Head and Hair

The word *sraj* denotes garland[403] but yet it seems to denote a ring of flower to wear it on the head of woman.[404] Such ring of gold was told *hiraṇyasraj*.[405] We find *stūpa* in another place[406] which denoted a kind of diadem or crown. *Kurīra*[407]

---

388. *ṚV*, 1/20/7, 1/35/8; *AV*, 5/1/7, 7/14/4; *ŚB*, 5/3/1/1.
389. *ṚV*, 1/35/4, 126/4.
390. *Ibid.*, 1/64/7, 4/16/4; *AV*, 3/22/1 to 6, 4/36/9; 6/38/2, etc.
391. *ŚYV*, 18/13 & *ŚB*, 13/2/2/18.
392. *AV*, 4/10/1 to 5.
393. *AB*, 8/13.
394. *Ibid.*, 1/14.
395. *Ibid.*, 6/24/1.
396. *ṚV*, 5/9/5.
397. *Ibid.*, 10/72/2 & *ŚYV*, 16/27.
398. *ṚV*, 4/2/17.
399. *Ibid.*, 8/8/2.
400. *ŚYV*, 30/17.
401. *Ibid.*, 30/17.
402. *Ibid.*, 30/17.
403. *SEDM*, p. 1274.
404. *ṚV*, 4/38/6, 5/53/4; *AV*, 1/14/1, 10/6/4.
Read, *hiraṇya srak* — *AV*, 10/6/4; *ŚB*, 5/4/5/22; *TB*, 8/9/8.
405. *AV*, 10/6/4; *ŚB*, 5/4/5/22; *TB*, 8/9/8.
406. *ŚYV*, 2/2; *ṚV*, 1/24/7; 7/2/1; *ŚB*, 1/3/3/5 & 3/5/3/4, etc.
407. *ṚV*, 10/85/8; *ŚYV*, 9/56; *AV*, 6/138/3.

and *opaśa*[408] were the ornaments of head which were used by the bride at the time of marriage. On the other hand, we find another type of ornament used on head named as *śipra*.[409] The words *hiraṇyaśipra*[410] and *hiriśipra*[411] denote that *śipra* was made of valuable metal. Another ornament of head was *śṛṅga* which is found in the Vedas and the *Brāhmaṇa* literature as well.[412] The word *hiraṇyaśṛṅga*[413] indicates that perhaps the strings were made of silver and other metals also. *Kumbha*[414] and *tiritas*[415] were such head-ornaments which were very important in those days.

Ornaments for Ears

We get a few ornaments for ears used in the Vedic Age. The names of the ornaments of the ears are as follows : *karṇa-śobhana,*[416] which was expected to get after the victory over an enemy. Secondly, *hiraṇyakarṇa*[417] or rings were worn by both males and females. Another type of ring which was called *cakra*[418] was also used by women. An ornament of ear named *prakāśa*[419] was presented to *hotā* at the time of sacrifice. Again an ornament *pravarta*[420] was found in the *ŚB*.

---

408. *ṚV*, 1/173/6; 8/14/5; *AV*, 6/138/1 & 2 *AV*, 9/3/8; *TB*, 4/1/1; 13/4/3.
409. *ṚV*, 5/54/11; 8/7/25, etc.
410. *Ibid.*, 2/34/3.
411. *Ibid.*, 2/2/5.
412. *ṚV*, 1/140/6; 163/11; *AV*, 9/4/17; 19/36/2; *AB*, 6/18.
413. *AV*, 19/36/5.
414. *Ibid.*, 6/138/3.
415. *Ibid.*, 8/6/7.
416. *ṚV*, 8/78/3.
417. *Ibid.*, 1/122/14.
418. *Ibid.*, 10/85/11 (*stotraṁ te cakre*).
419. *ŚB*, 5/4/5/22.
420. *Ibid.*, 3/5/3/16.

Ornaments of Neck

So far the ornaments of the neck are concerned, we find a *ṛk* mentioning about a garland made of *maṇi*.[421] Another word *mālā* also is met,[422] which perhaps was the original term of *mālā* or *mālya*. But, Macdonell and Keith mention it to be the dress of *ṛṣis*.[423] Secondly, our attention goes to *niṣka*[424] which has been described as "a golden ornamment for the neck or breast" by M.M. Willams.[425] Besides, Macdonell and Keith have also assumed it the same.[426] Thirdly, we get *rukma*,[427] which according to Monier, is a golden chain for the ornament of neck.[428] Another ornament *atkā*[429] denotes an armour also. We get some *maṇis* in the *AV* and other literature which are as follows : *maṇi*,[430] *hiraṇya-maṇi*,[431] *srāktya-maṇi*,[432] *sañjay-maṇi*[433] *deva-maṇi*,[434] *darbha-maṇi*,[435] *audumbara-maṇi*[436] *jaṅgiḍa-maṇi*,[437] *śaṅkha-*

---

421. *ṚV*, 1/122/14.
422. *Ibid.*, 10/136/2.
423. *VI*, 2/153.
424. *ṚV*, 1/129/2; 2/33/10; 5/19/3; *AV*, 5/14/3; *AB*, 11/4/1/8 & 13/4/1/7.
425. *SEDM*, p. 562.
426. *VI*, 1/513.
427. *ṚV*, 1/166/10; 4/10/5; *ŚB*, 3/5/1/20 & *AB*, 8/21/3.
428. *SEDM*, p. 882.
429. *ṚV*, 5/55/6.
430. *ŚYV*, 30/7; *AV*, 1/29/1, 2/4/1 & 2, 8/5/1.
431. *TS*, 7/3/4/1; *AV*, 10/6/4.
432. *AV*, 8/5/4.
433. *Ibid.*, 8/5/16.
434. *Ibid.*, 8/5/20.
435. *Ibid.*, 19/28/1, 19/30/5.
436. *Ibid.*, 19/31/1 & *TS*, 2/1/1/6.
437. *AV*, 2/4/1 to 6.

maṇi,[438] *varṇa-maṇi,*[439] *khadira-maṇi,*[440] *yava-maṇi,*[441] *parṇa-maṇi,*[442] *añjana-maṇi,*[443] and *pratisara-maṇi,*[444] etc. These are the prominent *maṇi*s used in the Vedic period.

Ornaments for Arms

A passage in the *ṚV* informs us that the people in the Vedic time used the ornaments in the arms also. A passage is used as a prayer to Indra to give the rings of the enemies that had been brought after they had been defeated.[445] A golden ring for arms was called *bhujī.*[446] Another ornament *khādi* is found in the *ṚV,*[447] *ŚB,*[448] and *AB.*[449] A Ṛgvedic passage describes about *narya*[450] used by Maruts in their arms. *Parihasta* was tied in the hands of the bride by a bridegroom with a view to bless her to beget children.[451] Another hand ring named *pratisara* was perhaps a kind of sharpened weapon and an ornament also, because it has been described as the means of killing enemies.[452] On the other hand, *hasti* was found as an ornament that was bright and lustred.[453] The ornament *bala* was also used as the ornaments of arm.[454]

438. *AV,* 4/10/1.
439. *Ibid.,* 10/3/1 & 3.
440. *Ibid.,* 10/6/6 & 7.
441. *Ibid.,* 9/2/13.
442. *Ibid.,* 3/5/4.
443. *Ibid.,* 4/9/3.
444. *Ibid.,* 6/138/3; 8/5/1.
445. *ṚV,* 8/97/2.
446. *Ibid.,* 8/8/2.
447. *Ibid.,* 1/168/3.
448. *ŚB,* 3/6/1/7 & 3/6/2/12.
449. *AB,* 3/5.
450. *ṚV,* 1/166/10.
451. *AV,* 6/8/1 to 3.
452. *AV,* 2/11/2, 4/40/10, 8/5/1 to 4; *ŚB,* 5/2/4/20.
453. *AV,* 3/22/1.
454. *AB,* 6/7.

Rings

The term *hiraṇya*[455] seems to be used for rings. The term was used as an adjective of the sun.[456] Thirdly, the word *ānūka* was met to denote rings.[457] The verse having the word *ānūka* has been translated as "guerdon" by Griffith.[458] Macdonell meant it to be an ornament simply.[459] On the other hand, an ornament *hiraṇya* was meant a type of ring which was used in the Vedic Age and the evidences are found in the *AV*[460] and *ŚB*.[461]

Ornaments of Waist

Nyocanī of the *ṚV*[462] has been guessed by scholars to be a chain worn round the waist. Another *varuṇapāśa*[463] meant the girdle of the *muñja* grass. *Hiraṇyavartanī*[464] was perhaps the chain of gold worn round the waist. We find *rāsanā*[465] though it is obscure in meaning. But we find its use in the age of the *Brāhmaṇa* also.[466] *Ināha* of the *AV* also denoted such an ornament.[467] The word *mekhalā* appears in the *AV*.[468] *Yoktra* was used by women as their favourite

455. *ṚV*, 1/22/5.
456. *Ibid.*, 1/35/9.
457. *Ibid.*, 5/33/9.
458. *ṚVg*, p. 252.
459. *Vedic Index*, 1/66.
460. *AV*, 2/36/7.
461. *ŚB*, 3/3/2/2.
462. *ṚV*, 10/85/1; *AV* 14/1/7.
463. *Ibid.*, 6/74/4, 7/88/7; *AV*, 4/16/6; *TS*, 2/2/5/1.
464. *ṚV*, 5/75/2 & 3.
465. *ŚYV*, 1/30, 9/59, 38/1, etc.
466. *ŚB*, 6/2/2/25 & 6/5/2/11.
467. *AV*, 19/57/4.
468. *Ibid.*, 6/133/1.

ornaments.[469] M.M. Willams, on the other hand, meant it as "any instrument for tying to or fastening a rope."[470]

Ornaments for ankle

We find a term *patsu khādi*[471] which perhaps meant to be an anklet. Another term, *vṛṣakhādi* is also met[472] which according to Max Müller was a thick anklet.[473] The word *hiraṇyapava* also perhaps meant the same.[474]

469. *ŚB*, 1/3/1/13 to 17.
470. *SEDM*, p. 854.
471. *ṚV*, 5/54/11.
472. *Ibid.*, 1/64/10.
473. Quoted from *VYBAG*, p. 30.
474. *ṚV*, 9/86/43.

9

Religion and Philosophy

Religion

Religion is a personal matter through which a man approaches to God. Yet the Vedic people utilized it in the both lines, personal and social. Religion is based on worshipping or *upāsanā*, which is being studied here.

WORSHIP OR UPĀSANĀ

As the root *'ās'* (to sit) is attached with the suffix *'yuc'*[1] and another sūtra adds the suffix aṇ.[2] The term should have used as neuter gender but a sūtra makes it feminine gender[3] and so the suffix *'tāp'* is used, thus, the word *'upāsanā'* comes into being. It is remarkable that the prefix *upa* is placed at the very beginning of the formation of the word.

Śarmopāsyāma[4] and *upāsanā*[5] of the *ṚV* and *upāsyāmī*[6] of the *AV* mean to worship, to serve and to be present. The words *upāsatai*,[7] *arcā*,[8] *vandāmahe*,[9] *havāmahe*,[10]

1. Read, *nyasāsrantho yuc, Aṣṭ* 3/3/107.
2. *Ibid.*, 7/1/1.
3. *Ibid.*, 3/3/93.
4. *ṚV*, 2/27/7.
5. *Ibid.*, 10/154/1.
6. *AV*, 6/24/2.
7. *Ibid.*, 10/8/22.
8. *ṚV*, 1/54/2.
9. *Ibid.*, 3/8/9.
10. *Ibid.*, 1/106/6.

dhīmahi,[11] *milate*,[12] *manāmahe*,[13] *arādhi*,[14] *upāsva*,[15] and *yajāmahe*[16] are such words which are scattered in the Vedic literature to denote worship or *upāsanā*.

Describing the importance of worship, the *R̥V*[17] proclaims, "None other comforter is found save only these: longings and my hopes are fixed upon the gods."[18] In the other place we get, "Let us if we have power, pay the God's worship."[19] God should be worshipped through adulations and salutations.[20] He may be worshipped through songs also.[21] Sometimes Vāśiṣṭhas are found worshipping gods.[22] A seer in the *AV* prays God to protect Him.[23] Thus, gods were supposed to be contented.[24] On the other hand, "Certainly to whole is Brahmā. So a man should worship him in peace."[25] We find somewhere *upāsanā* as the means of salvation also.[26]

Using the word *ayajanta* to denote *upāsanā* or worship, a R̥gvedic passage informs that *yajña* was performed for the sake of *yajña* by the gods and these were the first *dharma*

---

11. *R̥V*, 3/62/10.
12. *Ibid.*, 10/80/3.
13. *Ibid.*, 5/13/2.
14. *Ibid.*, 1/70/4.
15. *TS*, 10/8.
16. *R̥V*, 7/59/12.
17. *Ibid.*, 10/64/2.
18. *R̥Vg*, p. 578.
19. *R̥V*, 1/27/13.
20. *Ibid.*, 5/40/8.
21. *Ibid.*, 9/97/4.
22. *Ibid.*, 10/65/15.
23. *AV*, 19/27/1.
24. *Ibid.*, 11/5/2.
25. *ChU*, 3/14/1.
26. *Ibid.*, 8/12/3.

of the cosmos.[27] As He was thought to be "the sole ruler"[28] the people worshipped Him in order to throw away the evil thoughts and acquire the ideal qualities.[29] A person cannot achieve God without his suffering.[30] That was the cause of the worship of God. A person was advised to worship the God whom he liked most.[31] He who worships such gods remains for ever.[32] A worshipper realizes God to be his father, mother, sister and all.[33] The Vedic devotee believed that the climax of worship or *upāsanā* is to realize immortality of the soul and the God. A verse of the *ŚYV* proclaims that this and only this is the way to realize God.[34] We may come to the conclusion of the discussion after the mentioning of Śaṅkarācārya in the commentary on the *ŚBG*[35] as:

> *Upāsanā* is to stay approaching and centralizing one's intelligence to the *upāsya* or God according to *śāstra*s or holy books. It must be like the flow of oil.

GOD AND HIS DESCRIPTION

The word *svayambhū* of the *ŚYV* indicates that the Vedic people thought of Almighty God from whom Prajāpati sprung. He is the first existent and preserver of the seed of

27. *ṚV*, 1/164/50.
28. *ṚV*, 10/21/3. See in *The Hymns of the Ṛgveda* by Griffith. p. 625.
29. *ṚV*, 5/82/5.
30. *Ibid.*, 9/83/1.
31. Read, *ātmānam priyamupāsīta, BU*, 1/4/8.
32. Read, *ya ātmaneva priyamupāste hāsya priyaṁ pramayukam bhavati, BU*, 1/48.
33. *AV*, 20/108/2.
34. Read, *tameva viditvāti mṛtyumeti nānyaḥ panthā vidyatehyanāya, ŚYV*, 31/18.
35. Read, *upāsanaṁ nāma yathāśāstramupasyāsyārthasya viṣayīkaraṇena sāmīpyamupāgamya tailadhārāvat samānapratyayaprāvaheṇa dīrghakālaṁ yadāsanaṁ tadupāsanamācakṣate.* Śaṅkarācārya's commentary on *ŚBG*, 12/3.

creation.[36] The characteristics of that Supreme Soul or God have been described as follows :

1. He is the preserver of wealth (*hiraṇyagarbha*).
2. He is the only master of the created creatures.
3. He is the base of the world (*pṛthivīṁ dādhāra*).
4. He himself is the form of happiness (*kaḥ devaḥ*).[37]

On the other hand a Yajurvedic verse describes as :[38]

1. He is the only enlightening power of all the moving things of the world.
2. He is of the man and of the animals.

Moreover, He is described as the Supreme luster[39] and so on. While describing Him as Supreme existence *KaṭhU* says that He is the powerful controller of Sūrya, Agni, Indra and Yama.[40] The *BU* gives a very clear description of God whom it reveals to be perfect or *pūrṇa* and if a part or whole is taken out from Him, He remains the same.[41] If a man could not realize God in his life, he was thought to have lost everything.[42]

We find Supreme God being named as *skambha* in the *AV* in which he has been described to be the base of existence of Brahmā.[43] He has preserved fire, sun, moon, earth, air, space and heaven.[44] The 33 gods also are in

---

36. Read, *subhuḥ svayambhūḥ prathamohantar mahatyarṇave dadhe ha garbhamṛtviyam yato jātah prajāpatiḥ, ŚYV*, 23/63.
37. *ŚYV*, 25/10.
38. *Ibid.*, 25/11.
39. *Ibid.*, 19/9.
40. *KathU*, 2/3/3.
41. Read, *pūrṇamadaḥ pūrṇamidaṁ pūrṇātpūrṇamudacyate. pūrṇasya pūrṇamādāya pūrṇamevāvaśiṣyate, BU*, 5/1/1.
42. *KenU*, 2/5.
43. *AV*, 10/7/11.
44. *Ibid.*, 10/7/12.

Him.[45] He has been described as the originator of *ṛṣis*, earth, *ṛk, sāma* and *yajus.*[46] He has been believed to exist in both, life and death.[47] *Ṛṣis* of Aṅgiras race are the eyes and Yajus are the limbs of Him.[48] The whole cosmos, past and future, were believed to be originated from Him.[49] Another passage prays Indra as such : "I know you all O Indra, you all are in the *skambha*."[50] *Skambha* of the *AV* has been translated by Monier-Williams as Brahmā, the Supreme Being.[51] Two *sūktas* of the *AV* describe *skambha* elaborately.[52] On the other hand, the *ŚYV* in one place says that the Supreme God itself is the Agni, Āditya, Vāyu, Candramā, Śukra, Brahmā and Prajāpati.[53] It is because He is neither understood nor realized by general people because the unexpected and Supreme soul may be the ultimate goal of human being.[54]

GODS AND THEIR NUMBERS

It is a difficult matter to find a fixed number of gods as depicted in the Vedas. A Ṛgvedic passage says that though God is one yet scholars have described Him by different names.[55] So we find a great number of gods in the Vedic literature. The passages themselves reveal the facts. A passage of the *ṚV* clearly says that the numbers of gods is 33 and they reside in the sky, earth and space equally. Each

45. *AV*, 10/7/13.
46. *Ibid.*, 10/7/14 & 20.
47. *Ibid.*, 10/7/15.
48. *Ibid.*, 10/7/18.
49. Read, *bhūtaṁ ca yatra bhāvyaṁ ca sarve lokāh pratiṣṭhitāh*, *AV*, 10/7/22.
50. *Ibid.*, 10/7/30.
51. *SEDM*, p. 1, 2, 5 & 6.
52. *AV*, 10/7 & 10/8.
53. Read, *tadevāgnistadādiyastadvāyustadu candramā.*
    tadeva śukraṁ tad brahma tapaḥ sa prajāpatiḥ, *ŚYV*, 32/1.
54. *ŚYV*, 31/18.
55. Read, *ekaṁ sadviprāḥ bahudhā vadanti*, *ṚV*, 1/164/46.

place has eleven gods.[56] Another passage reveals the same number.[57] An Atharvanic passage also mentions the number of gods to be 33.[58] Though a Ṛgvedic passage mentions the number of gods to be 33[59] but yet it differs from the passage (*ṚV* 1/139/11) regarding the divisions of the gods, such as : Vasus 8, Rudras 11, Ādityas 12, Indra 1 and Prajāpati 1. The *ŚB* also counts in the same way.[60] On the other hand, an Atharvanic passage describes of 21 gods[61] whereas we find the numbers to be 3339 in some other places.[62] A Ṛgvedic passage also mentions it.[63] Thus, we get different views regarding the numbers of gods but yet it was not a matter of conflict as there was no difference between two or among many gods.[64]

THE NAMES OF THE GODS

So far the names of different Gods are concerned we may go through A.B. Keith as follows:[65]

The Great Gods — Celestial

1. Dyaus, the father
2. Varuṇa, Mitra and the Ādityas
3. Sūrya, Savitrī and Pūṣan
4. Viṣṇu
5. Vivasvān
6. The Aśvins

---

56. *ṚV*, 1/159/11.
57. *Ibid.*, 1/34/11.
58. *AV*, 10/7/13.
59. *ṚV*, 8/28/1.
60. *ŚB*, 11/3/6/5.
61. *AV*, 1/1/1.
62. *ŚB*, 11/6/3/4 *SāṇSS*, 8/21/14.
63. *ṚV*, 3/9/9.
64. *Ibid.*, 8/30/1.
65. *RPVUK*, preface XIV.

7. The goddess Dawn (Uṣas)
8. The moon (Soma).

The Great Gods — Aerial

1. Indra
2. Trita Āptya
3. Apām Napāt
4. Ahi Budhnya
5. Aja Ekapād
6. Mātariśvan
7. Vāyu and Vāta
8. Parjanya
9. The waters (Āpaḥ)
10. Rudra
11. The Marutas or Rudras.

The Great Gods — Terrestrial

1. Agni
2. Bṛhaspati and other forms of Agni
3. The God Soma
4. The Rivers
5. The Earth
6. The Sea

The Minor Gods of Nature

1 Ṛbhus and Ṛjus
2 The Gandharvas and Apsaras
3 Spirits of the Forest, the Trees, the Plants
4 Spirits of Agriculture, Pasture and the Mountains
5 Deities of the House
6 Divine implements
7 Divine Animals
8 Totemisms
9 The lesser Nature Goddesses.

The *Vedic Mythology*, on the other hand, informs the names

of goddesses as follows[66] : Sarasvatī, Pṛthvī, Rātri, Vāk, Purandharī, Dhīṣaṇā, Ilā, Bṛhaddīyā, Rākā, Sinīvalī, Guṅgu, Kuhu, Pṛṣṇi, Saraṇyu, etc. Moreover we get duel gods[67] and eight groups of gods.[68]

Whatever the list of the gods there may be, we find some departments alloted among gods as such :

No.	*Head Gods*	*Departments*	*References*
1.	Agni	*Vanaspati*	*AV*, 5/24/1 & 2
2.	Dyāvā-Pṛthvī	*Dātā* or donor	*Ibid.*, 5/24/3
3.	Varuṇa	*Apa* or water	*Ibid.*, 5/24/4
4.	Mitrā-Varuṇa	*Vṛṣṭi* or rainfall	*Ibid.*, 5/24/5
5.	Marutas	*Parvata* or mountain	*Ibid.*, 5/24/6
6.	Soma	*Latā* or creepers	*Ibid.*, 5/24/7
7.	Vāyu	*Antarikṣa* or Space	*Ibid.*, 5/24/8
8.	Sūrya	*Cakṣu* or eyes	*Ibid.*, 5/24/9
9.	Candramā	*Nakṣatra* or stars	*Ibid.*, 5/24/10
10.	Indra	*Dyu-loka* or heaven	*Ibid.*, 5/24/11
11.	Marutāṁ Pitā	*Paśu* or animals	*Ibid.*, 5/24/12
12.	Mṛtyu	*Prajā* or people	*Ibid.*, 5/24/13
13.	Yama	*Pitṛ* or forefathers	*Ibid.*, 5/24/15

Moreover, we find some animals treated as gods in the Vedas such as cow,[69] bull,[70] tortoise,[71] etc. While discussing about such gods and goddesses, Sudhakar Chattopadhyaya mentions,

> The association of dogs, the son of Saramā, Sārameya with Yama is found both in the *ṚV* and the *AV*. Indra is designated

66. *VMM*, pp. 332-37.
67. *Ibid.*, pp. 326-37.
68. *Ibid.*, pp. 338-39.
69. *AV*, 12/4/5.
70. *Ibid.*, 9/4/3.
71. *Ibid.*, 19/53/10.

> as a bull in the *ṚV*, horse is the symbol of sun and fire, the twin Vedic gods. Agni is again designated as a bird, while the owl and pigeon are differentiated from others of the same species as messenger of all evils.[72]

On the other hand, Dayānanda Sarasvatī gives the meaning of the names of gods[73] but Sukumari Bhattacharya has opposed such attempts of finding out the meaning of gods. She writes,

> The prevalent tendency of scholars to derive God-names from one particular root with one particular meaning has an essential drawback, it limits the connotation to one particular time and meaning. Mythology as long as it has any validity, has dynamism, and to confine a name to a fixed significance is to deaden it for all subsequent time.[74]

But Dayānanda Sarasvatī says that by knowing the names and deriving them, one would be able to understand the characteristics of the gods as well as the unity in diversity in the names of gods.[75] It has clearly been mentioned in various books.[76]

ONENESS IN MANY GODS

Though we find the existences of several gods in the Vedic literature, yet the passages of the Vedas[77] frequently clarifies the sense by saying :[78]

> They (Scholars) call Him Indra, Mitra, Varuṇa, Agni and He is heavenly nobly winged Garutman. To what is One, sages give many title : they call it Agni, Yama, Mātariśvan.

---

72. *EEAHS*, p. 27.
73. *SPD*, p. 9.
74. *ITS*, p. 17.
75. *SPD*, p. 8.
76. *ṚV*, 1/164/46, *SV* 6/8/2, *MS* 12/123.
77. *ṚV*, 1/164/4.
78. *ṚVg*, p. 113.

In the footnote Griffith clearly says,

> All these names, says the poet are, the names of One and the same divine being of the One Supreme Spirit under various manifestations.[79]

The devotee was advised to feel oneness among the gods Agni, Āditya, Vāyu, Candramā, Śukra, Brahmā and Prajāpati with the Supreme Spirit.[80] Among them none is greater and none is inferior.[81] Griffith translated as, "Nor one of you, ye gods is small, none of you is a feeble child : All of you, verily are great."[82] Yāskācārya also admits that, "God is one but He has been prayed in different ways."[83] Another Ṛgvedic passage[84] reveals, "Him with songs in many figures."[85] The passages of a *sūkta*[86] ends with, "You are only great Existence of all the gods."

VEDIC PRAYERS

Almost all the *ṛk*s of the *ṚV* are the prayers to God. But we get some important prayers in the Vedas that inspired the people. Some of them are as follows :

1. O God, let us live for hundred of autumns, study for hundred years, etc.[87]
2. A Yajurvedic passage runs thus, "O God, you are

---

79. Footnote on 1/164/46 by Griffith, *ṚV*, p. 113.
80. *ŚYV*, 32/1.
81. *ṚV*, 8/30/1.
82. *ṚVg*, p. 624.
83. Read, *mahābhāgyāt devatāyāḥ eka ātmā bahudhā stūyate, Nir*, 7/1/4.
84. *ṚV*, 10/114/5.
85. *ṚVg*, p. 624.
86. Read all in the passage of the *sūkta*, *mahaddevānāmasurat-vamekam. ṚV*, 3/55.
87. Read, *paśyema śaradaḥ śatam, jīvema śaradaḥ śatam. budhyema śaradaḥ śatam. rohema śaradah śatam. pūṣema śaradaḥ śatam, bhavema śaradaḥ śatam. bhūyema śaradaḥ śatam. bhūyāsīḥ śaradaḥ śatam, AV*, 19/67.

like enlightening fuels. You are lustre yourself. Please put that lustre in me."[88]

3. Another passage goes as, "You are lustre yourself and please put this in me. You are vigour yourself. Please connect me with that. You are strength and bestow that quality to me. You are wrath yourself and bless me with such anger. You are endurance yourself and please penetrate that in me."[89] The same feeling is reflected in the *AV*, also.[90]
4. "Obedient to the rein of Law Eternal, give us each thought that more and more shall bless us."[91]
5. "Ye Gods, raise up once more the man ye have humbled and brought low."[92]
6. "Let the part which does not take birth (*ātman*) be made splendid."[93]
7. "O God, please protect me from sinful actions."[94]
8. "O God, please make my mind full with good wills."[95]
9. Another passage prays gods as : "O God, please throw out the disasters from the surrounding environments and enable us to acquire the perfect, sweet and ideal things."[96]

Yajña or Sacrifice

The importance of *yajña* or sacrifice in the life of the Vedic people appears from the fact that the people were advised

---

88. *ŚYV*, 38/25.
89. *Ibid.*, 19/9.
90. *AV*, 2/17.
91. *ṚV*, 1/123/13; *ṚV*, p. 85.
92. *ṚVg*, p. 632.
93. *ṚV*, 10/16/4.
94. *Ibid.*, 10/128/4.
95. Read, *tanme manaḥ śiva saṅkalpamastu*, *ŚYV*, 34/1 to 6.
96. Read, *yadbhadram tanna āsuva*, *ŚYV*, 30/3.

to perform sacrifices one after another like one collects fruits from one tree and others.[97] Secondly, *yajña* was compared with Viṣṇu.[98] It was said that first of all Indra worshipped God through *yajña* and then people also started to do the same.[99] *Yajña* was said to be the essence of life of people and by performing the sacrifices people acquired prosperities.[100] Gods performed *yajña* through the Supreme God.[101] We find various types of descriptions regarding *yajña* as (i) Sacrifice itself is the Earth,[102] (ii) Cosmos is itself a *yajña*,[103] and (iii) *Vajra* also is itself a *yajña*.[104] So, it was not a general matter but a noble phenomenon in the Vedic India.

PURPOSES OF ORGANIZING GENERAL YAJÑAS

The people of the Vedic ages continued *yajña*s to get prosperities.[105] They wanted the results of the deeds they performed.[106] On the other hand, a Ṛgvedic passage goes thus, "O Mitrā-Varuṇa, I make oblations to you through sacrifices so that the celestial rain may remove our sufferings."[107] The *MS* also expresses the same view.[108] The

---

97. *ṚV*, 2/5/4.
98. Read, *yajño vai viṣṇuḥ*, *ŚB* 1/1/2/13 & *TS* 1/7/4.
99. Read, *manuḥ ha vai* (*prajāpatiḥ*) *agre yajñena* i.e., *tadanukṛtya imāḥ prajāḥ yājante*, *ŚB*, 1/5/2/7.
100. Read, *sarveṣāṃ vai eṣa bhūtānām, sarveṣāṃ devānām ātmā yad yajnāḥ. tasya samṛddhaṃ anuyājamānaḥ prajayā paśubhiḥ ṛdhyate.* *ŚB*, 1/5/2/7.
101. *ŚYV*, 31/16.
102. Read, *yajño vai bhuvanam*, *TS*, 3/3/7/5.
103. Read, *virāṭ vai yajñah*, *ŚB*, 1/1/1/2.
104. Read, *virājaḥ yajñaḥ*, *GB*, 1/5/24.
105. *ṚV*, 2/2/1.
106. *Ibid.*, 2/11/12.
107. Read, *ā vāṃ mitrāvaruṇā havyajuṣṭiṃ namasā devāvavasā vavṛtyām asmākaṃ brahma pṛtanāsu sahyā asmākaṃ vṛṣṭirdivyā supārā.* *ṚV*, 1/152/7.
108. *MS*, 3/76.

ŚBG also depicts it on the other way.[109] A passage of the *AV* says that the sacrifices or the *yajña*s make the rivers flow and they make the air blown. The sacrifices were done for the sake of birds and it was the means of production of offspring and wealth of the *yajamāna*. It was able to bestow peace.[110] On the other hand, an Atharvanic passage says thus: "Let the *yajña* throw the wickeds just like flood throws the foams."[111] So one of the purposes to constitute the *yajña* was to purify all the directions in the world.[112] The *ŚBG* also says that one gets heaven by performing *yajña*.[113] *Ghī* must be used in the *yajña* as it was thought to be its life.[114] People believed that sunrays took shelter in banyan tree, fig, wild fig and *Ficus infectoria* trees[115] for which those were preferred for the fuels of *yajña*. *Palāśa* also was an important fuel for *yajña*.[116] The whole world was supposed to be the *yajñavedī* and the residence of gods.[117] So the people were perhaps inspired to go everywhere and perform *yajña*s. The gods and the brāhmaṇas who were ready to help others in their disasters got their respective seats in the *yajña*s.[118] *Kuśa* was offered for the seats to gods and the sons of Aditi.[119] A *ṛtvik* was considered to be a worthy[120] whereas Brahmā

109. *ŚBG*, 3/14.
110. *AV*, 9/1/1.
111. Read, *idam haviryātudhānān nadīphenamivāvahat*, *AV*, 1/8/1.
112. *ŚYV*, 22/24.
113. *ŚBG*, 3/14.
114. Read, *eṣa vāva yajñaḥ yad ājyam. tasmāt ājyasya eva yajet*, *TS*, 2/6/3, *ŚB*, 2/4/3/1.
115. Read, *prāṇāḥ vai yajñasya samidhaḥ. naiyagrodhaḥ audumbaraḥ plākṣaḥ iti idhmo bhavati. ete vai gandharvāpsarasāṃ gṛhaḥ*, *ŚB*, 1/5/4/1.
116. *ŚB*, 1/3/3/19.
117. Read, *pṛthivī vai sarveṣāṃ devānām āyatanam. sā vai iyaṃ sarvā eva vediḥ*, *ŚB*, 14/1/1/1 & *TS*, 6/2/4.
118. *ŚB*, 1/3/3/9.
119. *ṚV*, 10/110/4.
120. *ŚB*, 3/1/1/5.

was thought to be the worthiest because he was supposed to be the medician among the *ṛtviks*.[121] Describing about the management of *yajña* a *ṛk* has allegorically been expressed thus: "A *hotṛ* recites *ṛks*, an *udgātṛ* sings the *sāman*, Brahmā corrects the errors and Adhvaryu lays down the rules."[122] In the footnote of the passage (*ṚV* 10/71/11) Griffith writes,[123] "Repeating rears or verses of the *ṚV*, this is the duty of the *hotṛ*, the holy psalm; the *gāyatra* or *sāman*, the *udgātṛ* or chanter, one of the four priests is intended. . . ." That is called *yajña* where Brahmā exists.[124] A story of Dīrghatamas of the *ṚV* says that he sat as Brahmā in the *rājasūya yajña* instituted by Bharata at his age of 90 years.[125] Brahmā was expected to be expert in everything.[126] The oblations were performed with five *vyāhṛtis* or statements.[127] The *ŚB* describes about it.[128] The *GB* gives more detailed description and mentions those *vyāhṛtis* such as, (*oṁ*) 1. Make me listen or *āśrāvaya*, 2. Let you hear or *astu śrauṣaṭ*, 3. Perform sacrifices or *yāja*, 4. We perform sacrifices or *ye yajāmahe*, and 5. Let the oblations reach or *vauṣaṭ*.[129] After the completion of *yajña*, the *yajamāna* must give the *dakṣiṇā* to the priest which only lead the *yajña* to the success.[130] The *ṚV* also emphasizes upon *dakṣiṇā*.[131]

---

121. *ŚB*, 1/8/1/28 & 1/7/4/19.
122. *ṚV*, 10/71/11.
123. *ṚVg*, p. 585.
124. Read, *yatra brahma tatra vai yajñaḥ sthitah, GB*, 2/1/4.
125. *ṚV*, 1/158/6.
126. Read, *brahma sarvavidyāḥ sarvaṃ veditum arhati, Nir*, 1/8.
127. Read, *vyāhṛti* is "statement", *SEDM*, p. 1039.

    caturbhiśca chaturbhiśca dvābhyāṁ pañcabhireva ca
    hūyate ca punar dvābhyāṁ sa me viṣṇu prasīdati.

128. *ŚB*, 12/3/3/3.
129. *GB*, 1/5/10.
130. *TMB*, 16/1/4.
131. *ṚV*, 1/107/2.

SERIAL ORDER OF THE YAJÑAS

The *GB* gives a sequential list of order of the *yajña*s such as: *agnyādhāna, pūrṇāhuti, agnihotra, darśapūrṇamāsa, āgrāyanam, cāturmāsya, paśubandha, agniṣṭoma, rājasūya, vājapeya, aśvamedha, puruṣamedha, sarvamedha, dakṣiṇāvanta, sahasradakṣiṇāvanta.*[132]

FORMS OF YAJÑAS

Agnyādhāna and Pūrṇāhuti

Agnyādhāna or the establishment of fire was compulsory for all the *yajña*s.[133] On the other hand, the *GB* says that *pūrṇāhuti* should be performed just after *agnyādhāna.*[134]

Agnihotra

So far *agnihotra* sacrifice is concerned it is said to be the mouth of all the sacrifices.[135] It has been compared with the fore part of an arrow[136] and was to be performed in the morning and the evening.[137] The evening oblations are offered to Agni and the morning oblations are for the sun.[138] It is said *jarāmarya* sacrifice also.[139] *Jarā* means oldness and *marya* denotes for death. Hence, it is clear that this sacrifice

---

132. Read, *athāto yajñakramāḥ. agnyādheyamagnyādheyat pūrṇāhutiḥ. pūrṇāhuteragnihotram agnihotrāddarśapūrṇamāsau darśapūrṇamāsābhyām, āgrāyaṇam āgrāyaṇāt cāturmāsyāni, cāturmāsyebhyaḥ paśubandhaḥ, paśubandhādagniṣṭomaḥ, agniṣṭomād rājasūyo rajasūyā-dvājapeyaḥ vājapeyādaśvamedhaḥ aśvamedhāt puruṣamedhaḥ, puruṣa-medhāt sarvamedhaḥ, sarvamedhāt dakṣiṇavanto dakṣiṇavadbhyo dakṣiṇā adakṣiṇāḥ sahasradakṣiṇe pratiṣṭhāmsteva ete yajñakramāh, GB,* 1/5/7.
133. Read, *agnyādhānapūrvā vai sarve yajñāḥ, tasmāt agnim ādahīta, TB,* 11/2.
134. *GB,* 1/5/8.
135. Read, *yajñamukhaṃ vai agnihotram, TS,* 1/6/10.
136. Read, *yathā vai iśo anīkam evaṃ yajñānām agnihotram, ŚB,* 2/3/3/10.
137. Read, *sāyaṃ prātaḥ agnihotraṃ juhoti, TS,* 3/4/10.
138. *ŚB,* 2/3/3/10.
139. Read, *etadavai jarāmaryaṃ satraṃ yad agnihotram, jarayā vā hi eva asmāt mucyate mṛtyunā vā, ŚB,* 12/4/1/1.

is to be continued until one becomes old or dies. The *agnihotra* is done by pronouncing two Yajurvedic verses.[140] A priest or a son is placed to perform the sacrifice if the sacrificer falls ill.[141] Sitanath Dey mentions about some secondary items of oblations that consist of gruel, rice, paddy and butter.[142]

Darśapūrṇamāsa

Darśapūrṇamāsa sacrifice seems to be another important sacrifice performed by the Vedic people. Gods are called in the previous day in order to perform the *yajña.*[143] Mainly Agni, Viṣṇu, Sarasvatī and Sarasvān are the gods to whom the *yajamāna* has to oblate in this sacrifice.[144] It is *iṣṭi* type of sacrifice and is done on the day of new and full moon. *Darśa* means new moon and *pūrṇamāsa* means full moon. The *ĀpGS* says that a married couple after observing a fast has to hold the sacrificial activities.[145] The ceremony consists of two days in full moon and two days in the dark moon.[146] The sacrificer performs six types of oblations as follows : 1. *Puroḍāsa*s were given to Agni, 2. Curd and milk for Indra in every *amāvasyā* alternatively, 3. *Puroḍāsa*s with *aṣṭa kapāla* for Agni, 4. *Apāṁśu yāja* with *ghī* for Agni and Soma, and 5. The *puroḍāsa yāja* with *ekādaśa kapāla* was offered on *pūrṇimā.*[147] The first and the second chapter of the *ŚYV* has been used to describe the *darśapūrṇamāsa* sacrifice. In order to perform this sacrifice one should invite four priests such as : Hotṛ, Adhvaryu, Agnidhra and Brahmā.[148]

140. *ŚYV*, 3/9 & 10.
141. *ILSYVS*, p. 125.
142. *Ibid.*, p. 126.
143. *GB*, 2/2/24.
144. *Ibid.*, 2/1/12.
145. *IVKR*, p. 399.
146. *IABJr*, p. 155.
147. *VSR*, pp. 259-60.
148. *VPJr*, pp. 124-25.

Cāturmāsya

The sacrifice *āgrāyana* is obscure and hence we find *cāturmāsya* sacrifice after this. *Cāturmāsya* sacrifice is supposed to get victory over the whole year.[149] One should start the *cāturmāsya* on the date of *Phālguna pūrṇimā.*[150] It occupies an important place in the animal sacrifice or *paśu yajña.*[151] Baladev Upadhyaya informs us that[152] the *yajña* started from the *pūrṇimā* of *Phālguna* is called *vaiśvadeva.* Secondly, *varuṇa praghās* or the sacrifice starts from the *pūrṇimā* of *Āṣāḍha.* Thirdly, the *śākamedha* starts from the *Kārttika pūrṇimā* and at last *sunasirīya* is held on the *pratipadā* of *Phālguna śukla.* Thus, the *cāturmāsya* sacrifice rotates in a year. It was told the sacrifice of medicines.[153]

Agniṣṭoma

Agniṣṭoma or *soma yajña* holds an important place among the Vedic people. *Iṣṭis* have been made by God for which He is regarded as the rebirth form of *agniṣṭoma.*[154] This sacrifice has been compared with the sun.[155] We find a story of how the *agniṣṭoma* sacrifice was started in the world, that runs as follows :

> Some poor *ṛṣis* saw this one-footed sacrifice *agniṣṭoma* and they carried it to their home through which they performed the sacrifice and as a result of this they reached the heaven.[156]

---

149. Read, *akṣayyaṃ vai sukṛtaṃ cāturmāsyayājino bhavati sambatsaram hi jayati, ŚB,* 2/6/3/1.
150. Read, *phālgunyāṃ paurṇamāsyāṃ cāturmāsyāni prayuñjīta, GB,* 2/119.
151. Read, *mukhaṃ vai etad sambatsarasya, GB,* 2/1/19.
152. *VSSB,* p. 511.
153. Read, *ato ete vai bhaiṣajyā yajñāḥ. yat cāturmāsyāni, GB,* 2/1/19.
154. Read, *tad vai etad agniṣṭomasya janma, ibid.,* 2/4/7.
155. *Ibid.,* 2/4/10.
156. *GB,* 1/3/7.

The *ŚB* has a long description of the *agniṣṭoma* or *soma* sacrifice. The sacrificer has to cut his nail, hairs in the midst of the utterance of some Yajurvedic passage.[157] He has to bath[158] and put on new dresses.[159] About the altar of the sacrifice, the *ŚB* clarifies : There has been a big pillar in the eastern part of the sacrificial house wherefrom one has to go forward three steps towards east and put a stake there which is named as *antaḥ-pāta*. This *antaḥ-pāta* is regarded to be the centre of the *yajñaśālā* wherefrom fifteen step southward and northward two stakes are put and they are named as *dakṣiṇaśroṇi* and *uttaraśroṇi* respectively. The sacrificer again has to move 36 steps towards east and put a stake named as *pūrvārdha*. He has to go 12 steps towards south from the centre and put a stake there. That is named as *dakṣiṇoṁśaḥ*. In the same way, we get *uttaroṁśaḥ* by putting a stake at the distance of twelve steps from the centre.[160] The sacrificer remains on fasting to stay in meditation until sunset. He has to go to bed after that, after offering his prayers to Agni[161] through a Yajurvedic passage.[162] He has to pray in the next morning as such : "I have got my thoughts returned and my life, breath and soul also have followed me accordingly."[163] The next day is followed by animal sacrifice for which one has to go to fetch a tree[164] and that is oblated in fire with a *mantra*, i.e., a passage of the *ŚYV*.[165] After that though we get a slaughtering scene

157. *Ibid.*, 3/1/2/2 to 9.
158. *Ibid.*, 3/1/2/10.
159. *GB*, 3/1/2/13.
160. Read, *tad vai etad agniṣṭomasya janma*, 3/5/1/1 to 6.
161. Quoted from *SRSBN*, p. 27.
162. *ŚYV*, 4/14.
163. *Ibid.*, 4/15.
164. *ŚB*, 3/6/4/15.
165. *ŚYV*, 6/8.

in a passage of the *ŚB*[166] but yet it is obscure how it is done. Naama Drury remarks, "The slaughterer could either choke the animal by keeping its mouth closed or strangle it with a noose."[167] Whatever the fact there may be, next programme follows with *soma* sacrifice. The *soma* is brought from Muñjavān mountain or from the Himālayan range by a brāhmaṇa by purchasing it from śūdra or a man of Kutsa tribe."[168] After the completion of that day's sacrifice the priest, *hotā*, *yajamāna* and others sit to drink *soma* and have it.[169] Thus, the *agniṣṭoma* sacrifice comes to an end.

While describing and defining *agniṣṭoma*, Acarya Baladev Upadhyaya mentions that the *soma* song of the *ṛk*[170] is said to be *agniṣṭoma*.[171] The *agniṣṭoma* sacrifice is performed in three ways, these were :

1. *Ekāha* or one day sacrifice.
2. A sacrifice which is performed for two to twelve days, and
3. *Satra* or such a sacrifice which is held for more than 30 days to 1000 years.

SACRIFICES RELATED WITH POLITICS

Though the sacrifices are related with the personal life but yet, we find the Vedic *ṛṣi*s connecting them with the social and political life also. We get the list of order of the *yajña*s in the *GB*[172] in which the first eight types of sacrifices are totally personal whereas the latter *rājasūya*, *vājapeya*, *aśvamedha*, *puruṣamedha* and *sarvamedha* are related with

166. *ŚB*, 3/89/1/15.
167. Quoted from *SRSBN*, p. 29.
168. *SRSBN*, p. 36.
169. *ŚB*, 4/2/1/29.
170. *ṚV*, 6/48/1.
171. *VSSB*, p. 512.
172. *GB*, 1/5/7.

politics and society. After studying the passages of the *ŚB,*[173] *GB,*[174] and *SS*[175] we find ourselves puzzled as to which one should be first performed between the two, *rājasūya* or *vājapeya*.

Rājasūya Sacrifice

We are going to first describe the rituals of the *rājasūya* sacrifice. We find Varuṇa describing about *rājasūya* sacrifices performed by Hariścandra.[176] A passage of the *AB* mentions that the *rājasūya* sacrifice of Hariścandra had four main priests. They were Viśvāmitra, Jamadagni, Vaśiṣṭha and Āyasa as Hotā, Adhvaryu, Brahmā and Udgātā[177] respectively. Śunaḥśepa was brought to offer to Varuṇa in that sacrifice.[178] The *rājasūya* sacrifice is known as *varuṇāsava* also.[179] The king who wished to go to heaven after death, performs this sacrifice. *Soma* sacrifice, *havi* sacrifice and *sarvadarvī* sacrifice also are inferior to *rājasūya* sacrifice.[180] After all, this sacrifice is a consecration ceremony of a king. Varuṇa is known as Dharmapati[181] and the *rājasūya* sacrifice is performed to worship Varuṇa.[182]

In the starting, the priests utters, "Quicken him O God, to be unrivalled, for great kingship, for self-controlling power. . . ."[183] The *adhvaryu* sprays the holy water to the

---

173. *GB,* 1/5/7.
174. *Ibid.*
175. *ĀpSS,* 11/9/9.
176. Read, *tasmā etaṃ rājasūyaṃ yajñakratum provāca, AB,* 7/3/3.
177. *Ibid.,* 7/4/4.
178. *Ibid.*
179. Read, *yo rājasūya sa varuṇasava, TB,* 2/7/6/1.
180. Read, *sarvān vai yajñakratum avasandhe, sarvāḥ iṣṭiḥ api darvī homān yo rājasūyena yajate, ŚB,* 2/5/3/9.
181. *ŚYV,* 9/39.
182. *TB,* 2/7/6/1.
183. *ŚYV,* 9/40.

king and blesses him as : "O Gods, inspire the king by making him free from all enemies, it is for the status of a great *kṣatra*, for the status of a great king and for the vigour of Indra."[184] In the same way, a passage of the *TS* also was uttered.[185] Sitanath Dey, after Mahīdhara, says as follows :

> Holy waters are collected from the seven different sources consisting of river, pools, wells, dew-drops, floods, rain water, seas, etc.

He further informs that "the water collected from those different sources are mixed in a wooden *udumbara* vessel."[186] The sprinkling ceremony is commenced after reciting the verses, said to Śunaḥśepa and the brothers of Madhucchandā by Viśvāmitra.[187] The verses are five in numbers. The Hotā tells the story sitting on the cot of gold.[188] The Adhvaryu pronounces *oṁ* in each *gāthās* and *mantras* when the Hotā sings.[189] After that, perhaps the *pārtha* oblation follow in which Agni, Soma, Savitā, Sarasvatī, Pūṣan, Bṛhaspati, Indra, Ghoṣā, Śloka, Aṁśa, Bhaga and Aryamā are oblated through *agnaye svāhā*, etc.[190] The *yajamāna* has to wear new dresses such as *tārpya, paṇḍva, adhivāsa* and *uṣṇīśa* after that. That is regarded as the new birth of the *yajamāna*.[191] The next ritual follows by performing the mounting of four quarters wearing the skin of tiger and then the blessing of Adhvaryu to the king follows as such :

184. Read, *rajyāyendrasyendriyāya imamamuṣya putramamuṣyai putramasyai viśa eṣavohmi, ŚYV*, 10/18.

185. *TS*, 1/8/12.

186. *ILSYS*, p. 73.

187. *AB*, 7/3/6.

188. *Ibid.*

189. Read, *omiti vai devam, AB*, 7/3/6.

190. *ILSYVS*, p. 74.

191. *Ibid.*

> I am going to sprinkle you to acquire the light, lusture and intelligence, collecting from Soma, Agni and Sūrya, respectively. So you must become worthy of administering and protecting the state.[192]

After that the king has to mount on the chariot and look down the earth so that he can pray the mother earth. The king who completes the above-mentioned rituals is called *dhr̥tavrata.*[193] The sacrifice comes to its end after the priest recites the verses of the *ŚYV.*[194]

Visvanath Pratap Varma gives the summary of the rituals of the *rājasūya* sacrifice as follows :[195]

1. Oblation of *apāmārga.*
2. Oblation of eight Devāsus.
3. Spreading the skin of an antelope.
4. Bringing the two *hiraṇyamaṇi*s in motion.
5. Wearing *tārpya, paṇḍva, adhivāsa* and *uṣṇīśa* by the king *yajamāna.* After that Adhvaryu gives three arrows, namely, *dr̥vā, rujā* and *kṣumā.*
6. Bringing the king in front of his subjects or *marya.*
7. Taking the skin of an antelope, and
8. Lifting the king by Adhvaryu.

So far the gift or *dakṣiṇā* to the priest is concerned, we find Jogiraj Basu mentioning as :

> There are special injunctions as regards the gifts meant for priest. Two mirrors studded with gold are meant for Adhvaryu, a gold necklace for Udgātr̥, a round gold ornament for Hotr̥, horses for the priest *Prasastr̥* and *Pratihartr̥,* ten pregnant cows are meant for brāhmaṇa, one sterile cow for Mitrā-Varuṇa, a bullock for *brāhmanacchaṁsī,*

192. *ŚYV,* 10/17.
193. *ŚB,* 5/4/4/5.
194. *ŚYV,* 10/34.
195. *VRV,* p. 149.

> clothes for *neṣṭr̥* and *potr̥*, a cartload of barley for *ācchāvaka* and an ox to *agnidhna*.[196]

On the other hand, the *AB*[197] suggests that *dakṣiṇā* such as, one thousand cows, golden seat, chariot fastened with strong and white horses, should be given to Hotā. Remarkable fact is that the horses of the chariot must be decorated with silver. Hundred cows, and a golden seat should be donated to Adhvaryu.

Vājapeya Sacrifice

The *vājapeya* sacrifice is performed by a monarch who has already performed *rājasūya* to become an emperor.[198] The verse of the *ŚYV* from 9/1 to 9/34 are related with the *vājapeya* sacrifice.[199] We find the term *vājapeya* used in the meaning of *annapeya*.[200] Again, the *TB*[201] says that God wishes to obtain strength (*vājam*) through the *vājapeya* sacrifice.[202] Both the kṣatriya and brāhmaṇas can perform this sacrifice. For example, both Br̥haspati and Indra performed the sacrifice once.[203] The *vājapeya* sacrifice stands for the temporal power of lordship of a kṣatriya and the spiritual lordship of a brāhmaṇa.[204] Sitanath Dey observes that it was a one-day *soma* sacrifice.[205] We get a clear

196. *IABJr*, p. 166.
197. *AB*, 7/3/6.
198. Read, *rājā vai rājasūyeneṣtvā bhavati samrādvājapeyena*, *ŚB*, 5/1/1/3.
199. Read, *navamedhyāye vājapeyamantrāḥ ucyante catustrimsat kaṇḍikā paryantam*. Mahīdhara on *ŚYV*, 9/1.
200. Read, *annapeyena taṃ ha vai nāmaitad yad vājapeyam annaṃ vā eṣa ujjayati yo vājapeyena yajate*, *ŚB*, 5/1/5/25.
201. *TB*, 1/3/2/3.
202. J.R. Basu translated *vājam* as strength in *IABJr*, p. 91.
203. *ŚB*, 5/1/1/11.
204. Quoted from *IABJr*, p. 94.
205. Quoted from *ILSYVS*, p. 67.

description of the sacrifice in the commentary of the *ŚYV* by Jvala Prasad Misra. Misra observes that the oblation of *ghī* is performed with the passage of *ŚYV* in the beginning of the ritual.[206]

1. The priests call *āgrāyana* and *ṣoḍaśī grahas*[207] at first and then they go to call *aindragraha*.[208]
2. The next ritual follows by landing the chariot and placing it on the altar made for this purpose.[209]
3. The horses are taken to bath and were consecrated. They are brought and fastened to the right and left order.
4. The Brahmā rides on the wheel of the chariot and utters the passage of the *ŚYV* with a view to making *yajamāna* reach the heaven with the permission of the god Savitā.[210]
5. He then recites the *mantras*, "I mounted there with the desire to get heavenly position."[211]
6. The next ritual follows by king's ascent on the chariot[212] after the *dundubhi* was blown.[213]
7. After that *ghī* is offered in oblation with the *mantras* of the *ŚYV* from 9/14 to 9/18 and the horses also are sprinkled.[214]

206. *ŚYV(J)*, 9/1 vol. I, p. 342.
207. *Ibid.*, p. 343 commentary on *ŚYV*, 9/2.
208. Read, *prathamaindra grahodbodhane viniyogaḥ*, Misra on *ŚYV*, 9/2; vol. I, p. 343.
209. Read, *rathamupāvaharati*, Mahīdhara on *ŚYV*, 9/5.
210. Read, *vedimadhye rathasthāpane viniyogaḥ*, *ŚYV*, 9/5. J.P. Misra's commentary vol. I, p. 346.
211. Read, *devasyāhaṃ savituḥ save satyaprasavasa indrasyottamaṃ nākamāruham*, *ŚYV*, 9/10.
212. Read, *rathamārohati yajamānaḥ*, Mahīdhara on 9/13.
213. *ŚYV*, 9/13.
214. *Ibid.*, 9/14, J.P. Misra's commentary, vol. I, p. 353.

8. Then the *yajamāna* rides on the chariot and lands down from it while the *mantra* 9/19 of the *ŚYV* is being recited. Moreover, he has to touch the *caru* and pronounce the same *mantra.*
9. The *yajamāna* has to prepare smelt *soma* for the horses.[215]
10. After that, he has to oblate four times with *ghī* reciting the verse 9/20 of the *ŚYV* and then oblates with *caru* and *puroḍāsa.*[216]
11. After this the king, along with his wife, has to climb the pillar by saying,[217] "We have become the offsprings of Prajāpati." Thus, he should touch the flour of wheat after landing down the pillar.
12. The *yajamāna* should look all the directions[218] while standing on the top of the pillar. Then he looks beneath and proclaims, "I salute the mother earth from here."[219]
13. The skin of a goat is spread on the seat of *udumbara* wood[220] and thus he takes his seat.[221]
14. Then the *yajamāna* accepts the seat and the ritual of oblating *ghī* or *ājyāhuti* takes place.[222]
15. Whatever the oblating materials remain in the sacrifice, all of those are sprinkled by *purohita* to the

215. Read, *yajuryuktān āghrāpayati vājina iti,* Mahīdhara on *ŚYV* commentary 9/19, p. 160.
216. *ŚYV,* 9/20 Misra's commentary, vol. I, p. 357.
217. *ŚYV,* 9/20 Misra's commentary, vol. I, p. 357.
218. Read, *yuparudha eva yajamāno diśaḥ paśyati,* Mahīdhara on *ŚYV,* 9/22.
219. Read, *yuparudha eva yajamāno bhūmim paśyati,* Mahīdhara on *ŚYV,* 9/22.
220. Read, *uttaravedimapareṇa udumbarīmāsandiṃ vastācarmaṇāstṛṇātiyaṃ ta iti,* Mahīdhara on *ŚYV,* 9/22.
221. *Ibid.,* 9/22.
222. *Ibid.,* 9/23/29.

yajamāna[223] and then seventeen more *ghī* oblations have to be performed.[224]

After the completion of the sacrifice the *yajamāna* is entitled as an emperor[225] because it is told *samrāṭsava* for a kṣatriya and *bṛhaspatisava* for a brāhmaṇa.[226]

Towards the end of the discussion of the *vājapeya* sacrifice, we want to quote Visvanath Prasad Varma regarding the sacrifice as :

> Perhaps the root of *vājapeya* is same as *ugra, ojas, ojman* and *vajra.* The *vājapeya* is a one-day *soma* sacrifice. This sacrifice was performed in the ancient times by political and military elites. Generally after the completion of *rājasūya* and *bṛhaspatisava,* the *vājapeya* sacrifice is constituted. Its aim is to have such a drink through which one could get power and strength.[227]

Aśvamedha Sacrifice

The *aśvamedha* sacrifice was regarded as the prominent sacrifice in the Vedic age. So the *aśvamedha* sacrifice was called the king of the sacrifices.[228] The *ṛṣis* invite all the gods in the sacrifice, a sacrifice which meant that the sacrificer have conquered all the directions.[229] People believed *Rāṣṭra* to be wealth and *aśvamedha* in itself.[230] The sacrifice is thought to be able to remove all the sins of the sacrificer.[231]

---

223. *ŚYV,* 9/30. Misra's commentary.
224. *Ibid.,* 9/31/34, Mahīdhara's commentary.
225. Read, *yo vai vājapeya sa samrātsava, ŚB,* 2/7/6/1.
226. Read, *bṛhaspatisavo vā yadvājapeyaṁ, ŚB,* 5/2/1/19.
227. *VRV,* p. 156.
228. Read, *rāja vai eṣa yajñānaṃ yad aśvamedha, ŚB,* 13/2/21.
229. Read, *sarvāḥ vai devatāḥ aśvamedhe anvāyattāḥ. tasmād rāṣṭrī aśvamedhayājī sarvāḥ diśo jayati, ŚB,* 13/2/2/1.
230. Read, *śrīrvai rāṣṭram. rāṣṭraṃ vai aśvamedhaḥ. tasmād rāṣṭrī aśvamedhena yajeta, ŚB,* 6/7/2/7 & 13/1/6/3.
231. Read, *sarvasya vai eṣa pāpmanaḥ prāyaścittiḥ. sarvasya vai etad bheṣajam. sarve vai etena pāpmānaṃ devāḥ atāran, TS,* 5/3/2.

Whatever the descriptions of the sacrifice there may be, we find that the sacrifice is started from the eighth day of the Phālguna *śukla*.[232] The ritual runs as follows :

1. *Adhvaryu* puts the garland of *niṣka* on the neck of the sacrificer reciting the verse of *ŚYV* (22/1).[233] After that the *yajamāna* takes a rope to bind the horse and speaks the verse 1/10 from the *ŚYV*.[234]
2. The horse is bound with that enchanted rope.[235]
3. The sacrificer seeks the permission from the Brahmā to bind the horse by saying, "O Brahmā, I want to bind it now."
4. Why horse is chosen as the prominent animal for the sacrifice has been described by the *ŚB* as :
   (i) Horse is thought to be the most intelligent animal.[237]
   (ii) No other animal is faster than a horse.[238]
   (iii) Horse is the most famous animal.[239]
   (iv) All the gods follow a horse.[240]
5. The horse is brought near the fire and fastened it in

232. Read, *sarvakāmasya rājñaḥ aśvamedhaḥ phālguna suklāṣṭamyāmārambhaḥ*, Mahīdhara on *ŚYV*, 22/1.
233. Read, *taṃ (niṣkaṃ) yajamānakaṇṭhe pratibadhnan adhvaryuḥ tejohasīti pāhi*, Mahīdhara on 22/1.
234. Read, *devasyatvetyādi mantreṇa* (*ŚYV*, 1/10) *trayodasratniṁ darbhamayīṁ dviguṇam aśvabandhanārthaṃ rajjumādāya....* Mahīdhara on *ŚYV*, 22/1.
235. Read, *prajāpataya ityantena rasanayāśvaṃ badhnāti*, Mahīdhara on *ŚYV*, 22/1.
236. Read, *brahman, aśvam bhantsyāmi*, Mahīdhara on *ŚYV*, 22/1.
237. *ŚB*, 13/1/2/6.
238. *Ibid.*, 13/1/2/7.
239. *Ibid.*, 13/1/2/8.
240. *Ibid.*, 13/1/2/4.

a post. Then the oblation follows with some passages of the *ŚYV*.[241]

6. God Savitā is then called in the sacrifice and a seat is offered.[242] It indicates that Savitā occupies an important place in the *aśvamedha* sacrifice.
7. After that Brahmā orders the Advaryu to kindle the fire in the sacrificial fireplace as : "O Adhvaryu, kindle the fire with your prayers and put the fuel in it. The fire is immortal."[243] Another passage is recited to offer a seat to him.[244]
8. The Adhvaryu and the *yajamāna* whisper a *mantra* in the ear of the horse.[245]
9. After that the ritual of *audgarbhaṇa* oblations begin and continue with *ākutyai prayuje*[246] for four times and *kāya svāha*[247] thrice a day for seven days.[248]
10. The Adhvaryu puts thirteen fuels in the fire and recites a verse of the *ŚYV* (22/22).
11. The sacrificer has to collect (i) *ghī*, (ii) powder of parched wheat, (iii) paddy, and (iv) parched paddy[249] for oblations. After that they had to oblate by saying, *prāṇāya svāhā*.[250]
12. A golden statue is laid down and worshipped by a

---

241. *ŚYV*, 22/6 to 8.
242. *Ibid.*, 22/9 to 14.
243. *Ibid.*, 22/15.
244. *Ibid.*, 22/17.
245. *Ibid.*, 22/19.
246. *Ibid.*, 4/7.
247. Read, *kāya svāhā*, *ŚYV*, 22/20 & 21.
248. *ŚB*, 13/1/7/2.
249. Read, *ājyasaktudhānalājānām ekaikaṃ juhoti*, Uvaṭa on *ŚYV*, 22/23.
250. *ŚYV*, 22/23 to 34.

yajamāma.[251] A passage of the *ŚYV*[252] is recited to make the golden statue alive. That was done by gods in ancient times.[253] That statue is supposed to become alive after the recitation of three *mantra*s of the *ŚYV.*[254]

13. The *purohita*s invite two *graha*s (Mahimānasas)[255] and they are requested to take their seats also.[256] After that the *yajamāna* offers the oblations to them.
14. After performing this ritual, the horse is fastened to the chariot in the midst of the recitation of the *ŚYV* (23/2, 3 & 4). Three more horses are fastened later on.[257]
15. The Adhvaryu and the *yajamāna* get into the chariot and go to the pond or river. They collect water from there after the horse enters the water. The ritual runs through the *ŚYV.*[258]
16. The chariot is brought to the sacrificial place, the horses are united and the wives of the king sprinkle holy water on the horses. At that time they recite the passage of the *ŚYV* (23/8).[259]
17. Brahmā asks Hotā like, "Who are around the sacrificial fire?"[260] A ritual of such conversation included in five passages of the *ŚYV* (23/9 to 23/13) is performed.

---

251. *ŚYV*, 23/1, Mahīdhara's commentary.
252. *Ibid.*, 23/1 & 13/4.
253. Read, *atha sāmagāyati etadvai.... ime vai lokāḥ sarpāḥ*, *ŚB*, 7/4/1/22.
254. *ŚYV*, 13/4, J.P. Misra mentions about *ŚYV*, 13/6; 7 & 8.
255. *Ibid.*, 13/1, Mahīdhara's commentary.
256. *Ibid.*, 23/2.
257. *Ibid.*, 23/5 & 6.
258. *Ibid.*, 23/7.
259. *Ibid.*, 23/9, Mahīdhara's commentary.
260. *Ibid.*, 23/9.

18. After that conversation, the horse is given a little water of the *prokṣaṇī* to drink.[261]

19. All those rituals of the *pariplava* legend are performed within ten days.[262] A period of 12 moons is allowed for the horse to move.[263] During this period the priest tells him about all royalties, all regions, all Vedas, all gods, and all beings; and whomsoever verily know these, attains to fellowship over all people, secures for himself all the Vedas and by gratifying the gods finally establishes himself on all beings. The same legend revolves again and again.[264]

20. On the other hand, Naama Drury informs that the stallion wanders for a year.[265] He further informs, "When the stallion and its entourage departs from the sacrificial enclosure, the Adhvaryu places a cushion of gold thread to the south of the *vedī* and on this the Hotṛ sits himself. The *rājā* sits upon the stool of gold and on his right, on the gold wrought cushions, sits the brāhmaṇa and the Udgātṛ. About this group or cluster the people wait to hear the *pariplava* legend. This was a cycle of teaching which lasts for almost a year, made up of mini-cycles each of ten days."[266]

21. Regarding stallion's wandering Jogiraj Basu says, "Before the actual performance of the *aśvamedha*, the sacrificial horse is let loose to roam over the whole country from place to place. It is a challenge

261. *ŚYV*, 23/17.
262. *SRSBN*, p. 55.
263. *Ibid.*
264. *ŚB*, 13/4/3/15.
265. *SRSBN*, p. 45.
266. *Ibid.*, p. 44.

to all the contemporary ruling chiefs, princes and monarchs. If anyone seizes the horse, it meant he opposes or stands in the way of the sacrificers attaining paramount sovereignty. In that case the attandants of the horse fight with that king who seizes the horse. If they fail to defeat him and win back the horse the sacrificer cannot perform the *aśvamedha.* A large number of royal attendants consisting of various types of figures numbering the five hundred heads guard the sacrificial horse and follow in its wake all over the country prepared for any eventuality. It is their sacred duty to protect the horse from all dangers and calamities and bring it back unscathed to the sacrificer. The varied and the large number of attendants forms a part of royal paraphernalia bespeaking the military strength of the king."[267]

22. The *pariplava* legend[268] of ten days goes as follows :
    (i) The legend of the king Manu Vaivasvata.[269]
    (ii) The legend (story) of Yama Vaivasvata.[270]
    (iii) The story of the conversation between Āditya and Varuṇa.[271]
    (iv) The story of Soma Vaiṣṇava.[272]
    (v) The story related with the king Arbuda Kādraveya.[273]

---

267. *IABJr,* p. 95/96.
268. *ŚB,* 13/4/3/3.
269. *Ibid.,* 1/8/1/1.
270. *Ibid.,* 13/4/3/6.
271. *Ibid.,* 13/4/3/7.
272. *Ibid.,* 13/4/3/8.
273. *Ibid.,* 13/4/3/9.

(vi) The legend of the king Kubera Vaiśravaṇa.[274]

(vii) The story of king Asita Dhānva.[275]

(viii) The story of the king Matsya Sammada.[276]

(ix) The story of the king Tārkṣya Vaipaśyata.[277]

(x) The story of the king Dharma Indra.[278]

The *ŚB* further remarks, "This very same legend revolves again and again for a year, for 36 periods, each period being of 10 days."[279]

After the Horse is Returned

After the return of the horse the king is accompanied with his wives. The wives are known as *mahiṣī, vāvātā, parivṛktā* and *palāgalī.*[280] They talk with Brahmā, Udgātā, Hotā and Kṣattā, respectively. Sitanath Dey mentions the first three queens as follows[281] :

(i) *Mahiṣī* is the chief,

(ii) *Vāvātā* is the favourite queen, and

(iii) *Parivṛktā* is the neglected wife.

According to Jogiraj Basu, *Palāgalī* is "Inferior to other three queens."[282]

1. The coronation ceremony starts after that. The holy water of the several sacred rivers and seas is collected and mixed. The priest sprinkles it on the *yajamāna* by reciting, "Quicken him, O gods to be unrivalled,

274. *ŚB*, 13/4/3/10.
275. *Ibid.*, 13/4/3/11.
276. *Ibid.*, 13/4/3/12.
277. *Ibid.*, 13/4/3/13.
278. *Ibid.*, 13/4/3/14.
279. *Ibid.*, 13/4/3/15.
280. *ŚYV*, 23/24 to 30.
281. *ILSYVS*, p. 80.
282. *IABJr*, p. 97.

O gods, so far as to be without enemy, for great freedom, for great chiefdom, for great lordship for man-rule."[283]

2. After that the king assures the mother earth by saying, "Mother earth, don't injure me and I also will protect you."[284]
3. The horse is then slain and the priest prays for the breath to enter in him again. He prays for that with a passage of the *ŚYV* (23/18).
4. All the wives of the lord, then sprinkle water on the horse from the water pots holding in their hands in order to put breath into the horse with three *mantra*s each.[285]
5. The chief queen *mahiṣī* sleeps with the horse[286] and others pray the horse as, "Establish your sperm in this woman. Such is wished by the lady also."[287]
6. At last, the skin of the horse is snatched away with a sword,[288] but before this the chief queen is taken out from the ditch.[289]

Thus, the sacrifice is brought to its end by paying homage to gods with a Yajurvedic passage[290] which is recited by all the people who attended.

Yajña : In General

All the sacrifices are to be performed with some particular

283. Read, *imaṃ deva asapatnam..... mahate jānarājyāya, ŚB,* 5/3/3/13.
284. *ŚB,* 5/4/3/20.
285. *ŚYV,* 23/19, Mahīdhara's commentary.
286. Read, *yajamānena prāṇaśodhane kṛte mahiṣī aśva samīpe śete,* Mahīdhara on *ŚYV,* 23/19.
287. *Ibid.,* 23/11.
288. *Ibid.,* 23/33.
289. Read, *yajamānena prāṇaśodhane kṛte mahiṣī aśva samīpe śete,* Mahīdhara on *ŚYV,* 23/32.
290. *AV,* 5/8/1 & *ṚV,* 1/153/2.

fuels. The sacrifices are found to have constituted with a view to rooting the diseases out.[291] The medicines which are used in the oblations are *gulgulu, pilā, nāladi, aukṣagandhī* and *pramardanī.*[292] The *AV* opposes the oblations with the organs of the creatures.[293] In the same way, we get a passage avoiding goat sacrifice also.[294] So far the gods of the sacrifices are concerned, we find the Agni,[295] Sūrya,[296] Indra,[297] Marutas,[298] Aditi,[299] Viṣṇu,[300] Tvaṣṭā,[301] Savitā,[302] Somadeva,[303] Bṛhaspati and Aśvins.[304]

On the other hand, after the sacrifice comes to its end, the gods are made to depart as : O gods, we have made your path easy,[305] O *yajña,* please go to Viṣṇu.[306] Let the oblation of *ghī* be received by god Agni.[307] Let the gods whom we have not worshipped and those whom we have worshipped wrongly, also get the oblation of *ghī* accordingly.[308]

---

291. *AV,* 4/37/3.
292. *AV,* 7/5/5.
293. Read, *eṣa vā aparimito yajño ya aja, AV,* 9/5/21.
294. *Ibid.,* 5/26/1.
295. *Ibid.,* 5/26/2.
296. *Ibid.,* 5/26/3 & 11.
297. *Ibid.,* 5/26/5.
298. *Ibid.,* 5/26/6.
299. *Ibid.,* 5/26/7.
300. *Ibid.,* 5/26/8.
301. *Ibid.,* 5/26/9.
302. *Ibid.,* 5/26/10.
303. *Ibid.,* 5/26/11.
304. *Ibid.,* 5/26/12.
305. *Ibid.,* 7/97/4.
306. Read, *eṣa vā aparimito yajño ya aja, AV,* 7/97/5.
307. *Ibid.,* 7/97/6.
308. *Ibid.,* 5/8/7.

Theory of Devotion or Bhakti

As devotion is an important factor of *upāsanā,* we get its instances in the Vedas. A passage of the *AV* read as follows: "Let the Agni not carry his oblation of sacrifice who does not possess the devotion in their heart."[309] On the other hand, we get a passage of the *R̥V* expressing the friendly devotion to gods.[310] A devotee never sacrifices from what he acquired in the spiritual field and proclaims,[311] "Neither the right nor the left do I distinguish, neither the east nor the west Ādityas. Simple and guided by your wisdom of Vasus may I attain the light that bring no danger."[312] In the other place the devotee again says, "May I obtain the broad light free from peril : O Indra, let not during darkness seize us."[313] We find a devotional *sūkta* in the *R̥V* which gives us the following informations :

1. Devotion causes to kindle the fire of *agnihotra* and oblation.[314]
2. Devotion inspired people to give or bestow to the needy persons.[315]
3. The gods put their faith on their devotee as to : "We shall get victory over the Asuras" for which they could win them. So devotee is able to bestow the luxuries to the person who performs the sacrifice with the hope of getting something.[316]

---

309. *AV,* 5/8/3.
310. *R̥V,* 10/133/6.
311. *Ibid.,* 2/27/11.
312. *R̥Vg,* p. 148.
313. *R̥V,* 2/27/14.
314. *Ibid.,* 10/151/1.
315. *Ibid.,* 10/151/2.
316. *Ibid.,* 10/151/3.

4. All the gods and *yajamānas* have continued their efforts to acquire "devotion."[317]
5. For the purpose of acquiring utmost devotion to God people offer their oblations in the morning, midday and evening.[318]
6. In another place devotion has been told as the daughter of Sūrya.[319]

Philosophy

Two terms "philos" and "sophia" form the word "philosophy." The term means "love to knowledge." Pythagoras used the word "philosopher" for the first time which meant "the admirer of knowledge."[320] The word *darśana* in India expresses different meaning. We may go through a passage of the *ŚYV* in this regard.[321] It indicates that the purpose of *darśana* is to open the cover of ignorance.[322] We know that the people were eager to discover the mysteries from the time immemorial. We get such an example in the *R̥V*[323] as follows :[324]

1. Who hath beheld him as He sprang to being ?
2. How the boneless one supports the bony ?
3. Where is the blood of earth, the life, the spirit ?
4. Who may approach the man who knows, to ask it ?

The *R̥V* goes further to ask again.[325]

5. Was He an unborn image?

---

317. *R̥V*, 10/151/4.
318. *Ibid.*, 10/151/5.
319. *Ibid.*
320. *DDO*, p. 36.
321. *ŚYV*, 40/15.
322. Read, *hiraṇmayena pātreṇa satyasyāpihitaṃ mukham*, *ŚYV*, 40/15.
323. *R̥V*, 1/164/6.
324. *R̥Vg*, p. 110.
325. *R̥V*, 2/164/6.

6. Who did establish these six regions ?

We get such questions in large number in the Vedas. Those may be regarded as the roots of the Indian philosophy. Whatever the fact there may be, Om Sivaraj tries to define the term *darśana* as, "The chain of ideologies wherefrom the *satya* and *dharma* are realized or seen is called *darśana*.[326] When knowledge-wisher falls in puzzle he claims as :[327]

1. Neither the right nor left do I distinguish, neither the east nor the west.
2. Please guide me by your wisdom.
3. O Vasus, may I attain the light that brings no danger.

THE CREATOR

We get a word *tataḥ* to denote the existence of the supreme and highest authority from which the element *virāṭ* came into being. That *virāṭ* begets *adhipuruṣa* which torn into pieces and thus the universe, planets, stars, etc., were formed.[328] That *tat* is described in a passage of the *ŚYV* as, He is spreading everywhere, Almighty, Boneless, Spotless, All-knowing element, Self-made, Perpetual, and so on.[329] A passage of the *ṚV* mentions Him to be Sovereign Ruler, the Undecaying One.[330] That all-pervading power has been prayed as *abhaya jyoti* or the light which yields fearlessness.[331] Again, He is in *parama vyoman* or the Supreme Divine,[332] and *parama pada* or the Supreme Existence.[333] The *ŚB*

326. Read, *dṛśyate jñāyate satyadharmohaneneti darśanam, DDO*, p. 33.
327. *ṚV*, 2/27/11.
328. Read, *tato virāḍajāyata virājohadhi pūruṣaḥ.*
sa jāto atyasricyata paścāt bhūmimatho puraḥ, ŚYV, 31/5.
329. *ŚYV*, 40/8.
330. Read, *yudhmasya te vṛsabhasya svarāja ugrasya yūnaḥ sthavirasya ghṛṣve.......... śrutasya mahato mahānī, ṚV*, 3/46/1.
331. *ṚV*, 2/27/11.
332. *Ibid.*, 1/143/2.
333. *Ibid.*, 1/22/20 & 23.

describes Him as Prajāpati from which the creation came into being.[334] In the same way the *BU* also says that He takes shape and becomes shapeless also, He is mortal and immortal as well; He is stable and dynamic, and He is existent and unexistent as well.[335] That All-pervading and the Supreme God exposed Himself as many.[336] This Supreme God expressed Himself as *ātman* and *paramātman*.[337] Griffith translated the passage as :

> Two birds with fair wings knit with bond of friendship, in the same sheltering tree have found a refuge. One of the twin eats the sweets fig tree's fruitage, the other eating not regardeth only.[338]

Another passage also expresses the same idea.[339] On the other hand, a Ṛgvedic passage declares the two creating elements, i.e., female and male existent in the name of *puruṣa* and *prakṛti*.[340] Om Sivaraj regarding the aforesaid that passage says, "It seems that Kapila has extracted the original theme of the Sāṅkhya philosophy from this passage."[341] According to Om Sivaraj the passage means, as,

> At the time of creation the *puruṣa* takes birth and the life being connected with the body comes to be enlightened at that time and Aditi served Mitra and Varuṇa for its birth. This *puruṣa* becomes regularly dynamic, consumer of several enjoying things and the existence of having endurance in it.

---

334. *ŚB*, 7/1/417 & 23.
335. *BrU*, 2/3/1.
336. Read, *indro māyābhiḥ pururūpa īyate*, *Ṛ*V, 6/47/18.
337. Read, *dvā suparṇā sayujā sakhāyā*, *Ṛ*V, 1/164/20.
338. *ṚV*, 1/164/20. Griffith's commentary.
339. *ṚV*, 1/164/21 & 22.
340. *Ibid.*, 10/64/5.
341. Quoted from *DDO*, p. 118.

> In several births of these unequal conditions, Hotā accompanies Him always.[342]

Thus, *jīvātmā* becomes immortal after knowing Him and no other way is there in the world to attain truth.[343] He becomes all-knowing then. The passage of the *ṚV* reflects the collective prayer also.[344] People thought that a man knows anything if God blesses him.[345]

ṚTA : AN IMPORTANT PHENOMENON IN THE VEDIC PHILOSOPHY

We get a large number of passages in the Vedic literature mentioning *ṛta* as an important phenomenon of life. At first, before the creation nothing existed except the Omnipotent One.[346] He desired to bring the creation into existence.[347] As such He constituted penance and as a result of that *ṛta* and *satya* are begeted.[348] That *ṛta* has been translated as "Eternal Law" by Griffith.[349] All the gods obtained mighty powers from *ṛta*.[350] Thus, the term *ṛta* denotes perpetual law of *dharma*[351] through which the existence came into being.[352] Thus, *ṛta* has been prayed by the sages as, "To Law (*ṛta*) belongs the vast deep earth and heaven."[353] Moreover, the foundation of Eternal Law or *ṛta* is firmly

342. *DDO*, p. 115.
343. *ŚYV*, 31/18.
344. *ṚV*, 1/17/9.
345. *ṚV*, 1/17/9.
346. *Ibid.*, 10/129/2.
347. *Ibid.*, 10/129/4.
348. *Ibid.*, 10/190/1.
349. *ṚVg*, p. 561.
350. *ṚV*, 1/2/8 & 7/60/5.
351. *ŚB*, 5/3/3/9, 5/4/4/5.
352. *ṚV*, 3/55/5 & 1/156/3.
353. *Ibid.*, Griffith on 4/23/10.

fixed.[354] On the other hand, H.N. Tripathi says that the expansion of *ṛta* is known as *sattva, raja* and *tama* or Sentimental principle, Motivational principle and Static principle, respectively."[355] Thus, *ṛta* is thought to be the phenomenon that leads the creatures to right path.[356] It has been explained as those that are able to remove the transgressions,[357] inspires to live for long,[358] and so on. In this context we may quote Visvanath Prasad Varma as follows :

> Though the theory of *ṛta* was introduced in the *ṚV*, yet we can erect a vast foundation of politics supporting its spiritual, moral and ideal literature.[359]

THEORY OF CREATION

In order to go through the theory of creation, we must first apprehend the Creation Hymn of the *ṚV*.[360] The importance of the *sūkta* appears in the comments of Vincent A. Smith when he says, "From among the many versions of the created Hymn, 'The earliest specimen of Aryan Philosophic thought'. . . ."[361] Almost all the scholars of the Vedas are astonished to read this *sūkta*. All the seven passages of the *sūkta* bear deep knowledge. Ramgovinda Trivedi says that all the six schools of philosophy of India are evolved out of this *sūkta*.[362] This *sūkta* has been translated by A.C. Das in

354. *ṚV*, 4/23/9.
355. *PBRNH*, p. 217.
356. *ṚV*, 1/24/3.
357. *Ibid.*, 4/23/8.
358. *Ibid.*, 4/23/9.
359. Quoted from *VRV*, p. 262.
360. *ṚV*, 1/129.
361. *OHIS*, p. 48.
362. *VSR*, p. 411.

a poetic manner.[363] After a study of these passages we firstly come to the following points:

1. Before creation came into being, there existed neither the existent nor the non-existent.
2. Both the mortality and immortality were absent, and no sign of the day's and night's divider existed.
3. Only the one named *ānīdavātam* was in existence.
4. There existed only darkness. The *ānīdavātam* remained covered and, as such, could not be seen.
5. This *ānīdavātam* desires to be exposed and first cause of creation comes out.

---

363. Read, "No-being then existed not, nor being;
There was no air, nor heaven which is beyond it;
What motion is there ? Where ? By whom directed ?
Was water there and fathomless abysses ?

Death then existed not, nor immortal;
Of neither night nor day was any semblance.
The One breathed calm and wideness by self-impulse;
There was not any other thing beyond it.

Darkness at first was covered-up by darkness;
This universe was indistinct and fluid.
The empty space that was void by hidden,
That One was by the force of heat engendered.

Desire then at first arose in it;
Desire which was the earliest seed of spirit.
The bond of being in non-being sages
Discovered searching in their hearts with wisdom.

Who knows it truely ? Who can here declare it ?
Whence was it born ? Whence issued this creation ?
And did the Gods appear with its production ?
But then who knows from whence it has arisen ?

This world-creation, whence it has arisen,
Or whether it has been produced, or has not,
He who surveys it in the highest heaven,
He only knows, or e'en He does not know it."

— Quoted from *RCD*, p. 537

6. The desire of *ānīdavātam* creates the consumers and the consuming things.
7. The begetter get mighty forces and free actions in left and right and *svadhā* is placed beneath Him whereas *prayāti* is placed above.
8. All the gods come into being after this creation.
9. This theory of creation is obscure one.

The Vedic philosophy informs that this is not the first creation rather uncountable creations had taken place before this.[364] Kunwarlal Vyasasisya admits in this regard as, "Modern scientists also have confessed that this creation hadn't sprung out accidently, this universe also dies like a life."[365] So far the sequential order of creation is concerned, three Ṛgvedic passages[366] inform as follows :

1. *Ṛta* and *satya* or Eternal Law and Truth.
2. Day and night.
3. Seas, ocean and rivers.
4. *Saṁvatsara* spring out from ocean.
5. God then divides times into day, night, hour and so on.
6. God then creates the Sun, Moon and other planets as He did before.
7. At the end He made the Heaven, Earth and Sky.

People thought that existent sprang from the non-existent in the earlier age.[367] On the other hand, if we study the *puruṣa sūkta*, we find some other informations such as :

1. This *puruṣa* is the only existent wherefrom all the visible are exposed.[368]

---

364. Read, *dhātā yathāpūrvam akalpayan*, *ṚV*, 10/190/3.
365. *BIPK*, p. 22.
366. *ṚV*, 1/190/1, 2 & 3.
367. *TU*, 2/7.
368. *ŚYV*, 31/2.

2. This *puruṣa* begets *virāṭ* from which the *adhipuruṣa* springs out and that created *adhipuruṣa* exposes itself in the land of stars, planets, etc.[369]
3. He (the *puruṣa*) constitutes a *yajña* wherefrom the consuming things, forests, its inhabitants, villages and animals came into existence.[370]
4. Other than those the *yajña* was able to create the *Ṛgveda*, *Sāmaveda*, *Chanda* and the *Yajurveda* from Him.[371]
5. Not only this, God then creates horses, cows, goats and other creatures.[372]
6. God creates the moon from His mind, the sun from His eyes, the air from His ears and the fire from His mouth.[373]
7. The space is His navel, heaven is His head, earth is His feet and directions are His ears.[374]

If one asks as to what type of *yajña* was held, then we will have to go through a Ṛgvedic passage[375] where questions has been put as, "What were the rules, the order and the model ? What were the wooden tender and the butter ? What were the Hymns, the chants the reciations and when do all the Deities paid worship to God?"[376] That *yajña* is supposed to have performed with the passages of the particular metres which are connected with particular gods such as :[377]

369. *ŚYV*, 31/5.
370. *Ibid.*, 31/6.
371. *Ibid.*, 31/7.
372. *Ibid.*, 31/8.
373. *ŚYV*, 31/12.
374. *Ibid.*, 31/13.
375. *ṚV*, 10/130/3.
376. *ṚVg*, p. 634.
377. *ṚV*, 10/130/5 & 6.

No.	*Name of the metre*	*God connected with that metre*
1.	*Uṣṇik* and *Uktha*	Sūrya
2.	*Gāyatrī*	Agni
3.	*Anuṣṭup*	Candramā
4.	*Bṛhatī*	Bṛhaspati
5.	*Virāṭ*	Mitra and Varuṇa
6.	*Triṣṭup*	Indra
7.	*Jagatī*	With all the gods together

On the other hand, the answers of the questions are got in the *ŚYV* also as follows[378] :

1. When *puruṣa* constitutes the *yajña,* He uses *sattva* or Sentiment principle as *ghī, grīṣma* or *rajas* Motivational principle as fuel, and *śarad* or *tamas* or Static principle as *puroḍāsas.*[379]
2. We get seven types of fuels.[380] Here the term "Seven types of fuels" indicates seven *padārtha*s such as earth, water, lustre, air, sky, desire or mind and intelligence.[381]
3. The *puruṣa* or God collects 21 pieces of fuels.[382] The term 21 pieces of fuels indicates the sum of five *mahābhūta*s, five *tanmātra*s, five *jñānendriya*s, five *karmendriya*s and mind.[383] Wisdom and *jñāna* is

378. *ŚYV,* 31/14.
379. Read, *itarayāge vasantaśabdena sātviko guṇa ucyate grīṣmaśabdena rājasaḥ śaracchabdena tāmasah,* Uvaṭa in *ŚYV,* (31/14). Moreover H.N. Tripathi mentions *sattva, raja* and *tama* as Sentiment principle. Motivational principle and Static principle. See *PBRNH,* p. 217.
380. Read, *saptāsyāsan paridhayaḥ, ŚYV,* 31/15.
381. Read, *paridhiśabdena pṛthivyāptejovāyurākāsaṁ manobuddhirityete paridhayaḥ kalpyante,* Uvaṭa on 31/15.
382. Read, *trisapta samidhah kṛtāḥ, ŚYV,* 31/15.
383. Read, *trisapta samidhaḥ. pañcamahābhūtāni pṛthivyādinī. pañcatanmātrāni rūpādīni. pañca buddhīndriyāṇi śravtrādīni. pañcakarmendriyāṇi pāṇyādīni manaśca.* Uvaṭa on *ŚYV,* 31/15.

discovered in this *yajña*.[384]

In the same way, the Upaniṣads also give a light to the theory of creation. They are found to be ́different.[385] On the other hand, the *TU* mentions about the Supreme God from whom the universe sprang and in whom all gets mingled after destruction.[386]

THE DOCTRINE OF NON-DUALITY OR ADVAITA

So far the doctrine of Advaita, is concerned we get a long description of it in the *ŚYV*.[387] The Advaita school of thought emphasizes upon the oneness between *Brahman* and *ātman*. Secondly, it is believed that whatever we see here as existent, is actually non-existent and has sprung as a result of *māyā* of that Brahmā. Thus, Brahmā is true and the creation is false. God is one and He is Existent, Spirit and Pure happiness. How this doctrine is reflected in the Vedic literature is being discussed here.

1. God is one.[388] A devotee prays God as "You are the only master of this world."[389] A passage of the *ŚYV* describes the Almighty God to be far from ignorance, Great and Self-lightened.[390] He is *hiraṇyagarbha*[391] and the only Creator.[392] He Himself has revealed as Agni, Āditya, Vāyu, Candramā, whiteness, Brahmā,

384. Read, *abadhnan puruṣaṁ paśum, ŚYV*, 31/15.
385. The *BU* (1/4/1) says about the springing of *puruṣa* and *ChU*, explaining about the creation that started from *ākāśa* (1/9/1).
386. Read, *yato vā imāni bhūtāni jāyante, yene jātāni jīvanti. yat prayantyābhi saṃviṣanti, TU*, 3/1.
387. *ŚYV*, 40/1 to 17.
388. Read, *eko viśvasya bhuvanasya rājā*, *ṚV*, 3/46/2.
389. *Ibid*, 10/101/3.
390. *ŚYV*, 31/18.
391. *Ibid.*, 13/4.
392. *ṚV*, 10/82/1 to 7.

water and Prajāpati.[393] The *ŚYV* (32/1 to 32/11) has a long description regarding this Omnipotent One.

2. The theory that God and spirit is one, is an important theory of the Advaita philosophy. The Spirit or *ātmā* has been described as *vijñānamaya* and *ānandamaya* in the *TA*.[394] The *AB* describes *ātmā* as the same as *ākāśa* which is in the middle of heaven and earth.[395] Moreover, the *AA* goes one step further and says that this creation has been taken from *ātmā* and the spirit of a creature is indifferent to Brahmā.[396]
3. So far the description of Brahmā is concerned, we get some sentences such as Brahmā is *ānanda*.[397] *Ānanda* must be known as Brahmā[398] and Brahmā is itself revealed as *vijñāna* and *ānanda*.[399] He is non-measurable, static, more intangible than sky, birthless, *ātman*, great and non-destroying phenomenon.[400]
4. In the same way we get a lot of passages in the Upaniṣads regarding illusion or *māyā* but a passage of the *ṚV* also supports that this term was well known to the Vedic people. The passage says that God exposes Himself in many forms, through illusion or *māyā*.[401] On the other hand, we get an information from the passage of the *ŚYV* that truth is covered with an attractive cover of gold.[402] Here

393. *ŚYV*, 31/1. See Mahīdhara's commentary.
394. *TA*, 9/1395. *AB*, 1/3/8.
395. *AB*, 2/4/1.
396. *AA*, 2/4/3.
397. *TU*, 2/4.
398. TU, 3/6.
399. *BU*, 3/9/28.
400. *Ibid.*, 4/4/20.
401. Read, *indro māyābhi pururūpa īyate*, *ṚV*, 6/47/18.
402. Read, *hiraṇmayena pātreṇa satyasyāpihitaṃ mukham*, *ŚYV*, 40/15.

the golden cover is nothing but *māyā*. This *ātmā* is true and undestructive. It is unborn, perpetual and everlasting element.[403] An Atharvanic passage also informs that the Brahmā is the seed of all the existing and non-existing things.[404]

Thus, the Advaita philosophy believes in the fact that every thing is the manifestation of Brahmā. The *ChU* also admits the fact.[405]

Though we have analysed the Advaita philosophy in the Vedic passages, yet the theory of Advaita also is found. The *KenaU* clearly mentions two elements Brahmā and other.[406] We get another passage in *R̥V* where two different elements denoting *jīvātmā* and *paramātmā* are mentioned as two birds.[407] Whatever the fact there may be, all the branches of Vedānta philosophy are reflected in the Vedic literature. Other schools of philosophy like Mīmāṁsā, Sāṅkhya, Vaiśeṣika, Yoga and Nyāya, also are sprung from the Vedas and the seed of all these schools of philosophy hides in.[408]

TRANSMIGRATION OF SOUL OR REBIRTH

So far the theory of transmigration is concerned, the *R̥V* mentions about Vāmadeva[409] describing about his previous births. Another R̥gvedic passage informs that the sage Bharadvāja prays Agni to rescue him from the sins of the previous births.[410] A *jīvātmā* or personal spirit sinks in the

---

403. *KaṭhU*, 1/2/18.
404. *AV*, 4/1/1.
405. *ChU*, 3/14/1.
406. *KenaU*, 1/5.
407. *R̥V*, 1/164/16.
408. *VSR*, p. 411.
409. *R̥V*, 4/26/27.
410. *Ibid.*, 6/2/11.

worldly measures as a result of the activities of the previous births.[411] A devotee prays God not to make him suffer for the deeds of the previous births.[412] The desires, knowledge, and the result of the deeds follow a man who falls to death.[413]

We get a lot of information regarding transmigration in the passages of the Vedas and the Upaniṣads, because it was thought that the *ātman* is a helpless phenomenon confined in the body of the creatures. Mind, intelligence and body generally conduct the creatures and its *ātman*.[414]

After all, regarding the philosophy in the Vedic literature, Umesh Misra observes as :

> The Vedas have no any particular theory on philosophy such as the later works like Nyāya and Vaiśeṣika have. The Vedas are the results of penances constituted by the sages through their experiences. So it has neither a particular philosophy nor a particular comment.[415]

---

411. Read, *dvā suparṇā sayujā sakhāyā, samānavṛkṣaṃ pariṣasvajāteḥ,* — *ṚV*, 1/164/2.
412. *Ibid.*, 7/52/2. (*mā vo bhujema anyajātam*).
413. *BU*, 4/4/2.
414. Read, *atmanam rathinam biddhi. ....* *KaṭhU*, 1/3/3.
415. *BDU*, p. 37.

10

Military Aspect

THIRST of power and rights have been the cause of wars among the different societies from the very beginning of the human civilization. We may count a lot of causes for which the battles and wars took place but a Ṛgvedic passage says that fights and battles have taken place to get victory over enemies and thereby acquiring wealths.[1] Satavalekar informs with the reference to a Ṛgvedic passage[2] that *mama satyam* or "mine is truth" will remain till the human civilization exists. Wars are bound to be held where such people stay. In a nutshell, the probability of war will remain always in human society. The people of three different nature namely, monstrous or *rākṣasī,* humane or *mānavī* and divine or *daivī* nature remain in men. The monstrous nature becomes inclined to war by saying "mine is truth."[3]

After the decision of war is taken, people of several groups start to seek the support and help of other kings and warriors.[4] On the other hand, in the ancient times the fighters and the kings performed some religious rituals so that they could acquire divine bliss at the time of war. So we find references in which they are found praying God for victory,[5]

1. *ṚV,* 6/35/2.
2. *Ibid.,* 10/42/4.
3. Quoted from *Vaidik Sainya Vyavasthā* by Satavalekar from *SAG,* p.96.
4. *ṚV,* 5/61/3.
5. *Ibid.,* 1/30/7 & 8.

for strength[6] and are also described as praying Indra to bestow victory to them.[7] We get another information from a passage of the *Ṛgveda* that the people and the kings performed the *yajñas* in order to defeat the enemies. It was believed that he who did not perform the sacrifices before the wars could not get victory over his enemy.[8] In the same way an Atharvanic passage also informs that the people of the Vedic period worshipped Indra before the wars took place.[9] It has been mentioned that the arrows were purified with sacred texts or *mantras* perhaps in pre-war rituals.[10] In some passages we find the victorious people performing *yajñas*[11] and praying Indra[12] after the war also. A passage clearly mentions that the king or a warrior performed sacrifices and prayed by saying, "We desire victory and let our sacrifices annihilate our enemies, let the gods Soma and Agni throw them. So wishing the defeat of the whole army of the enemies, I do hereby offer the oblations."[13] Thus, it is clear that the people of the ancient times had performed some religious rituals before the war started.

Perhaps the king assured the subjects by saying, "Let us cast away misfortunes and keep away those who hate us from a distant place."[14] An Atharvanic passage also presents such a statement which perhaps was uttered by the *purohita* to the soldiers at the time of war as such "O soldiers, let you show your vigour along with the king, let you be ready for war and follow such king who is wealthy, victorious and

6. *ṚV*, 1/8/1.
7. *Ibid.*, 6/49/17.
8. *Ibid.*, 8/30/16 & 17.
9. *AV*, 6/44/17.
10. *ṚV*, 6/75/16.
11. *Ibid.*, 7/34/6.
12. *AV*, 20/54/1.
13. *Ibid.*, 6/97/1.
14. *ṚV*, 5/45/5.

accustomed to archery."[15]

Formation of Army Troops

An army troop consisted several types of experts among them. We collect some from the *ŚYV* as such:[16]

(a) Soldiers
(b) Captain or *senāpati*
(c) Charioteer or *rathī*
(d) Chariotless or *arathī*
(e) Collector or *saṅgrahitṛ*
(f) Chariot-maker or *rathakāra*
(g) Blacksmith or *karmāra*

On the other hand, we find the soldiers wearing armour and also those who did not have armour, charioteers and cavalries.[17] Army troops were formed in such way in the Vedic period. We find the following characterstics of the army troops[18] :

(a) They were terrible and strong.
(b) They were stout and vigorous.
(c) They were brave.
(d) They were capable of controlling sky and earth.

A Yajurvedic passage informs one more quality as to acquiring victory over enemies.[19] In this respect, the term *maruta* bears important meaning as follows:[20]

(a) They were moderate in speeches (Marutāḥ = *mitar-avināḥ*)
(b) They were polyglots (Marutāḥ = *amita-ravināḥ*)
(c) They lit the light (Marutāḥ = *mitarocanāḥ*)

---

15. *AV*, 6/97/3.
16. *ŚYV*, 16/26 & 27.
17. *AV*, 11/10/22 & 24.
18. *ṚV*, 6/66/6.
19. *ŚYV*, 17/82
20. Compare *Nir*, 11/2/1 and 12/2/1.

(d) They have immense light (Marutāḥ = *amitarocanāḥ*)
(e) They made vital sound (Marutāḥ = *mahat ravanti*)
(f) They moved forward with unobstructed steps (Marutāḥ = *mahat dravanti*)

Moreover Satavalekar gives three more meanings for the term as:[21]

(a) They never weep (*mārud*)
(b) They are moderate in speeches (*mārut*)
(c) They perform their duties until their deaths (*marut*).

After the discussion of the term, *maruta*, we come to know that the term was used to denote the meaning of a soldier.

Uniform

The soldiers were expected to put on well-dressed uniform. The matter was expressed through a passage of the *Ṛgveda* as such: "Those warriors became well dressed like women."[22] Satvalekar mentions that the term *ajina* was used to mention uniform,[23] which were worn by Marutas and were seen very beautiful.[24] They were indifferent in wearing ornaments also. So the uniform appeared very similar.[25]

Discussing the characteristics of Marutas a Ṛgvedic passage says that they were not seen unequalled.[26] Griffith translates the verse as: "Having no eldest and no youngest, pre-eminent they have waxed in might."[27]

Division of Army

The warriors were divided and the Marutas were included

21. *Vaidik Sainya Vyavasthā* by Satavalekar, *SAG*, p. 101.
22. *ṚV*, 1/85/1.
23. *Vaidik Sainya Vyavasthā* by Satavalekar, *SAG*, p. 100.
24. *ṚV*, 1/85/3.
25. *Ibid.*, 8/20/22.
26. *Ibid.*, 5/59/6.
27. *ṚVg*, p.270.

in those groups[28] and thus they were entitled as the master of the groups.[29] Each group consisted of seven soldiers.[30] Some passages of the *ṚV*[31] and the *AV*[32] give a clear picture on the matter that the soldiers made their groups in seven in numbers. Another group is made of 63 soldiers having seven primary groups and fourteen securities. Thus, it becomes 63 in numbers.[33] Griffith translated the passage thus: "Thrice sixty Marutas waxing strong, were with thee like piles of beaming light worthy of worship."[34] Griffith says as such: "Thrice sixty; or sixtythree according to Sāyaṇa nine companies consisting of seven each."[35] We find three types of units of army, namely, (i) *sārdha*, (ii) *vrāta* and (iii) *gaṇa*,[36] which have been translated by Griffith as troops, band and company, respectively.[37] The numbers of warriors were expected to be 3000 in number.[38] Another passage advises that the king or the rulers must have innumerous warriors.[39] Moreover, we find a description of an army group of 300,000 people.[40]

Drum or Dundubhi

After the studies of the *AV* we come to know that the warriors were advised to beat the big kettle-drums before

28. *TMB*, 19/14/2.
29. *TA*, 3/11/4/2
30. Read, *sapta hi maruto gaṇah*, *ŚB*, 5/4/3/17.
31. *ṚV*, 1/85/1 & 6; 6/52/17; 8/20/23.
32. *AV*, 13/1/3.
33. Read, *tri ṣaṣṭi tvā maruto vāvṛdhānā*, *ṚV*, 8/96/8.
34. Quoted from *ṚVg*, p. 458.
35. *Ibid.*, Footnote on *ṚV*, 8/96/8, p. 458.
36. Read, *sārdhaṁ sārdhaṁ vā yeṣāṁ vrātaṁ vrātaṁ gaṇaṁ gaṇaṁ susastibhiḥ*, *ṚV*, 5/53/11.
37. *ṚVg*, p.266.
38. *ṚV*, 4/30/21.
39. *Ibid.*, 3/16/5.
40. *Ibid.*, 4/30/21.

the war started. The drum was beaten for several purposes such as:

1. To destroy the strong feelings of the enemies.[41]
2. To create the desire of victory and acquring wealths of the enemies.[42]
3. To create zeal among friends.[43]
4. To establish inspiration in the hearts of the warriors.[44]
5. To dispel the wives of the enemies from the battle fields along with their children after they heard the sound of the drums.[45]
6. To protect the people from the enemies.[46]
7. To bestow strength to one's own warriors and to create fear among foes.[47]

The drums were made of woods covered with skin.[48] Specially the skin of deer was used to cover the drum.[49] Strength was supposed to be the important element of getting victory in the battle[50] and the warriors drank *soma* juice to acquire triumph.[51]

Protection

People of the Vedic age were conscious in the matter of protection also. They were aware of their warriors for which they took measures so as to protect them. Such measures were as follows:

---

41. *AV*, 5/20/1.
42. *Ibid.*, 5/20/3.
43. *Ibid.*, 5/29/7.
44. *Ibid.*, 5/20/9.
45. *Ibid.*, 5/20/5.
46. *R̥V*, 6/47/28.
47. *Ibid.*, 6/47/20. & *AV*, 5/21/3 & 7.
48. *AV*, 5/21/2.
49. *Ibid.*, 5/21/7.
50. *R̥V*, 1/64/14.
51. *Ibid.*, 9/88/2.

1. The people made plans and programmes for their protections as well as the destruction of their enemies.[52]
2. They eagerly collected the unknown means of protections also.[53]
3. We find about armour used by the warriors at the time of wars.[54]
4. The armour were made of iron[55] and gold.[56]
5. The word *varman* was used in the *R̥V* to denote armour or a coat.[57] We find the same in the *AV* also.[58]
6. The armours were sewed but yet, we do not get such references that mention about the materials of which the armours were sewed.[59]
7. The term *kavaca* was used frequently in the *AV* and later literatures to denote chest plates or corsets.[60]
8. The word *śipra* also was used to denote helmet,[61] which was perhaps made of *āyasa*,[62] *hiraṇya*[63], *hari*[64] and *hiri*.[65]

A *R̥V* passage, on the other hand, mentions that Aśvinī-kumāras had possessed well and most powerful means of

52. *R̥V*, 6/25/2.
53. *Ibid*., 5/42/18.
54. *Ibid*., 6/46/12.
55. *Ibid*., 6/75/1.
56. *Ibid*., 1/25/13.
57. *Ibid*., 1/31/15; 140/10; 6/75/1; 10/107/7.
58. *AV*, 8/5/7; 9/5/26 & 17/1/27.
59. *R̥V*, 1/31/15 & 10/101/8.
60. *AV*, 9/10/22; *ŚYV*, 16/45; *AB*, 3/48; *ŚB*, 13/1/6/3, etc.
61. *R̥V*, 5/54/11; 8/7/25.
62. *Ibid*., 4/37/4.
63. *Ibid*., 2/34/4.
64. *Ibid*., 10/96/4.
65. *Ibid*., 2/2/3.

securities.[66] Again we get another information where we come to know that not only the men but also animals, like horse which was used for the purpose of war, also was covered with armours.[67] Thus, we find the people adopting the means of protection in those days.

Types of Wars

The strong warriors were advised to protect the weaks[68] in the battlefields. Secondly, the warriors were asked to search an appropriate rival in the battle. For example, a teenage boy should get the chance to fight with the boy of the same age.[69]

WAR WITH WEAPONS

People were found fighting with different types of weapons. Bow was one of the most important weapons in the Vedic period. He, who could throw the arrows on the goal without failure was called to be an expert archer.[70] First of all attempts were made to make the enemies exhausted of the arrows.[71] Whatever the fact there may be, the warriors of that time used various types of weapons in the wars. We find the reference of the sharpened weapons used in those days.[72] So far the different types of weapons used by the warriors of the Vedic period are concerned, we find the following weapons:

---

66. *Ṛ̥V*, 8/9/14.
67. *Ibid.*, 1/162/18.
68. *Ibid.*, 1/174/3.
69. *Ibid.*, 2/25/2.
70. *Ibid.*, 10/42/1.
71. *AV*, 1/2/3.
72. *Ṛ̥V*, 1/8/3.

No.	*Name of the weapons*	*Reference*
1.	Quiver of the *tūṇīra*	*Ṛ̥V*, 1/31/3 & 6/75/4
2.	*Vajra*	*Ibid.*, 1/40/8 and a lot
3.	Sword	*Ibid.*, 1/166/6 and others
4.	Dagger	*Ibid.*, 1/167/3
5.	Spear	*Ibid.*, 1/129/8
6.	Arrows	*Ibid.*, 1/144/5 and others
7.	*Aśuni* (the tip of missile)	*Ibid.*, 10/87/4
8.	Canon	*AV*, 1/26/1
9.	A canon	*Ibid.*, 1/26/1
10.	A bullet of lead	*Ibid.*, 1/16/2
11.	*Ādān* trap	*Ibid.*, 6/104/2
12.	*Sandāna* trap	*Ibid.*
13.	Electric weapon	*Ibid.*, 9/12/14
14.	A spade	*Ibid.*, 11/9/2
15.	*Apavṛ̥ta tamasāśtra*	*Ibid.*, 3/2/6
16.	*Hastaghna*	*Ṛ̥V*, 6/75
17.	A spear or *rambhinī*	*Ibid.*, 1/168/3
18.	*Srakti*	*Ibid.*, 7/18/7
19.	A Lance (*sṛ̥k*)	*Ibid.*, 1/32/12 & 10/180/2
20.	Scabbard	*ŚYV*, 30/14
21.	Daggar or *kṛ̥ti*	*Ṛ̥V*, 1/168/3
22.	*Paraśu* (battle-axe)	*Ibid.*, 1/127/3
23.	Lighting bolt (*kuliśa*)	*Ṛ̥V*, 3/2/1 & 1/35/5
24.	A club (*vighana, drughana, pināka*)	*TS*, 3/2/4/1; *AV*, 7/28/1; *AV*, 1/27/2 respectively
25.	*Adri*	*Ṛ̥V*, 1/51/3
26.	*Dhmā*	*Ibid.*, 10/72/2
27.	*Lohāyasa*	*ŚB*, 5/4/1/2
28.	*Karṣṇāyasa*	*ChU*, 4/17/7 & 6/1/5
29.	*Cakra*	*Ṛ̥V*, 8/96/9

CHARIOTING AND CHARIOTEERING

We find the warriors fighting on chariots. A passage of the *ṚV* compares a fighter of the chariot with space.[73] So far the parts of chariots are concerned, a passage of the *AV* mentions about chariots, chariot-lap pole, chariot-mouth and a charioteer.[74] Another passage mentions about the charioteer and the chariot in which fire was supposed to be in the company of Indra.[75] Somewhere the existence of the spokes of the chariot also is referred.[76] Moreover we get two[77] and three[78] wheeled chariots in the Vedas. In other places we find the metal tyres fixed in the chariots.[79]

TYPES OF CHARIOTS

We find several types of chariots in the Vedas mentioned everywhere. We are going to furnish the description of those chariots.

1. The description of general type of chariots are found in the entire Vedic literature. Among those evidences we mention only two, one from *ṚV*[80] and the other from *AV*.[81]
2. The *ṚV* gives an instance of the existence of horseless chariot.[82] The passage runs thus:
   "Where with ye made Rasa swell full with water flood and urged to victory the car without a horse."[83]

---

73. *ṚV*, 1/11/1.
74. *AV*, 8/8/23.
75. *Ibid.*, 3/21/3.
76. *ChU*, 7/15/1 & *ṚV*, 1/32/15; 1/101/9, etc.
77. *ṚV*, 8/5/29; *ChU*, 4/16/5.
78. *ṚV*, 8/8/33; 1/34/2 & 9; 1/47/2.
79. *Ibid.*, 1/180/1; *ŚB*, 5/4/3/16.
80. *ṚV*, 8/5/29, etc.
81. *AV*, 14/1/40, etc.
82. *ṚV*, 1/112/12; 120/10.
83. *ṚVg*, p. 73.

3. Moreover we find such a chariot which moved in water and on earth as well.[84] Griffith has clearly translated the verse as follows: "In the wide space your chariot reach the heaven, what time is turnth hither from the ocean."[85]
4. Further we find Ṛbhus as the chariotmakers for Aśvins.[86] They were able to build such chariots which could run everywhere.[87]
5. Again we find a term *kār* in the sense of chariot itself.[88] Sivapujan Singh Kusvaha translated the passage as "A wise drives the car in the waves of oceans and all other lands."[89]
6. Another passage of three storeyed chariot is met in the *ṚV*[90] as follows: "That he may move, they yoke him to the three-backed-tripple-seated car."[91]
7. Somewhere we get such a chariot which were conducted through gases.[92] The word *vāyu* was used to denote gas.
8. Electrical or lightening chariots also are found in the Vedic literature. A Ṛgvedic passage[93] informs about the electrical chariot such as[94] "Agni, the son of strength, whose car is lightening."
9. Another type of chariot named *aśvaparṇa* also was

---

84. *ṚV*, 4/43/5.
85. *ṚVg*, p. 229.
86. *ṚV*, 1/20/3.
87. *Ibid.*, 10/39/12; 1/92/28; 129/4; 5/75/3, etc.
88. *Ibid.*, 9/14/1.
89. "Yatāyātke Prācīn Vaijñānik Sādhan" by Sivapujan Singh Kusvaha in *HSA*, p. 729.
90. *ṚV*, 9/62/17.
91. *ṚVg*, p. 491.
92. Read, *pra vo vāyuṁ rathyujam kṛṇudhvam*, *ṚV*, 5/41/6.
93. *ṚV*, 3/14/1.
94. "Yatāyātke Prācīn Vaijñānik Sādhan" by S.P. Singh in *HSA*, p. 729.

in existence.[95] Satavalekar explains the cause of naming so as to have the speed of the chariot, like horses.[96]

Moreover we find such chariots which were pulled by horses,[97] chariots made of gold[98] and iron,[99] and tri-seated chariots.[100] Another passage of the *ṚV* again informs that a triangle of three woods also was used in the chariots.[101] We get a list of the things to build the chariots in general as such:

1. Woods specially preferred for Khayar, Śiśapa and so on.[102]
2. *Akṣa* or axle to connect two wheels of the chariot.[103]
3. Iron was an important metal for chariot-making.[104]
4. Aristocratic people generally decorated their chariots[105] with gold.[106]
5. A leather rope to tie the parts of the chariots.[107]

The chariot-maker after collecting the required materials build the chariot with his keen attention.[108] A passage says that Bhṛgus made the chariots of the gods in general.[109] It was expected that an expert chariot-maker would make

95. *ṚV*, 1/88/1.
96. *Vaidik Sainya Vyvasthā* by Satavalekar, *SAG*, pp. 107-08.
97. *ṚV*, 1/14/6.
98. *Ibid.*, 1/30/16 & 8/529.
99. *Ibid.*, 10/20/9.
100. *Ibid.*, 1/34/9; 42/2; 118/1 & 7/71/4.
101. *Ibid.*, 1/47/2 & 1/118/2.
102. *Ibid.*, 3/53/19.
103. *Ibid.*, 3/53/19 & 5/43/8.
104. *Ibid.*, 10/20/9.
105. Read, *eṣām rathāḥ sthirāḥ susaṁskṛtāḥ*, *ṚV*, 1/88/12.
106. *ṚV*, 1/30/16 & 8/5/29.
107. *Ibid.*, 10/102/8.
108. *Ibid.*, 5/73/10.
109. *Ibid.*, 4/16/20 & 10/39/14.

strong chariots[110] which must be beautiful to look at.[111] The expert horses created magic when they were fastened to the chariots.[112]

Flags also were the important phenomenon for the chariots.[113] The colour of the flag was saffron like fire.[114] We find the same in the other passage of the *ṚV* also.[115] Another two passages of the *AV* refer to the flags having the colour of the rising sun.[116] The commander was advised to ride the chariot which possessed the flag.[117]

USE OF ELEPHANTS IN THE WARS

So far the use of elephants in the war is concerned we do not get ample evidences in the Vedic literature but yet, some instances make it clear that the soldiers used elephants in the war at that time. First of all we get the description of four-fold army in the *ṚV* in which the term *caturaṅga* has been used.[118] Sarvadaman Singh with special reference to the *Śamavidhāna Brāhmaṇa* says that the elephants were among the four divisions of army.[119] He further informs that the people of Vedic age used elephants in war and were "seized, together with the female slaves from the worsted army."[120] An elephant was given so much importance because:

1. The elephant was regarded as the administrator of

---

110. *ṚV*, 6/47/26.
111. *Ibid.*, 6/47/27.
112. *Ibid.*, 5/75/5.
113. *Ibid.*, 1/50/3.
114. *Ibid.*, 1/64/7.
115. *Ibid.*, 8/43/4 & 10/12/2.
116. *AV*, 11/10/2 & 7.
117. *Ibid.*, 11/10/1.
118. *ṚV*, 10/92/11.
119. *AIWS*, p. 8.
120. *Ibid.*, 11/10/1.

all other animals of the forest.[121]

2. It was regarded to be the most important animal of the world.[122]
3. The elephant possesses unequalled strength.[123]
4. If trained, it rushes after enemies in wars[124] and so on.

Thus, a sacrificer prays God to bestow him the protector and the taming person of the elephant.[125] The elephant controller used goad to control the elephant in time.[126] Perhaps *soma* juice also was offered to the elephants before they were sent to the wars.[127]

CAVALRY

At first we may quote Sarvadaman Singh regarding cavalry as:

> Looking back as we do across the many millennia of past history in quest for origines of war like techniques and equipments we have to trace first the story of horse's domestication, before we set out to demonstrate its use as a machine of war.[128]

He further adds:

> There are a number of passages in the *ṚV* and the rest of the Vedic literature where single horses are mentioned without being specifically associated with the chariot; the inference that many of them must have been ridden is quite justifiable. Though chariots with only one horse were not unknown they formed exceptions rather than the rule on the field of

121. *AV*, 3/22/6.
122. *Ibid.*, 3/22/3.
123. *Ibid.*, 3/22/1.
124. *ṚV*, 8/83/8.
125. *ŚYV*, 30/11.
126. *ṚV*, 10/106/6.
127. *Ibid.*
128. *AIWS*, p. 53.

battle.[129]

Considering the horse to be energetic and strong one, a Ṛgvedic passage describes thus:[130]

> A body formed for fight hast thou, O charger; swift as the wind in motion is thy spirit. Thy horns are spread abroad in all directions: They move with restless beat in wilderness.[131]

Thus, the *ṚV* appreciates the presentation of a horse to a proper rider.[132] We get a legend of the birth or incarnation of a horse in a passage of the *ṚV*[133] as follows:

> What time first springing into life, thou neighest, proceeding from the sea or upper waters. Limbs of deer hadst thou and eagle pinions. O Steed, thy birth is high and must be lauded.[134]

The horse-keeper was respected by the people of that time[135] and they prayed God to beget horsekeeper on the earth.[136] They latter also was advised to look after the horse accordingly. The horsekeeper decorated the horse by fixing gold on its head and iron on the hoofs.[137] Moreover, it was covered with clothes[138] and was decorated with different types of leaves and others.[139] Griffith has translated the passage as follows; ". . . all these attend the charger."[140]

129. *AIWS*, p. 66.
130. *ṚV*, 1/163/11.
131. *ṚVg*, p. 109.
132. *ṚV*, 1/163/13.
133. *ṚV*, 1/163/1 and *AIWS*, p. 66
134. *ṚVg*, p.108.
135. Read, *aśvebhyo aśvapatibhyasca vo namo namo* ....., *ŚYV*, 16/24.
136. *Ibid.*, 30/11.
137. *ṚV*, 1/163/9.
138. *Ibid.*, 1/162/2 & 16.
139. *Ibid.*, 1/162/13.
140. *ṚVg*, p. 108.

We meet a seer asking a horse rider,[141] "Where are your horses? Where the reins? How came ye? How had ye the power? Rein was on nose and seat on back." This shows that the soldier rode on such a horse which was well-equipped and decorated with soldierly arms. The horses of gods possessed bright seats on their backs.[142] On the other hand, the horse-keepers were advised to look after the horses and not to keep them barebacked.[143]

The whip was essentially used to beat the horse on its thigh[144] so that it may stretch their thighs apart. While running in a line, the horses looked very attractive, which we find thus: "Put forth their strength, like swans in lengthened order, when they, the steeds, have reached the heavenly cause way."[145] On the other hand, we find the descriptions of dust raising tramp of horsemen in a passage of the *AV*.[146] Another passage of the same gives a description of day's journey of a horsemen in which it is said that a horseman can run a distance of ten *yojana* in a day.[147]

It is found that the soldiers first of all wanted to kill the soldiers riding the horse.[148] A soldier has been described in a passage of the *ṚV* as riding a horse freely in the battlefields.[149] So the horse which rushed towards the

141. *ṚV*, 5/61/2.
142. *ṚV*, 1/162/7.
143. *Ibid.*, 1/162/18.
144. *Ibid.*, 5/61/3.
145. *ṚVg*, 1/163/10; (see Griffith notes)
146. *AV*, 4/21/4.
147. *Ibid.*, 6/131/3. Regarding *yojana* Sir M.M. Williams writes, measure of distance sometimes regarded as equal to 4 or 5 English miles, but more correctly = 4 *krośa* or about 9 miles, according to other calculation = 2½ English miles, and according to some = 8 *krośas*. *SEDM*, p. 858.
148. *AV*, 11/10/24.
149. *ṚV*, 9/100/4.

battlefield was considered praiseworthy.[150] The expert horse-rider could dispel the enemies with the help of their horses.[151]

Saying about the use of horse in war in the *sūtra* period, Ram Gopal with special reference to the *PGS* (3/15/4) and the *KauS* (17/22) mentions,

> Though the *sūtra*s give no definite information about the existence of cavalry, it is quite certain that the horse was used for riding in the age of the *sūtra*s.[152]

Sarvadaman Singh informed that Roth translated the word *akra* as horse.[153] If so, we get a lot of description of *akra* in the *R̥V*.[154] In the same way, the term *sada* or *sadas* meant for *aśvārūḍhaḥ* or mounting on horses.[155] Thus, the word *āsada* also was translated as "foot soldier."[156]

Thus, cavalry seems to be an important aspect of war in the Vedic age according to the description of the Vedic literature.

INFANTRY

A passage of the *R̥V* mentions of an army of 300,000 soldiers as follows[157]: "Indra with his magic power and weapons sent the 300,000 *dāsa*s to slumber." Another passage also mentions about innumerable soldiers.[158] Thus, infantry was an important group of army. On the other hand, Sarvadaman Singh observes, "A literal acceptance of the

150. *R̥V*, 1/163/22.
151. *Ibid.*, 1/8/2.
152. *IVKR*, p. 184.
153. *AIWS*, p. 59.
154. *R̥V*, 1/143/7; 189/7; 3/1/12; 4/6/3; 10/77/2.
155. *Ibid.*, 1/162/17; 5/61/2; *AV*, 11/10/24.
156. *AIWS*, p. 59.
157. *R̥V*, 4/30/21.
158. *Ibid.*, 3/16/5.

inflated figures would indeed be open to questions; but an acquaintance with armies of considerable size would alike be undeniable."[159] A man is found in the *ṚV*[160] praying Agni thus: "Please protect us, our sons and grandsons who have gathered in the battlefield to fight against enemies." Thus, we come to know that sometimes the people of three generation also came together in the battlefields to fight against the enemies. The *AB* mentions about the array of soldiers as: "Agni arranged the army in three lines and three arrays in order to defeat the Asuras."[161] The people assembled from all directions[162] and performed *yajña* and then they attacked their enemies. Another passage of the *ṚV* informs us that Śambara had an army troop of 1000 people whom Indra killed in war.[163] An Atharvanic passage mention of an army with *sabhā* and *samiti*[164] and expresses the importance of army in the nation. The *AV* in one place mentions about *patti*[165] which according to Satavalekar denotes infantry.[166] Thus, the *ŚYV* also mentions about the commander of the infantry as *pattināṁ pati.*[167]

An Atharvanic passage mentions about four types of army such as charioteers, chariotless, horse-rider and infantry.[168] A seer in another passage prays God to enter into the infantry of the enemies to destroy them.[169] Other one speaks of "sharpening up clan or clans in order to

159. *AIWS*, pp. 8-9.
160. *ṚV*, 8/23/12.
161. *AB*, 3/14/1.
162. *ṚV*, 4/24/4.
163. *Ibid.*, 6/26.5.
164. *AV*, 15/9/2.
165. *Ibid.*, 7/62/1.
166. *AMSS*, p. 327.
167. *ŚYV*, 16/19.
168. *AV*, 11/10/24.
169. *AV*, 11/10/18.

fight."[170] We get sufficient evidences of infantry in the passage of the Vedic literature because "man found his feet on land, and on foot he first fought."[171]

Forts

We find different types of forts described in the Vedic literature. The word *pura* was frequently used in those days to denote "fort."[172] Thus, the word *pura* was found frequently in the Vedas,[173] the *Brāhmaṇas*[174] and the Upaniṣads.[175] But the *Ṛ̥V* has a lot of evidences of destroying forts by Indra. Somewhere Indra has been presented[176] as the destroyer of the forts who annihilated them one after another. He was called Purandara for destroying the forts.[177] Indra destroyed 100 forts of Śambara and bestowed them to Divodāsa.[178] In the same way, we find Agni related with forts in many passage of the *Ṛ̥V*.[179] Agni also got respect for destroying the forts of the enemies.[180] Forts were named as *pṛ̥thvī, urvī* and *śāśvata* for its length, width and strength, respectively.[181] The *AV*, in a place mentions that forts are god-made structures.[182]

TYPES OF FORTS

Vedic people were expert in making forts in different ways.

170. *AV*, 4/31/4.
171. *AIWS*, p. 7.
172. *VI*, 1/163.
173. *Ṛ̥V*, 1/58/8; 166/8; 3/15/4; 4/27/1, etc.
174. *AB*, 1/23; 2/12; *ŚB*, 3/4/4/3; 6/3/3/25; 11/1/1/273, etc.
175. *ChU*, 8/5/3.
176. *Ṛ̥V*, 1/53/7; 63/7.
177. *Ibid.*, 2/20/7.
178. *Ibid.*, 4/30/20.
179. *Ibid.*, 1/32/6; 33/12; 61/5; 130/7; 131/4; 174/2 & 3/34/1, etc.
180. *Ibid.*, 6/16/39.
181. *Ibid.*, 3/189/2.
182. *AV*, 12/1/43.

The followings are the types of forts:

1. ***Forts of stones*** : We find the forts of stones described in the passage of the *R̥V* where it has been said that Indra bestowed those forts to Divodāsa after killing Śambara.[183]
2. ***Forts made of iron*** : A R̥gvedic passage was used to pray Agni as the bestower of iron forts to his devotee.[184] Another passage of the *R̥V* says that the Dasyus had the forts of iron with them.[185] The seer Vāmadeva says in a place that he was brought up in the 100 forts of iron.[186] The seer in one place mentions about 100 forts of iron[187] whereas, another passage was used to describe the current of Sarasvatī river compared with the fort of iron.[188]
3. ***Āmā or the forts of bricks*** : A passage of the *R̥V* mentions about the fort made of bricks as such : "Dwelling at a distance in forts."[189] That was supposed to be of bricks.[190] Regarding this passage Amit Ray remarks, "It seems that sometimes the walls were built also of sun-dried bricks."[191] In the same way Sarvadaman Singh also observes, "The epithet *āmā* perhaps refer to unbaked (literally raw) brick walls."[192]
4. ***Forts made of three metals*** : The two passages of the *R̥V* indicate the existence of the forts made of

183. *R̥V*, 4/30/20.
184. *Ibid.*, 1/58/8.
185. *Ibid.*, 2/20/8.
186. *Ibid.*, 4/27/1.
187. *Ibid.*, 7/3/7.
188. *Ibid.*, 7/95/1.
189. *Ibid.*, 2/35/6.
190. *Vedic Index*, 1/163.
191. *VTSBAIA*, p. 64.
192. *AIWS*, p. 125.

three metals.[193] The term *tridhātu* have been translated by Griffith as "a home of triple refuge" as well.[194] On the other hand, V.R. Ratate seems to be correct to translate the passage as, "Let the fort made of three metals protect us."[195] He further informs that the term *tridhātu* denoted iron, silver and gold.

5. ***Forts made of hundreds of iron walls*** : We find the description of such a fort which had hundreds of iron walls.[196] The passage runs thus: ". . . and irresistible, be thou a mighty iron fort to us, with hundred walls for man's defence."[197] The word *śata* or 100 may be considered to be the numbers of the walls or pillars.[198]
6. ***The autumnal or śāradī fort*** : V.R. Ratate mentions that this type of fort was constructed to fight in the autumn season only.[199] The Dāsas were the masters of such forts.[200] A passage of the *AV*[201] gives a description of such fort. The same passage is repeated in the *R̥V* also.[202] Another R̥gvedic passage also informs the same.[203]
7. ***Gomatī forts*** : As cows were considered as the general expression of wealth,[204] its milk was drunk[205]

193. *R̥V*, 6/46/9 & 8/40/12.
194. *R̥Vg*, p. 310 & 428.
195. *ARV*, p.123.
196. *R̥V*, 7/15/4.
197. *R̥Vg*, p. 340.
198. *R̥V*, 1/166/8.
199. *ARV*, p. 123.
200. *Ibid.*
201. *AV*, 20/75/2.
202. *R̥V*, 1/131/4.
203. *Ibid.*, 1/174/2; 6/20/10.
204. *Ibid.*, 1/33/1; 1/191/4; 9/112/3; 109/166/1, etc.
205. *R̥V*, 1/120/9.

for acquiring strength,[206] it was offered as *dakṣiṇā* to the priests[207] and was entitled as "Inviolable" or *aghnyā*,[208] hence people thought to protect the cows so that the invaders could not loot them and thus the *gomatī* forts came into being. We get two instances in the *AV* in this context.[209]

8. ***Thorny forts*** : The Vedic literature mentions the forts encircled with thorns in the *R̥V*[210] The passage says that Puru had such forts in which he took shelter and Agni destroyed it in a war.
9. ***Mahāpuram*** : *Mahāpuram* or the great fort has been mentioned in the *TS* and *KS*[211] and the *Brāhmaṇas*.[212] The *GB* says that the *mahāpuram* or the great forts were defeated by the people.[213]
10. ***Mobile forts or sacalam puram*** : We find a reference of the mobile forts in the *R̥V*.[214] But yet the passage is obscure. V.R. Ratate compares such forts with rockets and luntures of the modern ages.[215]

Towards the end of the chapter we may quote Sarvadaman Singh as "Warfare led to the growth of states and goverment. Out of war arose kingship with its corollaries, heredity and despotism."[216]

Thus, the wars became deciding factors to the stability of the kingdoms or states and sometimes to nation also.

206. *R̥V*, 3/30/14.
207. *Ibid.*, 10/166/1.
208. *Ibid.*, 1/164/27 & 40.
209. *AV*, 20/71/4 & 20/81/2.
210. *R̥V*, 7/5/3.
211. *TS*, 6/2/3/1; *KS*, 24/10.
212. *AB*, 1/23/2.
213. Read, *mahāpuram jayantīti*, *GB*, 1/2/7.
214. *R̥V*, 8/1/28.
215. *ARV*, p. 124.
216. *AIWS*, p. 170.

11

Miscellaneous

Lipi in the Vedic Age

It is generally alleged that the people of the Vedic age did not know how to write. But the evidences mainly of the *R̥V* tell that the people of the Vedic India were acquainted with scripts. There are ample references which evidently prove the existence of scripts or *lipi* in those days in India. Some of these references are being mentioned below:

1. The word *brahmaṇacchaṁsī* denotes that the brāhmaṇas had to read the written texts in the different types of rituals.[1]
2. We get *pañcākṣara* up to *saptadaśākṣara* in some of the passages of the *ŚYV*.[2] Here *akṣara* meant alphabets which could form the metres.
3. A passage of the *ŚYV* goes as, "He who reads and recites. . ." speaks of the existence of scripts or *lipi*.[3]
4. We all know that the written document only can be seen. Otherwise a narrated speech can be heard but not seen. But the line *uta tvā paśyan na dadarśa*,[4] or one is unable to see yet he looked, denotes the existence of *lipi*.

---

1. *TS*, 1/8/18.
2. *ŚYV*, 9/32; 33 & 34.
3. Read, *yaḥ śaṃsate stavate* ..... *ŚYV*, 33/50.
4. *R̥V*, 10/71/4.

5. A Ṛgvedic passage clearly mentions about the existence of scripts in the Vedic India.[5] Griffith has translated the passage as follows: "The triplet with the two or four foot measure and with the syllable they form seven metres."[6]
6. In the same way, another passage informs that the people knew to count syllables and compose poems in several metres.[7]
7. A symbolical passage,[8] which according to Sāyaṇa, Mahīdhara and Patañjali, expresses the grammatical knowledge of the Āryans where four *pada*s, three tenses, two suffixes (*tinanta* and *suvanta*), seven cases and three types of speeches are mentioned.[9]
8. The word *aṣṭakarṇya* is met in the *ṚV* which describes about such cows whose ears are stamped with the digit eight. Hence the existence of writing alphabets and digits are found in the ancient literatures.[10]
9. We met with two particular words *svādhyāya* and *pravacana* in the *TU*.[11] *Svādhyāya* is impossible without the existence of letters and books.
10. The *ChU* says that Agni is the vowel *i*. The knowledge of vowel proves the existence of *lipi* in those days.[12]
11. We get a passage, mentioning two, four and six-footed metres and the composition of metreless sentences (*bicchandā*) in the Vedic literatures distinctly.[13]

---

5. *ṚV*, 1/164/24.
6. *ṚVg*, p. 111.
7. *ṚV*, 10/164/41.
8. *Ibid.*, 4/58/3.
9. *Mahābhāṣya* of Patañjali on *ṚV*, 4/58/3.
10. *ṚV*, 10/63/7.
11. *TU*, *Śikṣā vallī*/11.
12. Read, *agnirikāraḥ* ..... *ChU*, 1/13/1.
13. *ŚYV*, 23/34.

12. The names of the metres as the Vedas reveal are, *gāyatrī, triṣṭup, jagatī, anuṣṭup, paṅkti, bṛhatī* and *uṣṇik.*[14] Nobody can tell that the metre can be used without the knowledge of scripts.
13. We find that the *ṛṣi*s were able to write and count up to *ayuta,*[15] *niyuta,*[16] and even up to 10000000000,00,00,000.[17] It is beyond imagination that such people did not have the scripts to write down.
14. R. Roth is correct to say that none could compose *prātiśākhya*s without the existence of the written documents of the Vedas.[18]
15. Prof. Hansraj Agrawal says that Indians had the knowledge of *lipi* from the very dawn of human civilization and later they had discovered the huge numbers and grammar in the due course of time. The existence of oral teaching does not mean that there was no use of letters.[19]
16. It is said that oral teaching or *śruti* itself denotes that there was the absence of *lipi*, but "The term *śruti*", says Khagendra Dasgupta, "is named, for those sentences or songs which were sung by Gods and those songs that were listened by the *ṛṣi*s."[20]

After all, to say that the people who were expert in chariot and house buildings, trade and commerce, establishing forts and villages, and also those who possesed the knowledge of art and literatures, physics, astronomy, mathematics, medical science and chemistry, etc., were ignorants in

---

14. *ŚYV*, 23/33.
15. *ṚV*, 8/34/15.
16. *Ibid.*, 6/60/2.
17. *ŚYV*, 32/2.
18. Quoted. from *VSRH*, p 71.
19. *Ibid.*, 6/60/2.
20. *ASSK*, p. 75.

writings and they had no knowledge in scripts or letters, is meaningless and unbelievable. But unfortunately it is not exactly known as to what types of letters were used in those days.

Geography

The Āryans had the knowledge of Geography and we get sufficient evidences regarding that. So far the Natural Geography is concerned we get some evidences, such as:

1. This universe was created like a building — a miraculous feat of engineering or the result of the mechanical production.[21]
2. We find the mentionings of the premordial substance or unit of which the universe was developed.[22]
3. We have already discussed about astronomy in the Vedic ages which gives an idea of astronomical and mathematical geography.
4. A Ṛgvedic passage[23] presents an interrogator asking some questions as such:
   (a) What is the uttermost end of the world?
   (b) Where is the centre of the world?
   (c) What is the fecundating power of the rain-shedding steed?
   (d) What is the fountain source of speeches?
5. We get some evidences replying such questions as:
   (a) The earth is a fiery ball[24] and Agni or fire is the centre of the earth.[25]

---

21. *ṚV*, 10/129/6;7; 10/72/3 & 4; 10/81/24.
22. *Ibid.*, 1/164/6; 10/82/6.
23. *Ibid.*, 1/164 34.
24. *Ibid.*, 10/81/1.
25. *Ibid.*, 1/59/2 & 7/4/5.

(b) Sometimes we are informed of "making the earth firm," tranquillising mountains and consolidating the heaven.[26]

6. Information of earthquake is also got in the same[27] and the *AV*.[28]
7. The sages came to know that this earth was solidified and became fixed after its genesis.[29]
8. We find a passage mentioning about volcano also.[30]
9. We get lakes and waterfalls,[31] mountainous lands,[32] snowy mountains,[33] and deserts.[34] Moreover the descriptions of river banks[35] and the erosion by the Sarasvatī river[36] also are met.
10. The *TS* informs us about cleft or Irina, stony place of *śilā*, habitable place or *kṣayaṇa*, difficulty communicating forests or *kaṭa*, lake or *hrada*, rugged or *lopa*, etc.[37]

Regarding the geographical knowledge, Maya Prasad Tripathi mentions,

> It is but a truism to remark that Indians from the hoariest past had come to have a concept of Geography and had realized the importance of geographical knowledge and actually endeavoured to put it on record, of course, in their own primal

---

26. *R̥V*, 2/12/2.
27. *Ibid.*, 1/37/7.
28. *AV*, 19/9/8.
29. *Ibid.*, 20/34/2.
30. *Ibid.*, 2/3/7.
31. *Ibid.*, 8/7/10.
32. *Ibid.*, 8/85/2.
33. *Ibid.*, 10/121/4 & 5.
34. *Ibid.*, 6/62/2.
35. *Ibid.*, 6/61.
36. *Ibid.*, 6/61/2.
37. *TS*, 4/5/9/1.

> fashion, creating a separate section, which is found in their extant tomes or written documents of literature, culture and civilization.[38]

What did they tell and what types of picture do they present regarding the geographical description of Vedic India is an important matter to discuss.

INDIA : AS WE FIND IN THE VEDAS (NATURAL GEOGRAPHY)

Oceans and Seas

We have discussed in the first chapter that the people of the Vedic age had the knowledge of oceans and seas. While discussing the geographical situation of the Vedic India, a Ṛgvedic passage says that the two rivers, Śutudrī and Vipāśā, flow towards ocean and mingle.[39] Perhaps two eastern and western rivers surrounded modern Punjab and the Ganges valley.[40] It is supposed that the Vedic eastern sea was concealed[41] or extended up to the Bay of Bengal. Moreover the Vedic people lived in the land surrounded by four oceans in four main directions.[42] Khagendra Dasgupta says in this regard that a large proportion of the Thar desert was sea and it was enjoined with the present Rann of Kaccha. The Arāvalī was in the east. So the sea was a part of the present Sindhu Sāgara or the Arabian sea.[43] H.D. Sankalia also is found supporting the fact as:

> Rajputana was a sea during the time of Indus civilization and perhaps much earlier. This also supports the theory of some geologists that during a still earlier geological period, an area

---

38. *DGKAIM*, p. 319.
39. *ṚV*, 3/33.
40. *Ibid.*, 10/136/5.
41. *VSR*, p. 281.
42. *ṚV*, 9/33/6.
43. *ASSK*, p. 88.

> of the Arabian sea went along where the Vindhyas Hills are now.[44]

On the other hand, the *Encyclopaedia Britannica* informs regarding the northern ocean that there was vast ocean in Asia in the north of Balkh and Persia which has been named as Asian Mediterranian. It was so vast that it was connected with the Arctic ocean. The European Mediterranian was close by. The land of the Mediterranian was higher in the ancient times than the European ocean. Some natural changes caused the water of the Asian sea to be mixed with the European ocean. Thus, the ocean dried and it was changed into four seas such as Black Sea, Caspean Sea, Aral Sea and Lake Balkash. These seas were the parts of the northern ocean.[45]

Thus, we get a vast land named as Āryāvarta. The *MS* clearly mentions about the land of Āryāvarta to be in between the two eastern and western oceans.[46] Sometimes natural calamities occurred and the ocean turned into lands and mountains. In the same way, the places where the mountains existed turned into seas or lands. So the *ṛṣi*s prayed Indra to make the mountain fix and stable.[47] Perhaps the lands of modern south India, which has not been referred in the Vedic literature, was hidden under the water and it came out only in the later ages.

Mountains and Deserts

We get a term *himavanta*[48] in the *ṚV*. Perhaps it was another name of the Himālayas. On the other hand, the same informs about Mujavat or Kailāsa mountain.[49] The *TS* informs that

44. *ASSK*, p. 88.
45. Quoted from *VSR*, p. 281.
46. *MS*, 1/141.
47. *ṚV*, 1/62/3 & 2/12/2.
48. *Ibid.*, 10/121/4.
49. *Ibid.*, 10/34/1.

the Mujavān was in Gāndhāra.[50] Again the *MB* indicates it to be in the Himālayas.[51] The *TA* mentions of three mountains — the Sudarśana, Krauñca and Maināga.[52] The mountain Mahāmeru is referred in another place.[53]

On the other hand, we also get informations about the three deserts.[54] In the tenth book of the *R̥V* a desert has been mentioned to exist in the south of the Indus belt.[55] It is not known whether it was one among the three deserts or a fourth one.

RIVERS

The Indian people respected rivers very much. We find the names of some rivers in the present age as we get in the Vedic literature. But some rivers are known by some other names now. We are going to present the list of the names of the rivers as we get in the Vedic literature.

No.	*Name of the*	*Reference rivers*	*Modern names*	*Other informations*
1.	Aṅśumati	*R̥V*, 8/95/14	-	
2.	Añjasī	*R̥V*, 1/104/4	-	Perhaps it was a river of north-west.
3.	Anitabhā	*R̥V*, 5/3/9	-	It seems to be the sub river of the Indus.
4.	Asiknī	*R̥V*, 10/75/5	Cenāb or Candrabhāgā	Medicinal herbs were found here in large quantity

50. *TS*, 1/8/6/2 & *AV*, 5/22.
51. Read, *girerhimavataḥ pr̥ṣṭhe muñjavān nāma parvataḥ*, *Mbh*, 14/8/1.
52. *TA*, 1/31.
53. *TA*, 1/7.
54. *R̥V*, 1/35/8.
55. *Ibid.*, 10/63/15.

No.	Name of the rivers	Reference	Modern names	Other informations
5.	Āpayā	*R̥V*, 3/23/4	-	The *Mbh* informs that it flowed in Kurukṣetra. *MB* 3/63/68
6.	Ārjīkīyā	*R̥V*, 10/75/5	-	Yāska says that it was another name of Vipāśā. *Nir*, 9/26.
7.	Kubhā	*R̥V*, 5/53/9 & 10/75/6	Kābul	The Greeks called it Cofen.
8.	Kuliśī	*R̥V*, 1/104/3	-	Perhaps it was a river of Bāhlīk province.
9.	Krumu	*R̥V*, 5/53 & 10/75/6	Kurram	
10.	Gaṅgā	*R̥V*, 10/75/5 *ŚB*, 13/5/4/11 *TA*, 2/20, etc.		
11.	Gomatī	*R̥V*, 10/75/6 & 5/61/19	Gomala of Afghanistan	"It is not the present Gomatī." *VSR*, p. 289
12.	Jāhnavī	*R̥V*, 3/58/6		"There is a province Jāhnavī in the west of the Indus." *Ibid.*
13.	Tr̥ṣṭāma	*R̥V*, 10/75/6		"It flows eastward in Citrāl" *Ibid.*
14.	Dr̥ṣadvatī	*R̥V*, 3/23/4 *TB*, 25/10/14	The concealed river Ghaghar	It is said that the Aśmanvatī of the *R̥V*, 10/53/8 is the another name of the Dr̥ṣadvatī
15.	Paruṣṇī	*R̥V*, 5/52/9; 7/18/8 & 9 10/75/5	Irāvatī of the Punjab or Rāvī	
16.	Marudvadhā	*R̥V*, 10/75/5	Maruvardavan.	It is in the east of Cenāb
17.	Mehatnū	*R̥V*, 10/75/6		

No.	Name of the rivers	Reference	Modern names	Other informations
18.	Yamunā	ṚV, 5/52/17 10/75/5 *AV*, 4/9/10; *ŚB*, 13/5/4/11; etc.	Yamunā 7/8/19;	Some say it to be Cenāb and some as Rāvī.
19.	Yavyāvatī	ṚV, 6/27/6 &	*TB*, 25/7/2	Sāyaṇa calls it Hariyūpīyā
20.	Rathasyā	*JB*, 3/235		
21.	Rasā	ṚV, 1/112/12; 5/53/9; 10/75/6	*JB*, 2/440	It flows in the north of Afghanistan and Baluchistan.
22.	Varaṇāvatī	ṚV, 4/7/1	Varuṇā of Kāśī	
23.	Vitastā	ṚV, 10/75/5.	Jhelum	
24.	Vipāśā	ṚV, 4/30/11; 3/33/1 & 2; *GB*, 1/1/27 *GB*, 1/1/27.	Vyāsa	
25.	Vibālī	ṚV, 4/30/12		
26.	Vīrapatnī	ṚV, 1/104/3		Perhaps, a river of Bāhlīk province.
27.	Śiphā	ṚV, 1/104/3		
28.	Śutudrī	ṚV, 3/33/1 & 10/75/5	Sutlej	
29.	Śvetyā	ṚV, 10/75/6	Arjunī of Ismail Khan district.	
30.	Sadānīrā	*ŚB*, 1/4/1/14		Some say it to be Karatoyā and some say it Gaṇḍakī
31.	Sarayū	ṚV, 4/30/18 5/53/9 10/64/9	Sarayū	
32.	Sarasvatī	ṚV, 2/41/16 *AV*, 6/30/1	At present this river is	

No.	Name of the rivers	Reference	Modern names	Other informations
		TS, 7/2/1/4 *AB*, 2/19, etc.	concealed	
33.	Sindhu	*AV*, 6/24/1 7/45/1; 12/1/3 *SYV*, 8/59, etc.	Indus	
34.	Sudāmā	*TanB*, 22/18/7		
35.	Suvāstu	*Nir*, 4/7/2.	Swāt of Afghanistan	
36.	Suṣomā	*ṚV*, 10/75/5	Sohan	Tributary of the east Sindhu.
37.	Susartu	*ṚV*, 10/75/6.	Swāt(?)	
38.	Hariyūpīyā	*ṚV*, 6/27/5.		

POLITICAL GEOGRAPHY

States or Provinces

We have discussed the Natural Geography of India as revealed in the Vedic literature. Now description of the states or provinces of the Vedic nation is being given below:

No.	Name of the States	References	Details
1.	Aṅga	*AV*, 5/22/14 & *GB*, 1/2/9	Though not exactly known, yet some believe it to be the districts of Bhagalpur and Munger.
2.	Andhra	*AB*, 7/18	The sons of Vīśvāmitra got the curse of their father and hence became Āndhra, Puṇḍra, Pulinda, etc. Later on the Āndhras came to south, *VSR*, p. 291.
3.	Kamboja	*VSR*, p.291	Perhaps the Kambojas were the north-western residents.
4.	Kāśī or Kāśya	*AV*, 5/22/14, *ŚB*, 13/5/4/19 *GB*, 1/2/9	It is not known whether the present Kāśī was Vedic or not.

No.	*Name of the States*	*References*	*Details*
5.	Kīkaṭa	*R̥V*, 3/53/14	Some say that Magadha itself was Kīkaṭa while some other say that Kīkaṭas were the Anārya people. But H.C. Chakladhar holds that they were not Āryans.
6.	Kuru	*R̥V*, 10/33/4	It was near modern Delhi.
7.	Uttara Kuru	*AB*, 8/14	It was in the north of the Himālayas.
8.	Kośala	*ŚB*, 1/4/1/17	
9.	Gāndhāra or Gāndhārī	*R̥V*, 1/126/7 *AV*, 5/22/14,	The *R̥V* passage informs that the sheeps had hair in their bodies. *ChU*, 6/14/1
10.	Cedi	*R̥V*, 8/5/37 &	Perhaps this land was in a thick 8/5/39and dense forest.
11.	Naiṣidha	*ŚB*, 2/3/2/1; 2	It was situated in the south, but not known distinctly where it was.
12.	Puṇḍra	*AB*, 7/18	Perhaps the Vedic Āndhra and Puṇḍra were neighbours as Āndhra and Puṇḍra are mentioned together in the *AB*.
13.	Bāhlīk	*AV*, 5/22/5; 7 & 9 *ŚB*, 1/2/9/3	The *AV* indicates that this was in the northern part of India.
14.	Bharata	*R̥V*, 7/18/5; 3/33/11;12; 3/23/4 *JB*, 3/237	The Bharatas seems to had been the strongest group of people who were spread over the banks of the Paruṣṇī, Vipāśā, Śutudrī, Sarasvatī and Dr̥ṣadvatī, The *JB* informs that they resided in the Indus Valley, *VSR*, p. 301.
15.	Magadha	*ŚYV*, 30/32 *AV*, 5/22/14; *TB*, 3/4/1/1	It is not clear which land indicated Magadha. Vedic Magadha seems different to the present Magadha.
16.	Matsya	*ŚB*, 13/5/4/9 & *GB*, 1/2/9	The present Rājpūtānā was the Vedic Matsya province, *VSR*, p. 303.

No.	*Name of the States*	*References*	*Details*
17.	Madra	*BU*, 3/3/1; 3/7/1	It seems to be the land of the Himālayan Range.
18.	Mahāvṛṣa	*AV*, 5/22/4; 5 & 8 *JB*, 1/234 *ChU*, 4/2/5	It was the northern part of India.
19.	Vaṅga	*AA*, 2/1/1	The present Bengal including all other eastern part was perhaps known as Vaṅga.
20.	Videha	*ŚB*, 1/4/1/10, *TB*, 25/10/17	It was perhaps with Kośala in the western part of the country.
21.	Vidarbha	*JB*, 2/442	It is obscure whether the present Vidarbha was the Vedic one.

Towns

The people of the Vedic India were able to live the urban life as we get ample evidences of cities and towns in the Vedic literature. This is evident from the fact that the Āryans were expert in trade and commerce, crafts and industries,[56] housing and clothings, in using medicines and planes, etc.[57] Though we get the term *pura* several times in the Vedic texts[58] but the word *nagara* is perhaps found for the first time in the *TA* in the sense of town.[59] The *AB*[60] and the *JU*[61] introduces the adjectival term *nagarīm*. In the following list, some of the important towns along with their introductory descriptions are being given:

56. *ṚV*, 1/53/7; 58/8; 131/4; 166/8; 3/15/4; 4/27/1, etc.
57. Chapter VIII of this book.
58. *ṚV*, 1/58/8, 166/8, 3/15/4, 4/27/1, etc.
59. *TA*, 1/11/18; 1/31/4.
60. *AB*, 5/30.
61. *JU*, 3/40/2.

No.	*Name of the towns*	*References*	*Details*
1.	Kāmpilya	*TS*, 7/4/19/1, *ŚYV*, 23/18 *TB*, 3/9/6, *ŚB*, 13/2/8/3	Perhaps it was the capital of Pañcāla.
2.	Kārapaśava	*TMB*, 25/10/23	It was situated on the bank of the river Yamunā.
3.	Kārotī	*ŚB*, 9/5/2/15	
4.	Kauśāmbī	*ŚB*, 12/2/2/1	
5.	Tūrghna	*TA*, 5/1/1	The northern land of Kurukṣetra was known as Tūrghna.
6.	Triplakṣa	*TMB*, 25/13/4	It was on the bank of the river Yamunā where the river Dṛṣadvatī seems to have vanished.
7.	Nāḍapit	*ŚB*, 13/5/4/13	Bharata was born in this place from Śakuntalā.
8.	Naimiṣa or	*TMB*, 25/6/4 *JB*, 1/36/3 *ChU*, 1/2/13	Here 88,000 *ṛṣis* listened 18 Purāṇas from Sūta.
9.	Parīṇāha	*TMB*, 25/13/1 *JB*, 2/300	It is supposed to have been situated in the west of Kurukṣetra.
10.	Raikvaparṇa	*ChU*, 4/2/5	Perhaps it was in the State of Mahāvṛṣa
11.	Saryaṇāvat	*ṚV*, 8/6/39	The passage informs the place to be near Kurukṣetra.
12.	Śaciguṇa	*AB*, 8/23	It is located in west India.

Theory of Āryan Race

The theory of Āryan invasion and migration has left a landmark in the history of India. In the absence of the conception of the term *ārya* and their native land, one cannot enter into the theory of Nation and Nationalism in the Vedic literature. This theory has led to the question that whether they were nation from the very beginning of the human civilization. On the otherhand if we suppose that they were migrants and have entered into India on invading the

Indian people, we cannot go back more than three or four thousand years. Moreover, such conception misleads us to find the truth. Therefore, it is necessary now to examine the fact with keen eyes. Our research in this context goes as follows:

CONCEPT OF ĀRYAN RACE

The word Āryan in the sense of a race was first used by Lassen in the year 1847 in his book *History of Ancient India.*[62] Maxmüller also had been supporting the theory up to 1871, but this year he realized that he had committed a mistake. Sri Ram Sathe informs,

> In fact he became antagonistic to his own views and changed his theory. He started repeatedly thereafter, till the end of his life — and this also with full vigour — that by the term Āryan he did not mean a race in the sense of a group of people with distinct blood and physical and mental characteristics.[63]

He further informs,

> The term Āryan in the sense of a race was also used by Edward Thomas in 1866.[64]

This theory was put into discussion by Thomas in a meeting of the Royal Asiatic Society in London on 9-8-1866 and its report was published in 1871.[65]

EVIDENCES OF ĀRYAN'S MIGRATION AND INVASIONS COLLECTED BY WESTERN SCHOLARS

So far the term Āryan is concerned, it has wrongly and intentionally been explained by several scholars, such as Lassen, Maxmüller and Edward Thomas, etc., as a caste.

62. *AWTR*, p. 1.
63. *Ibid.*
64. *Ibid.*
65. *Bhāratīya Itihāsamālā* by Shri Ram Sathe, p. 99.

The word *ārya* is met 33 and 16 times in the *ṚV* and the *AV*, respectively.[66] Each times it reveals an adjective. The Western scholars put the following evidences to show the Āryans migration and invasion:

1. The word *dāsa varṇa* occurring in the *ṚV*[67] was considerd to allude to the black skin of the aborigines.
2. The term *kṛṣṇagarbha* of the same[68] was expressed to denote *anārya*.
3. *Dāsa*s were thought to be *anāsa*[69] which has been translated as noseless[70] or snub-nosed. Griffith describes it to be, "the flat nosed barbarians."[71]
4. The European scholars have taken the terms, *dāsa* and *dasyu*, as communities. That helped them to show that the Āryans were migrants and invaders and the Indian origins were called *dāsas* and *dasyus* by them.
5. The Western scholars accused that the Āryans hated phallus worship. With the help of a *ṛk* they argue that the non-Āryans were phallus worshippers.[72]
6. The fact that Indra snatched away the wealth hidden in the hundred-doored castle of the enemies and killed *śiśnadeva*s,[73] is presented to prove the Āryans' invasion.
7. The Āryans were white-skinned people[74] whom Indra gave horses, the sun and cows because those

66. *Bhāratīya Itihāsamālā* by Shri Ram Sathe, p. 99.
67. *ṚV*, 2/12/4.
68. *ṚV*, 1/101/1.
69. *Ibid.*, 5/29/10.
70. *ṚVg*, p. 249.
71. Footnote of Griffith on *ṚV*, 5/29/10.
72. *ṚV*, 7/21/5.
73. *Ibid.*, 10/9/9.
74. *Ibid.*, 3/34/9.

were thought to be the sources of money, enjoyments and land.

8. The Āryans killed 30,000,[75] 1,00,000,[76] and 50,000[77] Anāryas in different wars.

EXAMINING THE FOREIGNERS' ABOVE ASSESSMENTS

So far the word *dāsa varṇa* is concerned, the word *varṇa* has been translated by the Western scholars in the sense of race. Thus, they meant the *ṛk* as the description of the conflict between the Āryans and the non-Āryans. Ram Sathe says,

> This meaning is rendered absurd by the clear statement that the release of the sun was one of the result of the conflict. Is the sun a tennis ball which the non-Aryans could steal and keep in their pocket?[78]

Mentioning the meaning of the term *varṇa*, Sathe further remarks:

> The word (*varṇa*) usually means colour, the western scholars shouted eureka. They took the word to refer to the colour of the skin and saw the white-black conflicts in the *Ṛgveda*. Amara's lexicon mentions many words meaning it race which makes clear that the word *varṇa* is not one of them by mentioning it separately. Meanings of the word *varṇa* are colour, praise, letter, etc. The lexicon *Medinī* mentions *varṇa* to mean brāhmaṇa, kṣatriya, etc.[79]

The term *kṛṣṇagarbha*[80] has been translated by Griffith as "dusky brood."[81] On the other hand, in the footnote he meant the term as "the dark aborigines who opposed the

75. *ṚV*, 4/36/21.
76. *Ibid.*, 4/30/15 & 7/99/5.
77. *Ibid.*, 4/16/13.
78. *AWTR*, p. 52.
79. *Ibid.*
80. *ṚV*, 1/101/1.
81. *ṚVg*, p. 64.

Āryans."[82] Again, Sāyaṇa has translated the term as, "the masses of the clouds that are black inside."[83] We get another *ṛk*[84] where the word *kṛṣṇa* means "the cloud of dark colour."

The term *anāsa* does not mean snub-nosed. According to Sāyaṇa, "One who makes sound would be *nāsa* and the silent one *anāsa*."[85]

Dāsa, on the other hand, are not mentioned as community but *varṇa*.[86] Another passage clearly means the term in the sense of a slave.[87]

Had the sense of blackness expressed the meaning of *anārya*, we would not have got the relationship of blackness with gods and Āryans. But we meet Indra described as a black god in a passage of the *ṚV*[88] The seer Kaṇva also has been described to be black.[89] A seer prays Tvaṣṭā to bestow him the *piśaṅgarūpa* or tawny offsprings.[90]

The term *śiśnadeva* was supposed to be phallus-worshipper. This meaning given by the Western scholars is baseless because Yāska meant it to be licentious one.[91] Sāyaṇa has explained it as, "One who sports with the generative organ."[92] Vidhusekhar Bhattacharya explains the word *deva* as:

> The term *deva* when added with another term, it bears the meaning of 'devotion' and 'connected with.' For instance

82. *ṚVg*, footnote on 1/101/1.
83. See Sāyaṇa on *ṚV*, 1/101/1.
84. See Sāyaṇa's commentary on *ṚV*, 7/17/14.
85. *Ibid.*, 5/29/10.
86. *ṚV*, 2/12/4 & 10/22/8.
87. *Ibid.*, 8/56/3.
88. *Ibid.*, 4/17/4.
89. *Ibid.*, 10/3/11.
90. *Ibid.*, 2/3/9.
91. Read, *abrahmacaryaḥ śiśnena snathate*, 4/19.
92. See Sāyaṇa's commentary on the *ṚV*, 2/3/9.

> *mātṛdeva* and *pitṛdeva*, etc. A term *strīdeva* is met in the Purāṇic literature which means devoted and connected with women. In the same way the term *śiśnadeva* means 'to be devoted and connected with phallus.'[93]

On the other hand, there is no any relationship of the term *śiśnadeva* with the first three feet of the passage[94] and the meaning of the last foot is, "Let not the licentious approach our sacrifices." The theory of phallus-worship on the basis of this passage has become baseless.

Had the enemies of the so-called Āryans been called as *anārya*s or non-Āryans, then we would have got some passages in the *ṚV* where the Āryans would have been mentioned as the enemies of the seer.[95]

Thus, the theory of Āryans' invasion, which was propounded by the Western scholars on the basis of the misinterpretation of some Vedic passages, seems to become meaningless.

THE NAMES AND MEANINGS OF DASYUS IN THE ṚV

We find some terms and names of *dasyu*s in the *ṚV* as follows:

1. *Aja* (*ṚV*, 3/45/2) and *Ajāsaḥ* (*ṚV*, 7/18/19)
2. *Arnaśani* (*ṚV*, 8/32/2)
3. *Ahīśuva* (*ṚV*, 8/32/2)
4. *Arbuda* (*ṚV*, 2/11/20)
5. *Ilibiśa* (*ṚV*, 1/33/12 & *Nir.*, 6/19)
6. *Urana* (*ṚV*, 2/14/4)
7. *Aurṇavābha* (*ṚV*, 2/11/18)
8. *Kimīdina* (*ṚV*, 7/104/2)
9. *Kṛṣṇa* (*ṚV*, 1/73/7, 58/4, 115/5, 140/5, 146/3, 4/7/9, 7/8/2, 8/73/18 and *AV*, 6/22/1, 9/10/22, 10/20/9)

93. Quoted from *VRDB*, p. 67.

94. *ṚV*, 7/21/5.

95. *ṚV*, 6/60/6; 10/38/3 & 10/83/1.

10. *Kuyava* (R̥V, 7/19/2)
11. *Cumuri* (R̥V, 2/13/9, 6/18/8, 20/13, 26/6, 7/19/4)
12. *Tugra* (R̥V, 6/26/6)
13. *Tutuji* (R̥V, 6/20/8)
14. *Turukṣa* (R̥V, 8/46/32)
15. *Daśoṇi* (R̥V, 6/20/8)
16. *Dr̥bhīka* (R̥V, 2/14/3)
17. *Druha* (R̥V, 6/20/5)
18. *Dhuni* (R̥V, 1/174/9)
19. *Namuci* (R̥V, 5/30/8)
20. *Navavāstva* (R̥V, 1/36/18, 6/20/11, 19/49/6)
21. *Balbūtha* (R̥V, 8/46/32)
22. *Pipru* (R̥V, 5/21/11)
23. *Vr̥ṣaya* (R̥V, 1/93/4)
24. *Br̥hadratha* (R̥V, 1/36/18)
25. *Mr̥gaya* (R̥V, 4/16/13, 8/3/19, 10/49/5)
26. *Rudhikrā* (R̥V, 2/14/5)
27. *Varcin* (R̥V, 4/30/15)
28. *Vala* (R̥V, 1/32/5)
29. *Viśiśiśipra* (R̥V, 5/45/6)
30. *Viśvarūpa* (R̥V, 2/11/19)
31. *Vr̥ṣaśipra* (R̥V, 71/19/4)
32. *Veśa* (R̥V, 7/99/4)
33. *Vyaṁsa* (R̥V, 2/14/5)
34. *Śambara* (R̥V, 4/26/3)
35. *Śuṣṇa* (R̥V, 1/11/7, 4/30/13)
36. *Smadibha* (R̥V, 10/49/4)
37. *Svaśna* (R̥V, 2/14/5)
38. *Sr̥binda* (R̥V, 8/32/2)

A *R̥V* passage[96] gives the following characteristics of the *dasyus*: He is (a) riteless, (b) void of sense, (c) inhumane, and (d) keep alien laws. Another passage indicates that

96. *R̥V*, 10/22/8.

the term is an adjective, clarifying the meaning of *varṇa*[97] but not *jāti*. Again we find the *dasyus* being converted to Āryan by reforming their lives.[98] It was difficult to separate the Āryas from the non-Āryans.[99] Because the term Āryans neither denotes community nor a man of special body construction.

THE TERM ĀRYA : AS THE TEXTS REVEAL

1. The term *ārya* was used to address the respected one so Śāśvatī calls her husband as *ārya*.[100]
2. Had *ārya* been used as a community of people then how is it possible that the Yadus and the Turvasas were considered neither the *ārya*[101] nor the *anārya* or non-Āryan.[102]
3. *Ārya* denotes *varṇa* but not *jāti* or commune.[103]
4. A *Ṛ̥V* passage advises to change the people of the world by making them *ārya*.[104] This obviously meant an adjective and not a noun.
5. The passage, "we have deprived the *dasyus* of the holy name of *ārya*"[105] indicates the term to be an adjective.
6. We get a passage where an *ārya ṛ̥ṣi* wishes to make a *dasyu* an *ārya*.[106] It also has been used as an adjective.
7. In a *Ṛ̥V* passage,[107] where the term has been

97. *Ṛ̥V*, 2/12/4 & 10/22/8.
98. *Ibid.*, 8/51/9.
99. *Ibid.*, 1/51/8 & 9.
100. *Ṛ̥V*, 8/1/34.
101. *Ibid.*, 10/62/10.
102. *Ibid.*, 8/6/48.
103. *Ibid.*, 3/34/4.
104. *Ibid.*, 9/63/5.
105. *Ibid.*, 10/49/3.
106. *Ibid.*, 8/51/9.
107. *Ṛ̥V*, 1/103/3.

translated by Griffith in the sense of "non-Āryan inhabitants of the land,"[108] the term *ārya* denotes a *jāti* but Sāyaṇa meant it to be a scholar who performs *yajñas*.[109]

8. Again Sāyaṇa has meant the term *ārya* as the praying scholars,[110] who are the best *varṇa*,[111] the persons having humane behave[112] and the ones who are active.[113]

SOME OTHER DEFINITIONS FROM THE CLASSICAL LITERATURE

We have presented the evidences from the R̥gvedic texts that the term *ārya* was not used in the sense of a caste or creed rather it denoted some qualities. Other Sanskrit literatures also reveal the same. Some of the important examples are as follows:

1. The term *anārya* used in the *MB* also indicates the sense of adjective.[114]
2. The term *ārya* meant great, noble, good-looking and a personality which is capable of moving everywhere.[115]
3. The *SBG* also expresses the term *anārya* in the sense of a quality.[116]
4. A clear definition of *ārya* has been presented in the *MB* as follows : He who does not revive the enmity

108. *R̥Vg*, p. 66.

109. Read, *āryaḥ viduṣohanuṣṭhātr̥n*. See Sāyaṇa on 1/103/3.

110. Read *vidvāṃsah stotāraḥ*, *R̥VSāy*, 1/130/3.

111. Read, *uttamavarṇa* in *R̥VSāy*, 3/34/9.

112. Read, *mānave* in *R̥VSāy*, 4/26/2.

113. Read, *karmayuktāni*, *R̥VSāy*, 6/22/10.

114. *MBh*, Yuddha 16/11 & 14.

115. Read, *sarvadabhigataḥ sadbhiḥ samudra iva sindhubhiḥ āryaḥ sarvagamaścaiva sadaiva priyadarśanaḥ*, *Rām*, 1/1/16.

116. Read, *kutastvā kaśmalamidaṁ viṣame samupasthitam. anāryajuṣṭamasvargyamakīrtikaramarjuna*, *ŚBG*, 2/2.

which is once calmed down, one who is not egoistic or hopeless, who is not much joyous due to his pleasures and who is not pleased seeing others suffer and who does not repent after giving gifts is *ārya*.[117]

5. The *AK* means the term as (i) a man of family, (ii) a gentleman fit to attend the meetings, (iii) good natured, and (iv) righteous.[118]
6. Sri Ram was an *ārya*, because he cared for all with equality and who was dear to others like the moon.[119]

INDIA : ĀRYĀVARTA OR THE LAND OF THE CIVILIZED PEOPLE

We come to know from the above analysis that the term Āryan does not denote the meaning of a mere community but an adjective used in the sense of great, noble, ideal and humane. Such culture that flourished in India was named as Āryāvarta. The idea that the Āryans or civilized people came from outside India, invading its aborigines, is baseless. The *ārya*s or the civilized people were of the Indian origins according to the following Vedic evidences:

1. The God built land, washed and purified with the water of the Sindhu and the Sarasvatī, was the land of the civilized people.[120]
2. The *ārya*s are found praying Sarasvatī as the best

117. Read, *na vairamuddīpayati praśāntam na darpamārohati nāstameti na durgatohsmīti karotyakāryam tamāryaśīlaṃ paramāhurāryaḥ.*

&

na sve sukhe vai kurute praharṣam
nānyasya duḥkhe bhavati prahṛṣṭaḥ
datvā na paścāt kurutehnutāpam
sa kathyate satpuruṣārthaśīlaḥ,
— *Mbh,* Udyoga 33/117 & 118.

118. Read *mahakulakulīnāryaḥ sabhyasajjana sādhavaḥ, AK,* 2/7/3.

119. Read, *āryaḥ sarvagamaścaiva, Rām,* Bāl 1/16.

120. *ṚV,* 3/33/4.

goddess, best river, etc.[121] Had the Āryans been the foreigners they would not pray the Indian rivers as such.

3. On the other hand, the Vedic people prayed the seven Sindhus also in a *ṛk*.[122]
4. We do not get a single evidence of the motherly love to the foreign land in the Vedas which inspires us to accept the Indian origin of the Āryans.

The Indian people went abroad to spread their humane feelings and nobility in order to make the people of the world cultured.[123] This we have already discussed in the first chapter under the sub-topic, Vedic Nationals : Outside India.

Swāmī Vivekānanda exclaimed sorrowfully,

> And what your European *pundit*s say about the Aryans swooping down from some foreign land, snatching away the lands of the aborigines and settling in India by exterminating them, is all pure nonsense, foolish talk. Strange that our Indian Scholars too, say amen to them; and all these monstrous lies are being taught to our boys. This is very bad indeed. . . . In what Veda, in what Sūkta do you find that the Aryans came into India from a foreign country ? Where do you get the idea that they slaughtered the wild aborigines ? What do you gain by talking such nonsense?[124]

---

121. *ṚV*, 2/41/16 & 17.
122. *Ibid.*, 10/60/5.
123. *ṚV*, 9/63/5.
124. *The East and the West*, Lectures of Svami Vivekanada, p. 104.

Conclusion

OUR motto of this research was firstly to show that the theory of Nation and Nationalism first originated in India in the Vedic era. Some Western scholars have misguided the people by saying that India did not have any national feeling in the past. It was said so only to vilify the national life of India.

Secondly, Indian Nationalism is culture-based nationalism and not political one. We have discussed the conception of culture in the chapter that dealt with miscellaneous topics. Indian conception of Nationalism is based upon the aforesaid elements. This is the only cause for which India has retained its perpetual national life till now.

Thirdly, the theory of Nation and Nationalism is vague. It has not been defined by UNO also. The Western concept is therefore obscure.

On the other hand, the concept of political aspects in the Indian nation such as having parliaments and assemblies named as *sabhā, samiti,* and *vidatha,* kingship, types of states, are found scattered in the Vedic literature. The *varṇa* and *āśrama vyavasthā* were the pillars of social structure which were used to conduct the social and individual lives respectively. Again eternal theories of economics have been found in the Vedas by M.G. Bokare. Not only this, even the existence of several types of industries, trade and commerce also are described in the Vedas. The primary needs of people are found to have shelter, food and dresses, amusements medicines and ornamentations, etc. So far the Vedic religion and philosophy is concerned, it differed from the present practice of rituals. The *yajña* was supposed to be the main religious function. Vedic philosophy is known through the *Nāsadīya Sūkta* where the Vedic view of the theory of creation is sung. The *AV* and its *Saṁjñāna Sūkta*s are the storehouse of Indian philosophy. Several types of thoughts of schools were developed later on. The military aspect gives more evidences of missiles, planes, organiza-tions, several types of forts and invasions. The chapter, Miscellaneous, includes the achievement of science in India, its geographical descriptions, a new light on the vague Āryan theory, etc. In the course of our studies we came to know and realize the following informations:

1. First of all, we have tried to find out the definition of the term *rāṣṭra* according to the Vedic sources. In the course of treatment, we come to present the following definition of the term: **A *rāṣṭra* is such a geo-cultural territory of land having warrior protectors, awaken *purohita*s, concious and well-organized society whose social organizations are conducted by a powerful administration in which the people should have their cultural heritage, national and motherly feelings nurtured towards their territory of land.**
2. Whatever the Vedic people thought about *rāṣṭra* and their heritage in the everyday life of society, we find nationalism in marriage festivities, administrations, schools, wars, religious rituals and all other activities.
3. *Varṇāśrama vyavasthā* was not created out of hatred but it was observed to make the social life run smoothly.
4. There was a difference between *rāṣṭra* and *rājya*. A *rāṣṭra* was supposed to be a geo-cultural entity whereas a *rājya* was purely a political unit.

5. The theory of Āryans' invasion was found to be baseless as everywhere in the Vedic and classical literature, we find the terms used in the sense of an adjective. We can say, in a nutshell, that the term has been used to denote civilized and cultured one. Such cultured and civilized people had first originated in India and became the offsprings of this soil. None but such people of India were the root of human civilization. They went out for trade and commerce and there they bestowed a new light to the people.
6. The Indian intellectuals were able to set-up the several types of states such as *sāmrājya* (overlord-ship), *bhaujya* (self-rule), *pārameṣṭhya* (kingship), *rājyam* (great king-ship), *ādhipatyamaya* (sovereignty) and so on.
7. The Vedic states were conducted and administered with the help of parliaments or *Samiti*, state assemblies or *sabhā*s and village congregations or *vidatha*s.
8. There were ideal educational systems where the curriculums for the development of the four important elements of the human beings, i.e., soul, mind, body and intelligence were introduced.
9. Moreover we find the theories of economics such as price, supply, marketing, coinage, etc., in the Vedic literature.
10. Though we do not find the four *puruṣārtha*s mentioned systematically in the Vedic literature, yet we get so in the later literatures and the seeds of it was hidden in the Vedas and Upaniṣads as well. These *puruṣārtha*s directed human and national life towards perfection. Generally we find emphasis on *kāma* and on *artha* or finance. But the Indian system

emphasized not only upon *artha* and *kāma* but also used *dharma* and *mokṣa* to control upon them.

Thus, this research is expected to give a new light on the theory of Nationalism in the midst of the scholars to cogitate over. The theory of Nationalism based upon political and economic foundation is new and obscure. On the other hand, the culture-based theory of Nationalism is perpetual and perfect. We hope that this book will bestow a thought anew.

Appendix I

Culture : Definition and Aspects

So far the term "culture" is concerned we get the meaning of the said term as, follows:[1]

1. Advanced development of human powers; development of the body, mind and spirit by training and experience.
2. Evidence of intellectual development (of Arts, Science, etc.) in human society.
3. State of intellectual development among people.
4. All the arts, beliefs, social institutions, characteristics of community, race, etc. On the other hand, the term *saṁskṛti* is first met in the *ŚYV*.[2] The passage says that *saṁskṛti* is the manifestation of ideal deeds which are well respected by the whole world.

Discussing the difference between the words *saṁskṛti* and culture Ram Sarma says,

> The word 'culture' in English denotes the way of life and thinking which becomes as lovely as family, language, land and so on. Such love may lead a man or a group of men towards hatred and aggressions. We get a large numbers of instances in the world.[3]

---

1. *Oxford Advanced Dictionary*, ed. A.S. Hornby, p. 210.
2. Read, "*Sā Prathamā saṁskṛtirviśvavārā*" *ŚYV*, 7/14.
3. *Samasta Viśva ko Bhārat ke Ajasra Anudāna* by Sri Ram Sarma, p. 1.3.

Characteristics of Saṁskṛti

The word *saṁskṛti* expresses an important meaning and hence it has become necessary to peep into the matter. The characteristics of *saṁskṛti* are as follows:

1. *Saṁskṛti* can never be attached with a certain group of people, creed or land but it is universal and humane.[4]
2. *Saṁskṛti* is the worship of universal and perpetual beauty.[5]
3. T.S. Eliot in his *Survey of Culture* writes that the characteristic of culture is faith which compels to abide by the humane highness.[6]
4. Brahmananda Sarasvati says that the customs and thought that help to uplift the position of wordly and divine life is culture.[7]
5. *Saṁskṛti* is the congregation of our internal qualities, it is an inspiring energy which decides the social behaves, and begets languages and institutions.[8]

On the other hand, we get such descriptions that distinctly differs culture from civilization. Swami Satyadevji Parivrajak distinguishes the fact as: "Civilization is an expression of flesh, while culture is the manifestation of soul."[9]

Thus, the studies of the term leads us to think that the culture is something abstract and spiritual which inspires people to follow the path of virtue.

---

4. *Samasta Viśva ko Bhārat ke Ajasra Anudāna* by Sri Ram Sarma, p.1.4.
5. *Ibid.*
6. *Ibid.*
7. *Hindu Saṁskṛti* by Swami Brahmananda Sarasvati in *HSA,* p.24.
8. *Mānava Saṁskṛti* by Bhagavandas in *HSA,* p.176.
9. *Sabhyatā aur Saṁskṛti: Ek gṛdhra dṛṣṭi* by Swami Satyadevji Parivrajak in *HSA,* p. 234.

As *saṁskṛti* has been described as *viśvavārā*,[10] it means the actions respected by all the people of the world.[11] Thus, *saṁskṛti* or culture is the base of a *rāṣṭra* or nation which exists in the world on account of the culture it follows. Hatred, non-endurance, non-cooperation, and diversity cause a nation to vanish from the map of the world.

So we are going to discuss what the Vedic people attained in that field of culture.

1. ***Truth*** : As the path of truth was supposed to be easygoing,[12] so the people of high status supported and followed the path of truth.[13] The wicked people cannot step into the path of truth[14] whereas a pious one can walk easily.[15] So the people believed that people should be refrained from false[16] and follow truth.[17] God has established *śraddhā* or respect on the base of truth[18] for which a liar becomes impure[19] and a truthful becomes victorious always.[20] The truth bestows heaven[21] and protects nations.[22] So the Vedic persons wanted to make their desires truthful.[23] The people thought that the *vedatrayī* are the touchstones

---

10. *ŚYV*, 7/14.
11. Read, *viśvaṁ vṛṇoti iti*, Mahīdhara on *ŚYV*, 7/14.
12. *ṚV*, 8/31/13.
13. *Ibid.*, 4/33/6.
14. *Ibid.*, 9/73/6.
15. *Ibid.*, 9/73/1.
16. *ŚYV*, 1/5.
17. *Ibid.*, 7/45.
18. *Ibid.*, 19/77.
19. *ŚB*, 3/1/3/18.
20. *Ibid.*, 3/4/2/8.
21. *TMB*, 18/2/19.
22. *AV*, 14/1/1.
23. *ṚV*, 10/67/11.

of truth.[24] On the other hand, an ideal man tries to avoid untruth.[25] A liar makes false speeches[26] and reduces his lustre.[27] But once he realizes his sinful act, he resolves to abide by truth only and not the untruth.[28] He thus owns truth and dispels untruth.[29] He prays God to help him to attain the truth in speeches[30] and also that the truth may protect him.[31]

2. ***Character building*** : A Vedic person wanted to be great always.[32] He even wished to be considered so by his enemies also.[33] He tried his best to follow the grand and ideal customs in life so that his offsprings also may imitate those ideals[34] and believed that he, who disobeys the divine rules cannot get the life of hundred years.[35] So he wished that the honest earnings only may beautify the home.[36] It was believed that the wise persons got victory over death through the strength of penance, i.e, *brahmacarya*.[37] Drinking wine[38] and playing dice[39] were condemned as immoral deeds. Moreover delusion, wrath and

24. *ŚB*, 9/5/1/18.
25. *Ibid.*, 3/1/3/18.
26. *TMB*, 8/6/13.
27. *ŚB*, 2/2/2/19.
28. *AV*, 4/9/7.
29. *Ibid.*, 8/4/12.
30. *ŚYV*, 39/4.
31. *R̥V*, 10/37/2.
32. Read, *māmuttaraṁ kr̥dhi*. *AV*, 2/27/7.
33. *R̥V*, 1/4/6.
34. *AV*, 6/17/7.
35. *R̥V*, 10/33/9.
36. *AV*, 7/115/4.
37. *Ibid.*, 11/7/19.
38. *R̥V*, 8/2/2.
39. *Ibid.*, 10/34/15.

malice to own castes was considered wrong and the people wanted to be released from such state of mind.[40] This fact has allegorically been described.

These understandings led the Vedic people to advise the younger generations as to go forward towards light (wisdom) from dark (ignorance)[41] and to rise but not to fall down.[42] For that, people used to pray God to make them the travellers of the path of benediction[43] and make them hear the benedictory speeches.[44] In short they were eager to be virtuous.[45]

3. ***Devotion or śraddhā***: So far the devotion or *śraddhā* is concerned, the Vedic sages believed that only devotion is able to kindle the fire of the *yajña*[46] and leads the devotee to God.[47] *Aśraddhā* or non-devotion was supposed to be based upon untruth whereas *śraddhā* on truth.[48] A man realizes truth through *śraddhā* or devotion.[49] A passage says to give something with *śraddhā*.[50] At last, *śraddhā* is regarded as God[51] in a whole *sūkta* and it is prayed to mingle in a devotee.[52]
4. ***Purity*** : On the other hand, people centralized their glances to purity also. People wanted to make their

40. *AV*, 8/4/22.
41. *Ibid.*, 8/1/8.
42. *Ibid.*, 8/1/6.
43. Read, *svasti panthāmanucarema*, *R̥V*, 5/51/15.
44. Read, *bhadraṁ karṇebhi śr̥ṇuyāmaḥ*, *ŚYV*, 25/21.
45. *Ibid.*, 4/28.
46. *R̥V*, 10/151/1.
47. Read, *śraddhayā vindate basu*, *R̥V*, 10/151/4.
48. *ŚYV*, 19/77.
49. *Ibid.*, 19/30.
50. Read, *śraddhayā deyam. aśraddhayādeyam*, *BU*.
51. *R̥V*, 10/15/1.
52. *Ibid.*, 10/151/5.

life a sacrifice in itself,[53] by discarding the internal and external dirt.[54] People thought that life of a man becomes pure, if he uses the pure and auspicious things[55] and also the longevity of his life increases.[56] We find a seer as if proclaiming the sin, "We leave you ourselves if you do not want to leave us."[57] Moreover people are found praying God to purify his whole nature.[58]

5. ***Charity*** : Charity was highly esteemed in the Vedic India. People were inspired to distribute to thousands of hands though the income is raised with hundred hands.[59] It was supposed that the wealth of charitable person does not decrease but increases.[60] Thus he who does not give was supposed to be the abject one.[61] It was further thought that a charitable person reaches the divine state[62] and acquires the luster and brightness as the sun.[63] Such homes where no chariatable actions or rituals are performed, cannot be called home.[64] So a man of *gṛhasthāśrama* should not be confined to oneself,[65] but should give to mendicants and guests.[66] In fact, by giving some eatables to a

53. *AV*, 14/2/67.
54. *ṚV*, 10/9/8.
55. *ŚYV*, 19/42.
56. *ṚV*, 10/67/18.
57. *AV*, 6/26/2.
58. *ŚYV*, 19/39.
59. *AV*, 3/24/5.
60. *ṚV*, 10/117/7.
61. *AV*, 20/128/4.
62. *ṚV*, 1/125/6.
63. *AV*, 20/128/5.
64. *ṚV*, 10/117/5.
65. *ṚV*, 10/117/6.
66. *Ibid.*, 10/117/5.

hungry beggar, a person gets the full fruits of performing *yajña*.[67] A charitable person has been warned not to give something to the person who commits sin.[68]

6. ***Social conduct*** : Establishing a cordial relationship with the people of society[69] and friendship with the wise,[70] one should help the friends[71] and come forward together.[72] We find emphasis upon the sweetness in speeches,[73] avoiding voilent nature[74] and expressing love through eyes.[75] The man should be loved by the people[76] and animals as well.[77] He should live in brotherhood[78] so that all may love him.[79]

   Uplifting the degarded ones,[80] casting away hatred and envy,[81] and not uttering false speeches,[82] were the ideals of the Vedic people. The youngsters were expected to be obedient to the parents[83] and not to quarrel with brothers and sisters.[84] The man was

---

67. *Ibid.*, 10/117/3.
68. *AV*, 20/82/1.
69. *ŚYV*, 36/18.
70. *Ṛ̥V*, 1/89/2.
71. *Ibid.*, 10/117/4.
72. *Ibid.*, 10/191/2.
73. *AV*, 3/30/3; 16/2/2 & 4; 1/24/1 and 5/7/4.
74. *Ṛ̥V*, 8/18/13.
75. *ŚYV*, 18/66.
76. *AV*, 17/1/3.
77. *Ibid.*, 17/1/4.
78. *ŚYV*, 40/6.
79. *AV*, 19/62/1.
80. *Ibid.*, 4/13/1.
81. *AV*, 12/1/24.
82. *Ibid.*, 23/25.
83. *AV*, 3/30/2.
84. *Ibid.*, 3/30/3.

advised to make their birth worthwhile.[85] The gods become the friend of such persons only[86] As such a man should throw envy and hatred[87] without neglecting other creatures.[88] Bringing such conducts into existence, people may uplift and progress[89] in life.[90]

7. ***Fearlessness*** : A Vedic hero thought that fearlessness is the connotation of success and he thinks himself to be Indra[91] whom none can hinder in bringing his decision into practice.[92] Such happens if the solemn promise is forwarded to lead.[93] He is found saying.
   1. I will not compromise with demons, dacoits and offenders.[94]
   2. I shall throw the earth[95] and the sun[96] like a ball.
   3. O, the people of the world, listen to me, the dacoits flee away wherever we go[97] because the dacoits and the wicked people consider me like a lion and tiger.[98]

---

85. *Ṛ̥V*, 10/16/4.
86. *Ibid.*, 4/33/13.
87. *ŚYV*, 5/26.
88. *AV*, 8/1/7.
89. *Ṛ̥V*, 10/128/4.
90. *AV*, 5/10/7.
91. *Ṛ̥V*, 10/48/5.
92. *ŚYV*, 10/27/15.
93. *AV*, 19/4/2.w
94. *Ibid.*, 4/36/7.
95. *Ṛ̥V*, 10/119/9.
96. *Ibid.*, 10/119/10.
97. *AV*, 4/36/8.
98. *AV*, 4/36/6.

4. I am able to make the envious people and women spiritless.[99]

One wishes that he should be lustrous like the burning charcoal and break the mountains[100] and wishes not to be tormented with any fear.[101] Furthermore, he wishes not to be afraid of anything.[102] After the establishment of friendship with a person, he does not remain rigid[103]

99. *AV*, 7/13/1.
100. *R̥V*, 4/2/15.
101. *AV*, 19/15/5 & 6.
102. *Ibid.*, 2/15.
103. *R̥V*, 8/4/7.

Appendix II

Scientific Achievement in the Vedic India

WE have already discussed in the previous chapters about some scientific inventions and discoveries in medical science, architecture, technology of making awful weapons and ships, different types of charoits and planes and so on. But here we want to discuss the elements of science, especially physics, astronomy, chemistry, mathematics and goemetry.

Physics

So far the elements of physics in the Vedas are concerned, the facts that the planets and the stars of the space become spiritless[1] and hide[2] after the light of the sun falls on the earth, shows the height of the scientific thoughts of the Āryan sages. They knew that the dividing factor of time and space of this earth is the sun[3] which is the pivotal centre of the universe also.[4] The visibility of the Great Bears (*ṛkṣaḥ*, according to the Vedic term) or seven sages also occur due to the absence of the light of the of the sun.[5] The same thing

1. *ṚV*, 1/14/5.
2. *Ibid.*, 1/50/2.
3. *Ibid.*, 1/95/3.
4. *Ibid.*, 1/164/2 & 3.
5. *Ibid.*, 1/24/10.

has been explained thus, "The constellation pass away, like thieves together with their beams, before all behalding sun."[6]

On the other hand, we find the elements of the theory of gravitation also as, "Savitar fixed the earth with bands he binds it.[7] Another passage declares the theory of gravitation as, "Truth is the base that bears the earth and Sūrya are the heavens sustained."[8] The belief that Newton discovered the Theory of Gravitation in the world is put to question thus. Such attraction causes the earth and the planets to remain hung in the space.[9] Another passage informs about eclipse.[10] In another place we find that this whole universe is moving.[11]

Astronomy

Mentioning of Great Bears[12] (*ṛkṣaḥ)*, sun eclipse,[13] all the seasons, light and dark fortnights, *uttarāyana* and *dakṣiṇāyana*,[14] dates or *tithis* of lunar months,[15] stars or *nakṣatras* such as *Maghā, Pūrvāphālgunī* and *Uttarāphālgunī*,[16] fourteen *bhuvanas*,[17] six *lokas*,[18] and seven *lokas*[19] are some of the evidences that may claim the knowledge of astronomy of the Vedic *ṛṣis*.

---

6. See Griffith on *ṚV*, 1/50/1.
7. *ṚV*, 10/149/1.
8. *Ibid.*, 10/85/1.
9. *Ibid.*, 10/89/4; 3/55/20 & 1/33/8.
10. *Ibid.*, 1/40/5.
11. *Ibid.*, 8/12/30.
12. *Ibid.*, 1/24/10.
13. *Ibid.*, 5/40/5.
14. *ŚB*, 2/1/3/1.
15. *TS*, 7/4/8; *TB*, 1/2/2/8; *GP*, 1/6/19.
16. *ṚV*, 10/85/1.
17. *Ibid.*, 10/114/7.
18. *Ibid.*, 1/164/6.
19. *Ibid.*, 7/18/24.

Mathematics

We get a passage in the *ṚV* where a sage counts up to sixty thousands, and in the same passage there is another reference of ten thousands.[20] Counting so, addition, subtraction, multiplication and division also came into being in the Vedic age. Another passage of the *ŚYV* speaks of a huge number.[21] The passage presents the following informations:

1. Āryans knew G.P. series and the passage presents a ten multipled series.
2. The G.P. series goes up to 10^{17} or having seventeen numbers of zeros after one.
3. Though some scholare count up to 10^{12} in the passage as *eka, daśa, śata, sahasra, ayuta, niyuta, prayuta, arbuda, narbuda, samudra, madhya, anta* and *parārdha*.[22]
4. On the other hand, Uvaṭa, Mahīdhara[23] and J.P. Misra,[24] in their commentaries mention that it was 10^{17}.

Whatever the fact there may be, we get another instance of A.P. series in the two passages of *ŚYV*[25] as 1, 3, 5, 7, 9, 11, 13, 15, 17, 19, 21, 23, 25, 27, 29, 31, & 33 and 4, 8, 12, 16, 20, 24, 28,

---

20. *ṚV*, 8/56/22.
21. *ŚYV*, 17/2.
22. (a) *VHR*, p. 321.

    (b) *Aṅkavidyā, Gaṇit aur Jyotiṣ kā Mūlsrot Bhārat* by Śukadevji Pandey in *HSA*, p. 543.
23. Read, *abja samudrāntarvartinīnam kharba nikharba mahāpadma śaṅku saṅkhyānām upalakṣyakaṁ, tenābjaṁ daśaguṇam kharbaṁ, kharbaṁ daśaguṇam nikharbaṁ nikharbaṁ daśaguṇam mahāpadmaṁ mahāpadmaṁ daśaguṇaṁ saṅkuḥ saṅkurdaśaguṇaḥ samudraḥ*. See Mahīdhara on 17/2.
24. *ŚYV*, Commentary of J.P. Misra, p. 697.
25. *Ibid.*, 18/24 & 25.

32, 36, 40, 44 & 48, respectively. Those series have the common difference of 2 and 4, respectively.

The conception of geometry came first into the mind of the Āryan sages. A Vedic sacrificer decorated the altars of the *yajña*s with lines and circles and made the fire places in different shapes. A Yajurvedic passage mentions that the sacrificial fireplace was made the centre of the seven circumferences.[26] Ramgopal says about geometry as,

> The *Śulvasūtra*s, for example, lay down exact rules regarding the construction of squares and rectangles equal to squares and vice versa; and the construction of circle equal to squares and vice versa. Moreover the *sūtra*s show their knowledge of Pythagorean theorem, and give with its help the constructions for finding a square that will be equal to the sum or difference of two squares.[27]

R.G. Trivedi also comments as,

> Vedic literature must be respected as the father of geometry. The *Śulvasūtra*s describe the relationship between sides and hypotenuses, squares and circles, etc.[28]

Again squares, triangles and trough types of altars of *yajña* are described in the Vedic literature.[29]

Chemistry

The *ṚV* is able to express the theories of chemistry also. But it can be studied only on symbolical basis. Gurudatta has

26. Read, *saptāsyāsan paridhayaḥ*, *ŚYV*, 31/15.
27. *IVKR*, p. 338.
28. *VSR*, p. 322.
29. *ŚB*, 10/2/2/8 and *KS*, 21/4.

explained some passages of the *R̥V* in this context. He mentions that if Mitra, Varuṇa, Aryamā and Indra are supposed to be electron, proton, neutron and the atomic energy, respectively,[30] then some R̥gvedic passages of a *sūkta*[31] can give the following informations:

1. Atoms' particles are formed when energy becomes active.
2. *Apaḥ* are of three kinds, "electron, proton and neutron" or Mitra, Varuṇa and Aryamā.
3. Those three particles make atoms.
4. Neutrons move round the boundary of the atomic circle.
5. The neutron particles are Soma because of their chargelessness.

A R̥gvedic passage indicates that the atom becomes imbalanced when the will of Supreme rides upon it.[32] Gurudatta gives the following diagram for the expression:

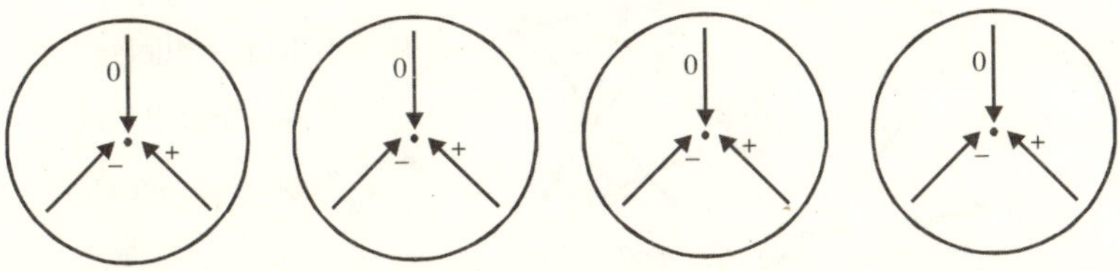

Atom becomes imbalanced when the *arvan* (the will of God) rides upon atom and the imbalancing happens when

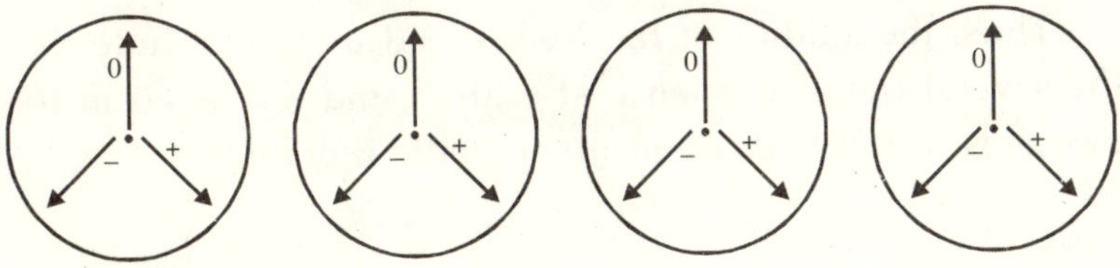

30. *Vedon me Soma* by Gurudatta, p. 13.
31. *R̥V*, 1/163.
32. *Ibid.*, 1/163/6.

the *tritas* split.[33] The above verse also presents the following diagram:

Ṛta was spread everywhere and it looked like having rays. The place of Mitra, Varuṇa and Aryamā seemed in *dyuloka*.[34]

Another passage says that the footless and handless Vṛtra or the chargeless particle challanged Indra or the charged one. Consequently, Indra or charged particle smote the uncharged one. Thus, the emasculated Vṛtra or uncharged particles lie[35] with scattered limbs. A special interaction was happening between the *vajra* of Indra and Vṛtra and thus the proton particles contract with neutron particles.[36] Gurudatta presents the following diagram to express the above description.

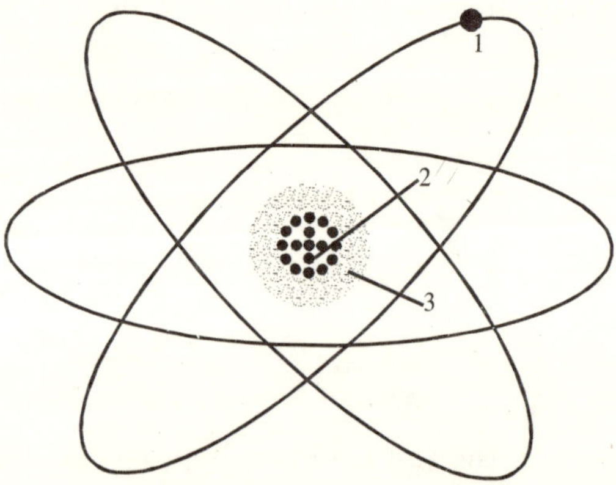

1. Mitra (Electron)
2. Varuṇa (Proton)
3. Soma (Neutron)

Thus, the studies of the Vedas lead us to conclude that the several fields of science also are found discussed in the passages of the Vedas and other Vedic literature.

---

33. *ṚV*, 1/163.
34. *Ibid.*, 1/163/1.
35. *Ibid.*, 1/32/7.
36. *Ibid.*, 1/32/8.

Appendix III

Christian Conspiracy of Misinterpreting Indian Literatures

Nations feel proud of their rich past and glorious history if they possess that. They try their utmost to discover the glorious elements of their history. India has ample evidences of such things and can discover a lot. But unfortunately, some Christian scholars have intentionally tried to vilify the Indian art, literature, philosophy, religion, history and culture.

After the establishment of British rule in India, some curious and studious persons intended to study Indology. William Johns was the first European foreigner to study Sanskrit in the middle of the eighteenth century.[1] He established the Royal Asiatic Society of Bengal to promote the Sanskrit education in 1783, the expenditure of which was borne by the East India Company for seventy years.[2] Secondly, the Boden Chair was introduced in Oxford University by Sir Colonel Boden in AD 1811 for the sake of promoting Sanskrit education.[3] A lot of foreigners, including Grim Bapp, Muir, Macdonnel, Winternitz, were inclined to

---

1. *Bhāratīya Itihās: Punarlekhan Kyoṅ ? Evam Purāṇo me Itihās Vivek* (*BIP-PIV*) by Dr. Kunwarlal Vyassisya, p. 16.
2. *Bhāratīya Itihās Mālā* (Political) Pt. I, by Shri Ram Sethe, p. 98.
3. *A Sanskrit-English Dictionary* by M.M. Williams, preface p. IX.

the Sanskrit education. For the first time the Western scholars analysed the Sanskrit texts with indifferent view.

The Western Scholars: In the Beginning

We get some European scholars in the beginning who studied Indology and commented without prejudices. We get Schopen Hauer declaring the Upaniṣads to be a "Production of highest human wisdom."[4] and "In the whole world there is no study as beneficial and elevating as that of the Upaniṣads."[5] Saint Thoreau remarks, "Where is fear when the Mother Gītā is there to protect."[6] Winternitz expressed in his views in the lecture given in Calcutta University as, "When Indian literatures became first known in the West, people were inclined to ascribe a hoary age to every literary work hailing from India. They used to look upon India as something like the cradle of mankind or at least of human civilization."[7]

The Western Christian Scholars and Their Role

On the other hand, another section of foreigners tried their best to vilify the Indian way of life. First of all they tried to reduce the historical data of timing and did not allow to cross the human history before 5472 BC because Christians believed that Adam lost Paradise in 5472 BC[8] and the human society came into being in the world only after that. The Christians were afraid of the Sanskrit literature, for F. Bodmer observes, "Custodians of the Pentateuch were alarmed by the prospect that Sanskrit would bring down the tower of

4. Quoted from *BIP-PIV*, p. 16.
5. Quoted from *Hindu Saṁskr̥ti me Īśvaravāda* by Bankebihari Das, in *HAS*, p. 132.
6. *Ibid.*, p. 133.
7. Quoted from *BIP-PIV*, p. 17.
8. *Hamārī Sānskr̥tik Dharohar* by Gurudatta, p. 103.

Babel."[9] A Christian scholar Sir Cononel Boden opened the Boden Chair in Oxford University, "to enable his countrymen to proceed in the conversion of natives of India into the Christian religion."[10]

English Education

Right from the beginning of the nineteenth century, a controversy between the scholars supporting the oriental and occidental style of education took speed. The controversy had raised at its worst when Macaulay landed in India as a member of the Governor-General's Council.[11] William Benetic appointed him as the Chairman of the Society of Public Instructions of Bengal to submit detail about education policy. Macaulay advocated the English education and submitted accordingly. His aim of introducing English education in India reflects from,

> We must do our best to form a class of such persons who may be interpreters between us and millions, whom we govern a class of persons, Indian in blood and colour, but English in tastes, in opinions, in morals and in intellect.[12]

Secondly he sent a letter to his father after introducing his policy of education in Bengal where his intention reflects as such.[13]

> Culcutta
> October 12, 1839
>
> My Dear Father,
>
> Our English schools are flourishing wonderfully. . . . the effect

9. *The Loom of Language* by Frederic Bodmer, New York, 1944. p. 174.
10. *A Sanskrit-English Dictionary* by M.M. Williams, preface p. IX.
11. *History of Indian Education* by P.L. Rawat, Agra, 1989, p. 152.
12. *Shri Ramakṛṣṇa aur Uccaśikṣā* by Videhatmananda in Śikṣāṅka (Kalyāṇ) p. 255.
13. *Hamārī Sāṁskṛtik Dharohar* by Gurudatta, p. 99.

> of this education on the Hindoos is prodigious. No Hindoo who has received our English Education ever remains sincerely attached to his religion. Some continue to profess it as a matter of policy and some embrace Christianity. It is my belief that, if our plans of education are followed up, there will not be a single idolator among the respectable castes in Bengal, thirty years hence, and this will be affected without any efforts to proselytize, without the smallest interference with religious liberty by natural operation of knowledge and reflection. I heartily rejoice in this prospect. . . .
>
> Ever yours,
> Most affectionately,
> T.B. Macaulay

Such was Macaulay's aim in introducing English education in India, as a result of which he wanted to create the enemies of Indian culture so that it would be easier to spread Christianity in the country.

Maxmüller

Maxmüller was a German scholar who studied the Vedic and other literatures of India and abroad. As a result of that he propounded the theory of Āryan's migration into India. Whatever the fact there may be, he studied the Indian literatures with keen attention. He was Christian by religion and wanted to vilify the Indian culture and beliefs. Lord Macaulay met Maxmüller, on the 28 December of 1855.[14] Maxmüller, after that meeting, completely changed his ideas regarding India and he was sent to Oxford University to translate the Indian Literatures, with a view to misleading the Indian people.[15] In that connection he writes, "I went back to Oxford as a sadder man and a wise man." (*SBI*, vol

14. *BIP-PIV* p.17.
15. *Hamārī Sāṁskṛtik Dharohar* by Gurudatta, p. 100.

VI, 1932).[16] Why he studied the Indian literatures becomes clear when he declared,

> To a missionary, an acute knowledge of the sacred books (of India) was as indispensable as the knowledge of enemy's country to a General.[17]

Reveals Intolerant and Christian View

Maxmüller completed his translations of the Vedas in 1866[18] and wrote a letter to his wife on 9/12/1866 mentioning his motto of the translations as, ". . . This edition of mine (of the *Ṛgveda*) and the translations of the Vedas will hereafter tell to a great extent on the fate of India and on the growth of millions of souls in the country. It is the root of their religion and to show them what the root is, I feel sure, 'the only way of uprooting all that has been sprung from it during the last three thousand years.'[19] On the other hand, he is found to be anxious when he exclaims in a letter dated 16/12/1868, written to the Duke of Argile with great hope, "The ancient religion of India is doomed and if Christianity does not step in, whose fault will it be ?"[20] Thirdly, he wrote a letter to his son where he shows his partiality to the Christian religion as, "Would you say that any one sacred book is superior to all others in the world ?. . . I say the *New Testament*. After that, I should place the Koran, which in its moral teachings, is hardly more than a later edition of the *New Testament*. Then would follow the *Old Testament*, The Southern Buddhist *Tripiṭaka*. . . . The Veda and The Avesta."[21]

Dayānanda was a great Vedic scholar who translated and explained the Vedas in glorious way. He even

16. *BIP-PIV*, p.17.
17. *APIIAI* by R.S. Sharma, p. 1.
18. *Vaidik Viśvarāṣṭra kā Itihās*, by P.N. Oak, vol. IV, p. 297.
19. *Vaidik Sāhitya Kī Rūparekhā* by Prof. H.R. Agarwal, p. 21.
20. *Ibid.*, p. 21.
21. *Hamārī Sāṁskṛtik Dharohar* by Gurudatta, p. 101.

challenged Max Müller for an open debate[22] on the objectionable contents that he entered intentionally but he, instead of accepting that challenge, comments in a letter to his friend Byramjee Malabari as, ". . . You may see a painult instance in Dayānanda Sarasvatī's labour on the Vedas.[23] One of his friends E.B. Russey came to know his activities and praised as, ". . . Your work will be formed a new era in the efforts for the conversion of India."[24] Dr. Spiegel wrote that the idea of progress in the Zews came from the Persians.[25] Maxmüller could not bear it, supposing that he had opposed the Christian belief and writes thus,

> A writer like Dr. Spiegel should know that he can expect no mercy; nay, he should himself wish for no mercy, but invite the heaviest artillery against the floating battery which he has launched into the troubled waters of Biblical criticism.[26]

Though his prejudices gave a lot of wrong information regarding Āryans and India, yet he reveals true evidences when he joined his masters. We can quote two paragraphs of the letter which he wrote to Queen Victoria in the year 1858. The paragraphs go as follows:[27]

> If I were asked under what sky the human mind has fully developed some of its choicest gifts, have most deeply pondered on the greatest problems of life and has found solutions of some of them which well deserve the attention even of those who have studied Plato and Kant, I should point to India.
>
> And if I were asked myself from what literature we here in Europe, we who are nurtured almost exclusively on the

22. *Hamārī Sāṁskṛtik Dharohar* by Gurudatta, p. 107.
23. *Vaidik Sāhitya kī Rūparekhā* by H.R. Agarwal, p. 21.
24. *Ibid.*
25. *Hamārī Sāṁskṛtik Dharohar* by Gurudatta, p. 106.
26. *Ibid.*
27. *Hindu Saṁskṛti me Īśvaravāda* by Bankebihari Das, in *HSA* p. 135.

> thought of Greeks and Romans and of the Semitic race, the Jewish, may draw that corrective which is most wanted in order to make our inner life more perfect, more universal, in fact more truly human, a life not for this life only, but a transfigured and Eternal life, again I should point to India.

All the other Western scholars who came after Maxmüller, followed him[28] and those interpretations got place in the social, political, economic, and religious histories of India. A lot of Eastern scholars and students also inclined to such studies and they are continuing their researches. Unfortunately, the translations and commentaries of Dayananda, Satavalekar, Jwala Prasad Mishra, Sāyaṇa, Mahīdhara, Uvaṭa, Ram Sharma, etc., are being ignored. India's blood and soul remain alien to the foreign scholars like Maxmüller and others who did not step into this country even for once.

---

28. *Vaidik Sāhitya kī Rūparekhā* by H.R. Agarwals, p. 21.

Appendix IV

The Range of Vedic Literature

VEDIC literature occupies a vast range of studies including *mantra Saṁhitās*, *Brāhmaṇas*, Upaniṣads, *Āraṇyakas*, *Prātiśākhyas*, *Kalpasūtras*, Upavedas and Vedāṅgas. We want to present the sketch of the range of Vedic literature as follows :

Sheet No. 1

No.	*Vedas*	*Upavedas*	*Brāhmaṇas*	*Śākhās*	*Āraṇyakas*	*Upaniṣads*
1.	*ṚV*	*Āyurveda* Dhanvantarī	*Aitareya* *Kauṣitakī* or *Śāṅkhāyana*	*Śākala* *Bāṣkala* *Āśvalāyana* *Sāṅkhāyana* *Māṇḍūkyāyana*	*Aitareya* *Kauṣitakī* or *Śāṅkhāyana*	*Aitareya* *Kauṣitakī* Other eight Upaniṣads
2.	*ŚYV*	*Dhanurveda* Viśvāmitra	*Śatapatha*	*Mādhyandina* or *Vājasaneyī* having the same *Saṁhitās* along with *Kāṇva* *Saṁhitā*	14/1/1 to 3 of the *ŚB* is its *Āraṇyaka*	*Bṛhadāraṇyaka* and *Īśa* others 17

	Kṛṣṇa YV	*Dhanurveda* Viśvakarmā	*Taittirīya*	*Taittirīya* *Maitrāyaṇī* *Kāṭhaka* *Kapiṣṭhal* *Kaṭha* having same *Saṁhitās*	*Taittirīya* *Maitrāyaṇī*	*Kaṭha* *Taittirīya* *Śvetāśvatara* *Kaivalya* and others 28
3.	*SV*	*Gānddharvaveda* Bharatmuni	*Tāṇḍya* or *Pañcaviṁśa* *Chāndogya* *Brāhmaṇa* *Ārṣeya* *Sāmabidhāna* *Vaṁśa*, *Jaiminīya* *Daivatādhyāya* *Saṁhitopaniṣads*	*Rāṇāyanīya* *Kauthumīya* *Jaiminīya* Other 10 *Śākhās* are not found today	*Talavakāra* *Chāndogya*	*Kena* *Chāndogya* *Maitrāyaṇī* Others 13
4.	*AV*	*Sthāpatyaveda*	*Gopatha*	*Śaunakīya* & *Paippalāda* with *Saṁhitā*		*Praśna* *Muṇḍaka* *Māṇḍūkya*

Sheet No. 2.

No.	Vedas	Prātiśākhyas	Sūtra Literature				Vedāṅgas
			Śrauta	Gṛhya	Dharma	Śulva	
1.	*Ṛ̥V*	*Prātiśakhya of Śākala Śākhā* Composed by Śaunaka	*Āśvalāyana & Śāṅkhā yana*	*Aitareya Śāṅkhāyana* or *Kauṣitakī*	*Vaśiṣṭha*		*Śikṣā Vyākaraṇam Chanda Niruktaṃ Jyotiṣa Kalpa*
2.	*ŚYV*	*Vājasaneyī Prātiśākhya*	*Kātyāyana*	*Pāraskara*	*Hārīta Śāṅkha*	*Kātyāyana*	
	Kṛ̥ṣṇa YV	*Taittirīya*	*Baudhāyana Āpastamba*	*Baudhāyana Āpastamba*	*Baudhāyana Āpastamba*	*Baudhāyana Āpastamba*	
			Hiraṇyakeśī or *Satyasādha*	*Hiraṇyakeśī Kāṭhaka Mānava*	*Hiraṇyakeśī Baikhānasa*	*Mānava Hiranyakeśī*	Do
			Vaikhānasa Mānava Bhāradvāja Varuṇa	*Bhāradvāja*	*Viṣṇu*		
3.	*SV*	*Sāma Prātiśākhya Puṣpasūtra Pañcaviṁśasūtra*	*Ārṣeya* or *Masaka Lāṭyāyana Drāhyāyana Jaiminīya*	*Drāhyāyana Jaiminīya Gobhila Khadira*	*Gautama*		Do
4.	*AV*	*AV Prātiśākhya-sūtra*	*Vaitāna*	*Kauśika*			Do

Bibliography

Original Texts and Commentaries (Vedic Section)

Atharvaveda (School of the Śaunaka), Sāyaṇa commentary and translation of R.C. Sharma, Sanatana Dharma Yantralaya, Muradabad, VS 1986.

Āpastamba Dharmasūtra, with Ujjvalavṛtti of Haradatta, ed. Mahadeva Sastri, Mysore, 1998.

Āpastamba Śrautasūtra, Rudradatta's commentary, ed. Garbe, India, 1902.

Āśvalāyana Gṛhyasūtra, ed. P. Sastri, Poona, 1936.

Īśādi Nau Upaniṣad, ed. Harikrsnadas Goyanaka, Gita Press, Gorakhpur, VS 2047.

Īśāvāsyopaniṣad, See *Īśādi Nau Upaniṣad* above.

Ṛgveda,

———, Satavalekar's commentary, Pardi, 1940.

———, Sāyaṇa's commentary, Mumbai, 1810, ed. Poona.

———, Griffith's commentary and translation, *The Hymns of the Ṛgveda,* Motilal Banarsidass, Delhi, 1973.

Aitareya Brāhmaṇa, Sāyaṇa's commentary, ed. Sudhakar Malaviya, Chowkhamba Prakashan, Varanasi.

Kaṭhopaniṣad, See *Īśādi Nau Upniṣad,* above.

Kāṭhaka Saṁhitā, ed. Satavalekar, Aundh, 1943.

Kātyāyana Śrautasūtra, ed. Vidyadhar Sharma with his own commentary, Achyuta Granthamala, Varanasi, 1930.

Kenopaniṣd, See *Īśādi Nau Upniṣad,* above.

Kauṣitakī Brāhmaṇa, ed. Pragna Devi and Medha Devi, Hindi translation by Ksemakarandas Trivedi, Chowkhamba Sanskrit Pratisthan, Delhi, 1993.

Gobhila Gṛhyasūtra, Bhaṭṭanārāyaṇa's commentary, ed. Cintamani Bhattacharya, Calcutta, 1936.

Chāndogya Upaniṣad, Gita Press, Gorakhpur, VS 2045.

Jaiminīya Upaniṣad Brāhmaṇa, ed. Pandit Ramdev, Delhi, 1921.

Jaiminīya Gṛhyasūtra, with Srinivasadhvari commentary, ed. W. Caland, Lahore, 1922.

Tāṇḍya Mahā Brāhmaṇa, Commentary of Cinnasvami Sastri, Chowkhamba, Varanasi, vs 1991.

Taittirīya Upaniṣad, with Sāyaṇa's commentary, Anandasram Sanskrit Granthavali, 1901.

Taittirīya Saṁhitā, with Sāyaṇa's commentary, Anandasram, Sanskrit Granthavali, 1901.

Nirkuta and Nighaṇṭu, ed. and tr. in English by L. Sarup, New Delhi, 1967.

———, *Pāraskara Gṛhyasūtra,* ed. Uma Śankar Sharma, Chowkhamba Vidya Bhavan, with Harihar Gangadhara commentary by Sudhakar Malaviya, Chowkhamba Sanskrit Sansthan, Varanasi, vs 2037.

Pañcaviṁśa Brāhmaṇa, ed. A. Vedanta Vagisa, Calcutta, 1986-74.

Praśnopaniṣad, See *Īśādi Nau Upaniṣad* above.

Bṛhadāraṇyakopaniṣad, Hindi tr. by Ashok Kausik, Lokapriya Series, Delhi, 1986.

Baudhāyana Dharmasūtra, with Govinda Svami's commentary, ed. Cinnasvami Sastri, Varanasi, 1934.

Baudhāyana Śrautatsūtra, B. Call and Asiatic Society, Calcutta, 1904.

Muṇḍakopaniṣad, See *Īśādi Nau Upaniṣad* above.

Śatapatha Brāhmaṇa, with Ratnadipika Hindi commentary, ed. Ganga Prasad Upadhyaya, Pracin Vaignanikadhyayan Anusandhan Sansthan, New Delhi, 1967.

Śāṅkhāyana Gṛhyasūtra, ed. S.R. Sahagal, Delhi, 1960.

Śukla Yajurveda, with Uvaṭa and Mahīdhara's commentary, ed. Panduranga Javji Sresthi, Mumbai, 1929.

———, Commentary of Jvala Prasad Misra, Venkates Mudranalaya, Mumbai, 1969.

———, Commentary of Dayananda Sarasvati, Sarvadesik Arya Pratinidhi Sabha, VS 1947.

Original Texts and Commentaries (Classical Section)

Amarakośa, with Maniprabha Hindi commentary, Chowkhamba, Varanasi, 1976.

Aṣṭādhyāyī of Pāṇini, Chowkhamba, Varanasi, 1950.

Arthaśāstra of Kauṭilya, ed. R. Sarma Sastri, Mysore, 1919.

Kumārasambhavam of Kālidāsa, Chowkhamba Surabharati, Varanasi, 1983.

Mahābhāratam, Gita Press, Gorakhpur, 1982.

Manu-Smṛti, Nirnaysagar Mudranalaya, Delhi, 1946.

Raghuvaṁśam, Chowkhamba, Varanasi, 1983.

Rāmāyaṇam of Vālmīki, Rāmābhinandinī Bhāsaṭīkā, Pandit Pustakalaya, Kāśī, 1951.

Viṣṇu Purāṇam, Venkatesvara Press, Bombay, 1910.

Śrīmad Bhagavad-Gītā,

———, Śaṅkarācārya's commentary, Gita Press, Gorakhpur, 1935.

———, Jayadayal Goyanka's commentary, Gita Press, Gorakhpur, vs 2045.

———, Ramsukhadasa's commentary, Gita Press, Gorakhpur, vs 2053.

Śrīmad Bhāgavat Mahāpurāṇa,

———, English Translation, S. Subba Rao, Tirupati, 1928.

———, Hindi Translation, Gita Press, Gorakhpur, VS 2050.

Siddhānta Kaumudī,

———, Motilal Banarsidass, Delhi, 1979.

———, With Tatvabodhinī commentary by Gnanendra Sarasvati, Motilal Banarsidass, Delhi, 1979.

Secondary Sources

Altekar, A.S., *State and Government in Ancient India*, Motilal Banarsidass, Delhi, 1992.

Bokare, M.G., *Hindu Economics*, Janaki Prakashan, Delhi, 1993.

Bhattacharjee, Sukumari, *The Indian Theogony*, Firma KLM Pvt. Ltd., Calcutta, 1978.

Bhattacarya, A. Taranath, *Vācaspatyam*, vol. IV & VI, Chowkhamba, Varanasi, 1970.

Bhide, N.N., *Kiṁ Rāṣṭraṁ Kaśea Rāṣṭrīya*, Babasaheb Apte Smarak Samiti, Nagpur, 1992.

Bandhyopadhyay, Pranab, *The Aryans and the Holy Vedas*, United Writers, Calcutta, 1993.

Basham, A.L., *The Wonder that was India*, Rupa & Company, Calcutta, 1992.

Basu, J.R., *India of the age of the Brāhmaṇas*, Sanskrit Pustak Bhandar, Calcutta, 1969.

———, *Veder Paricaya*, Firma KLM Pvt. Ltd., Calcutta, 1993.

Chattopadhyaya, Sudhakar, *Ethnic Elements in Ancient Hinduism*, Calcutta Sanskrit College Research Series, Calcutta, 1991.

Drury, Naama, *The Sacrificial Rituals in the Śatapatha Brāhmaṇa*, Motilal Banarsidass, Delhi, 1981.

Dutta, N.K., *Origin and Growth of Castes in India*, Firma KLM Pvt. Ltd., Calcutta, 1986.

Das, A.C., *Ṛgvedic Culture,* Bharatiya Publishing House, Delhi, 1979.

Dasgupta, K.N., *Aryasabhyatār Sandhāne,* Sahityayan, Calcutta.

Dvivedi, Kapildev, *Sanskrit Sahitya kā Samālocanātmak Itihās,* 4th edn., Allahabad.

Dey, Sitanath, *Indian Life in the Śukla Yajurveda,* Firma KLM Pvt. Ltd., Calcutta, 1984.

Ghurye, G.S., *Vedic India,* Motilal Banarsidass, Delhi, 1979.

Gopal, Ram, *India of the Vedic Kalpasūtras,* Motilal Banarsidass, Delhi, 1979.

Gooch, G.P., *Studies in Modern History,* London, Longman, 1931.

Govt. of Chinese Republic, *Constitution of Chinese Republic,* Hong Kong, 1982.

Govt. of U.S.S.R., *Constitution of U.S.S.R.,* Moscow, 1977.

Gnani, Shivadatta, *Vedakālīna Samāj,* Chowkhamba Vidyabhavan, Varanasi, 1967.

Gurudatta, *Vedon me Soma,* Delhi, 1993.

Hayes, Curlton J.H., *Essays on Nationalism,* New York, Macmillan, 1926.

Haradas, Balasastri, *Vaidika Rāṣṭradarśana,* Suruci Sahitya, New Delhi, 1982.

Homby, A.S., *Oxford Advanced Dictionary,* Oxford University Press, Oxford, 1981.

Joshi, Kireet, *The Vedas and the Indian Culture,* Rastriya Veda Vidya Pratisthan, Delhi, 1992.

Keith, A.B., *The Religion and Philosophy of the Veda and Upaniṣads,* vol. XXXI, Harvard University Press, London, 1925.

Kohn, Hans, *Idea of Nationalism,* London, 1960.

Kumar, Surendra, *Viśuddha Manusmṛti,* Arsa Sahitya Prachar Trust, Delhi, 1990.

Macdonell A.A., *Vedic Mythology,* Hindi translation by Suryakanta named as *Vaidik Devaśāstra,* Delhi, 1982.

Macdonell and Keith, *Vedic Index,* tr. in Hindi by R.K. Raj, Chowkhamba Vidyabhavan, Varanasi, 1962.

Maharaj, Svami Karapatriji, *Marxvāda aur Rāmrājya,* Gita Press, Gorakhpur, vs 2046.

———, *Vedārtha Pārijata,* vol. I & II, Gita Press, Gorakhpur, vs 2037.

Mazumdar, R.C., *Corporate Life in Ancient India,* Firma KLM, Pvt. Ltd., Calcutta, 1969.

Misra, Gangadhar, *Vaidik evaṁ Vedottar Bhāratīya Saṁskṛti,* Varanasi, 1981.

Misra, Umesh Chandra, *Bhāratīya Darśan,* Uttar Pradesh Hindi Sansthan, Lucknow, 1990.

Oaksmith, John, *Race and Nationality : An enquiry into the Origin and Growth of Patriotism,* New York, Stocks, 1919.

Pandey, Rajbali, *Hindu Dharmakośa,* Uttar Pradesh Hindi Sansthan, Lucknow, 1988.

Pillsbury, W.B., *The Psychology of Nationality and Internationalism,* New York, Appleton, 1919.

Pragyananda, Swami, *Historical Development of Indian Music,* Firma KLM Pvt. Ltd., Calcutta, 1983.

Ratate, V.R., *Atharvaveda Rājanīti,* Sampurnananda Visvavidyalaya Prakashan, Varanasi, 1989.

Ray, Amit, *Villages, Towns and Secular Buildings in Ancient India,* Firma KLM Pvt. Ltd., Calcutta, 1964.

Ray Govinda Chandra, *Vaidik Yug ke Bhāratīya Ābhūṣaṇa,* Chowkhamba Vidyabhavan, Varanasi, 1965.

Sarmah, T., *The Bhāradvājas in Ancient India,* Delhi, 1990.

———, *Vaidik Sāhityar Rūparekhā,* 1st edn., Guwahati, 1998.

———, *Vaidik Kāhini Prabhā,* Guwahati, 1990.

Sathe, Sri Ram, *Aryans : Who were They,* Bharatiya Itihas Sankalan Samiti, Mysore, 1991.

———, *Bhāratīya Itihāsmālā* (*Rājnaitik Khaṇḍa*),Bharatiya Itihas Sankalan Samiti, Delhi, 1993.

———, *Viśva me Rāṣṭrīyatā kī Vikās Yātrā,* Bharatiya Itihas Sankalan Samiti, Hyderabad, 1992.

Sharma, R.S., *Aspects of Political Ideas and Institutions in Ancient India,* Motilal Banarsidass, Delhi, 1991.

Sharma, S.N., *A History of Vedic Literature,* Chowkhamba Sanskrit Series Office, Varanasi, 1973.

Sharma, Sri Ram, *Samasta Viśva ko Bhārat ke Ajasra Anudāna,* Mathura, 1965.

Sastri, Satyananda, *Kyā Prācīn Ārya log Māṁsāhārī The,* Gaziabad, vs 2025

Sivaraj, Om, *Dharma aur Darśan,* Delhi, 1985.

Srinivasan, Doria, *Concept of Cow in the Ṛgveda,* Motilal Banarsidass, Delhi, 1979.

Srivastav, Balaram, *Trade and Commerce in Ancient India,* Chowkhamba Sanskrit Office, Varanasi, 1968.

Sahay, Shivapujan, *Hindu Sāmājik Saṁsthāyen aur Ārthik Jīvan,* Motilal Banarsidass, 1992.

Satavalekar, Sripad Damodar, *Atharvaveda : Mātṛbhūmi aur Svarājyaśāsan,* Svadhyay Mandal, Pardi, 1967.

Singh, Sarvadaman, *Ancient Indian Warfare,* Motilal Banarsidass, Delhi, 1989.

Sarasvati, Dayananda, *Satyārtha Prakaśa,* Arsa Sahitya Pracar Trust, New Delhi, 1981.

Sinha, N.K.P., *Political Ideas and Ideals in the Mahābhāratam,* Varanasi, 1964.

Smith, V.A., *The Oxford History of India,* Oxford University Press, London, 1982.

Tirtha Krsna, Bharati, *The Vedic Mathematics,* Motilal Banarsidass, New Delhi.

Tatacarya, A. Ramanuja, *Vedakālīna Janatantrasthānāni,* Rastriya Ṣanskrit Sansthan, Delhi, 1984.

Toynbee, Arnold J., *Nationality and the War,* London, 1915.

Tripathi, Hariharnath, *Prācīn Bhārat me Rājya aur Nyāyapālikā,* Motilal Banarsidass, Delhi, 1963.

Tripathi, M.P., *Development of Geographical Knowledge in Ancient India,* Varanasi, 1969.

Trivedi, Ramgovinda, *Vaidika Sāhitya,* Bharatiya Gnanpith, Kāśī, 1950.

Thengdi, Dattopanta, *Pūṇyāhavācan* in *Rāṣṭra* of M.S. Golvalkar, ed. by Bhanu Pratap Sukla, Panaki Prakasan, New Delhi.

Upadhyaya, Dindayal, *Rāṣṭra Jīvan kī Diśā,* Lokahita Prakasan, Lucknow, 1979.

Upadhyaya, Acarya Baladev, *Vaidika Sāhitya aur Saṁskṛti,* Sarada Samsthan, Varanasi, 1980.

Varma, Visvanath Prasad, *Vaidika Rājnītiśāstra,* Bihar Grantha Academy, 1975.

Vedalankar, Prasanta, *Vaidika Sāhitya me Nārī,* Basudev Prakasan, New Delhi, 1994.

Vivekānanda Svami, *Vivekānanda Sāhitya,* Hindi Translation of the lectures and letters of Svami Vivekananda, Advaita Ashram, Calcutta.

———, *Vivekānanda Sāhitya,* vol I, 1980.

———, *Vivekānanda Sāhitya,* vol II, 1981.

———, *Vivekānanda Sāhitya,* vol III, 1984.

———, *Vivekānanda Sāhitya,* vol IV, 1984.

———, *Vivekānanda Sāhitya,* vol V, 1985.

———, *Vivekānanda Sāhitya,* vol VI, 1985.

———, *Vivekānanda Sāhitya,* vol VII, 1985.

Vyasasisya, Kunwarlal, *Bhāratīya Itihās: Punarlekhan Kyon? Evam Purāṇo me Itihās Vivek,* Itihas Vidya Prakasan, Delhi, 1984.

Williams, M.M., *A Sanskrit-English Dictionary,* Motilal Banarsidass, Delhi, 1986.

Articles and Lectures

Devasarma, C. Nirajakanta, "Varṇāśram kī Aitihāsikatā," in *HSA*, Gita Press, Gorakhpur, 1950, p. 219.

Kumar, Basanta, "Janmanā Jāti," in *HSA* Gita Press, Gorakhpur, 1950, p. 227.

Kusvaha, S.P. Singh, "Yatāyāt ke Prācīn Vaijñānik Sādhan," in *HSA*, Gita Press, Gorakhpur, 1950, p. 723.

Sarma, Muralidhar, "Hindu Saṁskṛti, Uskī Ajeyatā aur Ādhārśilā," *HSA*, Gita Press, Gorakhpur, 1950, p. 386.

Sastri, Acarya Narendradev, "Hindi Saṁskṛti aur Pāścātyavāda," in *HSA* Gita Press, Gorakhpur, p. 171.

Sastri, Cinnaswami, "Synopsis on the Soma plant." *Our Heritage*, a bulletin of the Department of Post-Graduate Training and Research, Sanskrit College, Calcutta, vol. I, Part I, January to June, 1953, p. 85.

Satavalekar, Sripad Damodar, "Vaidik Rājyadarśan," *HSA*, Gita Press, Gorakhpur, 1950, p. 383.

———, "Vaidika Arthavyavasthā," in *SAG*, p. 119.

———, "Vaidika Sainyavyavasthā," in *SAG*, p. 93.

———, *"Ved me Darśāye Vividh Prakār ke Rājyaśāsan,"* Svadhyaya Mandal, Pardi, 1968.

———, *"Vaidika Svarājyaśāsan,"* Svadhyaya Mandal, Pardi, 1968.

———, *"Vaidika Devatāon kī Vyavasthā,"* Svadhyaya Mandal, Pardi, 1968.

———, *"Adhyātma Jñān se Vaiyaktik Divyajīvan aur Rāṣṭriya Unnati,"* Pardi, 1968.

Vedalankara, Jagannath, "Śikṣā evaṁ Guru Śabdon kī Nirukti," in *Śikṣāṅka Kalyāṇ*, 1988, Gita Press, Gorakhpur, p. 263.

Varma, T.P., "Indian Conception of History Writing", Research paper read in the Seminar, Sonitpur Through Ages, Tezpur, 1998.

Index